The Future of Islamic Finance

The Future of Islamic Finance: From Shari'ah Law to Fintech

EDITED BY

EDIB SMOLO

Effat University, Saudi Arabia

AND

MOHAMED MAHEES RAHEEM

Effat University, Saudi Arabia

emerald PUBLISHING

United Kingdom – North America – Japan – India – Malaysia – China

Emerald Publishing Limited
Emerald Publishing, Floor 5, Northspring, 21-23 Wellington Street, Leeds LS1 4DL

First edition 2025

British Library Cataloguing in Publication Data
A catalogue record for this book is available from the British Library

ISBN: 978-1-83549-907-8 (Print)
ISBN: 978-1-83549-906-1 (Online)
ISBN: 978-1-83549-908-5 (Epub)

Printed and bound by CPI Group (UK) Ltd, Croydon, CR0 4YY

To my dear family members, whose unwavering faith in me has been the driving force behind my accomplishments. In particular, I dedicate this book to my loving wife, cherished daughters, and late parents, whose love and encouragement have propelled me forward on this incredible journey.

Dr Edib Smolo

This book is dedicated to the Nameless and Faceless, who have lived and died striving for education and economic justice.

Dr Mohamed Mahees Raheem

Contents

List of Abbreviations

4IR	The Fourth Industrial Revolution
AAOIFI	Accounting and Auditing Organization for Islamic Financial Institutions
AI	Artificial Intelligence
APAC	North America and Asia-Pacific
APIs	Application Programming Interfaces
ASEAN	Association of Southeast Asian Nations
ATMs	Automated Teller Machines
BNM	Bank Negara Malaysia
BoP	Bottom of the Pyramid
CAGR	Compound Annual Growth Rate
CBDCs	Central Bank Digital Currencies
CCCA	Collective Commitment to Climate Action
CGC	Credit Guarantee Corporation Malaysia
CISL	Cambridge Institute for Sustainability Leadership
CSA	Community Supported Agriculture
CSR	Corporate Social Responsibility
ESG	Environmental, Social, and Corporate Governance
ETFs	Exchange-Traded Funds
G20	Group of Twenty
GCC	Gulf Cooperation Council
GDP	Gross Domestic Product
GFC	Global Financial Crisis
GHC	Global Health Crisis
GIFT	The Global Islamic Fintech
GMOs	Genetically Modified Organisms
HDI	Human Development Index
HPP	Home Purchase Plans
IBBL	Islamic Bank Bangladesh Limited

ICT	Information and Communication Technologies
IFI	Islamic Financial Industry
iFintech	Islamic Fintech
IFIs	Islamic Financial Institutions
IFSB	Islamic Financial Services Board
IME	Islamic Moral Economy
IRTI	Islamic Research and Training Institute
IsDB	Islamic Development Bank
ISF	Islamic Social Finance
ISFR	Islamic Social Finance Report
ITU-T	International Telecommunication Union Telecommunication Standardization Sector
KYC	Know Your Customer
LCTF	Low Carbon Transition Facilities
LMA	Loan Market Association
LSEG	London Stock Exchange Group
MENA	Middle East and North Africa
MSMEs	Micro, Small & Medium Enterprises
NFIS	National Financial Inclusion Strategy
NGOs	Non-Governmental Organizations
OIC	Organisation of Islamic Cooperation
P2P	Peer-to-Peer
PBUH	Peace Be Upon Him (Salutation Upon the Prophet Muhammad)
PLS	Profit-and-Loss Sharing
PoS	Proof-of-Stake
PoW	Proof of Work
PPS	Public/Private Partnerships
PRB	UN Principles of Responsible Banking
PSIB	Principles of Sustainable Islamic Banking
R&D	Research and Development
SC	Securities Commission
SDCs	Sovereign Digital Currencies
SDGi	SDGs Index
SDGs	Sustainable Development Goals

SMEs	Small and Medium Enterprises
SSLC	Sustainable Shipment Letter of Credit
SSOs	Standard Setting Organizations
SWT	Subhanahu Wa Ta'ala (Glorified and Exalted is He)
UN	United Nations
UNCTAD	UN Trade and Development
UNDP	United Nations Development Program
UNEP	United Nations Environment Programme
UNEP FI	United Nations Environment Programme Finance Initiative
UNFCCC	United Nations Framework Convention on Climate Change
VBI	Value-Based Intermediation
VBIAF	Investment Impact Assessment Framework
VBIT	Value-Based Intermediation Takaful model

About the Editors

Dr Edib Smolo is an Assistant Professor and former Chair of the Finance Department and Director of the Master of Science in Finance program at Effat University, Jeddah, Saudi Arabia. Prior to this position, he served as an Assistant Professor and Vice-Dean for Scientific and Research Activities at the International University of Sarajevo's Faculty of Business and Administration. During his time at International Islamic Liquidity Management Corporation (IILM), he developed the first short Islamic instrument with a global consensus that won the 2013 REDmoney global deal award. He holds a PhD from the International Center for Education in Islamic Finance (INCEIF), Malaysia's Global University of Islamic Finance. His degrees include a Bachelor of Economics (Honors) and a Bachelor of Islamic Revealed Knowledge and Heritage (Honors), as well as a Master of Economics from International Islamic University Malaysia (IIUM), Malaysia. In addition to writing and coauthoring several chapters in books, he also contributed to refereed journals on a variety of topics. He published "Introduction to Islamic Economics and Finance: Theory and Practice" in Bosnian in 2013. Additionally, he is a regular Speaker, Trainer, and Consultant on various Islamic Finance topics.

Dr Mohamed Mahees Raheem is an Assistant Professor of Finance, the Chair of the Finance Department, and Director of the Master of Science in Finance program at Effat University, Saudi Arabia. He holds a PhD in Islamic Banking and Finance from International Islamic University Malaysia and had previously worked as an Economic and Sustainable Development Consultant for a consultancy in Malaysia. He is a certified Fellow at Higher Education Academy (HEA) UK and a Young Fellow of the World Youth Network of the World Islamic Economic Forum (WIEF). With over 13 years of academic and industry experience, Dr Mohamed Mahees Raheem currently teaches at both the undergraduate and postgraduate levels and also serves as an Academic Advisor for finance students. He is also heavily involved in the development and review of program curricula, supervision of student internships and dissertations, and development of relationships with community. He was also instrumental in the development and implementation of the first postgraduate degree in Islamic Finance in Saudi Arabia and was involved in all aspects of course design and delivery and compliance.

About the Contributors

Syaima Adznan is a Senior Lecturer cum Researcher at the Faculty of Economics and Management under the Center of Global Business and Digital Economy studies (GLOBDE), Universiti Kebangsaan Malaysia (UKM), Malaysia. She is a Chartered Accountant (CA) of the Malaysian Institute of Accountants (MIA) and obtained her PhD from the International Center for Education in Islamic Finance (INCEIF) in 2022. She specializes in Islamic accounting, banking, and finance, and her research interests include intellectual capital, financial reporting, corporate governance, Shari'ah governance, and fintech. She has published and presented her research work in various conferences and journals. She is also a reviewer for *Management and Accounting Review*, *Asian Academy of Management Journal of Accounting & Finance*, *Asian Journal of Accounting and Finance*, and a few more journals.

Alija Avdukić is currently a Professor in Political/Moral Economy and Islamic Finance at University of Dundee School of Business. Alija holds a PhD in Islamic Economics and Finance (2016) from University of Durham and has an MA in Islamic Banking, Finance, and Management (2010) from Gloucestershire University. Alija's research interest is in Islamic economics and its various articulations, Islamic moral and political economy, and Islamic finance and banking. Alija teaches and supervises research on Islamic political and moral economy, Islamic banking, finance, and political economy of development in the Muslim world. Alija's recent research includes the construction of Islamic moral economy and Islamic political economy, both of which are considered as an incomplete project since early 1970s. Secondly, Alija develops the discourse around "social and developmentalist failure" of Islamic banking and finance in relation to the expressed ideals of Islamic moral economy by essentializing sharing and collaborative economy nature of Islamic finance. Alija is also involved in empirical research in various aspects and dynamism of Islamic banking and finance.

Issa Hamadou is a PhD student in Economics at the Faculty of Economics and Business at Universitas Islam International Indonesia (UIII). He completed his Master of Arts in Economics at the Faculty of Economics and Business at Universitas Islam International Indonesia (UIII). He got his Bachelor's degree and Master's degree in Applied Economics from the University of Maroua, Cameroon. His research interests include Islamic banking, Islamic Fintech, artificial intelligence, machine learning techniques, and SDGs. He is a hardworking student who participated and presented his papers at reputable international conferences in Malaysia, Indonesia, and Turkey. He is a contributor of Islamic finance about Islamic finance country report. His research publications appear in international journals such as *Muslim Business and Economic Review* (MBER) and the *Journal of Islamic Economics and Philanthropy*.

Sutan Emir Hidayat is an Associate Professor, and he is currently the Director of Islamic Economy Supporting Ecosystem at the National Committee for Islamic Economy and Finance (KNEKS), the Republic of Indonesia. He is a working group member of: Sustainability Working Group CIBAFI; Working Group FAS 1 AOIFI; Editorial Advisory Board, IFN Red-Money; Editorial Advisory Board, *International Journal of Islamic and Middle Eastern Finance and Management*, Emerald; and Editorial Advisory Board, *Journal of Economic Cooperation and Development*, SESRIC. He was recognized by ISFIN as one of the top influential 500 personalities on a global scale since 2015.

Norashikin Ismail is a Senior Lecturer at Faculty of Business Management, Universiti Teknologi MARA (UiTM) Johor. She graduated with a BA (Hons) in Accounting and Finance from the University of Lincolnshire and Humberside, United Kingdom in 1997. She was awarded with a Master of Business Administration from Graduate School of Management, Universiti Putra Malaysia in 2001 and received her PhD in Islamic Finance in 2011 from INCEIF. She has done research in the area of micro*takaful*, ESG, and *takaful* efficiency and published her research in refereed journal namely *International Journal of Economics and Management*, *Journal of Modern Accounting and Auditing*, and *Journal of Global Business and Economics*. Her current interest on research relates to ESG, crowdfunding, *takaful*, and corporate finance. She has presented papers in international and local conferences. She has also been involved in reviewing papers for local and international conferences and journals. Currently, she is the Coordinator for Doctor of Business Administration (DBA) at UiTM Segamat.

Abidullah Khan is an accomplished scholar specializing in Islamic finance. He obtained his PhD from Universiti Kebangsaan Malaysia in 2018, and his prior academic achievement includes an MBA in Islamic Banking and Finance from Graduate School of Business, Universiti Kebangsaan Malaysia in 2014. Dr Khan has made significant contributions to the field through publications in peer-reviewed journals. His research expertise lies in the intricate domains of Islamic social finance, Shari'ah disclosure practices, and the dynamics of Islamic banking. Dr Khan has been serving as an Assistant Professor at Sakarya University and an Assistant Professor of Islamic Finance (on leave) at Sukkur IBA University.

Shabeer Khan is an accomplished academic currently serving as an Assistant Professor at the College of Business Administration, Al-Yamamah University, Saudi Arabia. Prior to this, he held the position of Assistant Professor and Head of International Relations at the Department of Islamic Economics and Finance, Sakarya University, Turkey, and also served as an Assistant Professor at the Department of Business Administration at Sukkur IBA University, Pakistan. Dr Khan began his career as a Lecturer at Kohat University, Pakistan, and subsequently gained valuable research experience as a Research Assistant at INCEIF University Malaysia. Dr Khan's impressive academic journey includes attaining a PhD in Islamic Finance from INCEIF, Malaysia, as well as a Master's degree in Economics, a postgraduate degree in Shari'ah (Islamic Jurisprudence), and an MS degree in Social Science from Pakistan. He is highly regarded in the field of Islamic finance and economics and contributes actively to the industry. Dr Khan serves as a Shari'ah board member for Tayyib Advisory UAE and is a sought-after Shari'ah consultant for KalPay Financial Services, Pakistan, and Muawin, Pakistan. Additionally, he plays a pivotal role as a trainer and consultant with iFintel, Malaysia, where he imparts expertise in advanced econometric models, data analytics, and Islamic banking and finance.

Houda Lechheb is a Professor of Higher Education in the field of economics at Ibn Tofail University, Morocco. She has contributed significantly to the field of economics through her research, publications, and active participation in various academic events. She has also authored several pedagogical books and articles that enrich the understanding of economic concepts and theories. Her extensive teaching experience spans a wide range of economic subjects, including economics, management, quality management, and more. Her research interests encompass a wide array of economic topics, including economic growth, poverty, income inequality, impact evaluation, and more. She is frequently involved in various societal and economic issues where she shared her expertise through media appearances, public lectures, and consultations.

Abid Mahmood is a proficient academician and a scholar in the field of Islamic banking and finance. He obtained his PhD from University Kuala Lumpur in 2016. His prior academic achievements include a Master in Business Education in addition to Master of Islamic Studies. He has also attained the status of "Certified Shari'ah Advisor and Auditor" from AAOIFI, Bahrain. Dr Mahmood has made a significant contribution to the field of Islamic finance through his number of valuable publications in Scopus-indexed peer-reviewed international journals. His professional career as an adept educator expanded over 18 years. He has also contributed as a reviewer of high-worth international journals. Since 2022, Dr Abid has been serving Sukkur IBA University as an Assistant Professor of Islamic Finance.

Ziyaad Mahomed is an Associate Professor, the Lead Researcher (Shari'ah) for the Center of Excellence in Social Finance, and the Head of Online Programs at INCEIF University, Malaysia. He is also a consultant and Shari'ah advisor for almost 25 years and serves on several Shari'ah boards internationally, including HSBC Amanah in Malaysia and TajBank in Nigeria. Dr Ziyaad led several policy and strategy initiatives for financial institutions and governmental organizations in Islamic banking and *takaful*, sustainability, *sukuk*, fintech, and social finance. He has served as a consultant to the World Bank for Islamic finance development in South-East Asia and is an Adjunct Professor at the Asia School of Business in Malaysia. He holds a Master's and PhD in Islamic Finance from Malaysia, an MBA from South Africa, a BA (Hons) in Business (Finance) from the United Kingdom, and certification in the Islamic jurisprudence from South

Africa and Jordan. He lectures in Islamic Jurisprudence, Law of Contract, Sustainability and Social Finance, with almost 100 publications in academic and professional output.

Siti Masrohatin is an Associate Professor at the Faculty of Islamic Economics and Business (FEBI) and Program Coordinator of Master of Islamic Studies at School of Postgraduate, Kiai Haji Achmad Siddiq State Islamic University (UIN KHAS), Jember, Indonesia. She obtained her PhD in Management from Universitas Jember (UNEJ). She is currently a member of the Indonesian Association of Islamic Economists (IAEI) for the Commissariat of UIN KHAS and also a Companion to Halal Certification for Micro Small Medium Enterprises (MSMEs). She has published several books with national publishers and journal articles related to her research interests in human capital management, leadership, MSMEs, and halal tourism.

Hazik Mohamed is a multiskilled professional with substantial business management and varied experience in strategic, problem-solving, project management, and operational leadership roles. He has over 25 years of working experience and spent over 15 years building start-ups and business consulting, where he has consulted for MSMEs and MNCs on various business-related issues. His past corporate clients also include the ASEAN Secretariat, national finance offices, and the UNCDF. Hazik is the published author of *Belief and Rule Compliance* (Academic Press by Elsevier, 2018) on behavioral economics, *Blockchain, Fintech and Islamic Finance* (De|G Press by De Gruyter, 2019), and *Beyond Fintech* (by World Scientific, 2020). His wide research interests include financial inclusion, sustainable development, and new technology for disruptive socioeconomic advancement. Currently, he is working on business growth strategies for start-ups and engaged in various consulting projects.

Khairunnisa Musari is an Assistant Professor at Faculty of Islamic Economics and Business (FEBI) and Postgraduate Program, Kiai Haji Achmad Siddiq State Islamic University (UIN KHAS), Jember, Indonesia. She is a Secretary of the Indonesian Association of Islamic Economists (IAEI) for the Provincial Board of East Java since 2017. Her research interests are in *sukuk*, *waqf*, *esham*, fiscal and monetary policies, circular economy, halal logistics, sustainable finance, climate change, and Islamic microfinance and nanofinance. She has several book chapters with international reputable publishers such as IGI Global, Emerald Publishing Limited, World Scientific Publishing, Routledge, Springer, and Palgrave Macmillan. She has experience as a Senior Specialist for Islamic Finance of United Nations Development Program (UNDP) Indonesia and was listed as one of the Top 300 Most Influential Women in Islamic Business and Finance 2019, 2020, 2021, WOMANi Significancica 2022; WOMANi Academica 2023 by Cambridge-IFA.

Irum Saba has more than 19 years of progressive regulatory, research, training, and teaching experience with organizations of international repute. Currently, she is working as an Associate Professor and Program Director of MS Islamic Banking at Institute of Business Administration (IBA) – Karachi. She trained more than 6,000 employees in Pakistan's financial sector and taught more than 3,000 students in Pakistan. She has extensive regulatory experience with specific focus to promote women empowerment, organizational development, and Islamic banking and finance while working in the Islamic Banking Department of SBP. She is a Shari'ah-registered financial planner (Shari'ah RFP). She holds the Chartered Islamic Finance Professional (CIFP) credential from INCEIF with distinction and a PhD in Islamic Finance from INCEIF. She holds an MCom with distinction and a PGD in Islamic Banking and Insurance from Institute of Islamic Banking and Insurance (IIBI), London. Her areas of interest are political economy, management, Shari'ah, wealth planning and management, Islamic microfinance, corporate governance, and Islamic finance.

Soliha Sanusi is a Senior Lecturer at the Faculty of Economics and Management under the Center of Global Business and Digital Economy studies (GLOBDE), Universiti Kebangsaan Malaysia (UKM), Malaysia. She is a Chartered Accountant (CA) of the Malaysian Institute of Accountants (MIA) and obtained her PhD from the Universiti Teknologi MARA Malaysia in 2019. She was SLAB/SLAI scholarship recipient for her MBA and PhD studies. Her research interests are in the areas of direct tax, indirect tax, financial criminology, small–medium enterprises, mixed-method, and public sector accounting. She has published and presented her research work in various conferences and journals. At the moment, she is the editor of the *ASIAN Journal of Accounting and Governance*. She is also a reviewer for *Management and Accounting Review*, *Asian Academy of Management Journal of Accounting and Finance*, and a few more journals.

Umer Suleman is currently a Global Head of Risk, Compliance, and Shari'ah at Wahed based in the United Kingdom; he sits on the board of the UKIFC, is a member of the Islamic Finance Advisory, and is the cofounder of the National *waqf*. Umer has also been an advisor for several other Islamic Fintechs. Umer started his career as an Auditor at EY before holding senior positions in global finance institutions. Additionally, Umer has been actively involved in Islamic finance for the last 15 years, working with some of the most notable UK scholars on Shari'ah structuring and certifications. He was recognized for his work in 2016 as "one to watch" in London by the Brummel magazine. Umer studied Economics and Management at the Royal Holloway University of London and has subsequent postgraduate qualifications from Manchester Business School and Harvard University.

Putri Swastika earned her PhD in Islamic Finance from INCEIF, Malaysia. Prior joining the State Islamic Institute Metro (IAIN Metro), she was a Junior Fellow at Lehrstuhl für Sozial-und Wirtschaftsgesischte, Universität Leipzig, Germany. She authored Springer's Applying Risk Sharing Finance for Economic Development: Lessons from Germany (2021) and several Scopus-indexed and international journals.

Oumaima Tounchibine is a Moroccan-based Economist, Auditor, Management Controller, and Supply Chain Management Specialist. She holds a Master's degree in Management, Audit, and Financial Control. She was a Fellow at the

Division of Administration of the United Nations Economic Commission for Africa in Supply Chain Management Section. While continuing her PhD in the IIUM Institute of Islamic Finance (IIiBF), Oumaima participated as a Graduate Research Officer for the Government of Malaysia's sponsored Fundamental Research Grant Scheme (FRGS) research project titled "Humanitarian Sukuk: Developing an Alternative Financial Tool in Addressing Refugee Crisis." Simultaneously, she is also completing her PhD in Economic Science in Ibn Tofail University, the first world ranking research university in Morocco. In 2022, she received the best paper award on the recent research relating to refugee crisis from the Network for Education and Research on Peace and Sustainability (NERPS), Hiroshima University, Japan.

Syeda Beena Zaidi is specialized in the field of Finance. In 2014, she earned her Master's degree from Sukkur IBA University. She has extensive experience as a trainer of financial literacy and is presently serving as a Lecturer, Finance at Sukkur IBA University. Ms Zaidi is working toward a doctorate in Islamic and Sustainable Finance. Her research goals involve bridging digital and sustainable finance with Islamic finance.

Nor Razinah Mohd. Zain, PhD, is currently working as an Assistant Professor of Laws at IIUM Institute of Islamic Finance (IIiBF), Malaysia. She received her LLB (Honors), Master's of Comparative Laws (MCL), and PhD in Laws from International Islamic University Malaysia (IIUM). She is also an Advocate and Solicitor of the High Court of Malaya (nonpracticing). Since 2014, she worked with Ahmad Ibrahim Kulliyyah of Laws, Harun M. Hashim Law Center, and Kulliyyah of Economics and Management Sciences (KENMS). Her specialization focuses on comparative banking laws, Islamic finance, alternative dispute resolution, business law, and sustainable finance law. Currently, she is a Fellow under IIUM's Sejahtera Center that emphasized on Sustainable Development Goals' community-oriented engagements. She has contributed in several research projects from 2014 to 2023. She has written more than 70 research works (including articles and chapters). In her leisure time, she enjoys reading.

Hafizah Omar Zaki is a Senior Lecturer in Marketing at the Faculty of Economics and Management (FEP), Universiti Kebangsaan Malaysia (UKM). She is currently the Head of Emerging Technology and Big Data (ETBD) cluster at the Center of Global Business and Digital Economy (GloBDE), FEP-UKM. She holds a PhD in Marketing – specializing in advertising and branding from University of Malaya (UM), an MBA – specializing in Human Resource Management from UKM, and a degree in Multimedia Management from Multimedia University (MMU). Her research and publications involve advertising, branding, digital marketing, and digital business amid the advancement of technology use.

Preface

"The Future of Islamic Finance: From Shari'ah Law to Fintech" offers a comprehensive examination of the evolution, principles, and contemporary relevance of Islamic finance. Delving into its ethical, technological, and sustainable dimensions, this book explores the integration of Islamic finance with modern financial practices and its potential to foster sustainable development and financial inclusion. Through insightful chapters authored by experts in the field, readers gain a deeper understanding of Islamic finance's role in shaping the future of finance, navigating economic challenges, promoting social well-being, and leveraging technology-driven innovations. With a focus on ethics, sustainability, and technological advancements, this book serves as a valuable resource for practitioners, policymakers, researchers, and students seeking to explore the dynamic landscape of Islamic finance.

The book is organized into four interconnected parts, each offering a unique perspective on different aspects of Islamic finance.

Part One provides an overview of the foundational aspects of Islamic finance, tracing its historical evolution and exploring its fundamental principles. *Chapter 1* delves into the historical journey of Islamic finance, highlighting its unique features and key principles, while *Chapter 2* examines the relevance of Islamic economics in addressing contemporary challenges. Building upon this, *Chapter 3* explores the philosophical underpinnings of Islamic finance, emphasizing its enduring relevance in today's financial systems. Finally, *Chapter 4* discusses the contributions of Muslim scholars to economic theories, advocating for free trade and ethical market practices.

Part Two focuses on the ethical and socially responsible dimensions of Islamic finance, exploring its role in promoting sustainable development and social welfare. *Chapter 5* examines the integration of Islamic finance with the Sustainable Development Goals (SDGs), emphasizing its potential to alleviate poverty and promote environmental sustainability. This ethical imperative is further underscored in *Chapter 6*, which discusses the role of Islamic microfinance in fostering social well-being and financial inclusion. Additionally, *Chapter 7* explores the potential of Islamic social finance to address humanitarian challenges, particularly in Organization of Islamic Cooperation (OIC) countries, through mechanisms such as *zakah* and *waqf*. *Chapter 8* emphasizes the ethical imperative of Islamic banking, highlighting its role in promoting responsible financial practices and sustainability.

Part Three explores the intersection of technology-driven innovation with Islamic finance, addressing opportunities and challenges presented by fintech and digital currencies. *Chapter 11* discusses the potential of fintech to enhance financial inclusion and support sustainable economic growth within Islamic finance. This is complemented by *Chapter 12*, which analyzes the compatibility of digital currencies with Shari'ah principles and explores the regulatory framework needed for their integration into Islamic finance. Furthermore, *Chapter 13* examines the role of artificial intelligence in improving efficiency and risk management within Islamic banking while ensuring compliance with Shari'ah principles.

Part Four presents an in-depth exploration of the future landscape of Islamic finance, addressing key challenges and opportunities facing the industry. *Chapter 14* focuses on strategies for fostering financial inclusion, enhancing sustainability, embracing digitalization, and promoting industry harmonization within Islamic finance. Finally, *Chapter 15* concludes the book by emphasizing the need for a values-driven approach and the integration of Islamic finance with emerging technologies to drive ethical, equitable, and sustainable financial practices globally.

In short, "The Future of Islamic Finance: From Shari'ah Law to Fintech" presents a nuanced exploration of Islamic finance, spanning its historical roots to its contemporary applications. This comprehensive examination delves into the ethical, technological, and sustainable facets of Islamic finance, shedding light on its integration into modern financial practices and its potential to drive sustainable development and financial inclusion. Authored by experts in the field, each chapter offers unique insights into Islamic finance's role in shaping the future of finance, addressing economic challenges, promoting social welfare, and embracing technological innovations. Grounded in principles of ethics, sustainability, and technological advancement, this book serves as an invaluable resource for practitioners, policymakers, researchers, and students alike, providing a comprehensive understanding of the dynamic landscape of Islamic finance, its timelessness, and its profound implications for the global financial sphere.

Dr Edib Smolo & Dr Mohamed Mahees Raheem

Acknowledgments

We would like to express our sincere gratitude to all the individuals who contributed to the realization of this book. Their invaluable support, insights, and expertise have been instrumental in bringing this project to fruition.

First and foremost, we extend our heartfelt appreciation to the esteemed reviewers who dedicated their time and expertise to provide invaluable feedback and constructive criticism during the review process. Their meticulous attention to detail and insightful comments greatly enhanced the quality and depth of the book.

We extend our sincere thanks to Dr Amnisuhailah Abarahan, Dr Admir Meskovic, Dr Aida Hanic-Suceska, Dr Ashraf Iqbal, Dr Hazik Mohamed, Dr Moutaz Abojeib, Dr Muhammad Iman Sastra Mihajat, Dr Muhammad Mustapha Ishaq Akinlaso, Dr Mustapha Abubakar, Dr Norhanim Mat Sari, Dr Rashed Jahangir, Dr Syaryanti Hussin, and Mr Shazuli Raheem for their meticulous attention to detail and insightful comments, which greatly enhanced the quality and depth of the book.

We would also like to thank Dr Haifa Reda Jamal Al-Lail, the President of Effat University, for her support in the realization of this project.

We are also deeply grateful to our colleague, Dr Anna Visvizi, for her consistent support and encouragement throughout the entire duration of this project. Her insights and guidance were invaluable in shaping the direction of the book.

Furthermore, we would like to express our gratitude to the staff at Emerald Publishing for their outstanding assistance and support throughout the publication process. Their professionalism, expertise, and dedication ensured the successful completion of this book.

Last but not least, we extend our thanks to our families, friends, and colleagues for their unwavering support and encouragement throughout this journey. Their understanding, patience, and encouragement were essential in enabling us to devote the necessary time and effort to this project.

In short, we are deeply grateful to everyone who contributed to this book in any capacity. Your support and dedication have been invaluable, and we are truly honored to have had the opportunity to work with such talented individuals.

Editors

Chapter 1

A Brief Overview of Islamic Finance: From Madinah Market to Wall Street

Edib Smolo and Mohamed Mahees Raheem

Effat University, Saudi Arabia

Abstract

Many lessons have been learned by the global financial system at the aftermath of the Global Health Crisis (GHC), which could last till the financial crisis occurred in 2008–2009 (global financial crisis [GFC]). As such, the system started facing the deep-rooted questions about regulatory reforms. Amidst a perilous situation, Islamic finance (IF) had demonstrated clear evidence of strong muscles into something that countries appreciate as the tool for money intermediation. It constitutes a brief introduction to the way Islamic Financial System or IFS (1) came forth in the past and (2) continues nowadays. The paper starts with the stating the maqasid al-Shari'ah (goals of the Shari'ah), which are the fundamental objectives of the legal system in Islam. Then, it highlights the key concepts, unique features, and modes of financing that are unique within the IFS. The integration of Islamic financial institutions (IFIs) into the global economy is covered and IF as well as global financial dynamics at large discussed with the closing comments mirroring IF complexity on the background of global economy. This segment alone has posted very significant gain of almost US$3 trillion, which is projected to rise further to US$6.7 trillion by 2027 – a clear indication of its outreach and accessibility to all.

Keywords: Islamic finance; Islamic banking; Islamic Financial System (IFS); Shari'ah; Islamic law; Maqasid al-Shari'ah

Introduction

In the wake of the COVID-19 pandemic (although referred to as the GHC) that erupted globally and the echoes of the GFC in 2008–2009 are claimed to be the most severe since the Great Depression, imposing some stringent alternative

The Future of Islamic Finance, 1–14

doi:10.1108/978-1-83549-906-120241001

procedures and stress tests to evaluate the international financial system's strength became a pressing concern. These events prompted the world to go through the first comprehensive review of the current international financial system, and the interactions that were held were the first steps in determining the desired regulatory reforms. On the other hand, there also started a search for a dependable and clean long-term thing to solve the problems caused by these (Haneef & Smolo, 2013; Smolo, 2020; Smolo & Mirakhor, 2010).

In the midst of the devastating wreckage that the GFCs have brought upon the financial sector worldwide, IF has never ceased to grow and develop (Smolo et al., 2023). Increasingly seen as one of the most dynamic areas within the international financial innovation is of IF, and today, it has become well-accepted and widely practiced form of financial intermediation known for its market competitiveness and strength. Thus, it exceeds the boundaries of the realm of faith, which to a great deal is practiced by Muslims and non- Muslim people alike. The sector's surge is symbolized by the tremendous market share implying that the value of assets soared up to US$4.5 trillion in the year 2022 and is predicted to grow even higher to US$6.7 trillion by the year of 2027 (ICD-LSEG, 2023).

The present chapter is designed to explain the key principles and concepts of the IFS. Efforts are made to demonstrate the applicability of those ideas in the modern context by analyzing the current application of some of these key principles. The part two of the paper will present the summary of the IFS recording both its historical evolution and present situation. The *maqasid al-Shari'ah* (the objectives of Shari'ah) lies in the essence of the IFS; hence, the section three of this essay will examine the major concepts arising from these objectives. The IFS (which stands for the IFS) constitutes the specific type of financial intermediation form which is characterized by peculiar features that enable them direct the flow of funds toward the stimulation of the productive economic activity. On the contrary, I will be presenting the key syntheses as well as various forms of microfinance in part four and happening right after that in part five. Part 6 will emphasize on the placing the IFI in particularly global market and the transformation started from the local level to the international level. Lastly, the concluding section of this chapter will shed light with the insightful final remarks that put together the intricate fabric of IF on the loose sketched background of the global financial market.

The Islamic Financial System: An Overview

The realm of IF, rooted in the guidance of Shari'ah, embodies a unique ethos in financial dealings.[1] The Holy Qur'an and the *Sunnah* stand as the foundational

[1]Literally, Shari'ah means a path to a watering place, a clear path to be followed. This led to its use for the path which the believer has to tread in order to obtain guidance in this world and deliverance in the next.

sources of Shari'ah, complemented by the consensus of jurists (*ijma'*) and analogy (*qiyas*).[2] While Shari'ah staunchly prohibits the exchange of interest, characterizing the IFS merely as "interest-free" oversimplifies its intricate nature. Beyond this restriction, IF, as a reflection of broader Islamic principles, champions the preservation of property rights, ethical standards, risk-sharing, and the pursuit of social justice. It extends beyond profit to embody a broader societal responsibility, where investment activities align not only with Shari'ah ethics but also consider public interests (*masalih* pl. of *maslahah*).[3]

The roots of Islamic financial principles run deep through the annals of Muslim history. This has been discussed extensively in Chapter 4. The term "Islamic financial system," though coined relatively recently in the mid-1980s, encapsulates a tradition that spans centuries. Over the past four decades, and particularly in the last 20 years, IFIs have transcended regional confines to become integral components of the international financial system. Today, IFIs extend their influence across banking, insurance, and capital markets, a testament to their evolution and significance in the global economic landscape.

The utilization of Islamic financial instruments echoes through the corridors of time, with the first "modern" experiments in Islamic banking surfacing in the 1960s and 1970s. Mit Ghamr local savings bank of Egypt that initiated in 1963 is an Islamic bank of historical importance since it is the first one to be launched. The establishment of the Bank was done with a full success; then in 1967, after installation, the Bank of Nasir became the precursor of social banking accordingly to the principles of Shari'ah.

The entire historical road map of IF comprehensively depicts IF as an independent and separate financial paradigm from usual financial systems with experimentation intended for local interests only to one that has been globally accepted. The narrative that smoothly threads its way through time shows bright connection between the ethics of marketplace in Madinah to advanced tapestry of Wall Street, where IF has managed to reaffirm its significance and power.

The Market of IF came to attract not only Muslim but also non-Muslim investors and stakeholders too. Exploring the expansive global reach of the IFS, the following narrative derives inspiration from the comprehensive perspectives outlined in the "Islamic Finance Development Report 2023: Navigating Uncertainty" which came into existence through the cooperation between the Islamic Corporation for the Development of Private Sector (ICD) of the Islamic Development Bank Group and the London Stock Exchange Group (LSEG).

In the dynamic environment of global finances, IF resolved the challenge of insecurity in 2022, consequently delving into a macroeconomic system that was besieged by the fluctuations in world prices of commodities and a global supply chain that was still on its pre pandemic equilibrium. In the environment, the

---

[2]*Sunnah* is an Arabic word that means "habit" or "usual practice". Technically, this term refers to whatever was reported that the Prophet Muhammad (peace and blessings be upon him) said, did, or gave his tacit approval.

[3]The Holy Qur'an is full of references to *maslahah* (benefits). For example, see: (57:25), (16: 90), (2:151), (3:164), (2:185), (22:78), (2:286), (4:28), (27:77).

industry level, the growth has surged to 11% last year, which is lower than 17% peak recorded in the previous season. In the year 2021, the asset levels were at US$4.5 trillion.

Diverse sectors within IF experienced disparate fortunes. Islamic funds, both mutual funds and exchange-traded funds (ETFs), bore the brunt of adverse sentiment in equities due to multiple rate hikes. Consequently, assets under management for Islamic funds dipped by 10% to US$220 billion. Despite this downturn, notable launches, including Australia's inaugural Islamic ETF and environmental, social and governance (ESG) ETFs in various regions, injected a spark of innovation into the landscape.

Islamic banking, a cornerstone with assets totaling US$3.2 trillion, encountered headwinds as 24% of Islamic banks reported lower profits or higher losses. Inflationary adjustments, increased expenses for digitalization, and equity investment setbacks contributed to these challenges. However, some regions, like the Gulf Cooperation Council (GCC), exhibited positive performance driven by higher profit income and reduced impairment charges.

Sukuk, the second-largest contributor with US$788 billion in outstanding value in 2022, demonstrated resilience. Malaysian market issuances surged, but the GCC experienced a decline due to reduced funding needs from sovereigns and state-backed entities, which was attributed to a spike in oil prices. Noteworthy corporate issues arose in Sub-Saharan African nations like Tanzania and Nigeria.

Takaful (Islamic insurance), the third-largest sector with US$90 billion in total assets, expanded by 16% though only 52% of operators posted positive performance. Claims payouts in sectors like motor *takaful* and investment losses impacted results (Refer Fig. 1.1).

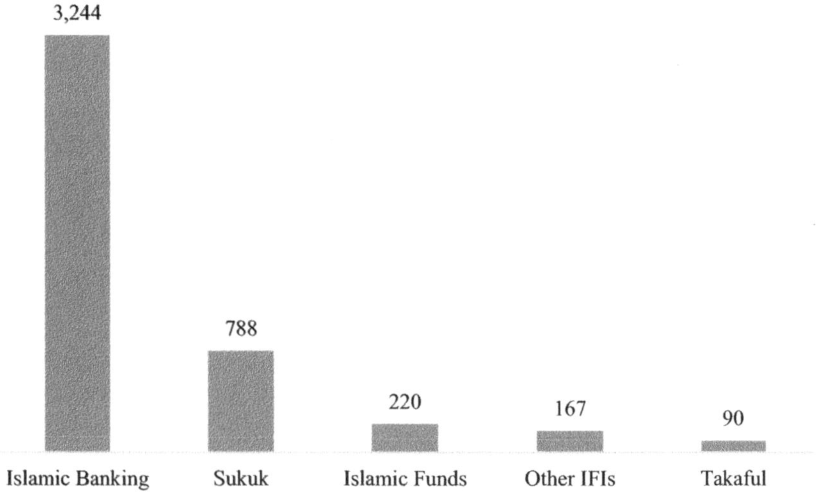

Fig. 1.1. Global Assets of Islamic Finance. *Source:* Adapted from ICD-LSEG (2023).

The other IFIs sector, valued at US$167 billion, saw Saudi Arabia leading in numbers, with a burgeoning IFS in Pakistan capturing attention. The Islamic Finance Development Indicator underscored Malaysia, Saudi Arabia, and Indonesia as the most developed jurisdictions among 136 countries, with Pakistan ascending to the sixth position.

Looking ahead, the IF industry anticipates a positive trajectory. In emerging markets, Russia and Uganda incorporate Islamic banking, while Algeria and Ethiopia lay the foundations for Islamic capital markets. Established Shari'ah-compliant markets witness advancements in governance in the UAE and strengthened Shari'ah governance in Pakistan and Saudi Arabia.

A burgeoning trend in Islamic fintech unfolds, with digital *takaful* operators launching in Malaysia, aligning with technological advances. *Sukuk*, a crucial asset class, awaits a growing pipeline, especially in ESG *sukuk*, aligning with sustainable economic goals. Increased efforts in knowledge and awareness are reflected in the growing importance of Shari'ah qualifications and Indonesia's national strategy for financial literacy.

With these multi-faceted growth channels and developments, the IF industry projects a growth trajectory, reaching US$6.7 trillion by 2027 (ICD-LSEG, 2023).

Maqasid al-Shari'ah (Objectives of the Shari'ah)

In the realm of IF, the principles embedded in *maqasid al-Shari'ah*, often referred to as the objectives or *maslahah* (public interest), play a pivotal role. This complex topic, briefly touched upon here, holds significance as it is commonly argued that *maqasid al-Shari'ah* forms the foundational basis of Islamic economics. According to Khan (2002), economic agents within an Islamic framework are oriented toward seeking *maslahah*, going beyond the conventional pursuit of utility.

The nuanced exploration of *maqasid al-Shari'ah* gained substantial attention only in the 11th century, notably by al-Ghazali (505H/1111 CE) and later by al-Shatibi (d. 790/1388). Ibn Qayyim al-Jawziyyah (d. 1356) emphasized that the Shari'ah aims at safeguarding people's interests in both this world and the hereafter (Ibn Qayyim, n.d.). Al-Ghazali eloquently expressed that the objective of the Shari'ah is to promote the welfare of human beings, encompassing the safeguarding of faith, life, intellect, posterity, and wealth (Al-Ghazali, 1937).

Classified by Muslim scholars into three main categories, *maqasid al-Shari'ah* includes *daruriyyat* (essentials), *hajiyyat* (needs), and *tahsiniyyat* (embellishments).[4] Muslim scholars define *maslahah* as "the preservation of the objectives of Shari'ah," signifying its primary role. The essential *masalih*, or *daruriyyat*, are divided into five, emphasizing the preservation of key aspects:

(1) Preservation of faith/religion (*Din*),
(2) Preservation of life (*Nafs*),

---

[4]For detailed discussion on different classifications see Ibn Ashur (2001), Kamali (1998, 2008), Vejzagic and Smolo (2011), and ISRA (2011, 2023).

(3) Preservation of lineage/descendants/procreation (*Nasl*),
(4) Preservation of property (*Mal*) and
(5) Preservation of intellect/reason (*'Aql*).

This comprehensive approach aligns with the multifaceted objectives of Shari'ah, ensuring not just the individual but also the communal well-being. Recognizing these objectives serves as a compass guiding IF practitioners (Smolo, 2013).

The Salient Features of Islamic Finance

In the intricate realm of IF, numerous scholars have delved into the foundational principles, drawing insights from key sources like the Qur'an, *Sunnah*, *ijma'*, and *qiyas* (Askari et al., 2012; Ayub, 2007; El-Gamal, 2006; Mirakhor, 2007; Smolo, 2013; Smolo & Ismail, 2011; Usmani, 2002). These principles, deeply rooted in Islamic jurisprudence, underpin the ethical and financial framework that transcends geographical and temporal boundaries. The most important are:

The Prohibition of Riba *(Interest or Usury)*[5]

At the heart of IF lies the unequivocal prohibition of *riba*, or interest and usury, as emphatically stated in the Qur'an. The verse declares, "Those who devour usury (*riba*) will not stand except as one stands whom Satan has driven mad by his touch. That is because they say, 'Trade is like *riba*,' whereas Allah has permitted trade and forbidden *riba*."[6] *Riba*, with its literal meaning of "excess," "growth," or "increment," holds profound implications for financial transactions.

The prohibition extends to two distinctive forms (Al-Zuhayli, 2003a):

(1) *Riba al-Fadl:* Primarily applicable to barter transactions, this form of *riba* involves the trading of one commodity within a category where the rules of *riba* apply for another commodity of the same category. An increase of one compensation over the other characterizes this exchange.[7]
(2) *Riba al-Nasi'ah:* Tailored specifically to loans, this type of *riba* encompasses any excess payment over the principal amount, acting as compensation for a delay in repayment.

---

[5]Some authors differentiate between usury and interest and say that *riba* refers to usury only while interest is not included in the prohibition. In this paper, the term *riba* refers to both interest and usury. For detailed discussion on the issue of *riba*, see: (Al-Zuhayli, 2003b, p. 309).

[6]Al-Qur'an, 2:275. In fact, the receipt of *riba* is forbidden in the Holy Qur'an, while the payment of *riba* is prohibited in the Sunnah of the Prophet (peace be upon him), and consensus (*ijma'*). In the Qur'an, the strongest prohibition is provided in the verses [2: 275–279].

[7]The following items are mentioned in a *hadith* to be *ribawi* and as such should be exchanged only in an equal measure or quantity: gold, silver, barley, wheat, salt and dates.

The meticulous classification of these two types underscores the depth and precision with which IF addresses various facets of financial transactions. This prohibition not only reflects a distinctive ethical stance but also emphasizes the importance of fairness, justice, and equitable dealings in the financial realm.

Prohibition of **Gharar** *(Excessive Risk and Uncertainty)*

Gharar, a term laden with meaning, encapsulates the concept of something with a pleasant appearance but an unpleasant reality. Defined as the sale of probable goods whose existence and/or characteristics lack certainty, *gharar* equates to a trade akin to gambling (Al-Darīr, 1995). Examples include the sale of fish in the sea, birds in the sky, or unripe fruits on the tree, all of which introduce excessive and avoidable uncertainty into transactions.

Prohibition of **Maysir** *(Gambling/Speculation)*

IF staunchly prohibits gambling and games of chance that involve the possibility of total loss to one party.[8] Described as a zero-sum game, *maysir* leads to a transfer of wealth without creating any new wealth. Beyond financial considerations, the prohibition of *maysir* is motivated by the potential for invoking enmity and distracting individuals from their worship.

Shari'ah-Compliant Activities

As a subscriber to Islamic tenets of trading, IFIs must operate upon to what will be permissible under Shari'ah guidelines. This means that Shariab pays an absolute disapproval of investing in casino business, tobacco production, alcoholic beverages, pork farming, pornography works, and the manufacture of guns and other things not associated with Islamic teaching.

Risk-and-Return Sharing

Unlike interest-based incomes, IF seeks to promote returns on investment by spreading the risk and reward among lending parties or monies given. Such kind of the approach stimulates business among the partners depending on the nature of human relationships not the system of base interests which are clubbed as the conventional interest system.

The Sanctity of Contracts

The contractual obligations not carried out according to Islamic way of life are also regarded as breach of trust in Islam.[9] Contracts involvement in the sanctity of

---

[8]Gambling is prohibited in the Qur'an [5:90–91].

[9]Refer to Qur'an, [5:1] where it says: "O you who believe! Fulfill (all) obligations."

contracts is another aspect which is marked the disclosure of full information, which is aimed to tackle the possession of the hazard and information asymmetry. This implementation allows for genuine business delicate deals under fair conditions.

Social Justice

Islamic system fully stands against the things that would lead or result in social injustice or the party doing exploitation. Furthermore, public interest is promoted ensured above the benefit of an individual. This is achieved by IF principals that oppose paying interest except on the basis of deferred payment (*riba*), risk-maximizing instruments (*gharar*) and gambling (*maysir*). IF then promotes fairness and justice through legitimate compensation for risk-and-return sharing as well as cooperation and *maslahah* (public interest).

Among other issues, community banking, ethical banking, and socially responsible investing are the basis of IF model. In this way, it endeavors to design a financial environment that not only be in accordance with the religious doctrines but also complies with the ethical values that people follow in the modern world. Being this ethos ponders as the passage from the antique markets of the town of Madina to the busiest financial structures of Wall Street the Islamic banking is the entrenched principle that it will stand the test of time.

The Basic Modes of Islamic Finance

As the landscape of IFIs has evolved, so too has the array of financial instruments at their disposal. These instruments cater to a wide spectrum of sectors, encompassing housing projects, car financing, working materials and equipment acquisition, funding business ventures, and addressing government deficits. A concise exploration of the fundamental modes of finance in IFIs reveals their versatility and applicability across various economic domains.[10]

Qard Hasan *(Benevolent Loan)*

Qard Hasan, translating to "good loan," is not merely a financial contract but a commitment grounded in social welfare. Technically, it functions as a loan agreement between two parties, with the amount borrowed being equivalent to the amount to be repaid. However, what distinguishes it is the benevolent nature allowing the borrower to repay more than the borrowed sum, provided such terms are not predefined at the contract's outset. This unique mode aligns with the spirit of mutual assistance and societal well-being, reflecting the ethos of IF.

---

[10]For a detailed discussion of the basic modes of Islamic finance, please see: Al-Zuhayli (2003a, 2003b), Ayub (2007), ISRA (2023), Smolo (2013), Smolo and Ismail (2011), Usmani (2002), etc.

Musharakah *(Active Partnership)*

Musharakah, translating to "sharing," epitomizes a profit-and-loss-sharing partnership, akin to a joint venture. In this collaborative framework, two or more parties contribute capital, be it in cash or kind, along with their labor. The essence lies in shared ownership and risk. Profits derived from the venture are distributed according to a pre-agreed profit-sharing ratio, fostering a cooperative approach. Conversely, losses are shared based on the capital contributions, emphasizing a shared responsibility in both success and challenges.

Musharakah Mutanaqisah *(Diminishing Partnership)*

Musharakah Mutanaqisah, a dynamic hybrid of *musharakah* and *ijarah*, orchestrates a unique financial alliance between a financier, often a bank, and a beneficiary, the client. The crux of this contract lies in joint ownership of an asset or property, with a distinctive condition. The financier gradually sells their shares to the beneficiary at a pre-agreed price and within a predetermined schedule. This evolving partnership captures the essence of shared ownership while facilitating the client's ultimate acquisition of the asset, offering a nuanced solution in IF (Smolo & Hassan, 2011).

Mudarabah *(Passive Partnership)*

Mudarabah stands as a special form of partnership, encompassing a capital owner (*rabb al-mal*) contributing capital and an entrepreneur or manager (*mudarib*) overseeing the business. The distribution of profits adheres to a pre-agreed ratio, yet the capital itself remains unguaranteed. Notably, in the event of a loss, it is the provider of capital who bears the financial burden, as they lack control over the management of the business. This passive partnership underscores the risk-sharing nature of IF, fostering collaboration while acknowledging individual roles.

Bay' al-Murabahah *(Cost-Plus Financing)*

Bay' al-Murabahah, often termed cost-plus financing, revolves around a transparent contract of sale and purchase.[11] Here, the bank acquires the requested asset from the supplier and discloses the cost along with a profit margin (mark-up) to the customer. The selling price, predetermined at the contract's outset, remains fixed and immutable. This mode provides clarity and fairness to the customer while adhering to Islamic financial principles.

---

[11]Also known as *al-murabahah lil-amr bi al-shira* (*Murabahah* for the Purchase Orderer).

Bay' al-Salam *(Future Delivery)*

Bay' al-Salam, representing a future delivery sale contract, introduces a distinctive temporal dimension to transactions. This payment method reflects the fact that the buyer pays the price from the beginning and requires the merchandise specified within the period of time. By this way of operation, the transactions are already made keeping in view the requirements of the present and the future and the cementation of the commitments, hence the flexibility of the IF system is quite evident.

Ijarah *(Leasing)*

Ijarah, the term depicting "to rent something," takes the shape of a lease agreement where a lessor, usually the bank or asset owner, leases out its underlying asset to the lessee. Such situation excludes alternation and is cost-effective after an approved lease rental for a specified time. However, among the essentials, the ownership of the lease's property stays with the landlord, whose role also includes the maintenance. A marvelous illustration of a mutual symbiosis relationship where the tenant gains from the use of the asset that does not imply ownership at the same time promotes flexibility and responsibility is the concept of *ijarah* which is an IF mode.

Ijarah wa Iqtina *(Lease Ending in Ownership)*

Ijarah wa Iqtina is similar to an *ijarah* contract only that it has a variant style and in fact, even more, complex than the *ijarah*.[12] It may look like the landlord's typical agreement, but it is the last part which makes it different from a regular contract. Here, what is being leased is the asset itself rather than the right to use it. This transmission is overseen through the second contract in which the leased asset is gifted to the lessee or he is also authorized to buy it from the lessor for a nominal price. This inclusion is the manifestation of a long-term utmost ownership granting that appeals to the basics of IF.

Istisna' *(Commissioned Manufacture)*

Istisna' happens to be this purchase order contract, where a buyer wishes a seller to work on a project for delivery at a future date. In this contract, the supplier is asked to complete a specific job as per the specification of the agreement. It fits into the Shari'ah standard which is peculiar for cases where the procurement of custom-made products is the only alternative for the buyer and witnesses the flexibility factor in the IF.

---

[12]It is also known as *Ijarah Thumma al-Bay'* or *Ijarah Muntahiyah bi-Tamlik*.

Sukuk *(Islamic Certificate/Bond)*

Sukuk commonly referred to as Islamic certificate or bond is a document that acknowledges one's ownership in divorced equity that is toward or backed by a definite project or investment activity. Just like normal bonds are traded in the stock market *sukuks* can also be traded among the traders. But it is also in accordance with the basic pillars of Shari'ah in the sense that it is a commodity-based bond proving the linkage of financial products and moral traits into Islamic banking.

The diversity in IF is depicted trough the various modes such as *qard hasan*, *mudarabah*, *musharakah* and *ijarah* to *murabahah*, *salam*, *istisna'* and *sukuk* which in turn indicate that Islamic financial instruments are very versatile and subtle. The emerging modes which are based on fairness, accountability, and moral criteria are proof of IF's adaptability and quest for innovation. To sum up, they are essential parts that constitute a business which is fair and based on interaction between different parties, the Islamic business system.

From Madinah Market to Wall Street

The rise of Islam in seventh century Mecca not only brought into being a very spiritual religion but also the beginning of an elaborate economic system. Koehler (2014) challenges traditional historical notions by presenting the scaling point of capitalism to be more on the Muslim civilization than on Medieval Europe. He is of the view that the capitalistic system was shaped and imbued with its organizational and ideological elements in an architecture of the Muslim world.

As the prophet Mohammed (pbuh – peace be upon him) (an experienced trader) and Mecca town (a center of trade and spirituality) were the core of this economy, the mercantilism created a new elegant type of business trade. The Islamic religion with sufficient input about the justice *('adl)* and the fairness over extensive trade, dealt with equitable trade. The teachings of these business codes stipulate the sacredness of the business contracts and encouraging the responsibility of contractual integrity as the civic duty and the religious obligation. Islam, which is a system of life taken in whole, is an ideal of the religious and mundane affairs and the economic relationship being all the time intertwined with each other. The fact that Islamic law guaranteed the right to private property, brought women and men on an equal ground, was an unconventional aspect of Islamic jurisprudence which dates back for more than 14 centuries.

Muhammad's (pbuh), great economic influence on the economy came after his immigration to Medina. Through the founding of a Muslim community, he has been critical in the setting up of socioeconomic "engines" whose function has been to propel the growth and development of his society. The Mosque of the Prophet started to be a place where the discussions to be made occurred; it was almost equal to a current day parliament or assembly then. Considering discussions of emerging problems and key decisions, this place served as forum where people and societal representatives were consulted and disputes were resolved.

In Medina, the preexistent market became the first of multiple setbacks that were caused due to the imposition of different taxes and their incompatibility with Islamic eternity values. The acceptance of these new reforms was distinctive and was attained under the command of the Prophet. He decreed that new business transactions within this market would be free of taxes and privileges. Trade in the market of this pattern was performed tax-free, no special privileges were indicated for any participant.

Economic ideas of Islamic economics have their origin in the teachings of Prophet Muhammad (pbuh), which create a prototype pattern for the whole mankind. After Muhammad, the Prophet of Islam, the religion had spread to all over the world encountered by the problems of diverse nature. However, the Islamic history also presents a case of continuous economic thought development which was equally implemented under Islamic rule as indicated in Chapter 4.

The authentication of changing Islamic economic principles speaks for many writings indicating the development of the science of economics in those countries wherever Islam was cultivated. In fact, the growth trajectory of the IF industry as shown in the "Islamic Finance Development Report 2023," and explained at the beginning this article, is a remarkable demonstrate of the industry's resilience. In the context of global economic uncertainties, the industry is still able to withstand challenges including commodity fluctuation and supply chain disruption in 2022. Its outstanding Those assets totaling $4.5 trillion today imply that IF has been able to penetrate deeper into the global financial space.

What is even more fascinating for the economic growth phenomenon is the different sectors of the industry, with the different performance. While the financial industry met various obstacles on its way, Islamic funds and banks demonstrated to be flexible and creative. Such as the emergence of newcomers, for instance, the introduction of Australian Islamic ETF and the ESG ETFs as a sign of dynamic revolutionary change of ETFs segment. Islamic banking's US$3.2 trillion in assets, resilience and outstanding performances in GCC show that the industry is able to navigate its way successfully in difficult times.

While the IFS emerged from the old Madinah market and is now ascending to the heights of the mighty Wall Street, it is increasingly being woven into the fabric of the global financial system. Islamic Financial Investment presents ample room for further growth in light of the emergence of Islamic fintech, a faster *sukuk* pipeline and the reinforced efforts aimed at increasing public awareness and knowledge. Boasting an estimated growth to reach a whopping US$6.7 trillion by end of 2027, the global IF sector is in line to be the ethical and sustainable power presiding over the future of global financial markets. Its journey from standing on traditional markets to delving into the intricacies of Wall Street demonstraes how it changes the financial landscape worldwide.

Concluding Remarks

To sum up, the path from Madinah Market to Wall Street proves the idea that IF is universal in its appeal, and it can stand the test of time. Its ability to evolve into a formal means of financial intermediation exemplifies a story of versatility and inclusivity. Therefore, for this financial system to strengthen and to keep us competitive in the complexities of modern financial landscape, we need to rely on its principles that serve as pillars.

Apart from economic metrics, the projected growth of the sector from $4.5 trillion in 2022 to a shocking $6.7 trillion by 2027 (ICD-LSEG, 2023) again demonstrates the industry's importance in economics and also its ability to transcend cultural and faith borders. IF as a player in international financial systems, Islamic is "not just a fly on the wall"; rather, it emerges as a driving force for the transformations and dynamics of the international financial system landscape. This is an example of the constant change dynamic in finance. On the one hand, traditional concepts remain at its core while; on the other hand, they push the financial ecosystem forward, determining the currents of the global economic change.

At its core, IF distills a philosophy that goes beyond mere numbers as they appear in the financial statements. It tells an original story about the ability of a culture to be flexible, inclusive, and perennial, all the while being relevant in today's larger global context and technology. What we see today as more products and services come on the IF scene is a continuous process of its growth in the global financial arena and the IF narrative is becoming an essential part of the evolving financial world history.

References

Al-Darīr, S. M. A.-A. (1995). *Al-Gharar wa Atharuhū Fī al-'Uqūd: Fī al-Fiqhi al-Islāmiyyi* (2nd ed.). Dallah al-Barakah.

Al-Ghazali, A. H. M. (1937). *Al-Mustasfā min cIlm al-Usūl* (Vol. 1). Al-Maktabah al-Tijariyyah.

Al-Zuhayli, W. (2003a). *Financial transactions in Islamic jurisprudence* (M. A. El-Gamal, Trans., Vol. 1). Dar al-Fikr.

Al-Zuhayli, W. (2003b). *Financial transactions in Islamic jurisprudence* (M. A. El-Gamal, Trans., Vol. 2). Dar al-Fikr.

Askari, H., Iqbal, Z., Krichenne, N., & Mirakhor, A. (2012). *Risk sharing in finance: The Islamic finance alternative*. John Wiley & Sons.

Ayub, M. (2007). *Understanding Islamic finance*. John Wiley & Sons.

El-Gamal, M. A. (2006). *Islamic finance: Law, economics, and practice*. Cambridge University Press.

Haneef, R., & Smolo, E. (2013). Reshaping the Islamic finance industry: Applying the lessons learned from the global financial crisis. In H. Ahmed, M. Asutay, & R. Wilson (Eds.), *Islamic banking and financial crisis: Reputation, stability and risks* (pp. 21–39). Edinburgh University Press. https://doi.org/10.3366/edinburgh/9780748647613.003.0002

Ibn Ashur, M. A.-T. (2001). *Maqasid al-Shariah al-Islamiyyah*. Dar- al-Nafa'is.

Ibn Qayyim, A.-J. (n.d.). *I'lām al-Muwaqqī'in* (Vol. 3). Idārah al-Tibā'ah al-Munīriyyah.

ICD-LSEG. (2023). *Islamic finance development report 2023: Navigating uncertainty*. The Islamic Corporation for the Development of the Private Sector (ICD) & the London Stock Exchange Group (LSEG). https://api.zawya.atexcloud.io/file-delivery-service/version/c:NWI4OWQ5MjctNWQ3NS00:NWM3MjBmN2ItYjNjMS00/IFDI%202023%20Report%20-%20Nov%2030.pdf

ISRA. (2011). *Islamic financial system: Principles and operations*. International Shari'ah Research Academy for Islamic Finance (ISRA).

ISRA. (2023). *Islamic financial system: Principles and operations* (3rd ed.). International Shari'ah Research Academy for Islamic Finance (ISRA).

Kamali, M. H. (1998). Al-Maqasid al-Shari'ah: The objectives of Islamic law. *The Muslim Lawyer*, *3*(1). Article 1.

Kamali, M. H. (2008). *Maqasid al-Shariah made simple* (Revised Edition). The International Institute of Islamic Thought (IIIT).

Khan, M. F. (2002). Fiqh foundations of the theory of Islamic economics: A survey of selected contemporary writings on economics relevant subjects of Fiqh. In H. Ahmed (Ed.), *Theoretical foundations of Islamic economics* (pp. 61–85). Islamic Research and Training Institute (IRTI). Book of Readings No. 3.

Koehler, B. (2014). *Early Islam and the birth of capitalism*. Lexington Books.

Mirakhor, A. (2007). *A note on Islamic economics*. Islamic Research and Training Institute (IRTI). IDB Prize Winners Lecture Series No. 20.

Smolo, E. (2013). *Uvod u islamsku ekonomiju i finansije: Teorija i praksa*. Dobra knjiga.

Smolo, E. (2020). Islamic finance and limited purpose banking (LPB): Two sides of the same coin. In A. Rafay (Ed.), *Advances in finance, accounting, and economics* (pp. 100–116). IGI Global. https://doi.org/10.4018/978-1-7998-1611-9.ch006

Smolo, E., & Hassan, M. K. (2011). The potentials of *mushārakah mutanāqisah* for Islamic housing finance. *International Journal of Islamic and Middle Eastern Finance and Management*, *4*(3). Article 3. https://doi.org/10.1108/17538391111166476

Smolo, E., & Ismail, A. G. (2011). A theory and contractual framework of Islamic micro-financial institutions' operations. *Journal of Financial Services Marketing*, *15*(4). Article 4. https://doi.org/10.1057/fsm.2010.24

Smolo, E., Jahangir, R., Nagayev, R., & Aysan, A. F. (2023). Performances of leading Islamic finance markets prior to and during the COVID-19 pandemic. *Heliyon*, *9*(1). Article 1. https://doi.org/10.1016/j.heliyon.2023.e12870

Smolo, E., & Mirakhor, A. (2010). The global financial crisis and its implications for the Islamic financial industry. *International Journal of Islamic and Middle Eastern Finance and Management*, *3*(4). Article 4. https://doi.org/10.1108/17538391011093306

Usmani, M. T. (2002). *An introduction to Islamic finance*. Kluwer Law International.

Vejzagic, M., & Smolo, E. (2011). Maqasid Al-Shari'ah in Islamic finance: An overview. In Z. Kefeli, N. Ahmad, A. Shaharuddin, Z. Shafii, & H. Misbah (Eds.), *Post-crisis economic challenges for the contemporary Muslim Ummah: Proceedings of the 4th Islamic economic system conference 2011 (iECONS 2011)* (pp. 511–527). Universiti Sains Islam Malaysia (USIM).

Chapter 2

Navigating Modern Economic Challenges: The Islamic Economics Paradigm in Focus

Edib Smolo

Effat University, Saudi Arabia

Abstract

The following chapter provides a summary of the global financial crisis (GFC) and how it impacted the global financial markets generally, emphasizing the Islamic finance industry (IFI) in particular. The GFC has been a catalyst for the supporters of the Islamic economic and finance principles. Minsky's claim (2008) that stability is the root of instability was gaining more and more supporters after the GFC, provoking more and more criticism of the conventional finance paradigm. Such shift elevated Islamic financial system as a potential alternative. Looking at the failures and lessons learned from the GFC in tandem with the relatively sound state of the Islamic financial industry implies a reexamination of this paradigm and proposal of the one based on Islamic economics and finance principles. Grounded in socioeconomic justice, introducing equality, responsibility, transparency, honesty, and morality, this paradigm can be successful if appropriately implemented. Nevertheless, a current bifurcation exists between the wings of Islamic economics and finance theory and their practical application. To tackle the current issues, innovative thinking has to be applied especially in Islamic economics and finance. Mimicking the conventional financing's methods and incorporating them through *Shari'atization* process gives rise to the risks of the traditional system's assimilation and system's breakdown. Therefore, building a framework and offering a tangible course of action is unavoidable for the management of the complexities and the risks involved.

Keywords: Islamic economics; Islamic finance; Islamic banking; conventional finance; paradigm; paradigm shift; Shari'ah compliant; Shari'atization; global financial crisis; Covid-19

The Future of Islamic Finance, 15–27

doi:10.1108/978-1-83549-906-120241002

Introduction

In the ever-evolving landscape of our globalized world, economic theories are continually under scrutiny to address pressing issues. The aftermath of the 2008–2009 GFC, extensively examined by analysts, highlighted vulnerabilities in the conventional financing system. Factors such as high leveraging, the complexity of financial transactions, and a disconnect between the real and financial sectors were brought to the forefront (Askari et al., 2010; Haneef & Smolo, 2013; Smolo & Mirakhor, 2010).

More recently, the unprecedented shock caused by the COVID-19 pandemic (now also referred as the global health crisis or GHC), coupled with widespread business disruptions, has further exposed weaknesses in the global economic structure. This has led to disruptions in global value chains, exacerbated unemployment, increased social inequalities, and even escalated poverty within and between nations. The economic downturn has been compounded by emerging challenges, including the digitization era affecting various facets of life, rising political and institutional risks worldwide, persistent global warming, and the degradation of biodiversity – all posing threats to humanity.

Amid these challenges, it is imperative to explore alternatives to the prevailing conventional economic paradigm, which has historically adopted a methodologically neutral stance on matters of morality, ethics, and religion (Li, 2019; Putnam & Walsh, 2012). Esteemed academics have called for a departure from neoliberalism, urging the exploration of new avenues rooted in morality, human and social sciences, and religious perspectives (Stiglitz, 2010, 2019).

From an Islamic standpoint, a substantial body of conceptual and empirical research suggests that the Islamic economic system, as prescribed in the Qur'an and practiced during the time of the Prophet (pbuh – peace be upon him), offers a viable alternative (Al-Jarhi, 2022; Iqbal & Mirakhor, 2013; Mirakhor & Askari, 2010, 2017; Mirakhor & Hamid, 2009).

This chapter aims to delve into the challenges facing contemporary economics, with a specific focus on the paradigm of Islamic economics as a promising alternative. The following key objectives will be addressed: (i) examine issues and critiques of conventional finance, emphasizing vulnerabilities exposed by the GFC; (ii) investigate whether Islamic finance can serve as a viable alternative to address the shortcomings of the current economic system; (iii) provide a justification for introduction of the new paradigm; (iv) briefly highlight principles of Islamic economics and finance; and (v) concisely elaborate the current dichotomy within the IFI and the way forward. By addressing these objectives, the chapter aims to contribute valuable insights into the ongoing discourse on reshaping economic paradigms in the face of contemporary challenges.

Unveiling Systemic Weaknesses: A Comprehensive Critique of Conventional Finance PostGlobal Financial Crisis (GFC)

The GFC's aftermath initiated a serious scrutiny of classical financial mechanisms that brought to light various deficiencies and a set of intertwined problems. This part provides a summary of a few research (Ahmed et al., 2013; Haneef & Smolo, 2013;

Smolo & Mirakhor, 2010), which provides a detailed critique of conventional financial system after GFC. The discussed problems pave the way for the consideration and investigation of Islamic economics as a possible alternative. Lessons which we gained from these papers identified common problems like wrong credit transfer, inadvisable credit expansion and failure to manage risks and opportunities properly. The similarity between these lessons highlights a systematic nature of the difficulties inherent for conventional finance. The issues raised and lessons learned from the GFC are briefly summarized below:

- *System Anchored in Interest and Indebtedness:* The instability of a largely interest-based and debt-ridden financial structure showed up. This debt-led architecture was unveiled as a risky gamble and an inevitable driver of the boom-and-bust process.
- *Subprime Mortgages and Securitization:* The upheaval resulted from the slump in property values and nonrepayment of the mortgage loans given to the people with worse-than-average credit scores. The combination of the "generate and disseminate" strategy and loan bundling instruments contributed to a rise in the dangers by creating a gap between lenders and borrowers. As a starting point, the quantity of sub-prime home loans jumped, and the bundling process did not improve new instruments' safety. This made the crisis come about.
- *Monetary Policy and Low Interest Rates:* Monetary policies, coupled with a long period of low interest rates, were among the causes of the financial meltdown. The low interest rate environment fostered the demand for housing. Consequently, prices went up, and there was an escalation of refinancing that intensified the risk in the financial industry.
- *Credit Expansion and Predatory Lending:* Excessive and insufficient monitoring of credit expansion, in combination with predatory lending activities, were the elements that make up the financial environment. Financial institutions, seeking higher gains, were pioneering opaque instruments and intricate off-balance sheet transactions, hence contributing to the financial crisis.
- *Risk Management Breakdown:* The crisis clearly showed the major weaknesses of the risk assessment approaches applied by both private and public entities. The lack of capital, sound liquidity planning, and effective risk management rendered, therefore, central to the reliable running of banks.
- *Complexity and Inadequate Risk Management:* Financial inventiveness and complexity of creative methods in product development revealed serious flaws in risk management. The crisis drew attention to how the increase in complexity of financial instruments was faster than capabilities of regulators and participants in the markets and in the end breached down risk management frameworks.
- *Liquidity, Leveraging, and Contagion:* The crisis highlighted the importance of the liquidity risk management and the use of leverage. Global awareness of contagion spread leads to instability in the interbank market and a need for deleveraging, which is a reflection of how advanced the financial systems and its vulnerability are.

- *Regulatory and Supervisory Failures:* Such issues as a low supervisory environment and a weak regulatory framework were seen as director factors fueling the crisis. The existence of appropriate government and supervisory mechanisms to regulate and manage risks was overlooked, thus fueling excessive risk-taking.
- *Transparency and Disclosure Issues:* Opaque information and market disorder presented uncertainties which downplayed the risks. The crisis shed a light on the importance of a complete disclosure that helps in creation of market confidence and constructive market discipline.
- *Role of Rating Agencies:* The credit rating agencies, who were supposed to protect the market, were in conflict and even contributed to the crisis by getting involved into the design and structuring of new products. Achieving dominance in the rating agencies' market gave an impulse to lower credit standards. This situation draws a conclusion that improvements in the system for rating are necessary.
- *Financial Globalization Impact:* Through the process of globalization, which involves an integration of economies globally, as well as instant information transfer, the GFC had a spillover effect contaminating economies all around. Globalization has quickly ballooned crises around the world, utilizing the speed of modern technology to create an entirely new level of economic interconnection. The factor that complicated the crisis even more was the role of strong international linkages and investments that lead to the spread of credit derivatives, particularly subprime instruments on a mass scale. The financial market got affected by all of this, and therefore, its functionality decreased rapidly. This clearly demonstrated the repercussions of financial globalization in its entirety.

In short, the extended period of "the great moderation," along with the irresponsible expansion of credit, lasted enough for the foundation of the crisis to be laid down. These components include loose monetary policies, unbridled credit and debt growth, inadequate regulatory control, introduction of complex and opaque financial products, wrong perception of risks and susceptibility of asset price bubbles, inadequate disclosure and transparency, predatory lending practices, and a high leverage. These factors, taken together, are widely considered the root causes of the crisis.

During the GFC inspection of the traditional financial system, a system that is a complex web of interrelated problems unfolds. These include, but are not limited to, problems in risk management, negative consequences of fast globalization and built-in deficiencies in policies based on lending money at interests. Through this elaborate analysis, the way to implement other models such as Islamic economics, which could provide effective solutions for some intricate problems in current finance, is paved. The reality of a paradigm shift crystallizes as soon as these complexities are overcome and the various lessons learned from the GFC are integrated. This will ultimately pave the way for an economic trajectory that will stand the test of time.

Islamic Principles and the Overhaul of the International Financial System

The aftermath of the GFC and the GHC that left many countries in financial and economical distress clearly point to the necessity to conduct a comprehensive audit of the world financial market. The call for restructuring is not novel, having been a prominent discourse, especially in the aftermath of recurring financial crises approximately every decade.

The so-called paradigm shift, which will be addressed shortly, is known to the conventional economic–financial system. This system, together with its paradigms, has evolved over centuries, influenced by ancient and medieval Muslim scholars, mercantilists, and classical and neoclassical economists, leading to modern economic systems like capitalism and socialism. While these systems share similar worldviews, their strategies diverge significantly. Despite recurrent revisions and abundant resources, Chapra argues that these systems failed to achieve their material goals due to inherent flaws in their worldview and strategies (Chapra, 1991). With the collapse of socialism and the conclusion of the Cold War, capitalism, along with its paradigm, emerged victorious as a model for the world. However, the avarice and self-interest in the capitalist financial system have contributed to the global financial crisis and its ensuing tribulations. Hence, a revision of the current financial system is imperative.

Kahf (2003) posits that the Islamic economy is a branch of economic science rather than a separate discipline. Nevertheless, many authors contend that the Islamic economy differs significantly from the aforementioned systems, relying on specific principles and a worldview derived from the Qur'an and the Sunnah of the Prophet Muhammad (pbuh) (Chapra, 1991; Mannan, 1983). The current analysis assumes that specific solutions to various economic issues lie within the Islamic economy, diverging from the basic assumptions of neo-classical and socialist–communist paradigms. This does not imply that every institution and practice in these systems is non-Islamic, as common assumptions and ideas exist. However, with its unique sources and characteristics, Islamic economics possesses an identity fundamentally distinct from existing paradigms that inadequately address the needs of the Islamic economic system.

In essence, Islamic economics and finance deviate from a neutral value system, contrasting with the conventional economic and financial system. Chapra's (1998) statement is pertinent here:

> Islamic economics is based on a paradigm which is not secularist and value- neutral. It treats all human beings as vice-regents of God and brothers unto each other. All resources at the disposal of human beings are a trust and must be used for the well-being of all in conformity with the values provided by the *Shari'ah*. However, well-being in Islam is not a function of just material possessions and unlimited consumption. It is rather a function of the balanced satisfaction of both the material and the spiritual needs of the human personality. This can be done by actualizing the *maqasid al-Shari'ah* (goals of the *Shari'ah*). (Chapra, 1998, pp. 104–105)

Defining a Paradigm

A paradigm can be defined as "a concept of reality that informs all thought within its frame of reference until unavoidable facts of reality conflict with it and cause its adherents to reject this first paradigm for another one." Thomas Kuhn defines a paradigm in one place as "an accepted model or pattern" while in another he defines it as "what the members of a scientific community share, *and*, conversely, a scientific community consists of men who share a paradigm" (Kuhn, 1996, pp. 23, 176).

Thus, for example, Thomas Kuhn and Imre Lakatos, who are the most famous critics of positivism, argue that theories are not rejected and replaced simply because their inaccuracy is repeatedly established through empirical testing. On the contrary, theories are subclasses of larger "paradigms" (Kuhn) or "scientific research programs" (Lakatos) that cannot be refuted by empirical testing. Thus, a science progresses through "scientific revolutions" (Kuhn) or "replacement of scientific research programs" (Lakatos) when existing "paradigms" or "scientific programs" are replaced by superior ones (Arif, 1986; Wisman, 1979).

This paradigm shift, according to Kuhn, represents a "scientific revolution" or a "paradigmatic revolution" that occurs when the existing paradigm fails to encompass and explain the whole of reality, and as a result, its supporters reject and replace that paradigm with a new paradigm. All this indicates that knowledge is not static as it progresses over time.

A Need for a New Paradigm

Taking into account the GFC whose consequences are felt even today, we can rightly say that this is one of the proofs that the market economy paradigm is not accurate and needs to be reformulated. Islam, as a way of life and guidance for all the humanity, has a potential to offer a new (old) paradigm that could be used to build a new financial system. Even the Vatican, in the midst of the 2008–2009 GFC, criticized the free-market model for its adverse overdevelopment in the past two decades. Furthermore, the Vatican called for restructuring of the conventional financial system, relying on ethical principles on which Islamic finance is based. Similarly, during protests organized by the "Occupy Wall Street" movement that started outside the New York Stock Exchange one could find a slogan that appeared on a protestor's placard saying "Let's bank the Muslim way." All this indicate the growing importance of Islamic finance globally. Hence, it is not a surprise that Islamic finance attracted a lot of attention in recent years.

All this points to the need to develop an Islamic paradigm. It is important, however, to note that the Islamic economic paradigm is not a new thing as it has been discussed before. As will be discussed more in Chapter 4, the Islamic economic and financial system can be traced to seventh century Madinah community that was established and nourished by the Prophet Muhammad (pbuh). Nevertheless, general critique of the current economic and financial system in the world offers a unique opportunity to make fundamental changes to the way how the conventional and Islamic financial systems work.

Some 40 years ago, Muhammad Arif, then a PhD student in the US, drew attention to the need to build an Islamic paradigm and its importance. Unfortunately, his vision and ideas fell on deaf ears as no one approach to this problem seriously. His insights and ideas were important back then, but they are probably even more important now.

The Western paradigm based on materialism – Arif argues – offers only a limited worldview and a certain theory of knowledge. This paradigm relies on an *invisible hand* and follows an ideology of self-interest, and these two have led to the GFC. First, self-interests, greedy and profit-motivated individuals (investors, banks, and corporations who are mostly speculating on the market in search of higher and higher profit) use all the means to earn extra profit and neglected their obligations to carry out necessary due diligence. Their thirst for extra earnings led them to lend even to individuals who were unable to repay it. Second, the invisible hand and free-market economy failed to adapt to the situation and alert us to the tsunami that hit the financial market. If free market theory is true, then we should not be facing this problem at all.

Keynes and Minsky envisaged that such a system in which wealth of individuals largely depends on markets ruled by debt-based contracts is altogether unstable. Minsky pinpointed that a system which "in which borrowing is necessary to repay debt is speculative finance" (Minsky, 2008, p. 48). Furthermore, he called financial institutions "merchants of debt" (p. 279). According to Mirakhor (2009), the factors that make banking operations unstable are interest and debt, two basic causes of the current financial crisis. Minsky's ideas, often referred to in the financial instability hypothesis, owe their origins to Keynes's General Theory, Irving Fisher's debt deflation theory, and Henry Simons' writings (Minsky, 2008, p. 192). The above hypothesis designates an interest-based debt contracts as the reason behind the instability in the entire economic system. Additionally, brief stability, itself, could eventually result in instability as it creates contentment that will follow with excessive risk-taking and high unpredictability (Buiter, 2009; Minsky, 2008; Yellen, 2009).

Therefore, it is obvious that the free-market paradigm is not efficient and that we need a new paradigm. This new paradigm should have certain characteristics that can answer questions that have emerged as a result of this crisis. We need a comprehensive approach or a worldview with a clear vision to support justice, accountability, transparency, fairness, and morality that were lost many years ago in the pursuit of profit maximization.

Today, not only is the modern economy and its survival at stake, but Muslims are also at a crossroads. This is also an opportunity for Muslim *Ummah* to ascend the world throne. To do so, Muslim scholars should be very careful to avoid mistakes made by the modern economic system. This means that this new paradigm should not be based on the ashes of classical or contemporary economic theories and practices. It simply means that if this paradigm were to be implemented then Muslims should not continue to copy the phenomena that originally caused this financial mess in the first place.

Thus, there is an urgent need for fresh ideas and innovative approaches to address these issues. This is true of all Islamic disciplines in general, and Islamic economics and finance in particular. Continuing to copy conventional financing methods and incorporating them into Islamic financial architecture through *Shari'atization* will lead Islamic finance to a dead end and eventual merge with the conventional system, ultimately leading to a collapse. Consequently, a good foundation and a clear vision are needed to get rid of these dangerous and difficult weather conditions.

In short, Islam, encompassing all walks of life, can provide one new, alternative paradigm. In fact, Islam in itself is inevitably the only overarching paradigm that can tackle the existing and upcoming issues. However, it is up to Muslim scholars how they will present this paradigm and whether they will succeed in bringing Islam to the center of the world stage. As things stand now, there is a clear gap between what Islam teaches and what can be seen in practice. This is exactly what Askari et al. (2012) speak when they say:

> There is, however, a paradigm gap between what Islam teaches and actual market behavior. For this reason, government actions (and the institutions they create) to remedy the deficit in informational, enforcement, and governance behavior and reduce the cost of participation in stock markets have to be stronger and more comprehensive than exist today. These policies, actions, and institutions should have the competence, efficiency, and enforcement capabilities such that they can elicit the kind of behavior that replicates, or closely approximates, those expected if market participants behaved in compliance with Islamic rules. (p. 122)

The Islamic economy, as mentioned earlier, is based on a paradigm that has socioeconomic justice as its primary goal. That is why it is up to us to show ourselves and others that the modern man can live in a peace, satisfying his worldly needs, and all in accordance with the Islamic paradigm that advocates justice, equality and gives priority to human values over material goods.

A Critique of Islamic Finance

The GFC made the IFI to come out of the shadow, so it was viewed as an alternative. Nevertheless, the IFI wasn't free from the crisis, having endured impact of a lesser magnitude. This raises the question over the potential existence of a link between the IFI and the conventional institution, where they share a framework and rules that are similar. The research conducted on the aftermaths of both the GFC and GHC on Islamic equities are congruent with this view (Smolo et al., 2022). Notwithstanding the uncertainties, Islamic equities may have some hedging advantages, even if they are not very significant (Smolo et al., 2023).

The opponents argue that IFI follows the rules of the conventional financial system, perceived by the some as a subsystem wherein the principles of Shari'ah are at times deviated. Critics focus on the practice of replicating the traditional mechanisms and doing a "Shari'ah make-up," according to which the nature of Islamic finance is seriously distorted. According to this perspective and thesis, Islamic finance acts thus not as an independent entity but is being made subordinate to the traditional financial system which finally makes it hinder its very own basic function of facilitating risk sharing.

As a niche market, IFI will face major obstacles. Whether this industry becomes a main alternative for the current global financial markets or rather a mere replication will depend on how the industry addresses and solves these challenges. Maintaining both regulatory compliance and following the Shari'ah principles is the key task for Islamic finance to stand out from the mainstream finance while at the same time being "ethical" and robust.

A Brief Description of Islamic Finance

The term "Islamic finance" is generally employed for financial activities driven by the principles of Shari'ah (Islamic law). Etymologically, Shari'ah, an Arabic term, implies "the way," "the path to the watering place," or more figuratively, "a clear path to follow," or even more specifically, "the path leading to a source." Conceptually, Shari'ah refers to the route a faithful adherent should follow as guidance for this world and salvation in the Hereafter.

The fundaments of Shari'ah are the Qur'an and the *Sunnah*. *Sunnah*, a common Arabic word for which the nearest English meanings include "custom," "action," or "practice," refers to whatever the Prophet Muhammad, peace be upon him, said, carried out, or implicitly accepted. The third and fourth fundamentals of Shari'ah are the consensus of the jurist (*ijma'*) and the analogy (*kiyas*). Alongside these ones, Shari'ah law staunchly prohibits both paying and receiving interest (*riba*). But, presenting the Islamic economic and financial structure as just "interest-free" does not correctly capture the full essence of it (Iqbal, 1997; Smolo, 2013). In Islamic world view, the concept of Islamic finance and banking is built on the basis of the following principles: protection of the rights of ownership, balancing ethical values and fighting uncertainty by spreading risk among members of society. In addition, projects that are put up should not only reflect the ethical precepts of Shari'ah but also the concerns of the public (*maslahah*).

The principles of Islamic finance have been practiced in the Muslim world for centuries (see Chapter 4). The term "Islamic financial industry" (IFI), however, is relatively young and originated in the mid-1980s (Iqbal, 1997; Smolo, 2013; Zaher & Hassan, 2001). However, since its inception about 60 years ago, and especially in the last couple of decades, IFI has evolved into a respectable and important part of the international financial system. As a result, IFI today comprises Islamic banking, *takaful* (Islamic insurance) and capital markets. It is further enhanced by the recent introduction of financial technology (fintech) solution that broadened its scope significantly.[1]

[1]For the latest development of the IFI, see DinarStandard (2023), IFSB (2023), and Deloitte (2019).

Although Islamic financial instruments have been used throughout the history, the first experiments with Islamic banks occurred much later, in particular during the 1960s and 1970s. Mit Ghamr, which was founded in Egypt in 1963, is considered the first Islamic bank. Subsequently, the Nasir Social Bank was established in 1967, and it was the first social bank to operate in accordance with Shari'ah principles. Today, Islamic finance attracts both Muslims and non-Muslims around the world with promising future growth prospects.

While Islamic financial instruments go back to ancient times, Islamic banks likely emerged in the 1960s and 1970s. It was Mit Ghamr, a bank founded in Egypt in 1963, that achieved the historical milestone of being the first Islamic bank. This was followed by the Nasir Social Bank starting its operations in 1967 which was the first social bank in the world and pioneered the social banking based on Shari'ah principles. However, today Islamic finance is gaining ground worldwide, with both Muslims and non-Muslims recognizing its potential. This opens the way for expansion in the long term. Nevertheless, the flight path of this progress is different from one country to another depending on the nature and the development of Islamic finance in those countries. As the Islamic Banker has pointed out, the marketplace is currently dominated by two main models. The first is a systematized approach indicated by Malaysia's parallel two-banking system which is symmetric in the sense that traditional and Shari'ah-compliant banking are both present: the former focuses on the conventional kind, while the latter concentrates on the other, with each of them having their corresponding separate rules and regulations. The second model in question is called "ad hoc approach," where both government and the regulator fail to recognize the demand for development of Islamic banking and regulatory framework as well as the law that would allow it to function properly (Islamic Banker, 2010, p. 2).

Conclusion

This chapter provides a brief revision of the GFC and its overall impact on global financial markets, including the IFI. The GFC provided a valuable incentive for advocates of the Islamic economic and finance. The claim by Minsky (2008) that stability breeds instability, i.e. his "financial instability hypothesis" that gained support in the aftermath of the GFC, led to growing critics of the conventional finance paradigm.

This development placed the Islamic financial system to the forefront as a possible alternative. Given briefly discussed failures caused by and lessons drawn from the GFC as well as a relative resilience of the Islamic financial industry, the Islamic economics and finance paradigm is revisited. It is believed that Islamic economy is based on a paradigm that has socioeconomic justice as its primary goal and advocates for equality, equality, accountability, transparency, fairness, morality, etc. In short, the Islamic economics and finance paradigm could provide solutions to the issues raised in this chapter if implemented properly. At the moment, however, there is a dichotomy between Islamic economics and finance ideals and reality.

The problems that we are facing now call for new ways of thinking and inventive mechanisms to handle this situation. This is the case with all Islamic subjects, however, with a more pronounced focus on Islamic economics and finance. Replicating the traditional forms of financing and blending them with the Islamic financial structure through the *Shari'atization* technique is a risky affair. It might culminate in complete assimilation with the conventional system and a possible breakdown. Consequently, it is necessary to have a foundation base here, but also put forward a realistic plan of action which will help to mitigate the dangers and complexity.

References

Ahmed, H., Asutay, M., & Wilson, R. (2013). *Islamic banking and financial crisis: Reputation, stability and risks*. Edinburgh University Press. https://doi.org/10.1515/9780748672370

Al-Jarhi, M. A. (2022). The Islamic macroeconomic model: How to apply it. In T. Eğri & Z. H. Orhan (Eds.), *Islamic monetary economics: Finance and banking in contemporary Muslim economies* (pp. 13–31). Routledge.

Arif, M. (1986, October). The Islamization of knowledge and some methodological issues in paradigm building: The general case of social science with a special focus on economics. In *15th Annual Conference of the Association of Muslim Social Scientists*, Indianapolis, USA.

Askari, H., Iqbal, Z., Krichene, N., & Mirakhor, A. (2010). *The stability of Islamic finance: Creating a resilient financial environment for a secure future* (1st ed.). Wiley. https://doi.org/10.1002/9781118390450

Askari, H., Iqbal, Z., Krichenne, N., & Mirakhor, A. (2012). *Risk sharing in finance: The Islamic finance alternative*. John Wiley & Sons.

Buiter, W. H. (2009, May 8). Lessons from the global financial crisis for regulators and supervisors. In *25th Anniversary Workshop "The Global Financial Crisis: Lessons and Outlook," of the Advanced Studies Program of the IFW*, Kiel, Germany, May 8–9, 2009.

Chapra, M. U. (1991). The need for a new economic system. *Review of Financial Economics*, *1*(1). Article 1.

Chapra, M. U. (1998). Relevance and importance of Islamic economics. In M. Kahf (Ed.), *Lessons in Islamic economics* (Vol. 1, pp. 99–114). Islamic Research and Training Institute (IRTI). Seminar Proceedings No. 41.

Deloitte. (2019). *Sharia economy: Boosting financial inclusion through Sharia economy in Indonesia*. PT Deloitte Consulting.

DinarStandard. (2023). *State of the global Islamic economy report 2023/2024*. DinarStandard with the support of Dubai's Department of Economy and Tourism (DET). https://www.dinarstandard.com/post/state-of-the-global-islamic-economy-report-2023

Haneef, R., & Smolo, E. (2013). Reshaping the Islamic finance industry: Applying the lessons learned from the global financial crisis. In H. Ahmed, M. Asutay, & R. Wilson (Eds.), *Islamic banking and financial crisis: Reputation, stability and risks* (pp. 21–39). Edinburgh University Press. https://doi.org/10.3366/edinburgh/9780748647613.003.0002

IFSB. (2023). *Islamic financial services industry stability report 2023*. Islamic Financial Services Board (IFSB).
Iqbal, Z. (1997, June). Islamic financial systems. *Finance & Development*, *34*, 42–45.
Iqbal, Z. & Mirakhor, A. (Eds.). (2013). *Economic development and Islamic finance*. International Bank for Reconstruction and Development/The World Bank. https://doi.org/10.1596/978-0-8213-9953-8
Islamic Banker. (2010, January–February). Prospect and challenges for Islamic finance in 2010: Fault lines of the Islamic finance industry. *Islamic Banker*, 168–169. Article 168–169.
Kahf, M. (2003). Islamic economics: Notes on definition and methodology. *Review of Islamic Economics*, *13*. Article 13.
Kuhn, T. S. (1996). *The structure of scientific revolutions* (3nd ed.). University of Chicago Press.
Li, C. (2019). Morality and value neutrality in economics: A dualist view. *The Journal of Philosophical Economics*, *XII*(2(Articles)), 10725. https://doi.org/10.46298/jpe.10725
Mannan, M. A. (1983). Islamic economics as a social science: Some methodological issues. *Journal for Research in Islamic Economics*, *1*(1). Article 1.
Minsky, H. P. (2008). *Stabilizing an unstable economy*. McGraw Hill.
Mirakhor, A. (2009, October–December). Recent crisis: Lessons for Islamic finance. *New Horizon*, (173), 12–15.
Mirakhor, A., & Askari, H. (2010). *Islam and the path to human and economic development*. Palgrave Macmillan.
Mirakhor, A., & Askari, H. (2017). *Ideal Islamic economy: An introduction*. Palgrave Macmillan. https://doi.org/10.1057/978-1-137-53727-0
Mirakhor, A., & Hamid, I. S. (2009). *Islam and development: The institutional framework*. Global Scholarly Publications.
Putnam, H. & Walsh, V. C. (Eds.). (2012). *The end of value-free economics*. Routledge.
Smolo, E. (2013). *Uvod u islamsku ekonomiju i finansije: Teorija i praksa*. Dobra knjiga.
Smolo, E., Jahangir, R., Nagayev, R., & Aysan, A. F. (2023). Performances of leading Islamic finance markets prior to and during the COVID-19 pandemic. *Heliyon*, *9*(1). Article 1. https://doi.org/10.1016/j.heliyon.2023.e12870
Smolo, E., Jahangir, R., Nagayev, R., & Tarazi, C. S. C. (2022). Performances of Islamic and conventional equities during the global health crisis: Time-frequency analysis of BRICS+T markets. *Review of Financial Economics*, *40*(3). Article 3. https://doi.org/10.1002/rfe.1152
Smolo, E., & Mirakhor, A. (2010). The global financial crisis and its implications for the Islamic financial industry. *International Journal of Islamic and Middle Eastern Finance and Management*, *3*(4). Article 4. https://doi.org/10.1108/17538391011093306
Stiglitz, J. E. (2010). *The Stiglitz report: Reforming the international monetary and financial systems in the wake of the global crisis*. The New Press.
Stiglitz, J. E. (2019, November 4). The end of neoliberalism and the rebirth of history. *Project Syndicate*. https://www.project-syndicate.org/commentary/end-of-neoliberalism-unfettered-markets-fail-by-joseph-e-stiglitz-2019-11

Wisman, J. D. (1979). Toward a humanist reconstruction of economic science. *Journal of Economic Issues*, *13*(1). Article 1.

Yellen, J. L. (2009, May). A Minsky meltdown: Lessons for central bankers. FRBSF Economic Letter No. 2009-15. http://www.frbsf.org/publications/economics/letter/2009/el2009-15.pdf

Zaher, T. S., & Hassan, M. K. (2001). A comparative literature survey of Islamic finance and banking. *Financial Markets, Institutions & Instruments*, *10*(4). Article 4.

Chapter 3

The Eternality of Islamic Teachings: The Adaptability of Islamic Finance Principles

Putri Swastika

Institut Agama Islam Negeri Metro, Indonesia

Abstract

To fully comprehend the significance of Islam in Islamic Finance, it is imperative to delve deeper into the ontology, epistemology and axiology of Islamic principles. Ontology is concerned with the foundation of reality, whilst epistemology covers the learning process. Then, axiology talks about the subject's values, norms and principles. This chapter covers the ontology of the Knowledge from an Islamic perspective, which, epistemologically speaking, is believed to be eternal, unchanging and universal by the believer. Therefore, having a profound understanding of the ontology and epistemology of the source and the Knowledge, the discussion continues the axiology of Islamic finance principles, which is paramount to understanding the role of Islam in modern financial systems.

Ontology is concerned with the foundational building blocks that become the governing rules, i.e. the relationships between the Almighty and His creations. It is crucial to acknowledge the eternality of the Creator, as He is not in comparison to His creation. The epistemology of Islam placed Al-Qur'an as the Book and Muhammad (Peace Be Upon Him – PBUH) and the Messenger of Allah (swt) as the Archetypal model. The Book is the Meta framework that serves as the ultimate authority. Muhammad (PBUH) led and taught his generation how to run a state, organize public affairs and restore justice in law and rulings. It is his sayings and behaviours that Muslims refer to ethics and good behaviour (akhlaqul karimah) as the axiology of Islam. These are fundamentals before embarking to the adaptability of Islamic finance principles into policy.

The Future of Islamic Finance, 29–47

doi:10.1108/978-1-83549-906-120241003

Keywords: Islamic finance principles; adaptability of Islamic finance; ontology and epistemology of knowledge; Islamic finance axiom; risk sharing in finance; Islamic economics

Introduction

To fully comprehend the significance of Islam in finance, it is imperative to delve deeper into its source and underlying principles. Islam organizes all human affairs and activities, from waking up to lying down and resting. Islam prescribes every activity in detail, not only a recommendation to do but it comes with real examples. There are no human affairs in Islam that have no examples. Such perfection is derived from the Divine Knowledge of the Creator. In Islam, the position of a man is a creation of Allah (*subhanahu wa ta'ala*– swt), like angels, demons (*jinns*) and all other creatures.[1] Yet, the Creator puts man in a place unlike other of His creations, as He (swt) teaches the Knowledge directly to a man. This relationship between the Creator and man as His creation is eternal, everlasting, unchanging and universal. It represents the building blocks of Islam.

A profound understanding of the building blocks is paramount to understanding the role of Islamic principles in modern financial systems. Acknowledging the eternal nature of God and man relationships will set a clear direction on to the Book and the Messenger, as the Meta framework and the Archetypal model, that explain, elaborate and give example to generations of generations of mankind. To differentiate between the Divine Knowledge from Allah swt and knowledge from human, the earlier is written as the Knowledge. It carries laws and rules and thereon the Knowledge becomes norms, values and principles to organize the daily life of a man. It is not restricted to a certain tribes or race; considering the relation between the Creator and man, the Divine Knowledge is universal. These principles can be applied to various contexts, including financial systems.

Islamic law can be perceived as a rigid and inflexible doctrine incompatible with modern financial systems for those who are adamant in understanding the ontological and epistemological aspects of Islam (Mirakhor & Smolo, 2011, 2012, 2014). Revisiting the source of Divine Knowledge and, step by step, following its axioms and laws in governing modern financial systems is mandatory for observers. The intriguing part is that understanding the ontological, epistemological and axiological of Islam would lead to dynamic, flexible and applicable principles of the financial system. Therefore, this chapter aims to address the misconceptions of Islam and demonstrates how Islamic axiology could stimulate the development of an innovative dynamic and modern financial system.

This chapter is organized as follows: The first part is to explain the ontological, epistemological and axiological of Islam. It includes the attributes of eternality and universality of Islamic law and principles. From there, it leads to the second

---

[1]Subhanahu wa ta'ala (SWT) is arabic terms referring to the characteristics of Allah SWT, which means 'Glorified and Exalted is He'. This phrase expresses respect and awe for Allah.

part of the adaptability of Islamic principles to modern finance. It includes historical proof that modern economies have used it to recover from crises. Despite such, the ongoing challenge to mainstream Islamic principles into macroeconomic policies is discussed in part three.

The Concept of Eternality and Universality of the Knowledge as the Source of Islam

The concepts of eternality and universality are closely intertwined. Eternality refers to something timeless and everlasting, while universality applies to everyone regardless of race, culture or background. Eternality refers to something inter-dimensional that exists across different dimensions of reality. A loving relationship between a mother and her sons is said to be eternal although the subject being is not. Eternality is also a distinct attribute of God – The Almighty that His existence is incomparable to men or other creations.[2] Universality carries an attribute of being relevant to a generation at all stakes. Being sincere and kind is a universal love language, or human rights apply for all mankind regardless their nations, race and creeds. It is also explained by the Qur'an that Prophet Muhammad (pbuh) was sent as a mercy for the universe.[3] Thus, the Almighty God is eternal, sent the book Al-Qur'an, where its content is preserved and unchanged, via a man whose task is to bring mercy for the universe.[4,5] It is a condition to submit into the relationships between the Creator and creation as the foundation to accept the knowledge.[6]

If western philosophers acknowledge active mind in the pursuit of knowledge, Islam puts heart as the gate for knowledge. Avicenna, in Metaphysics, addressed it as soul (Avicenna, 2005). Avicenna distinguished science to information because science would bring benefit to the happiness of soul in the hereafter. Information, science and knowledge are today's keywords that are used interchangeably. But we

---

[2]Refers to the attributes of Allah as explained in the Qur'an Surah 112 (Sincerity): 1–4; '*1. Say: He is Allah, the One and Only; 2. Allah, the Eternal, Absolute; 3. He begetteth not, nor is He begotten; 4. And there is none like unto Him*'. (Yusuf Ali translation)

[3]Refers to the Qur'an Surah 21 (The Prophets): 107; *"And We have sent you (O Muhammad SAW) not but as a mercy for the 'Alamin (mankind, jinns and all that exists)."* (Mohsin Khan translation)

[4]Refers to the Qur'an Surah 85 (The Big Stars): 21–22; *"Nay! This is a Glorious Qur'an, (Inscribed) in Al-Lauh Al-Mahfuz (the Preserved Tablet)."* (Mohsin Khan translation)

[5]Refers to the Qur'an Surat 6 (The Cattle): 115; *"And the Word of your Lord has been fulfilled in truth and in justice. None can change His Words. And He is the All-Hearer, the All-Knower."* (Mohsin Khan translation). The eternality and universality of Al Qur'an is known as I'jaz Al-Qur'an (inimitability of the Quran).

[6]Refers to the Qur'an Surah 6 (The Cattle): 14; *"Say, 'Is it other than Allah I should take as a protector, Creator of the heavens and the earth, while it is He who feeds and is not fed?" Say, [O Muhammad], "Indeed, I have been commanded to be the first [among you] who submit [to Allah] and [was commanded], 'Do not ever be of the polytheists.'"* (Sahih International)

should ask, how does a man know the reality in life? How does a man know the time and the direction to navigate a ship sailing in the ocean? Every affair in life requires knowledge, but we are overwhelmed with information. Avicenna conclude that information will introduce one to choices of good and evil, while science and knowledge elevate soul to God the All-Knowing.

The Knowledge thus becomes the life guidance. It is like the guiding light for a sailor to safely navigate their ships. A knowledge seeker will be unstoppable to learn and actively seek knowledge because his soul felt joy in the search. Losing the knowledge is like losing the beacon amidst the ocean darkness. Luckily, one who agrees to submit his life comprehensively into the endearing eternal relationships with his Creator is given a full set of the Source of Knowledge. It is Al-Qur'an and the Prophet Muhammad (pbuh).

Al-Qur'an is a manual to navigate a life with purpose and direction. If one dreams to have a successful life, he/she must have a vision of life, its essence and the purpose of existence – not only existing. Without knowing these, life (essentially) becomes less beneficial and useful even when one reads the Book. For such believer, Al-Qur'an thus has only a restricted role in navigating life occasions during sorrows or turbulences. Although materialistically successful, a life without reference to Al-Qur'an becomes less meaningful and empty-felt. It is like doing things without a certain purpose.

Besides book, knowledge transfer happens during interactions between teacher and student. This transfer of knowledge is known as teaching, a process involving direct communication between teacher and student. So as long as the student actively pursues and communicates with the teacher, transfer of knowledge continues to happen. The Teacher is Allah SWT the Omniscient and The Wise. It is said in the Qur'an, Surah (chapter) 2:

> (30) And (remember) when your Lord said to the angels: "Verily, I am going to place (mankind) generations after generations on earth." They said: "Will You place therein those who will make mischief therein and shed blood, - while we glorify You with praises and thanks (Exalted be You above all that they associate with You as partners) and sanctify You." He (Allah) said: "I know that which you do not know." (31) And He taught Adam all the names (of everything) , then He showed them to the angels and said, "Tell Me the names of these if you are truthful." (32) They (angels) said: "Glory be to You, we have no knowledge except what you have taught us. Verily, it is You, the All-Knower, the All-Wise." (33) He said: "O Adam! Inform them of their names," and when he had informed them of their names, He said: "Did I not tell you that I know the Ghaib (unseen) in the heavens and the earth, and I know what you reveal and what you have been concealing?" (Mohsin Khan translation).

Qur'an was revealed over period of 23 years. It is thus manifested and exemplified by The Messenger Muhammad (pbuh). The Prophet (pbuh) was given an immensely key role in implementing the Qur'an into organizing daily affairs. Not only received the revelation but he also enforced it with utmost authority in his daily life. He was the sole interpreter of the Qur'an, and his actions were a clear manifestation of the message in the Qur'an. He ensured that the rules prescribed in the Qur'an were strictly adhered to in all public domains, be it governance, legal matters, social issues or the economy.

As the acting agent, the Prophet (pbuh) implemented the divine teachings in all aspects of life and set a perfect example for his followers, from private life to organize a state of Yathrib by introducing rules, regulations and public consultation to arrive at an agreed policy. Muhammad's (pbuh) virtue was founded on the active–dynamic love relationship with Allah swt and humanity, known as *walayah* (Mirakhor & Hamid, 2009). The Prophet Muhammad (pbuh) set an outstanding example of how Islamic law could be used to govern a diverse and pluralistic society successfully. His teachings inspire and guide humanity towards a path of righteousness, compassion and love for others.

The implemented framework by the Prophet (pbuh) is referred to as the 'Archetype Model' (Mirakhor & Hamid, 2009). His leadership in Yathrib transformed the society from rule-non-compliance to become rule compliance, as such the city was called as Medina. For 13 consecutive years, the foundation for good governance, property rights, market structures, rules of participation, distribution and redistribution of resources, education, public projects and other government issues were laid. The Prophet's (pbuh) rules were primarily based on the Madaniyah chapters, which were continuously revealed to him through Divine Revelation.[7]

Islam is a profound legal system constructed on principles of mercy and compassion for others. These are two foundations for policymaking. While Al-Qur'an provides a means for man to communicate with the Creator, the Prophet Muhammad (pbuh) demonstrated the implementation through his actions and sayings. As such, it is a complete way of life which reduces the uncertainties amongst people (North, 1990) Referring to North's theory, Al Qur'an and Prophet Muhammad (pbuh) are a set of institutional scaffolding that construct a society. There is a popular testimony of Ja'far, a cousin of the Prophet (pbuh) who once presented to Negus the King of Ethiopia, which showed the transformation of the community:

> Your Majesty, before Islam we were a people who worshipped idols, ate the meat of dead animals, engaged in immoral acts, cut relations with our blood relatives, mistreated our neighbours and those with whom we had covenants. The powerful among us would exploit and destroy the powerless. This was our state of affairs until Allah appointed one among us, a messenger who was known for truthfulness, trustworthiness, and moral and ethical behaviour. He called us to know Allah in His Unity and to adore

[7]Madaniyah chapters are chapters or verses of the Qur'an which were revealed in Medina, usually consisted topics such as governance, legal, and community matters.

> Him, and abandon the idols which we and our forefathers were worshipping. He admonished us to be truthful and trustworthy; to establish ties with blood relatives; to treat well our neighbours and those with whom we had covenants; to abandon immoral and unethical conduct; to stop shedding blood; to avoid lying, stealing from the orphans, and destroying the reputation of innocent women by falsely accusing them. He ordered us to establish daily communion (salah); to pay zakah (the right of others in one's income and wealth), and to fast. (Atay, 2020)

The conversation between Ja'far and Negus, the King of Ethiopia, highlights the foundational change in the life of Muslims, a metamorphosis effect after the coming of Islam. The crucial transformation is to shape and instil institutional scaffolding enacting rule compliance mechanism that subsequentially transformed the society. The rule compliance is thence a result of being surrender to God – The Almighty, The Creator and The All Knowing.

The story of Ja'far also indicates the aspects rule compliance in reducing uncertainties. It is distinct from 'ethics' because ethics is not universal but rule compliance is. Ethics are relative and utilitarian since ethical decisions are made based on self-interest and needs. Rule compliance is strict and focus on the common objectives which protects the rights of others into one's activity. Utilitarianism also makes ethical decisions more ambiguous as they are based on cost–benefit analysis through logic which can suffer from dissonance and inconsistency at times. In contrast, the Archetypal model is eternal and universal because its principles of mercy and compassions ingrained within the souls. Even a non-believer of Islam can be expected to comply with the general rulings and not on the rituals. It is reflected in Al Quran chapter Al-Shuuraa (42) verse 23, where Allah said:

> That is (the Paradise) whereof Allah gives glad tidings to His slaves who believe (in the Oneness of Allah Islamic Monotheism) and do righteous good deeds. Say (O Muhammad pbuh): "No reward do I ask you for this except to be kind to me for my kinship with you." And whoever earns a good righteous deed, We shall give him an increase of good in respect thereof. Verily, Allah is Oft-Forgiving, Most Ready to appreciate (the deeds of those who are obedient to Him).[8]

One reflection of this verse is that the Prophet Muhammad (pbuh) clearly showed mercy and compassion to his family members, despite some of his family members were non-believers.[9] Love, mercy and compassion were the Divine

---

[8]Mohsin Khan translation (Khan, 1996).

[9]For instance, the two of his great protectors and defenders are his grandfather and uncle. They continued to defend the Prophet (pbuh) until their deaths as non-believers.

reasons that could alter an ignorant to become a rule compliant. Another recorded saying of Muhammad (pbuh) in Sahih Bukhari in Chapter 11, hadith number 2021, was

> Narrated 'Aisha radhiyaAllahu anha (may Allah be pleased with her): The Prophet (pbuh) said, "Jibrael (Gabriel) continued to recommend me about treating the neighbours kindly and politely, so much so that I thought he would order me to make them as my heirs." (Bukhārī & Khan, 1976)

Islam was and is never exclusively ordained for the believers only. Certainly, when it comes to rituals, the laws such as prayers, marriage, funerals, dietary laws and inheritance, the application is restricted only to the believers. However, laws and rules concerning resource allocation, rules of behaviours for exchange, production, distribution and wealth/income redistribution are legally inclusive and applicable to all members of society. The incentive structure for rule compliance is offered for all as Allah swt said:

> And if the people of the towns had believed and had the Taqwa (piety), certainly, We should have opened for them blessings from the heaven and the earth, but they belied (the Messengers). So We took them for what they used to earn. (Al-Qur'an, 7:96)[10]

The ontological, epistemological and axiological dimensions of Islam lie on the distinct characteristics of the Almighty Creator and the Archetypal Model. Islamic institutions underpin in all sets of standards in life. Islamic economics is a discipline that aims to establish social justice and well-being through application of rules and laws by the Creator. It supports the definition of modern economics that underlays the basic reason of exchange is essentially merging self-vested interest to support benefits for all society members (Smith, 1776).

Islamic economics concerns with organizing individuals to display the principles of love, mercy and compassion to others in production, distribution and consumption. The basic reason of exchange is not to reap maximum profits in all activities because it is not sustainable. Such principles have tremendous economic implications and consequences as it would ensure rule compliance through the right policies and incentives for sharing and caring the economy. By applying so, it converges with the vision of unity in Islam. The Islamic economic system is for everyone, as love for others should be applicable to all people of background, beliefs, universal and timeless.

Therefore, based on these reasons, Islam has embedded eternality and universality in its teachings. Even when it comes to a non-believer, the principles of mercy and compassion for others are two common building blocks and are implementable by a man's virtue. One could not reject those Islamic institutions,

[10]Mohsin Khan translation (Khan, 1996).

i.e. rules, regulations and principles, demonstrated 'care for others' and 'social justice' at its utmost form, from private to a pluralistic state affair. Although acknowledgement and acceptance are two different realms, no scholars have ever rejected the fact that Medina was the civilized society where Islamic institutions applied and impacted to significant development of such multi-faith community (Cook, 2004). As the Qur'an is preserved, the rules and regulations have unchanged, and the Archetypal model was accepted and implemented in open society, there is no hesitation to conclude Islam is the fountain of eternal and universal source of knowledge.

Adapting Islamic Finance Principles to Modern Financial Practices

Islam has established rules and conditions for an effective economic system that serves the welfare of society. There are two conditions that must be met for the Islamic economic system to function optimally (Mirakhor, 2009). The first condition is to prohibit the practice of risk-transfer and risk-shifting behaviours in the market. These behaviours are commonly seen in a market where resources are limited, and people's greed blinds them to the consequences of their actions. In such conditions, profit maximization becomes the ultimate goal, and externalities that may occur in the long term are shifted to future generations.

The second condition that Islam prescribes is the implementation of risk sharing (Mirakhor, 2011). This condition recognizes everyone, including future generations, as partners who own portions of the economy according to their roles. Risk-sharing behaviour promotes cooperation and coordination (Mirakhor & Smolo, 2011), which are often lacking in the existing economic system. It is an essential institution that has led to economic transformations throughout history. These conditions can be applied to economic policy and finance to overcome the current market failure and socioeconomic issues such as income inequality, unemployment and poverty. However, for this ideal economic system to work, all members of the community must comply with the rules by avoiding risk transfer, shifting behaviour and exercising risk sharing in economic and finance transactions.

Historians have extensively researched the impact of risk sharing and the neglect of risk transfer and shifting on economic progress across different regions and historical periods (Swastika & Mirakhor, 2021). The Middle East provides a noteworthy example, where merchants used risk-sharing agreements such as '*modaraba*' and '*musharaka*' to facilitate financial transactions between capital owners and entrepreneurs (Çizakça, 1996). Both parties shared the business risk based on their financial and labour involvement in the venture. European merchants later adopted these fundamental principles during the medieval era, which paved the way for the development of modern financial systems.

The prohibition of interest rate-based contracts in Islamic finance is a technical application of the risk-sharing paradigm in finance, which Islam condemns. It is based on the principle that all interest-based transactions feature an act of shifting or transferring risks to the counterparties, which violates property rights. As a result, it creates social division, stimulates social problems, such as racism, anarchy, chauvinism, income inequality and poverty, and aggravates socio-economic phenomena. In terms of finance, social problems are likely to lead to a problem in capital mobilization. Dividing society based on wealth, race or nationality status would prevent capital from finding its most productive use. This leads to an increase in the cost of financing for talented entrepreneurs without known reputation, which is detrimental to the economy (Chapra, 2006).

Institutions are effectively transmitted and enforced through government policy (Mirakhor, 2012; Mirakhor & Askari, 2017; Othman & Mirakhor, 2013). The government has the authority to arrange and regulate public system which interlinks with private decisions. Government's policy is a powerful driver to influence social structures; thus, any public policies would significantly affect structural changes in a nation. It is also argued that structural changes would steer a new government (Riha, 1985). Considering the importance of authority vested in the government, leaders must carefully manage people's risks without jeopardising good norms and values.

The institution of risk transfer and shifting systems move individual risks to bank runs (private risk) to sovereignty and circle back to tax payers' consent due to bails out. Mirakhor (2008) pointed out that risk transfer and shifting are two instable policy institutions that have triggered financial crisis. From social justice point of view, the government's decision of bailing out the too-big-to-fail companies is deemed unfair because economic risks are borne by current and future taxpayers. Other negative impact of risk transfer and shifting systems is the wide gap in income inequality, since the wealthy individuals enjoy exclusive protection by authority, while the rest of group pays the cost (Cingano, 2014).

The alternative system for risk arrangement is risk sharing. Indeed, shari'ah scholars have defined that Islamic finance is a system which promulgates risk sharing contracts (Bakkali & Mirakhor, 2021). Risk sharing means that property claims exist only when transacted parties share the transaction risk based on their ability to assume the risk. This is the legal maxim, i.e. the general rule and principle to ensures burden of economic and financial risks is divided amongst economic agents according to their capacity. The risk-sharing system also ensures that private risks are isolated to individual and cannot be transferred to the public because of barriers to shift and transfer. Risk sharing fences the system with a stable institutional scaffolding that promotes justice, rewards transparency and accountability and strong social capital. Due to its merits, risk sharing is an important institution of society, particularly in the economy. Risk sharing ensures socioeconomic orders and fixes other structural problems due to the imbalanced growth witnessed today. The government, as the ultimate risk manager of society, must always be vigilant to public risk and protect society at large from receiving unwanted risks from private sectors.

Risk-sharing system acknowledges people participation and unity in its principles. It encourages people to participate directly in financing national projects and ensures equal access to information and money capital. To enact, incentives are also given for households and private actors who supported national programs. Strong social capital improves market institutions; thence, cooperation, collaboration and coordination are fostered. Once it is achieved, risk sharing system will automatically reduce uncertainties. In economic policy, risk sharing unclogs obstructions in wealth circulation so that money would strictly follow the speed of real market transactions. Thus, risk sharing economy is an inclusive system, where talents and good values are valuable intangible collaterals for money to be invested.

Risk sharing in finance has long-known to advance human civilization. Economic historians have recorded that the application of risk sharing instruments in various parts of the world (Harris, 2009; Udovitch, 1962; Çizakça, 2011). Venetians' 'commenda' is known to be popular investment instrument at the times. In *commenda,* merchants and sailors are partners, each contributed to the human capital or skills and also sometimes participate in the monetary capital. Individuals who had extra savings invested to the sails with hope for positive return. This money thus recorded as shares with rights to receive dividends everytime the ships returned from their expeditions. Such instrument successfully replaced the conventional sea loan and thus financed Venetia's Renaissance era (Harris, 2009; Lara, 2006).

Meanwhile in France, another variation of *commenda* existed. It was not private transactions, instead it partnered private with public interest projects. Société Générale du Crédit Mobilier (shortened, Crédit Mobilier) was one of well-documented 'investment bank' which its vision is to invest depositor's funds into public projects, such as building railways and housings. Established in 1852, Emile and Isaac Pereire invited about one hundred investors of the bank with amount ranging from 10 to 800 shares. They also ventured with the investment bank of B.-L. Fould et Fould-Oppenheim operated in Germany and owned 30% of shares (Cameron, 1953). Crédit Mobilier invested investors' funds to the establishment of the Eastern, Western, Southern and Grand Central railway networks of France, reconstruction and beautification of Paris and the creation of a shipping company named Compagnie Générale Transatlantique. The profits earned from these projects were hence distributed to shareholders in the form of dividends and was reported to be higher than the average market profit rate.

Commenda and Crédit Mobilier are two 'old' risk-sharing instruments whose effectiveness will be questioned if it is applied to today's economies. One may argue on the complexity of modern economies, and innovative financial assets are incomparable with old-styled participation scheme. The *Commenda* and Crédit Mobilier thus are viewed as irrelevant to today financial system. However, without understanding the underlying principles that had made *Commenda* and Crédit Mobilier so successful in transforming the society, it would be hard to further advanced partnerships and implemented risk sharing in finance.

Risk-sharing macroeconomic policy allocates financial risks of a country to economic agents based on their ability to bear them. This policy is divided into two: monetary and fiscal policy. Monetary policy is about managing money supply, while fiscal policy concerns with managing government revenue and spending. Implementing risk sharing into monetary policy considers the use of money as a medium of exchange. The core of risk sharing monetary policy is on money circulation which it must follow real transaction. Further, it must not be accumulated out of love value. Interest rate mechanism acknowledges this peculiar relation between money and its holders since it continues to positively increase. Risk transfer and shifting monetary policy is putting love to money in the centre principle that defeats mercy and compassion for others. It encourages the competition to accumulate money, which in turn will lead to an inequitable distribution of wealth and slow growth of the real sectors.

The second part is risk sharing in fiscal policy. Fiscal policy which are oriented on improving society welfare takes different approach than fiscal management which is in favour of specific groups. The key principle here is to translate compassion to others into strategic plans for people's welfare. Fiscal policy is government tool to manage the risks of society to provide safety and security amongst its citizens. Through fiscal discipline and avoiding national debt, government demonstrates justice for current and future citizens. Tax system is built on the foundation of mercy and not as punishment for doing economic activity. The poor's living is guaranteed and taken care of adequately by budgets through various safety nets and social programs. This is done without shifting burdens to other segments in society, i.e. tax payers, as it is the responsibility of all members to participate in improving society welfare.

In risk-sharing fiscal system, national expenditures aim to alleviate the poor, provide basic needs for all citizens and prepare future generations for the nations. Its spending includes necessities, such as food, health and shelters, safety (education) and security. Construction projects would have no significant value to growth if it did not improve social capital. At this context, growth must be redefined as human progress and not GDP which is based on monetary value. The aspects of human development, including social capital and trust, all of these could be enacted and enforced under risk-sharing fiscal policy. Mercy and compassion would improve rule compliance and coordination amongst the society members, thus fostering social capital which necessary to build a strong nation.

One example of a risk-sharing macroeconomic policies was implemented by Germany from 1933–1936 (Swastika & Mirakhor, 2021). Studying Germany in the early 20th century, the country underwent a rapid transformation from a defeated nation to a hub of technological and automotive advancement. This shift occurred within a relatively short time frame, specifically during the interwar period, with the implementation of risk-sharing principles in public policies. Despite the National Socialist party's political domination, the country's control was finally returned to its citizens by letting direct participation from private and household sectors into macroeconomic policies.

There are three phases of Germany economy. The first four-year plan (1933–1936) carries different target and objectives than the Plans post 1938. War preparation was only expressed from 1937 onwards and not before. The macroeconomic policy of the first four-year plan was totally focussed on improving unemployment and living conditions of Germans (Balogh, 1938; Overy, 1992; Shirer, 1962). Job provision was the target. By targeting jobs growth, Germany invented job-creation bills called *Arbeitsbeschaffungswechseln* (Katona, 1936; Overy, 1975; Schwarz, 1933). These bills were launched in early 1933.

Arbeitsbeschaffungswechseln allowed entrepreneurs to undertake public projects that generated employment for people. By involving society in financing public projects, the bills put people at the main driver seat that control economy. The bills financed people's public project and tied financial sectors to support job creations instead of money creation. The bills were unlike bonds because the bills could only be redeemed once the project was completed and earned profits. It resembles to equity securities where people are investors ensuring the projects and its outcomes meeting its target.

The implementation of a risk-sharing policy has been witnessed in various examples, among others include Commenda, Crédit Mobilier and the German macroeconomic policy. People participation in the fiscal policy demonstrates the compassion of others, and replacing interest rate with the bills scheme that favours finance to be entangled with real sectors shows mercy and not self-interest. It enables a more inclusive environment and more importantly reduce economic uncertainty. The underlying mechanism of this policy follows a fundamental principle that money is a medium of exchange and economic policy values beyond money accumulation. Policy orientation like this would enable a more efficient distribution of monetary capital from a surplus to entrepreneurs seeking capital.

In the context of a risk-sharing fiscal system, national expenditures must be oriented towards human development. All other development or construction projects would have no significant value to economic growth if it is counterproductive to improving social capital. Human development projects entail fulfiling the basic needs of people, such as health, shelter and education. Growth should be redefined as human development – not GDP which is based on monetary value. The aspects of human development, including environmental quality, healthcare, education, energy and more, are feasible to be financed using risk sharing. The people-oriented policy would improve rule compliance and coordination amongst the society members, thus affecting trust ethics and fostering social capital within the society.

Implementing a risk-sharing principle at the national level can help to close the disparities that exist in our society today. Promoting mercy and compassion to be implemented in monetary and fiscal policies will arrive onto social justice within the current generation avoids burdening tax payers and future generations with intra- and inter-generational risks. Intragenerational risk occurs during times when current tax payers burden the economic risks arising from corruption, collusion and nepotism, and government is vested on self-interest. Intergenerational risk endangers future generations from excessive debts and repayments, poor social capital and bad society. Risk sharing policy promote and provide equitable wealth distribution and opportunities for all individuals to thrive and succeed, resulting in a more stable institutional scaffolding to be a prosperous economy.

Challenges and Opportunities in Implementing Islamic Finance

When it comes to challenges and opportunities in implementing Islamic finance, there is urgency to understand the status quo. Islamic finance is currently a subset of conventional system, whereby rules and regulations enforced are double standards. Islamic financial institutions must adhere to rules which are derived from conventional principles, while also fulfiling its set of regulations. Such compromise reduces the efficiency of Islamic finance because the Islamic financial institutions competitiveness becomes adrift. Islamic financial institutions thus are more costly than the conventional because customers must pay all the legal and administrative fees in exchange for contracts which are all written in foreign language and without clear explanation.

Islamic finance is also failed to pass the litmus test. The litmus test of any financial system is to achieve social welfare and prosperity. The efficiency of a system is measured whether it functions according to what it is supposed to do, thus in case of today, Islamic finance has yet to function as a just intermediary. There are no stark differences between the practice of Islamic finance and conventional system, except on the terminology of contracts. Fiqh muamalat has yet to successfully providing noticeable achievement that meets people's expectations about Islamic financial institutions. This disappointment has costed distrust in society that Islamic banks is like conventional.

Another ongoing misconception about Islamic finance is that it works only in a primitive economy. It is argued that fiqh muamalat is no longer compatible and applicable to today's rules and regulations. Fitting fiqh muamalat means to compromise between the strict and fixed rulings of Islamic scholars which most are lagging of the fast-paced conventional system. As such Islamic finance instruments could not adapt to our open and modern market, thus is ineffective to provide social welfare. The argumentation is also around the extra costs of Islamic scholars' opinion whenever society asks them to address the complexity and ambiguity of modern financial products. Different Islamic schools of thought introduce different rulings (*fatwas*), as such implementing Islamic finance principles is rigid and an expensive process, thus serves as the curfew for innovation and creativity in open modern and complex economy.

Certainly, these public perceptions are not criticizing Islamic finance per se. Public evaluates what today's Islamic bankers exercised and how they felt about Islamic financial institutions not meeting people's expectations. Islamic finance is the alternative to perilous conventional system, but human resources that work on the industry are still failing to push the application of Islamic finance principles in his policy. Islamic bankers are still preoccupied by the fiqh process without a thorough examination of economic implications on instruments. While Islamic scholars is not economists, the talents pool of Islamic scholars who understand economics becomes rare. Therefore, these challenges open opportunities for depth discussion on the application of Islamic finance.

Islamic finance principles are based on the axiology of risk sharing. As explained earlier, it prerequisites mercy and compassion, so agents are willing to accept and agree to share risks. Mercy and compassion are two ingredients that should be thought throughout the policymaking process. Whether it is an individual decision, industrial regulations, or macroeconomic policy, mercy and compassion must play active role in every consideration on todays and future implications. Mercy and compassion are the universal language and eternal values of risk sharing principles. This way, explaining Islamic finance principle becomes simpler and understandable by all people for generations.

The government has the authority to implement the principles into macroeconomic policies. In terms of fiscal policy, public financing based on Islamic finance would set participative mechanism between citizens and the private sector to public projects through a selection process based on meritocracy. The active participation of citizens and the private sector in public financing is essential, as this mechanism of budgeting would ensure that projects needed most by society are prioritized and prevent conflicts of political interest. In the monetary system, the principle is to engage money with lawful exchange transactions. To abolish interest rates, the monetary authority would need to introduce an alternative instrument that keeps money intact in real lawful transactions.

Debt is a significant challenge in modern economies. There are two sources of financing public projects that are tax collection and national debt. In recent times, debt has been increasingly relied to address fiscal gaps. Prominent economists have written on the potential risks of over-indebtedness, deflation and financial fragility during business cycles (Cordella et al., 2005; Huber & Runkel, 2008; Reinhart, 2013; Reinhart et al., 2003, 2015). Monetary instruments attempt to balance liquidity through a combination of policies, which may result in a long-term shift of debt and speculation. Intermediaries may unintentionally create a bubble economy where the accumulation of money is seen as a growth indicator. However, despite growth nominally improving, it is now evidence that jobs and productivity may continue to suffer.

Debt financing is a perilous policy for a country. It potentially undermines sovereignty and leads to significant economic fragility and social unrest. It is crucial for governments to consider alternative macroeconomic policies that can benefit everyone by sharing the risk. Sharing risk is a result of mercy and compassion as measures in public policymaking. It evokes active participation which helps to mitigate the risks of moral hazards and adverse selections and fosters social cohesion by encouraging rule compliance and building trust – both of which are essential components of social capital. By embracing this approach, governments can create a more stable and prosperous future for their citizens, while also building stronger, more resilient communities.

Conventional finance regards debt (and money) as a commodity; therefore, borrowing lending is a trade transaction. Interest rate is the price that balances supply and demand. Such approach invokes adverse selection during pre-borrowing, and moral hazards after the loan are granted due to information asymmetries. Financial intermediary theory reinforces this setup, with banking sectors playing a broker role. This has spurred debt, and despite the cost of funds getting more expensive, people become more and more indebted and increased social tension and distress.

As a solution for financial distress, Islam promotes risk sharing instruments of income distributions and redistributions. These instruments are mechanisms to demonstrate mercy and compassion for others, thus is risk sharing that aims for human progress. Throughout the time, economic growth is about constructing a civilized society. In a civilized society, trust is improved enabling cooperation, coordination and collaboration for reducing uncertainties and subsequently improving welfare. These are the importat but often neglected measures in finance, that is also held account for shaping structural changes in society.

Establishing trust is important tenet in ensuring healthy distribution and redistribution mechanism (Mirakhor, 2004). Trust in exchange and trust in redistributions are highly rewarded. In fact, Islam recognizes credit contracts are rooted in compassion and trust. *Qard*, or benevolent loan, allows individuals to provide financial assistance without expecting interest or principal repayment under the guarantee of Allah swt. Allah swt mentioned about *Qard*:

> Who is he that will lend to Allah a goodly loan, then (Allah) will increase it manifold to his credit (in repaying), and he will have (besides) a good reward (i.e. Paradise). Al Hadid Chapter 57: Verses 11[11]

Although repayment is not required, borrowers are still obliged to repay the loan. *Dayn*, a debt arising from exchange transactions, is profitable and commendable to record and witness. Islam enforces social capital and trust within Muslim individuals with a guarantee of stability in return.

It is important to note here that not all Muslim majority countries follow the same approach to Islamic finance because of different interpretation. Countries such as Iran, Pakistan and Sudan are the examples of countries which reject interest rate into banking system. Unfortunately, this principle is not followed by applying risk sharing, thus it meets the sufficient condition for Islamic finance to flourish but not the necessary conditions for the system to pass the litmus test of socio-economic problems. Beyond that, these countries are also politically limited by big finance, and so the leaders to compromise it to suit the interests of big finance and politics.

Another important challenge is to shift paradigm in government regulations. Regulation creates a standard, or rule of the game, for society members. To design a comprehensive, global and dynamic regulatory, prudential and supervisory framework, regulators must agree that the current paradigm in regulations is ineffective to avoid crisis. Policymakers must evaluate thoroughly, despite all the advancement in technologies and science, why regulation still failed to mitigate crisis. Regulators should continuously check what are missing elements in policy. After detail evaluation, then policy makers must be in consensus to initiate paradigm shift. And as part of Islamic finance recommendation is to instil mercy and compassion as measures of policy so that risk sharing could transform policy from dull and lagging to comprehensive, global and dynamic regulations.

---

[11]Mohsin Khan translation (Khan, 1996).

Investment in education and training programs must focus on building characters. Learning facility todays is engrossed so much on the transfer of knowledge and pay less attention on building values and characters of the students. Education should not only help individuals and businesses making informed financial decisions, it should also shape rule-compliant individual and build a strong social capital within community. Instilling a rule compliant, trust and social capital would help to accelerate the implementation of risk sharing and lawful exchange transactions into personal finance decisions, as well as more advanced topics such as investing, risk management and financial planning.

Finally, it is important to recognize that building a stable and sustainable economy is a long-term process that requires active-dynamic contributions from all members of society. This means that individuals, businesses and governments must work together to reset and re-instil good values and principles into economic policy so that more equitable access and prosperity benefit everyone. By planting participation and risk-sharing finance on top of good institutions as the ground, nations can build a better future for todays and future generations.

Risk sharing is an action of mercy and compassion. If today we witnessed that risk transfer and shifting flourish, it alarms that mercy and compassion have started decaying. This situation must be fought back by shifting social paradigm from the domination of risk transfer and shifting financial system to risk sharing. It is urgent to continuously and relentlessly promoting, elaborating and collecting proofs on the applied risk sharing finance and documents its implications to human progress and civilization. More importantly, keeping mercy and compassion at micro-level decision would promote risk sharing in community.

Conclusion

History have recorded adequate information that risk sharing is an effective principle to organize modern economies. Adopting risk sharing into economic policy entails putting mercy and compassion as measures and factors for policy making. Policymakers are individuals who must display mercy and compassion in every decision affecting society. Leaders put people's well-being at his shoulder and so we trust them to organize our risk and affairs. These are times and opportunities to select leaders who understand risk sharing principle and can enforce it into factors and measures for policy making process. Within this frame, young talented visioner leader must born as proof of risk sharing application in politics.

Discussions at earlier section have demonstrated that risk sharing financed transformation in the economy. It is urgent to explain and reiterate what the archival records and demonstrate it into scientific articles that risk sharing prevails in many countries at different times and occasions. We argue here that there should be no urgency to restrict risk sharing with Islam as label because this paper has shown the ontology, epistemology and axiology of Islam is universal and eternal. Thus, so long as the policy resonates the basic axioms of risk sharing, that is mercy and compassion, into the economic system, it is Islamic finance by default.

If one is on doubt whether is risk sharing is applicable, then mercy and compassion are inexistent in his life. Mercy and compassion are values for a strong solid society, and the inexistence of these values endangers our life. Omitting mercy and compassion from decision-making would put our life on risk because we could not trust other people. When man displayed distrust to others, no cooperation, coordination and collaboration would contribute to rising uncertainties. Risk transfer and shifting alienates a man, divided society into groups, creates disparities between government and people and fuel for civil war.

Therefore, this paper explains the evident that Islamic finance principles can be applied in modern economies to promote financial stability, economic growth and social development. The adoption of Islamic finance principles poses several challenges, including the need for leaders to recognize mercy and compassion in policy making process. As the ultimate risk manager of the people, the government is responsible for enforcing, protecting, preserving social order through mercy and compassion. Social order under violence and oppression is not sustainable and short-lived as history recounts falling dictators and regimes. Islamic bankers must also evaluate society perceptions, whether Islamic financial institutions have satisfied people's expectations.

References

Atay, R. (Ed.). (2020). *Islam through Hadiths* (Vol. 7). İleri Basım Matbaacılık A.Ş.

Avicenna. (2005). *The metaphysics of the healing: A parallel English-Arabic text.* Brigham Young University Press.

Bakkali, S., & Mirakhor, A. (2021). *Risk-sharing finance: An Islamic Jurisprudence (Fiqh) perspective* (Vol. 10). Walter de Gruyter GmbH.

Balogh, T. (1938). The national economy of Germany. *The Economic Journal, 48*(191), 461–497.

Bukhārī, M. I., & Khan, M. M. (1976). *Sahīh Al-Bukhārī: The translation of the meanings of Sahih Al-Bukhari: Arabic-English.* Dar Ahya Us-Sunnah.

Cameron, R. E. (1953). The credit mobilier and the economic development of Europe. *Journal of Political Economy, LXI*(6), 461–488.

Chapra, M. U. (2006). The nature of Riba in Islam. *The Journal of Islamic Economics and Finance, 2*(1), 7–25.

Cingano, F. (2014). Trends in income inequality and its impact on economic growth. *Trends in Income Inequality and Its Impact on Economic Growth, 163.* https://doi.org/10.1787/5jxrjncwxv6j-en

Çizakça, M. (1996). *A comparative evolution of business partnerships: The Islamic world and Europe, with specific reference to the Ottoman archives.* Brill Academic Pub.

Çizakça, M. (2011). *Islamic capitalism and finance: Origins, evolution and the future.* Edward Elgar Publishing Ltd.

Cook, M. (2004). *Commanding right and forbidding wrong in Islamic thought (first).* Cambridge Universty Press.

Cordella, T., Ricci, L. A., & Ruiz-arranz, M. (2005). *Debt Overhang or Debt Irrelevance? Revisiting the Debt-Growth Link,* IMF Working Paper.

Harris, R. (2009). The institutional dynamics of early modern Eurasian trade: The commenda and the corporation. *Journal of Economic Behavior & Organization*. https://doi.org/10.1016/j.jebo.2009.04.016

Huber, B., & Runkel, M. (2008). Hyperbolic discounting, public debt, and balanced budget rules. *Scottish Journal of Political Economy*, *55*(5), 543–560.

Katona, G. M. (1936). The “miracle” of German recovery. *Foreign Affairs*, *14*(2), 348–350. https://doi.org/10.1017/S1052703600007176

Khan, M. (1996). *The Noble Quran in the English Language*. King Fahd Printing Complex.

Lara, Y. G. D. (2006). The secret of Venetian success: Public-order yet Reputation-based Institutions. *Conference Proceeding. XIV International Economic History Congress.*

Mirakhor, A. (2004, April). Islamic finance and instrumentalization of Islamic redistributive institutions. *Ibn Rushd Memorial Lecture*.

Mirakhor, A. (2008). Lessons of the recent crisis for Islamic finance. *IIUM Journal of Economics and Management*, *16*(2).

Mirakhor, A. (2009). Islamic economics and finance: An institutional perspective. *IIUM Journal of Economics and Management*, *17*(1), 31–72.

Mirakhor, A. (2011). Risk sharing and public policy. *The 5th International Islamic Capital Market Forum*. Securities Commission of Malaysia.

Mirakhor, A. (2012, November). Shariah compliant macro-economic policy. Paper presented at Sisana Kijang, Bank Negara Malaysia.

Mirakhor, A., & Askari, H. (2017). Institutional structure of a sound economy. In *Ideal Islamic economy*. https://doi.org/10.1057/978-1-137-53727-0_4

Mirakhor, A., & Hamid, I. S. (2009). *Islam and development: The institutional framework* (Vol. 3). Global Scholarly Publications.

Mirakhor, A., & Smolo, E. (2011, August). Do conventional and Islamic finance share common epistemology? *GIF Islamic Finance*, 48–53.

Mirakhor, A., & Smolo, E. (2012). Discovering the roots of conventional and Islamic finance. In H. Dar (Ed.), *Global Islamic Finance Report (GIFR) 2012* (pp. 148–153). Edbiz Consulting Limited.

Mirakhor, A., & Smolo, E. (2014). Epistemological foundation of finance: Islamic and conventional. *Islamic Banking and Finance Review*, *1*(1). https://doi.org/10.32350/ibfr.2014.01.01

North, D. C. (1990). *Institutions, institutional change and economic performance*. Cambridge University Press. https://doi.org/10.1017/cbo9781139175302.016

Othman, A., & Mirakhor, A. (2013). Islam and development: Policy challenges. In Z. Iqbal & A. Mirakhor (Eds.), *Economic development and Islamic finance*. The World Bank. https://doi.org/10.1596/978-0-8213-9953-8

Overy, R. J. (1975). Cars, roads, and economic recovery in Germany. *The Economic History Review*, *28*(3), 466–483.

Overy, R. J. (1992). *War and Economy in the Third Reich* (2002 repri). Oxford University Press, Inc.

Reinhart, C. (2013). *Debt's impact on growth: Latest study doesn't settle debate* (pp. 4–5).

Reinhart, C. M., Reinhart, V., & Rogoff, K. (2015). Dealing with debt. *Journal of International Economics*. https://doi.org/10.1016/j.jinteco.2014.11.001

Reinhart, C., Rogoff, K., & Savastano, M. (2003). Debt intolerance. *Brookings Papers on Economic Activity*, *1*(13932), 1–74.

Riha, T. (1985). German political economy: The history of an alternative economics. *International Journal of Social Economics, 12*. https://doi.org/10.1108/eb013991

Schwarz, P. (1933, October 8). Germany presses recovery project. *The New York Times*, 1933.

Shirer, W. L. (1962). The rise and fall of the Third Reich: A history of Nazi Germany. *The American Historical Review*, *68*(1), 126. https://doi.org/10.2307/1847219

Smith, A. (1776). An inquiry into the nature and causes of the wealth of nations. In S. M. Soares (Ed.), *MetaLibri digital library*. (*Vols. I–IV*). https://doi.org/10.1057/9780230291652

Swastika, P., & Mirakhor, A. (2021). In H. Askari (Ed.), *Applying risk-sharing finance for economic development lessons from Germany*. Palgrave Macmillan.

Udovitch, A. L. (1962). At the origins of the Western Commenda: Islam, Israel, Byzantium? *Speculum*, *37*(2), 198–207. https://doi.org/10.2307/3210793

Chapter 4

Islam and Free Trade: The Contributions of Muslim Scholars to Modern Economic Theories

Edib Smolo

Effat University, Saudi Arabia

Abstract

Islamic economic ideology has exerted a profound influence on the evolution of the open market, particularly in the domains of individual property rights, unobstructed commerce, and restrained governmental interference. The Islamic doctrine pertaining to individual property rights underscores the entitlement of individuals to possess and exercise dominion over their possessions, and this fundamental doctrine has played a pivotal role in shaping the unrestrained market. Islamic economic philosophy also champions free trade, affording individuals the freedom to exchange commodities and services devoid of governmental constraints. This doctrine has contributed to the creation of a more efficient and prosperous economic milieu. Ultimately, Islamic economic thought propagates the concept of delimited governmental involvement in economic affairs. This principle affords enterprises the latitude to undertake risks, while empowering entrepreneurs to establish novel companies, both of which are integral to economic expansion. The undeniable contributions of Islamic economic thought to the maturation of the open market are incontestable. These principles have been instrumental in the establishment of a more efficient, flourishing, and vibrant economic landscape. As our world becomes progressively intertwined, it remains imperative to retain the insights gleaned from Islamic economic thought and persist in the pursuit of an equitable and free market system.

Keywords: Islamic economics; free trade; Madinah market; Muslim scholars; capitalism

The Future of Islamic Finance, 49–64

doi:10.1108/978-1-83549-906-120241004

Introduction

As Islam emerged in Mecca in the seventh century, knowledge expanded into different areas. Although some may attempt to overlook or diminish their impact, the contributions of Muslim scholars cannot be overstated. Thus, it is not surprising that Schumpeter attempted to mark this period as a "great gap" in the evolution and development of economic thought when he said: "So far as our subject is concerned we may safely leap over 500 years to the epoch of St. Thomas Aquinas (122574), whose *Summa Theologica* is in the history of thought what the south-western spire of the Cathedral of Chartres is in the history of architecture" (Schumpeter et al., 1994, p. 70).[1]

Similarly, in his work "The Protestant Ethic and the Spirit of Capitalism," Max Weber argues that the birth of capitalism began in Western Europe and spread to North America (Weber, 2001). By examining the connections between Muslim culture and capitalist development, Koehler (2014) questions whether Western historians have correctly attributed the birthplace of capitalism to medieval Europe. He suggests that it was the Muslim civilization that provided the organizational and ideological elements that were combined to yield some of the positive features of capitalism.

Koehler explains that the Prophet Muhammad, peace be upon him (pbuh), himself was an established entrepreneur, and Mecca was not just a holy place but also a significant trading center at that time. By promoting justice (*'adl*) and fairness, Islamic teachings provided extensive guidance on fair trade, emphasizing the importance of writing business contracts and honoring them as both a religious and civic duty.

Denying the existence of an economic system within Islam is equivalent to denying Islam itself. Islam as a faith represents a way of life that does not distinguish between the mundane and the religious or separate religious rituals from socioeconomic relationships. The right to private property for both men and women has been properly recognized in Islamic law for over 14 centuries. Islamic institutions and business practices were later adopted in Venice and Genoa. Other Islamic institutions that were assimilated in Europe included charitable foundations, *waqf* (endowments), and higher educational institutions, such as *madrasas* (Smolo, 2012; Smolo & Ismail, 2011). Koehler argues that these higher educational institutions served as models for the oldest colleges in Oxford and Cambridge (Koehler, 2014).

It is rightly said that Muslim scholars have left an indelible mark on the development of all disciplines, including economics, throughout the centuries. We must not forget that Islamic educational institutions were centers of learning where great minds from both the East and the West acquired knowledge. For centuries, educational institutions across the Muslim world were centers of advanced education and scientific achievement. These institutions foreshadowed today's high schools, colleges, and universities. Among the primary centers of learning were Baghdad in Iraq, Damascus in Syria, Bursa and Edirne in Turkey,

[1]Also known as the "Schumpeterian Gap."

Cairo in Egypt, where the University of Al-Azhar was founded in 975, and cities like Cordoba, Granada, Zaragoza, and Seville in Islamic Spain, among many others (Smolo, 2013). We should also not forget that the world's oldest university, the University of Al-Qarawiyyin, was founded in 859 in the Moroccan city of Fes by Fatima al-Fihri.[2] The fact that a woman founded this university speaks volumes about the status of women during that period and the freedoms that existed in that part of the world under Muslim rule.

From the scientific works of Western scholars, one can discern the ideas and teachings of Muslim scholars that preceded them. This is not surprising because Muslim scholars excelled in scientific inquiry. They supplemented existing knowledge of their time with translations of works by ancient Romans, enriched with Islamic principles and narrative. These enriched teachings undoubtedly left a mark on later Western scholars such as Roger Bacon and Thomas Aquinas. All in all, we can say that Islam significantly contributed to the development of modern sciences, including economics and what we now call the free market or *laissez-faire*.

However, the stagnation of Muslims led to a change in what is now called the "world order." The West capitalized on the achievements of the Muslim world and continued where Muslims had left off. In this process, the field of economics developed as a separate discipline (Sadeq & Ghazali, 1992, p. 10; Smolo, 2013, p. 134).

The modern economic thought, on the other hand, does not give much importance to Muslim scholars and their ideas. This Western approach is not surprising due to the influence of Christian thought and the Crusades on the development and Renaissance that occurred in Europe (Mirakhor, 1987). Nevertheless, the achievements of the Middle Ages and the translation of classical works available in educational centers in Muslim Spain (*Al-Andalus*) significantly impacted the development of the Renaissance and Enlightenment in Europe (Lane-Poole & Gilman, 1990).

In short, the development of economic science and the idea of a free market is not something that happened overnight. Rather, the history of economic thought represents a continuous progression of ideas composed of epochal contributions to the ever-expanding body of knowledge inherited from the past (Ekelund & Hébert, 2014, pp. 1–3; Islahi, 2014, p. 1). In the following sections, we will briefly outline the development of Islamic economic thought and its undeniable influence on the development of the free market as we know it today.

The Schumpeterian Gap

Economic historians, in their analyses, typically begin with Greek philosophers and Roman jurists and administrators. Occasionally, they also refer to the writings of certain early Christian scholars. They then jump to the Middle Ages and

---

[2]This university, which was originally a mosque, was included in the educational system of Morocco only in 1963.

Europe, which experienced the Enlightenment, leading to the development of natural and social sciences. This leap effectively skips over approximately five centuries (the same 500-year period Schumpeter bypasses in his work). During this period, historians tend to ignore that Muslims ruled over a significant portion of the known world, established powerful empires and developed economies, and contributed substantially to promoting culture and science, including economics (Islahi, 2014).

Islahi argues that skipping over this period is primarily seen in the context of economic thinking and institutions. He points out that the contributions of Muslim scholars to medieval Europe in fields such as philosophy, science, mathematics, geography, history, art, and culture are well-documented and known (Islahi, 2014, p. 75).

Nevertheless, there is a growing recognition of this injustice or oversight in scholarship, with more voices drawing attention to the significant contributions of Muslim scholars. Islahi cites Heaton, who states "Muhammadanism regarded trade as a worthy occupation, ties of rule and religion facilitated long-distance trade and travel and since the Asiatic and the Moslem world possessed many industrial or agricultural skills and products which were superior to those of the European end, the West benefited by the lessons it learned from its new masters" (Islahi, 2014, p. 78). Simultaneously, the Crusaders benefited from both commercial products and economic institutions of Muslim society, as well as from their scientific works. This is where terms such as *hisbah* (*agoranomos* – inspection), *mudarabah* (*commenda* – passive partnership), *suftajah*, *sakk* (*cheque*), *tariff*, and others originated (Islahi, 2014, pp. 78–79).[3–6]

Although the development of modern economic thought is often associated with Adam Smith and the 18th century, it does not imply that economic themes were not discussed in earlier societies, including the Muslim world, which had been at the forefront in various aspects. It is true that throughout human history, all cultures have had certain principles on which they based their social and economic-financial relationships. This also holds for Islam and Muslims. The Messenger of Allah, Muhammad (pbuh), was a respected merchant in Mecca even before receiving his prophethood. With the revelation of the Qur'an over 23 years and the development of the Muslim community (*Ummah*) in Medina, there

[3]*Hisbah* represents accountability institution or market inspection, and *muhtasib* is an inspector who oversees market operations (see Islahi, 2018, p. 59; Koehler, 2014).

[4]*Mudarabah* is a contract between the *rabb al-mal* (capital owner), who only contributes the capital, and the *mudarib* (entrepreneur, manager or commercial trustee), who runs and manages the entire business (see Smolo, 2013, pp. 79–80, 117–118, 271).

[5]*Suftaja* is a type of banking instrument that was used for lending in the Muslim state, especially during the Abbasid period. This instrument was used to collect taxes, pay government obligations, and transfer funds by merchants. It was mostly used by traveling merchants. *Suftaja* represents an early paper instrument that functioned as a check for long-distance payments and safe travel (Lydon, 2009, 2019; Smolo, 2013).

[6]The word *sakk* in Arabic means file, document, receipt, check, policy, bill, bond (see Muftić, 1997, p. 595).

was a transformation in business arrangements within this community. This doesn't mean that Islam introduced entirely new business principles.

On the contrary, by the Divine will and wisdom, the Messenger of Allah (pbuh) enriched the existing practices among the Arabs in three ways. First, he confirmed and approved specific methods that aligned with Islamic teachings. Second, practices that contradicted these teachings were rejected and prohibited. Third, some techniques contained elements of both the first and second groups. In such cases, if the forbidden parts were removable, Muhammad, (pbuh), removed them and allowed the purified principles to be used. Otherwise, he abolished them (Smolo, 2013, p. 116).

Therefore, the Messenger of Allah (pbuh) was the first person in Islam to establish economic and financial principles through his words, deeds, and tacit approval. The companions of the Messenger (pbuh) embraced this practice and passed it on to later generations. The result of such an approach is that today, we can find works discussing economic issues in all periods of Islamic history. In other words, we can conclude that economic and financial issues in Islam have had continuity from the beginning of the Islamic revelation to the present day.

For example, the contemporary principles of venture capital were extensively used in Islamic civilization based on the principles of *mudarabah* and *musharakah* (partnerships) and were adapted for long-distance trade in accordance with the skills and capabilities of workers and capitalists (Smolo & Hassan, 2011). Simultaneously, a monetary system based on gold and silver was sufficiently developed at that time to avoid problems associated with barter economics. Koehler writes, "In Baghdad, by the early tenth century a fully-fledged banking sector had come into being: exchanging gold and silver coins and lending money to government and to merchants who were able to pay money into accounts in one city and draw money in another. These drafts had several names – one of them was the Persian word *čak* that has come down to us as *check*." (Koehler, 2014, pp. 2–3).

Islamic Economics and Finance: A Brief Overview From Inception to Today

The fundamental sources of Islam are the *Qur'an*, *sunnah* (the actions and sayings of the Prophet Muhammad), *ijma'* (consensus of scholars), and *qiyas* (analogical reasoning). Therefore, the economic ideas of Muslims are based on Islamic teachings derived from these sources. The Qur'an is considered the Word of God revealed to the Prophet Muhammad (pbuh), and the *sunnah* represents the Prophet's practical demonstration and explanation, containing numerous economic teachings and principles applicable to various contexts.

However, you will not find a specific chapter (*surah*) in the Qur'an exclusively dedicated to economic issues. Instead, the Qur'an provides timeless guidance and inspiration, offering principles for all aspects of human life regardless of space and time. The Qur'an addressed economic issues as they arose in society during its revelation. Additionally, the Prophet Muhammad (pbuh) provided further explanations and guidance on economic matters when the need arose. Thus, during the period of Qur'anic revelation and the life of the Prophet Muhammad (pbuh), all questions arising in Islamic society were directed to him, and he, through Divine revelation, provided answers. Later, during the time of the four righteous caliphs, new questions were resolved through *shura* (consultation).

In general, Muslim scholars used the Qur'an and *sunnah* as starting points in their reasoning but relied on reason (*ijtihad*) to address issues in changing historical and economic conditions, following the principles of *ijma'* (consensus) and *qiyas* (analogy).[7] In this process, they did not rely solely on these sources and personal experiences. Whenever circumstances allowed, they used the knowledge and experiences of others, a practice that continued throughout Islamic history.

However, as Islam spread to other parts of the world, new discoveries and encounters between civilizations and cultures presented new challenges and questions that needed answers. This led to the development of *fiqh* (Islamic jurisprudence) as a science. *Fiqh* did not only deal with issues like ablution, prayer, fasting, almsgiving, and pilgrimage but covered all aspects of behavior, including economic matters.

As mentioned earlier, Koehler argues that Islamic civilization provided organizational and ideological elements that, when combined, contributed to some positive aspects of capitalism.

As an experienced merchant, the Prophet Muhammad (pbuh) was aware of the importance of the economy for societal development. After migrating to Medina and establishing a Muslim community with himself at its head, he initiated the establishment of socioeconomic institutions that furthered the development of society and the community. The Prophet's Mosque served as a center for gathering and what we might now call a parliament or assembly. Discussions on emerging issues, significant decisions, consultations with eminent representatives of society, and dispute resolutions were conducted there.

Before the arrival of the Prophet Muhammad (pbuh), Medina had a market where trade was conducted daily following the prevailing practices among the Arab community at the time. Participation in this market was taxed. Due to this practice and others inconsistent with Islamic teachings, the Prophet Muhammad designated a new place for all business transactions. In a hadith recorded by Ibn Majah in his Sunan, the Prophet Muhammad (pbuh) said: "This is your market; do not diminish it, and do not levy taxes on it."[8] Thus, trading in this market was not taxed, and no one had privileges. The first to arrive at the market each day could choose any place they wished, which was not the case before.

Considering this, it can be concluded that the principles of Islamic economics trace their origins back to the early days of Islam and the actions of the Prophet Muhammad (pbuh), who actively set rules that had to be followed.

---

[7]The *ijtihad* is "a creative and comprehensive intellectual effort by qualified individuals and groups to derive the juridical ruling on a given issue from the sources of Shari'ah in the context of the prevailing circumstances of society" (Kamali, 2008, p. 165).

[8]Hadith no. 2233. This narration is characterized as weak (*da'if*).

After the passing of the Prophet Muhammad (pbuh) and his companions, Islam continuously spread to other parts of the world, bringing with it new challenges. Nevertheless, Islamic history testifies to the continuous development of economic thought wherever Muslims ruled. There are many works that confirm this assertion, and we will mention some shortly.

With the expansion of the Caliphate, not only the economy but every aspect of life experienced development. During the Abbasid dynasty, Baghdad became the center of the Caliphate and international trade, experiencing its peak. Great attention was given to economic issues. The state budget was generously spent for the benefit of the people. During the reign of the second Abbasid Caliph, Al-Mansur, many books were collected from various fields. After him, his son Al-Mahdi became the Caliph, and his minister, Muawiyah bin Ubaydullah bin Yasir Al-Ash'ari, wrote the book "Kitab al-Haraj" (The Book of Taxation), which historians claim to be the first book on Islamic economics. There is no evidence of the existence of a copy of this book, but Dr Najatullah Siddiqi claims it to be the first book of its kind.

The second book of this kind is "Kitab al-Haraj" written by Imam Abu Yusuf (d. 798 CE) under the orders of Caliph Harun al-Rashid (Sadeq & Ghazali, 1992). This is one of the earliest works on the Islamic taxation system. There is also the book "Kitab al-Haraj" by Yahya bin Adam al-Kara'i (d. 818 CE) and "Kitab al-Amwal" by Abu Ubaydah al-Qasim bin Sallam (d. 838 CE). Scholars like Al-Mawardi (d. 1058 CE), Ibn Hazm (d. 1063 CE), Al-Ghazali (d. 1111 CE), and others wrote on economic issues in the early period of Islamic history (Azmi, 2002, p. 10).

After this period, many Islamic scholars wrote about economics within Islam, but space does not permit us to delve into their ideas regarding Islamic economics. It is essential to note that the term "iqtisad" (economics) emerged in the modern era, and economics as a modern concept was part of *Fiqh*.[9]

In summary, reflecting on the period from the early 15th century CE, Islahi (2014) divides the history of Islamic economic thought into three broad phases: (a) the formative period, covering the time immediately after the onset of revelation until the end of the time of the Companions (11–100 AH/632–718 CE); (b) the translation period from the second to the fifth century AH (8th to 11th century CE), during which Muslim scholars translated the works of other civilizations, utilized them, and advanced them; and (c) the period of retranslation and transmission, during which Greco-Arab Islamic ideas reached Europe through translation and other contacts (from the sixth to the ninth century AH/12th to 15th century CE).[10]

---

[9]For a more detailed description of the development of Islamic economy and finance, see (Smolo, 2013).

[10]For a detailed description of these stages, see (Islahi, 2014, p. 7).

The Development of Modern Economic Discipline: A Brief Overview

According to Western scholars, economics as a scientific discipline is relatively young. Scholars often refer to the mercantilists of the 17th and 18th centuries as the precursors to modern economics. Mercantilists promoted exports while minimizing imports, which also involved the promotion of imperialism, tariffs, and subsidies. It's worth noting that modern economic thought also draws on the teachings of ancient philosophers like Plato and Aristotle and later thinkers such as St. Thomas Aquinas.

However, the creator of modern economic discipline is considered to be Adam Smith (1776), who, in his book "The Wealth of Nations," advocated for a *laissez-faire* system. In this system, the government has minimal involvement, and individuals, guided by the "invisible hand" mechanism, seek to pursue their self-interests while simultaneously benefiting society. The fundamental ideas of economics proposed by Smith were further developed by classical economists of the late 18th and early 19th centuries (Malthus in 1778 and Ricardo in 1817), as well as by neoclassical economists of the mid and late 19th century (J.S. Mill in 1848, Walras, and Marshall in 1890). Keynes expanded the scope of economics and partially opposed certain principles of a free market economy. This forms the tradition of mainstream conventional economics. The radical strand emerged at the end of the 19th and the beginning of the 20th centuries with Karl Marx and Lenin (as mentioned in Sadeq & Ghazali, 1992, p. 4).

Based on the aforementioned facts, conventional economics emerged during the 17th century, at least according to the literature. Gordon, however, argues that this claim is entirely false and that the roots of modern economic analysis have deeper historical roots than many current economics students are aware of (Gordon, 1975).

Economic Issues Through the Works of Muslim Scholars

Discussing the contributions of Muslim scholars to the development of modern economic thought would require an extensive examination. In what follows, we will attempt to briefly introduce their teachings and perspectives on certain economic issues that are at the core of modern economics and free-market capitalism.

Private Property, **Laissez-Faire,** *and the Question of State Intervention*

Islam recognizes private property, but this ownership is not absolute as in Western civilization. Instead, private ownership in Islam is considered a trust (*amanah*) from the Almighty Allah, who is the ultimate owner of everything in the heavens and on earth (Qur'an, 20:6). Additionally, the practice of the Prophet Muhammad (pbuh) teaches us that working and engaging in economic activities are obligations for every Muslim and are considered a divine duty and a commendable virtue.

Social justice is the result of productive work and equal opportunities, allowing everyone to utilize their abilities in work and receive a fair reward for their labor. However, this work must adhere to the norms and principles of Islam. This perspective is shared by all Muslim scholars throughout Islamic history. Prominent scholars such as Ibn Taymiyyah (1263–1328), Ibn Al-Qayyim al-Jawziyya (1292–1350), and Ibn Khaldun (1332–1406) emphasize this idea.[11] However, despite individuals having the right to private property, these Islamic scholars believed that the state has the right to intervene for the sake of social interest (*maslahah*). Nevertheless, according to Ibn al-Qayyim's opinion, confiscated property must be compensated for.

In this regard, these scholars were strong proponents of the *laissez-faire* system or free-market capitalism that aligns with Islamic principles. In other words, their form of free market capitalism is not driven by selfishness, egoism, or other (mis) values promoted by the capitalist system. Instead, the *laissez-faire* system they advocated for is one where equality, justice, fair prices, fair wages, moral responsibility, and similar values are prevalent. The freedom to trade, including free access to the market (entry and exit), as established by the Prophet Muhammad (pbuh), is also a principle advocated by these scholars in their works. At the same time, they were against any form of monopoly and artificial price-fixing that would harm society. In short, Muslim scholars throughout the centuries advocated for a free market that promotes the public good (*maslahah*) and is regulated by Islamic norms. In such a system, there is neither absolute freedom nor absolute control of the market (Smolo, 2013).

The Theory of Price

In a *laissez-faire* system, the forces of supply and demand determine the price of products in the market. This theory was developed long before it became prominent in modern economic literature. Early scholars, including Ibn Taymiyyah and Ibn Khaldun, paid significant attention to this issue.

Ibn Taymiyyah stated: "If people are dealing their goods in the normal ways (*al-wajh al-ma'ruf*) without any injustice on their part and the price rises either due to shortage of the goods (i.e. decrease in supply) or due to increase in population (i.e. increase in demand), then it is from Allah. In such cases, to force the sellers to sell their goods at a particular price is a wrongful pressure (*ikrah bi gair haqq*)" (Islahi, 1988, p. 83). In other words, according to Ibn Taymiyyah, there are two reasons for an increase in prices:

(1) product shortages (i.e. supply shortage) and
(2) an increase in people's disposable income (i.e. an increase in demand).

[11] For a brief description of some economic ideas, see (Gusau, 1993; Islahi, 2014; Islam, 2016; Rizkiah & Chachi, 2020; Spengler, 1964).

To put it differently, the market price of a product is determined through the interaction of the forces of supply and demand in a free market. Thus, in the first case, the price increase is due to the shift of supply curve to the left (from Supply_1 to Supply_2), which results in a price increase from P_1 to P_2. In the second case, there is a shift in the demand curve (from Demand_1 to Demand_2) caused by an increase in people's disposable income. This shift in the demand curve also leads to an increase in price from P_1 to P_2. Graphically, these two cases are illustrated in Fig. 4.1 below. The first case is shown in Graph 1 and the second in Graph 2.

These early Islamic scholars recognized and articulated principles of supply and demand, which are foundational concepts in modern economics. Their insights into the determination of prices through market forces contributed significantly to economic thought and align with many aspects of modern economic theory.

Ibn Khaldun proposed that alterations in prices may arise from factors not previously discussed. One example is that shifts in production expenses can result in price fluctuations. Should production costs decrease, manufacturers can provide their products at a reduced price. Conversely, if production costs rise, the product's price will likely increase.

Additionally, overall economic conditions also influence changes in supply and demand in the market. For example, in a prosperous and developed city or region, there might be an increased demand for luxury goods. Competition among buyers to obtain these relatively scarce goods and the willingness of the wealthy to pay high prices for them can drive up prices in the market (Rizkiah & Chachi, 2020, p. 79).

All the points mentioned above, along with other analyses not covered here, indicate that Muslim scholars were well-acquainted with fundamental principles of modern economics, such as the laws of supply and demand. The graphical representation provided above is a well-known concept in economics. However, this type of representation of supply and demand is a product of later economic

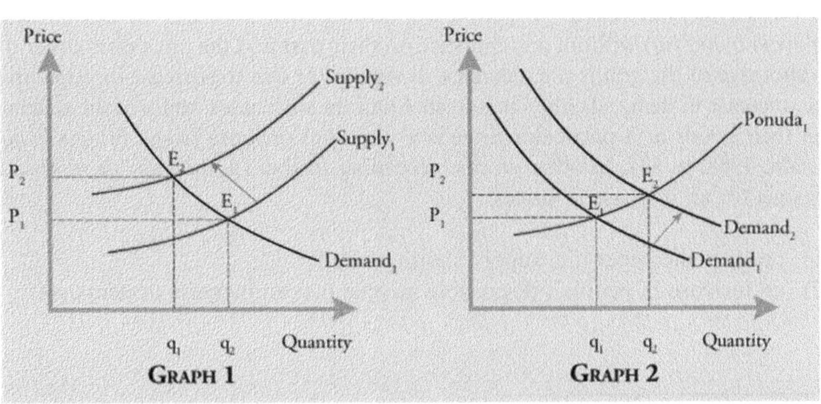

Fig. 4.1. The Laws of Demand and Supply. *Source:* Author's own.

analyses, and earlier scholars (including even Adam Smith) did not use it. Nevertheless, based on the examples provided, we can conclude that these scholars' ideas align with modern economic principles, and Ibn Taymiyyah and Ibn Khaldun were aware of these principles.

The Role of the State in the Market

Regarding the state's role in the market, there is a prevailing view that the market should be left to the forces of supply and demand. A well-known example is the Prophet Muhammad (pbuh), who refused to fix prices in the market, stating that it is from God. In other words, as long as market activities are per Islamic principles, the state should not intervene. Accordingly, among Islamic scholars (*'ulama*), the prevailing opinion is that price determination should be left to the market, i.e., the forces of supply and demand.

However, according to Ibn Khaldun, one of the state's primary functions is to establish and promote market justice (*'adl*) and fairness. By maintaining order and enforcing the law, the state will create a conducive environment for economic activities, leading to socially beneficial development. Therefore, if there is an abuse of power by individuals, such as hoarding goods (*ihtikar*) to increase prices or creating a monopoly, which threatens the public interest (*maslahah*), scholars allow state intervention through price fixing. Thus, the goal of price fixing in Islam is to maintain justice and enable the satisfaction of people's basic needs (Islahi, 1988).

Interestingly, Ibn Khaldun strongly opposes the state's participation in the market for commercial purposes. He believes the market is competitive, and the state's entry would create unfair competition. The reason is that ordinary traders cannot compete with the power of the ruler (the state) when buying or selling goods, which would significantly harm them. If this were to happen, such a practice would demotivate people from starting businesses and trading in those markets. This would further lead to a reduction in the tax base and, ultimately, a decrease in tax revenue. All of this would significantly negatively impact the overall development of society and the economy. Before him, Al-Dimashqi spoke on this topic, saying, "when a regent starts trading, his subjects are lost" (cited in Islahi, 1988, p. 207).

In summary, while the prevailing view in Islam supports market forces and non-interference by the state, there is a recognition that the state has a role in maintaining justice and preventing abuse in the market, even if it means intervening through price fixing in certain circumstances. However, the state's direct participation in commercial activities is generally discouraged, as it can distort competition and harm the economy.

Monetary Policy

As was the case with the global financial crisis, the COVID-19 pandemic has undeniably left a profound impact on the global economy. Most countries have resorted to monetary and fiscal policies to mitigate the adverse effects of the pandemic. It is evident that during this period, major economic powers have engaged in extensive money printing. Considering disruptions in supply chains and such monetary policies, it is no wonder that we are facing unprecedented global inflation, unlike anything witnessed in recent decades.

Money is an indispensable factor in the healthy functioning of an economy. Scholars, over centuries, have recognized the importance of money and its role in economic development. Therefore, it is unsurprising that a multitude of scholars, including Ibn Miskawayh (died 1030), Al-Ghazali (1058–1111), Ibn Taymiyyah, Ibn Al-Qayyim, Ibn Khaldun, and Taqi Al-Din Ahmad Al-Maqrizi (1364–1442), have written on this topic.

For instance, Al-Ghazali, Ibn Taymiyyah, and Ibn Khaldun delved into the nature of money and its functions. They believed that money primarily serves as a medium of exchange and a measure of value. Modern economists concur with these first two functions, but add a third: serving as a store of value. This means that money not only facilitates transactions and measures the value of goods and services but also serves as a store of value. Therefore, the first two functions align with the claims and teachings of earlier Muslim scholars. However, the last function of money, serving as a store of value, is not acknowledged by Muslim scholars. According to Al-Ghazali, money itself is not a commodity and, as such, lacks intrinsic value. Possessing money merely enables the owner to purchase any goods or services.

Ibn Taymiyyah emphasized the importance of money and its impact on the general well-being of society. He prohibited any form of currency debasement through the devaluation of silver by reducing the silver content in *dirhams*. He was also aware that an increase in the quantity of money would lead to a general rise in prices, commonly referred to as inflation (Islahi, 1988). In essence, Ibn Taymiyyah argued that trading currencies, printing money, or increasing the money supply would lead to monetary devaluation and inflation unless accompanied by concurrent increases in wealth and the global volume of transactions. Such actions would be tantamount to "appropriating the wealth of others" (Al-Qur'an, 4:29) and constitute unlawful enrichment for a small group of individuals. Al-Maqrizi also believed that the quantity of money in circulation affects inflation. This connection is explained in modern economic science through *the quantitative theory of money*. Al-Maqrizi further held the view that gold *dinars* and silver *dirhams* served as universal currencies, thereby supporting the gold standard, which remained in effect until 1971 when it was abolished by the United States.

Simultaneously, as far back as the 14th century, Ibn Taymiyyah and Al-Maqrizi pointed out that if a devalued or "bad" currency entered the market, its circulation and use would suppress "good" money from circulation. This phenomenon, observed in 14th century Egypt, is known today as Gresham's Law, named after Thomas Gresham, the financial minister to the Queen Elizabeth I, who famously stated that "bad money drives out good." In other words, when two forms of money coexist in a market, people tend to hoard the money they consider more valuable while spending the depreciated money (Hanson, 1974; Sadeq & Ghazali, 1992).

These historical perspectives underscore the enduring significance of sound monetary policies and the role of money in maintaining economic stability and fairness. Understanding these historical insights can assist policymakers in making informed decisions, especially in today's complex economic landscape.

Economic Development

Acquiring wealth in Islam is not only commendable but even deemed necessary for every capable Muslim. This is underscored by the practices of Allah's Messenger (pbuh) who himself engaged in trade and established the first free market based on Islamic principles. After all, for a Muslim to fulfill their fundamental obligations in Islam, such as *hajj* (pilgrimage), *jihad* (struggle), and *zakat* (almsgiving), it is necessary to have adequate income. The Prophet Muhammad (pbuh) stated, "A strong believer is better and more beloved to Allah than a weak believer, while there is good in both."[12] This reference encompasses not just physical strength but any form of strength, including material strength. Therefore, Islam does not endorse asceticism; in fact, it challenges it. On the other hand, Islam supports any form of success, development, and prosperity within Islamic norms.

Al-Tartusi emphasizes that economic underdevelopment or backwardness leads to political instability, which, in turn, weakens military power and eventually results in subjugation by stronger and more developed countries. Conversely, economic development leads to political stability and military strength, which in turn lead to control, dominance, and external security of the state. Furthermore, Ibn Taymiyyah considers any economic activity leading to economic development as a collective obligation (*fard al-kifayah*).[13]

Scholars like Ibn Hazm and Ibn Taymiyyah have advocated for the state's obligation to provide basic life necessities to enable individuals to fulfill their obligations to Allah and to their families and society as a whole. Ensuring the provision of basic needs for the population has only recently found its place in modern economic discourse, although Ibn Hazm (994–1064) advocated for this as early as the 11th century. According to Ibn Hazm, basic needs include food, drink, clothing, and shelter. Both Ibn Hazm and Ibn Taymiyyah believed that the state and affluent members of society should participate in fulfilling these needs.

Simultaneously, Islam opposes the concentration of wealth in the hands of a few. Allah, the Almighty, says, "And what Allah restored to His Messenger from the people of the towns - it is for Allah and for the Messenger and for [his] near relatives and orphans and the [stranded] traveler - so that it will not be a perpetual distribution among the rich from among you. And whatever the Messenger has

---

[12]The hadith is narrated by Abu Huraira and recorded by Muslim. See hadith no. 1840 in (El-Munziri, 2004, p. 825).

[13]*Fard* or *fardh* is what Allah, the Almighty, has decreed; strictly ordered to be perform. *Fard al-'ajn* is the duty of individuals, while *fard al-kifayah* is the duty of the community – congregation.

given you - take; and what he has forbidden you - refrain from. And fear Allah; indeed, Allah is severe in penalty" (Al-Qur'an, 59:7). In this regard, Shah Waliullah (1703–1762) argues that such practices lead to income inequality in distribution on the one hand and the production of luxury goods on the other hand (Sadeq & Ghazali, 1992).

The Taxation and Division of Labor

Basic taxation in Islam is defined by the Qur'an and the practice of the Prophet (pbuh) who established the foundations of Muslim society. Islam recognizes *zakat* as the obligatory property tax for Muslims, amounting to 2.5%. For non-Muslim minorities, another form of tax called *jizyah* was utilized. With the spread of Islam and the increase in administration, the need for funding also grew, and the funds from *zakat*, *jizyah*, and land taxes (*haraj*) proved insufficient. Therefore, scholars allowed the collection of other taxes, always emphasizing the obligation to consider the public interest (*maslahah*).

Ibn Khaldun devoted special attention to this issue, and his views on taxation are very similar to the principles we see today among proponents of supply-side economics. The main principles of this theory argue that reducing taxes and deregulation are necessary for economic growth. Advocates of this theory point to the multiplier effect of tax cuts on increased demand and production.

Considering the precepts of Islamic doctrine, Ibn Khaldun advocated for the establishment of tax rates that are optimized. Within the pages of the *Muqaddimah*, Ibn Khaldun articulates, "Comprehend that initially, the governing authority levies minimal taxes yet accumulates substantial revenue, whereas eventually, the state imposes numerous levies but garners meager income" (Ibn Haldun, 2007, p. 458). This line of thought closely resonates with the comprehensive historical scrutiny recently presented by Ray Dalio (2021).

Indeed, it is worth noting that the renowned Laffer Curve in the field of economics was originally discerned by Ibn Khaldun. The Laffer Curve illustrates that when the tax rate is set at 0%, the government is unable to generate any tax revenue, irrespective of the size of the tax base. Conversely, when tax rates reach 100%, individuals are disinclined to engage in economic activities since their income, after accounting for taxes, dwindles to zero, consequently yielding zero tax revenue (Laffer, 2004).

Al-Ghazali and Ibn Khaldun also contributed to the development of the labor theory of value and the division of labor. These topics were revisited many centuries later by Adam Smith and David Ricardo. In short, Ibn Khaldun, without the techniques or existing concepts available in the 18th century, elaborated on the necessity of the division of labor before Adam Smith; the value of labor before David Ricardo and Karl Marx; the theory of population before Thomas Malthus; fiscal responsibility of the state before J. M. Keynes, and cyclical analysis before Marx and Joseph Schumpeter. Islahi (2014) argues that many economists later discovered mechanisms that Ibn Khaldun had already found long before them.

Concluding Remarks

This work represents an attempt to briefly showcase the teachings of earlier Muslim scholars and attribute them the credit they greatly deserve. From the provided content, it is evident that many ideas and theories of contemporary economic thought were deeply rooted in the works of these Islamic thinkers and scholars, several centuries prior. Abraham Udovitch's words serve as confirmation when he said, "Some of the institutions, practices and concepts already found fully developed in the Islamic legal sources of the late eighth century did not emerge in Europe until several centuries later" (Udovitch, 1970, p. 261).

Regrettably, the historians of modern economic thought often attribute these ideas to Western scholars, ignoring the contributions of Muslim giants who preceded them. Nevertheless, an increasing number of individuals are pointing out these oversights and acknowledging the error. Langholm (1979) underscores the influence of medieval scholars on modern economics. He observes that it is currently effortless to overlook the fact that those who established the bedrock of contemporary economics in the 18th century were well-versed in the amassed knowledge of dogmatic analysis, much like how the typical economist of the 20th century remains oblivious to it. Crucial facets of innovative theories, which these early economists did not explicitly detail since they assumed them as given, can be traced back to the enduring legacy of medieval educational institutions.

Likewise, Watt (1972) does not hesitate to state: "For our cultural indebtedness to Islam, however, we Europeans have a blind spot. We sometimes belittle the extent and importance of Islamic influence in our heritage, and sometimes overlook it altogether. For the sake of good relations with Arabs and Muslims we must acknowledge our indebtedness to the full" (p. 2).

Therefore, without exaggeration, it can be said that capitalism and the free market in their current forms would almost certainly not exist without the contributions of Muslim scholars who wrote on these and other topics throughout the history of Islam.

References

Azmi, S. (2002). *Islamic economics: Public finance in early Islamic thought*. Goodword Books.

Dalio, R. (2021). *Principles for dealing with the changing world order: Why nations succeed and fail*. Avid Reader Press/Simon & Schuster.

Ekelund, R. B., & Hébert, R. F. (2014). *A history of economic theory & method* (6th ed.). Waveland Press.

El-Munziri. (2004). *Muslimova zbirka hadisa: Sažetak* (M. Mrahorović, Trans.). El-Kalem. www.temawy.com

Gordon, B. (1975). *Economic analysis before Adam Smith: Hesiod to Lessius*. Macmillan.

Gusau, S. A. (1993). Economic thoughts of Ibn Khaldun. *Journal of Islamic Economics*, *3*(1), 61–80.

Hanson, J. L. (1974). *A dictionary of economics and commerce, (with an English/Arabic glossary)* (4th ed.). Librairie Du Liban & Macdonald & Evans LTD.

Ibn Haldun. (2007). *Muqaddima* (T. Muftić, Trans., Vol. 1). El-Kalem.
Islahi, A. A. (1988). *Economic concepts of Ibn Taimīyah*. Islamic Foundation.
Islahi, A. A. (2014). *History of Islamic economic thought: Contributions of Muslim scholars to economic thought and analysis*. Edward Elgar.
Islahi, A. A. (2018). *Ibn Taymiyyina ekonomska misao* (D. Avdagić, A. Avdić, A. Džaferović, & R. Mehmedović, Trans.). Udruženje građana Multi.
Islam, M. H. (2016). Ibnu Taimiyah and his concept of economy. *Iqtishoduna*, *7*(1), 15–33.
Koehler, B. (2014). *Early Islam and the birth of capitalism*. Lexington Books.
Kamali, M. H. (2008). *Shari'ah law: An introduction*. Oneworld Publications.
Laffer, A. B. (2004). *The Laffer curve: Past, present, and future* (1765; Backgrounder, pp. 1–16). The Heritage Foundation. www.heritage.org/research/taxes/bg1765.cfm
Lane-Poole, S., & Gilman, A. (1990). *The story of the Moors in Spain*. Black Classic Press.
Langholm, O. (1979). *Price and value in the Aristotelian tradition*. Universitetsforlaget.
Lydon, G. (2009). A paper economy of faith without faith in paper: A reflection on Islamic institutional history. *Journal of Economic Behavior & Organization*, *71*(3), 647–659. https://doi.org/10.1016/j.jebo.2009.03.019
Lydon, G. (2019). Paper instruments in early African economies and the debated role of the Suftaja. *Cahiers d'Études Africaines*, *236*, 1091–1118. https://doi.org/10.4000/etudesafricaines.27569
Mirakhor, A. (1987). Muslim scholars and the history of economics: A need for consideration. *American Journal of Islamic Social Sciences*, *4*(2), 245–276.
Muftić, T. (1997). *Rječnik arapsko-bosanski* (3rd ed.). El-Kalem.
Rizkiah, S. K., & Chachi, A. (2020). The relevance of Ibn Khaldun's economic thought in the contemporary world. *Turkish Journal of Islamic Economics*, *7*(2), 70–90. https://doi.org/10.26414/A074
Sadeq, A. M., & Ghazali, A. (1992). *Readings in Islamic economic thought*. Longman Malaysia Snd. Bhd.
Schumpeter, J. A., Schumpeter, E. B., & Perlman, M. (1994). *History of economic analysis* (Reprinted 1994). Routledge.
Smolo, E. (2012). Islamic finance from local initiatives to a global market player: Can it bridge the East and the West? *Bulletin (European Association Banking and Financial History)*, *2*, 46–50.
Smolo, E. (2013). *Uvod u islamsku ekonomiju i finansije: Teorija i praksa*. Dobra Knjiga.
Smolo, E., & Hassan, M. K. (2011). The potentials of *mushārakah mutanāqisah* for Islamic housing finance. *International Journal of Islamic and Middle Eastern Finance and Management*, *4*(3). Article 3. https://doi.org/10.1108/17538391111166476
Smolo, E., & Ismail, A. G. (2011). A theory and contractual framework of Islamic micro-financial institutions' operations. *Journal of Financial Services Marketing*, *15*(4). Article 4. https://doi.org/10.1057/fsm.2010.24
Spengler, J. J. (1964). Economic thought of Islam: Ibn Khaldun. *Comparative Studies in Society and History*, *6*(3), 268–306.
Udovitch, A. L. (1970). *Partnership and profit in medieval Islam*. Princeton University Press.
Watt, W. M. (1972). *The influence of Islam on medieval Europe*. Edinburgh University Press.
Weber, M. (2001). *The protestant ethic and the spirit of capitalism* (T. Parsons, Trans.). Routledge.

Chapter 5

Integrating Islamic Finance Into the Sustainable Development Goals (SDGs)

Edib Smolo[a], *Irum Saba*[b], *Norashikin Ismail*[c] *and Ziyaad Mahomed*[d]

[a]Effat University, Saudi Arabia
[b]Institute of Business Administration (IBA), Pakistan
[c]Universiti Teknologi MARA Cawangan Johor, Malaysia
[d]International Centre for Education in Islamic Finance, Malaysia

Abstract

The announcement of the SDGs in 2015 marked a dramatic shift in global development, culminating in an age of international cooperation where the international community bands together to tackle the world's most pressing challenges. This chapter discusses the peculiar connection between Islamic financing and the SDGs and focuses on the possible harmony between these two sectors. It emphasizes the need for significant financial resources to advance sustainable development. Researchers argue it is crucial to bring digital technologies together with Islamic finance to reach sustainable economic growth through innovations like artificial intelligence (AI), blockchain, and fintech. In addition, the chapter explains core principles of Islamic finance that conform to Shari'ah, which will eradicate poverty and promote conscientious consumption. Islamic finance opens the opportunity for financially and socially excluded groups, poverty reduction, and environmental sustainability through programs like renewable energy projects. However, SDG integration with Islamic finance still poses some challenges, namely, Shari'ah scholars' understanding of the SDGs, regulatory and operational difficulties, the necessity for innovation, and measuring nonfinancial benefits. Through case studies, the authors provide pragmatic insights into successful integration processes as well as practical lessons for the concerned parties. The chapter ends by making policy recommendations grounded on active support by governments, compulsory educational initiatives, new interesting Islamic finance products, and

The Future of Islamic Finance, 65–82

doi:10.1108/978-1-83549-906-120241005

shared efforts (or undertakings) among various stakeholders. In short, this chapter positions Islamic finance as a potent catalyst for SDGs, furnishing a sustainable economic and social development framework while acknowledging and addressing challenges on the integration journey.

Keywords: Islamic economics; Islamic finance; sustainable development goals; SDGs; Shari'ah-compliant; Maqasid al-Shari'ah; digital finance

Introduction

Sustainable development is a wide-ranging, dynamic concept that has increased as an issue nowadays and is incorporated within Islamic finance. As the entire world arises to combat the issues of the environment, social and economy, the Islamic finance has been accepted widely as one of the effective ways to work toward the UN's 2030 SDGs Agenda. This part of the paper discusses the part that Islamic finance plays in the evolution of the sustainable development factoring in the uniqueness of the elements that are involved in the process prompting the conclusion that Islamic finance is an exceptional contributor in the sustainable development process worldwide.

The connection between Islamic finance and sustainable development rests on a set of concepts which are based on the pillars of Islamic banal laws. These principles not only include the prohibition of interest (*riba*) but also the establishment of ethical and responsible methods of money making. There are several Islamic financial tools, including *sukuk* (Islamic certificates/bonds), *zakat* (religious tax/almsgiving), and *waqf* (endowment) that have a direct bearing on the SDGs which incorporate objectives, namely, the elimination of hunger, emphasis on social justice, environmental sustainability and economic prosperity.

From extensive ethical business and sustainable development research, the discussions point out that Islam finance and development are interconnected in many aspects. The research study of Al-Roubaie and Sarea (2019) stresses the role of Islamic finance in environmental stewardship and sustainable development being in the nature of Islamic finance, which signifies the Islamic finance moral obligation in promoting environmental sustainability. Likewise, Mohammad and Abduh (2022) find that Shari'ah-compliant financing, especially through *sukuk*, can boost infrastructure that is resilient and innovative; these factors are key to achieving Goal 9 of the UNSDGs – "Industry, Innovation, and Infrastructure."

Numerous scholarly inquiries have delved into the intersection of Islamic finance and sustainable development, illuminating the multifaceted aspects of this connection. The research study by Al-Roubaie and Sarea (2019) underscores the role of Islamic finance in environmental stewardship and sustainable development, underscoring the moral duty of Islamic finance in fostering ecological sustainability. Similarly, Mohammad and Abduh (2022) investigate how Islamic financing, particularly through *sukuk*, can contribute to resilient infrastructure and innovation, both of which are pivotal to SDG 9 – "Industry, Innovation, and Infrastructure."

Furthermore, an article published by Harahap et al. (2023) gives the reader a systematic assessment of literature about the primary power of Islamic finance in supporting SDGs. Therefore, government and regulatory support is critical to boost the delivery capacity of Islamic finance in pursuing SDGs. And in the same vein, they tend to highlight the importance of Islamic finance in Bahrain's pursuit of sustainability development goals, showing similarities between principles of Islamic finance and sustainability objectives while operating within the particular context of a country (Ebrahim et al., 2021).

While the world suffers from the negative effects of the traditional economic system which are associated with resource depletion, wastes production and environmental pollution, Islamic finance is viewed as a possible solution. The findings of Hassan et al. (2020) has demonstrated that Islamic finance is the forerunner in the march toward a circular economy, which is a new paradigm of a cleaner and resource economizing economic structure. This transition is in line with SDG 12, which envisions "Responsible Consumption and Production." It also aligns with the UN 2030 Agenda for Sustainable Development's overarching goal to promote resource efficiencies and waste reduction across all industries.

This chapter seeks to draw from the conclusions obtained in the research projects and to venture into the larger issues of the consequences of Islamic finance on sustainable development. Its main goal is to provide clear information about the numerous ways that could be used by Islamic finance to help theSDGs, concurrently emphasizing the problems that need accurate consideration and thought. This pursuit then will remain key in the era marked by an increasing determination to build up a better and more just world for all of us.

Islamic Finance: Principles and Mechanisms

In financial systems, Islamic finance is governed by the Law of Shari'ah and thus seeks to be governed by adhering to the Islamic legal framework. It is through this sophisticated structure that is based on ethical and social duty that we are able to create fairness and equality in the society. For the Islamic finance, usury (*riba*) is a firmly rejected part of the Islamic finance, perceived as an act of unfair exploitation of weak financially.

Alternatively, Islamic finance uses *mudarabah* (silent partnership) and *musharakah* (partnership) whereas it is based on contribution and profit sharing with others. This strategy is developed to stimulate economic advancement, grow solidarity, and make sure that wealth is distributed in an equitable manner.

Islamic finance surpasses the limits of conventional banking by moving from the financial sector to other sectors like insurance (*takaful*) as well as bonding with *sukuk* and reaching the investment sector through mutual funds. These Financial Instruments are tested rigorously to ensure that they conform to the Islamic principles and guidelines. As a result, they are ideal for people who are looking for a financial undertaking that aligns with their religious beliefs and principles.

The global Islamic finance industry has seen an impressive growth with both conventional banks offering Islamic financial products and with prominent

Shari'ah-compliant banks gaining ground in the international arena. Interestingly, also non-Muslim countries have started looking at Islamic finance and see it as the opportunity to not only promote ethical financial practices but also sustainability.

This is an important factor because it means that this tool is not only targeted at the Muslim community but also echoes the sentiments of individuals who believe in an ethical alternative financial system. Its fundamental tenets of fairness, clear vision, and strong corporate culture are attractive to all types of investors and businesses, reflecting the fast-growing demand for moral and comprehensive financial services.

Sustainable Development Goals: An Overview

The year 2015 registered a historic shift in the global development agenda when the UN officially presented the SDG. These goals, which constitute 17 standards to attain and a total of 169 targets, became a follow-up action to the Millennium Development Goals, signaling a fresh period of global cooperation and making a resolve to fulfill the outstanding challenges around the (Cuervo-Cazurra et al., 2022). In this respect, the SDGs encompass a holistic set of goals that aim to eradicate poverty and inequalities, unsustainable consumption, production and resource utilization, climate change, environmental degradation and promote peace and justice by 2030 (Yu & Huang, 2021). Although the nations in the world are pursuing these goals globally with the deadline of 2030, attaining them might be not easy.

While SDGs are conceptualized around specific themes, they are interdependent and thus cannot be treated in isolation. Here the goals point to ending the confrontational approach of their ancestors, a conscious resolve that sustainable development cannot be seen as a collection of separate parts. Different than traditional definition, this trichotomy of economic, social, and environmental dimensions recognizes that they are not separate but to be considered in the totality (Cuervo-Cazurra et al., 2022).

The 17 SDGs along with their sub goals acts as an inclusive framework for identifying the most pressing problems and finding solutions at the global level. These topics include hunger and education, gender equality, energy access, the promotion of social equity, environment sustainability, economic growth and poverty eradication as well. These targets play a crucial role in charting the course of development for countries and their communities by supplying a framework in which they can work out their own problems within the framework of sustainable development. They symbolize a world-wide appeal and the way they are more manageable for multilateralism, they are not confined to certain nations, but it includes all regardless of their development status. This universality is a clarion call for global partnership and collaboration as these (SDGs) goals reconfirm that all the people regardless of being from affluent or poor countries should do this together in order to move toward a sustainable development.

But this broadness and brevity of the SDGs are also what makes them very general and undemanding in their approach. Unlike other treaties, they are rather providing a package of instruments and policy tools that serves the purpose of flexibility and enables each member nation to customize its tactics to fit their goals.

Financing is an important factor and deserves a comprehensive analysis in order to realize the SGDs. Sustainable development, to realize the eradication of poverty, education, health that cater for diverse needs and environmental protection, will take a lot of financial resources. Finance is both the lifeline and vehicle which steering these goals are made possible. The essential tip for the right utilization of resource, on both the national scale and through international divisions, is central for the matter.

With both the businesses and governments working toward establishing their by-laws on the lines of the SDGs, the role of the finance in this regard also become yet bigger. Not just ethical but also key thing to prioritize is financing sustainable solutions and technologies that are dedicated to achieving the SDG agendas. It assists in preparations for the changing horizons of the technological innovations and sustainability practices by ensuring the growth of the resilient and thriving society (Cuervo-Cazurra et al., 2022).

The Intersection of Islamic Finance and SDGs

According to Harahap et al. (2023), Islamic finance boasts amazing potential to contribute toward the fulfillment of SDGs which is the initiative of the UN geared toward human and environmental welfare wellness. The protection of humans from poverty or any other obstacles that might disturb their smooth development should be the aim of *maqasid al-Shari'ah* and SDGs. Two crucial trends that are responsible for the successful journey of SDGs are proper economic growth and globalization. The adaptation of both digital technologies and Islamic finance activities is required for maintaining the aligned pace with economic progress in accordance to the sustainable development guidelines mentioned in SDGs. Digital instruments including AI, blockchain and fintech can create an innovation and job creation-centric economy that leads to an overall digital transformation (Tlemsani et al., 2023). Also, digital technologies have enabled people in emerging economies to access various services including healthcare, education and financial services and thus improving the quality of life and reducing inequality.

In the context of globalization, the role of technology such as blockchain and fintech is attached to Islamic financial instruments to develop new business models as highlighted by study of Budalamah et al. (2019). It is proven that the development of technology has resulted to innovations in the field of Islamic finance such as *waqf* and *sukuk*. The innovation of these financial instruments would improve financial stability, achieve SDGs, and mitigate climate change and eventually improve efficiency.

Identifying the Alignment Between Islamic Finance Principles and SDGs

According to UNCTAD (2018), the achievement of the SDG's goal must start with economic development through fiscal and monetary policy development in underdeveloped economies. Basically, four principles of Islamic finance should be focused to help the heart of SDGs goal. First, the generation of wealth should originate from lawful trade and asset-based investments. Second, investments to the betterment of society by providing social and ethical benefits together with financial returns. Third, risk should be distributed and shared among involved parties. Fourth, the avoidance of engagement in any harmful activities strictly (Tlemsani et al., 2023).

In principle, Islamic finance is related to Shari'ah principles with the aim of achieving *maqasid al-Shari'ah*. The prohibition of *riba* and *gharar* (uncertainty) is mainly the concept of *Tawhid* (the oneness of God) in Islamic finance with the aim is to help humanity such as releasing oneself of poverty. Clearly, the Islamic financial system provides a protection of wealth for productive purposes, provides business opportunities, and eventually create employment among society. With the Islamic digital finance, it promotes responsible and ethical consumption by integrating Islamic principles into financial transactions. Following this, it inspires individuals and businesses to engage in socially and environmentally responsible practices aligning with the SDGs (Table 5.1 highlights the linkages between SDGs and Islamic finance).

In addition, Islamic finance is implementing risk sharing mechanism emphasizing the share ownership elements which create the community oriented shared economy such as profit-sharing financing (*mudarabah*) and partnership (*musharakah*). A study by Dusuki (2008) found that Islamic banking is more preferred by society because of its ethical purpose rather than its operating mechanism. This implies that Islamic finance principles are aligned with the social welfare goal of SDG No. 1, 2, 3 and 10 stressing no poverty, zero hunger, good health and wealth and reduced inequalities.

The protection of environment is crucial aspect that is also in compliance with Shari'ah and consistent with the SDGs, in particular environmental sustainability. The environmental domain in the SDGs covers clear water and sanitation (SDG 8), affordable and clean energy (SDG 9) and climate action (SDG13).

How Islamic Finance Can Contribute to Specific the SDGs

Moving toward the SDGs, the Islamic digital finance and SDGs are closely connected as both aim to promote sustainable economic and social development. It is noted that principles of Islamic finance would contribute to achieving the SDGs by promoting financial inclusion, reducing poverty, supporting sustainable economy growth and environmental sustainability by promoting green financing such as renewable energy projects and social sustainability by supporting projects that promote social welfare with providing affordable housing and health care projects.

Table 5.1. SDGs and Islamic Finance.

SDGs Number	SDGs Title	Integration of SDGs in Islamic Finance
1.	No Poverty	*Waqf*, *zakat*, Islamic microfinance, charity/donations, *takaful* are used for removing poverty, hunger and to support good health
2.	Zero Hunger	
3.	Good Health and Well-Being	
4.	Quality Education	The first verse of Holy Quran was about reading. Islam promotes education hence it is integrated in teachings of Islam
5.	Gender Equality	Women are given huge respect and appreciation in Islam
6.	Clean Water and Sanitation	Wastage of Water is strictly prohibited in Islam
7.	Affordable and Clean Energy	Islamic financial institutions should provide funding to the institutions who focus on circularity and sustainability of infrastructure and for economic growth
8.	Decent Work and Economic Growth	
9.	Industry, Innovation and Infrastructure	
10.	Reduced Inequalities	Islamic social finance can be used for reducing inequality
11.	Sustainable Cities and Communities	Anything that is against the public interest is prohibited in Islamic finance. Islamic financial institutions should support the industries who work on ecofriendly projects and sustainable industries
12.	Responsible Consumption and Production	
13.	Climate Action	
14.	Life Below Water	Islamic finance focus on preserving land and water. Islamic financial institutions can launch green or blue *sukuk* and provide financing to companies who are committed to protect environment, land and water
15.	Life on Land	
16.	Peace, Justice and Strong Institutions	Islamic economic system is against corruption. Hence Islamic finance supports peace, justice, and strong institutions
17.	Partnerships for the Goals	Collaboration is encouraged in Islam and Islamic financial institutions should work with different stakeholders for achieving SDGs

Source: Authors' compilation.

In attaining the welfare criteria in SDGs through poverty alleviation and sustainable development, long-term investments and equity financing is required. As asserted by Harahap et al. (2023), Islamic finance support efforts to meet the SDGs using five pathways: financial stability, financial inclusion, reduction of financial vulnerability, social and environmental activities. To support the welfare of community, the development of sustainable *waqf* will also contribute to the improvement of the socioeconomic status of Muslims by building sustainable and appropriate buildings in accordance with the current social need of Islamic development goals.

In addition, the emergence of the Shari'ah social bank is another strategy to enhance economy growth, which indicates poverty alleviation and community development and leads to environmentally friendly economic practices (Mohd Nor, 2016).

*Leveraging Islamic Social Finance (*Zakat/Sadaqah*) for Social Development*

The existence of the Islamic social finance (ISF) as a form of finance aims to promote social justice, economic progress and environmental sustainability emphasizing the ethical aspects of finance such as investing in socially responsible projects. There are a few mechanisms used in the ISF namely *zakat* (religious tax/almsgiving), *sadaqah* (voluntary charity), *waqf* (endowment) and *qard hasan* (interest free loan). This social financing mechanism would improve communal and individual well-being through monetary assistance which assists to accomplish SDGs.

As reported by the Organisation for Economic Co-operation and Development (OECD), the value of *waqf* assets is to be worth US$3 trillion with an expected return of 5% or US$150 billion annually that can be used for socio economic goals (OECD, 2020). A study by Rehman (2019) stated that the value of global *zakat* collection is over US$1 trillion per year with the help of the Islamic development bank (IDB) as the key participant in promoting the Islamic social financing. Apart from *waqf* and *zakat*, *qard hasan* is another mechanism which requires wealthy people to lend money to poor people without charging interest and providing flexibility to loan receiver for repayment (Zauro et al., 2020). Clearly, it shows that the primary objective of the Islamic social financing is in line with SDGs.

The Key Areas of Integration

The integration of Islamic finance and SDGs may exist in several dimensions such as education and human capital development, poverty alleviation and economic empowerment, infrastructure and renewal energy, healthcare and well-being, environmental conservation and finally gender equality and social inclusion. A further elaboration of each dimension would be discussed in this section.

Education and Human Capital Development

Education constitutes a fundamental facet of the human experience. In progressing toward the enhancement of human resources, diverse collaborations must be established by various stakeholders in the market and educational institutions. These alliances bridge the divide between institutions of higher learning and the industry's requirements. Significantly, such partnerships facilitate the creation of modules and curricula, equipping students with the necessary competencies per Islamic finance demands. Additionally, education and vocational training investments are imperative for attaining human capital development. Through these concerted endeavors, the realization of quality education, as outlined in SDG 3, becomes feasible, ultimately elevating the well-being of all individuals. Human welfare (*maslahah*) is crucial in Islamic finance, aligning with the Islamic wealth criterion.

Poverty Alleviation and Economic Empowerment

Islamic finance primarily centers on the *maslahah* of the Muslim community, aiming to diminish poverty and enhance the welfare of the community. Muslims are encouraged to boost community support through mudarabah, in addition to their funds which they can invest as partners in business. Through the contribution of capital for the various entrepreneurial activities, excellent business partnerships with profit sharing finance and also by improving the quality of the entrepreneur, economic prosperity is nourished. However, apart from profit-sharing financing, Islamic microfinancing you have tools not only for micro-credit provisioning but also for offering financial aid to SMEs (Smolo & Ismail, 2011; Smolo et al., 2020).

Last but not least, Islamic banking instruments such as qard and *waqf* fill the gap of SMEs' financial need. These financial instruments play a great role in fighting against large problems of poverty by creating more jobs and thus leading to the growth of the economy. Incorporating Islamic microfinancing, qard, *waqf*, and profit-sharing mechanisms such as mudarabah and musharakah, which help to solve poverty problem in the light of SDGs (the first goal), is a good idea.

Infrastructure and Renewable Energy

The combination of digital finance and Islamic finance in contribution SDG 7 is a key step to achieving a viable and sustainable energy system. The emergence of Islamic digital finance contributes to sustainable energy systems by supporting fresh initiatives of renewable energy such as solar and wind, which eliminate greenhouse gas emissions. Similarly, according to the studies conducted by Tlemsani et al. (2023), the Islamic digital finance maybe used in promoting responsible consumption, investment in clean energy, and encouraging conservation of land which are some of the targets of the SDGs.

However, apart from this, the lack of consistent Internet connection, cheap smartphones, and lack of necessary infrastructure impedes access to financial services by communities. In this regard, sustainable infrastructure that is funded through crowdfunding platforms can be the way to go when it comes to achieving the SDGs. The combination of crowdfunding platforms and Islamic finance is vital in SDGs.

Healthcare and Well-Being

The influence of the ISF such as zakat and *waqf* into the healthcare system proves important, especially during the COVID-19 pandemic, which has highlighted the role that the ISF can play. According to Ascarya (2022), ISF instruments, including zakat funds, have shown to help run the disease management agencies and meet the essential survival requirements. Furthermore, endowment funds aid in providing funds to health facilities. Another research study by Lawal and Ajayi (2019) affirm that zakat contributions are so substantial that could cater for the both the micro- and macro-humanitarian causes.

Embracing technology as an integral element in ISF ensures the collection and tracking of zakat toward humanitarian needs covering fields like housing, primary healthcare facilities, water, food and power supplies. Building up the zakat institutions becomes the key to the advancement of the country's economy through the improvement of the life condition of the people in Indonesia (Herianingrum et al., 2023).

Environmental Conservation

One of the priorities of SDGs is environmental sustainability. Hence, the incorporation of Islamic trade financing with SDG 7 becomes an important factor in achieving the soaring goal. Islamic banks are making efforts on financing renewable energy-related projects, such as solar and wind power, as well as the ones which aimed at energy saving. Moreover, Islamic commercial financing can be part of the enactment of SDG 12 through supporting the business corporations to use the manner that has low impact on the environment and adopt responsible natural management (Dirie et al., 2023).

Additionally, it shows that the combined responsibility of both Islamic social and commercial financing to achieve SDG 13 goal is also the effective way for it to finance climate change projects which cover food production and greening the environment. Sustainable farming, which is often geared toward lowering carbon emission and protecting people's environment, is also important. The other case for the facilitation of the public is seen on the investments made in the recovery and waste management processes.

Gender Equality and Social Inclusion

The fifth goal of UN SDGs that is gender equality encourages women to actively participate in different spheres including financial sector through the equal rights and opportunities. To achieve SDGs, inclusion is essential, and women's empowerment is an important prerequisite of global gender equality. The gender pay gap which is considered a major difficulty in Malaysia, according to Department of Statistics Malaysia, is applied to female workers who are earning RM66.67 for every RM100 revolved among male workers. Recognizing this issue directly requires the joint efforts of both the government and the private sector bodies (including the financial institutions) to ensure the sustainability of the development and equality.

This integration is the key driver for the future of sustainable growth. This is beneficial to everybody in a society (Harahap et al., 2023). Consequently, digital technologies have positioned as the fundamental building blocks of the Islamic finance industry to pursue the attainment of SDGs and creation of social benefits as well as economic development. This eventually will lead us to sustain the world for the future (Arner et al., 2020; Tlemsani et al., 2023).

Challenges and Opportunities

Integrating Islamic finance with SDGs presents several challenges:

- *The Understanding of SDGs Among Shari'ah Scholars:* There is a need for an improvement and enhancement of the SDGs recognizing among the Shari'ah scholars. We see this as a must because they not only include the approval of but also the advancements in Islamic financial products and services. The new guidelines issued by AAOIFI on Shari'ah decision-making have opened new opportunities for making sustainability requirements an integral part of Juristic consensus for the first time. If Shari'ah scholars adhere to this, the challenge becomes an opportunity for social impact through fatwa (Shari'ah resolutions).
- *Regulatory and Operational Challenges:* The significant amount of sustainability standards globally makes it challenging for institutions to apply a further filter of Shari'ah compliance in the sector. This poses both regulatory and operational challenges to move the Islamic finance sector forward.
- *Innovation in Islamic finance:* There is a need for more innovation in Islamic finance to support the SDGs. The development of green *sukuk* can significantly support the SDGs. However, there are only a limited number of issuances and concentrated in specific regions such as Malaysia, Indonesia and Turkiye. Furthermore, social impact *sukuk* issuances have been rare. Therefore, innovation that integrates sustainability and fintech solutions are expected to provide more opportunities for Islamic finance to support financial inclusion and reduce SDGs funding gaps.
- *The Measurement of Nonfinancial Performance:* Islamic financial institutions (IFIs) need to develop mechanisms to measure nonfinancial performance, including their contribution to the SDGs. Opportunities for implementing successful models like value-based intermediation (VBI) exist in Malaysia, but they have not been adequately replicated.

These challenges highlight the need for continued efforts in integrating Islamic finance with the SDGs. However, most of these challenges also provide opportunities for better integration and an increased social impact for Islamic finance.

Case Studies in Integration of Islamic Finance With the SDGs

Gatehouse Bank has introduced green home financing products in the United Kingdom (UK) to pursue environmental sustainability. Intriguingly, home buyers and landlords acquiring or refinancing more energy-efficient homes with an "A" or "B" energy efficiency rating receive a reduction in their monthly payments, coupled with offsetting the home's carbon emissions. Another noteworthy initiative is the Woodland Saver account at Gatehouse Bank, which has contributed to planting over 12,500 trees across the UK since its launch in 2021, with carbon credits registered on behalf of its customers. These instances underscore the commitment of the Islamic finance system to addressing environmental impact and aligning with SDG 7 for affordable and clean energy.

Shifting the focus to SDGs No. 1 and 8, addressing poverty and fostering economic growth, Indonesia has successfully implemented the digitization of the *waqf* program. The revenues generated from *waqf* are able to support numerous programs toward fulfilling the SDG goal of alleviating poverty and ensuring everyone has access to decent living. This integration of *waqf* and crowdfunding proves that digital economy is being applied, featuring the sustainability of Indonesia's economy. The proposal of digital *waqf* using crowdfunding platforms as opposed to traditional legislation in *waqf* administration in Thailand is brought about by the absence of such laws (Zain et al., 2019). Below is one of the Islamic finance accounts of its application integrated with Sustainable Development Goals.

Case Study 1: Value-Based Intermediation and Value-Based Intermediation **Takaful**

An Islamic finance regulatory framework of Malaysia was devised by the SDGs into the regulation system in the year 2020 (Ismail et al., 2020). VBI which stands for value added contribution to economy is the concept introduced by Bank Negara Malaysia (BNM) as early as 2017. Value-based intermediation takaful (VBIT) model was incorporated into the market, and the framework was demonstrated in *takaful* organization in year 2021 as an adaptation of the key components of VBI. They both seek to assume functions of intermediation of the *maqasid al-Shari'ah* through actions, services, and products that would contribute toward a positive and sustainable impact on the economy, society and the environment. In order to speed up the implementation of VBI credit, 15 Islamic banks, including BNM, got together in the VBI Community of Practitioners (COPs)'s technical support program to share their knowledge and skills to make VBI workable. From the initial white paper on VBI in 2017, BNM released the Investment Impact Assessment Framework (VBIAF) and six VBIAF Sectoral Guides that assist banks and corporates with standardized expectations for meeting sustainability targets.

The underlying principle of the VBI strategy stems from the unsustainable short-term goals prevalent in many financial sectors (BNM, 2018). The idea is to transition from a short-term perspective concentrating solely on profits to long-term objectives encompassing people, the planet, and profitability. VBI promotes a more holistic observation of Shari'ah by ensuring the offerings and practices of IFIs not only comply with Shari'ah requirements but also achieve the intended outcomes of Shari'ah. The intended outcomes of VBI are compatible with the sustainability agenda propagated by the SDGs and the Principles for Responsible Banking (PRB) promulgated in the UN Environment Program Finance Initiative.

More specifically, VBI activities align with SDGs that promote affordable and clean energy (SDG 7), decent work and economic growth (SDG 8), sustainable cities and communities (SDG 11), and SDG 13 on climate action. Institutions implementing VBI are expected to focus on four key pillars that serve as a framework of implementation and monitoring: entrepreneurial mindset, community empowerment, good self-governance, and best conduct.

The first pillar of the entrepreneurial mindset focuses on SME development and entrepreneurial support through financial empowerment strategies, networking, and advisory services, all offered through Islamic banks. SMEs are provided with Low Carbon Transition Facilities (LCTFs) and SDG-linked deposits to ensure sustainability. The VBI Report 2022 indicates that almost RM 1 billion (USD 215 million) of deposits were SDG-linked by the end of 2022, and more than RM 2.8 billion (USD 600 million) was allocated to SME and MSME financing in the same period (AIBIM, 2023).

For community empowerment, the focus is on solutions that provide social impact, including zakat, crowdfunding, education, and health services. A total of RM 14 billion (USD 3 billion) was provided for public health and education, RM 8 billion for affordable housing, and over RM 11 billion (USD 2.4 billion) was allocated for disaster relief and customers affected by COVID-19 pandemic. Good self-governance has promoted the establishment of group sustainability committees, more effective whistleblowing and anti-corruption policies, and the implementation of an ESG framework. For the pillar on best conduct, green learning, employee well-being, and financial literacy programs have been funded as corporate social responsibility initiatives for over RM110 million (USD 24 million).

VBIT has only recently been implemented, distinguishing itself from VBI by replacing the entrepreneurial mindset with financial resilience and adding capacity building as an additional pillar.

Both initiatives highlight the importance of revising the institution's corporate value intent, ensuring that the organizational culture is aligned with the SDGs, ESG targets, and the *maqasid al-Shari'ah.*

Case Study 2: Sukuk Prihatin

In September 2020, the Government of Malaysia introduced *sukuk* Prihatin, a financial initiative fully redeemed in September 2022.[1] The Malaysian Ministry of Finance disclosed that this USD 150 million *sukuk* formed a crucial element of the national economic recovery plan post-COVID-19 pandemic, channeling funds toward micro- and small businesses, public healthcare, and education. The issuance

---

[1]For details see MOF (2022).

reached approximately 2,500 individuals and businesses, facilitated through the digital banking platforms of 27 Malaysian banks. *Sukuk* returns enjoyed tax exemption, granting subscribers the choice to contribute a portion or the entire principal upon maturity.[2]

Case Study 3: Al-Rajhi Awqaf

The premier philanthropic entity in Saudi Arabia, the Sulaiman Al-Rajhi Charitable Foundation, has embarked on initiatives to fortify the nation's resilience and dependability of the food supply chain (SDG 2). Leveraging an Islamic endowment known as *waqf*, the Al Rajhi Foundation instituted a substantial SAR 1 million (USD 267,000) grant, renewed biennially, dedicated to advancing agricultural research for date palm cultivation, thus fostering innovation in programs addressing food security. The "Abdullah Sulaiman International Award for Scientific Innovation in Dates and Palm Trees" is a prestigious award granted to the most distinguished researchers whose outstanding innovations tremendously improve dates and palm trees' farming.

An alternative demonstration that creates a focus on *waqf* as the initiator of environmental conservation as well as food security can be seen with Saleh Al-Rajhi *awqaf's* initiatives. Growing date palm trees is in the core of the activities of Al-Rajhi *waqf*. And therefore, it has devoted extensive areas of almost 5,466 hectares to various sites for farms of about 45 types of these trees. Due to the huge work that it did in this field, it was entitled with the Guinness World Records in 2011.

Specifically, infrastructure development and finance are vital since it helps in the implementation of the SDG 7, 11, and 13 principles which prioritize sustainability and climate change. This alignment is clearly reflected in their dogged persistence organic farming and use of solar energy for energy purposes. ECOCERT has been the first institution to have bestowed Al-Rajhi *waqf* with certification back in 2007, well before the beginning of SDG (Sulaiman Bin Abdulaziz Al Rajhi Charitable Foundation, 2022).

Lessons Learned in Practice

The success of these projects has provided several valuable insights:

- *Innovation in Islamic Financial Instruments:* The interactive use of special Islamic financial instruments, such as *ijarah*, *mudarabah* and *wakala*, has

[2]Diverse instances globally highlight the usage of Islamic capital market instruments, such as *sukuk*, to address SDGs funding gaps. Illustrative examples encompass Tadau Energy and Quantum Solar Park *sukuk* in Malaysia, aligning with SDGs 7, 11, and 13. Additionally, the Ahmed Wardi Eye Hospital Cash *waqf* Linked *sukuk* in Indonesia contributes to SDG 3, while the Turkiye Emlak Katilim Bankasi (Emlak) green *sukuk* issued in 2022 aligns with SDGs 7, 11, and 13.

significant favorable impacts on the achievement of the SDGs. For example, the green *sukuk* has already led to more climate-friendly investments.

- *Alignment With Maqasid al-Shari'ah:* Generally, the SDGs have a related to the *maqasid al-Shari'ah*, but there are minor differences in certain aspects of Shari'ah. As the blockchain facilitates this ecosystem constellation, it creates a perfect option for the entire international financial system to obtain funds.
- *Role of Shari'ah Scholars:* The function of Shari'ah scholars should not be oversimplified by their sole role of auditing the fulfillment of product criteria but to take into consideration and incorporate SDG and values.
- *Philanthropic Instruments:* Pursuing SDGs in social and economic activities, charitable instruments, such as *waqf*, *zakat*, and *sadaqah*, will stay supremely important because of their impact on instilling cooperation, solidarity, and alternative finance.
- *Sustainable Sukuk:* The issuance of green *sukuk* has been a key element of the COVID-19 response by ensuring alignment with the main principles of Islamic finance.
- *Fintech and Innovation:* The rise of fintech in Islamic finance should stimulate the innovations by industry players and enhance creativity by giving the new perspectives and concepts for the financial transactions.

These takeaways stress the capability of Islamic finance to play a role in meeting the achievement of SDGs, and they therefore make a case for the need to cultivate efforts to this effect.

Policy Recommendations

By its very nature, Islamic finance in the true sense of the word is the tail wind for SDGs, which in turn should be the sole responsibility of governments to actively apply them for SDG attainment. A huge budget gap, from $5 to $7 trillion, indicates the potential of Islamic finance to address the financial needs for SDG implantation. The uprooting of Islamic finance not only covers SDGs but also provides solutions to the environmental, social and governance (ESG) issues as well.

Compulsory training in human resources and educational projects should not be limited to the business field. They should go beyond that and engage not only stakeholders, policymakers and the educational institutions as well, but everyone who would like to understand the principles of Islamic finance and SDGs. The intensive campaigns that target the entire population including children, youth, and adults have to be organized to increase the dissemination of knowledge.

Institutions with advanced, unique and Islamic financing concepts designed to enhance this sustainability in financial services should be recognized. These organizations should be required to supply impact reports, a review of their relation to the SDGs. Regulatory bodies should develop reporting templates for IFIs to ensure a clearer data collection and more transparency over the institutions' role in accomplishing SDGs.

Regulators are called upon to create and support R&D projects in the framework of SDGs and Islamic finance collaboration, which will be an impetus for new products compliant with SDG principles. IFIs could be promoted via tax incentives as they perform an essential role in the implementation of the SDGs.

Teamwork is vital in the realization of the objectives of Islamic finance and SDGs. The establishment of stakeholder dialogic platforms among civil society, IFIs, and local and international actors through private forums and networks is desirable. Public/private partnerships (PPPs) are essential building blocks in dealing with challenges and solving SDGs through Islamic finance. Immediate intentions of the international bodies should be to promote the operating models that would result in international money injections for the SDGs and the ultimate common progress on the world scale.

Conclusion

Islamic finance projects itself as a universal phenomenon. Through the illumination of the synergy between SDGs and the Islamic finance, explicit guidance originates from the Holy Qur'an and Sunnah. Esteemed Islamic scholars, including Imam Abu Hamid Al-Ghazali, delved into *maqasid al-Shari'ah*, aligning with SDGs: providing timeless wealth, preserving heritage, uplifting spirit through education, keeping faith and, last but not least, maintaining life (Al-Ghazali, 1937). Deeds which are based on the five mentioned objectives are praiseworthy, they conserve the public interest (*maslahah*), and whatever is not in line with these principles should not be followed. The significance of these goals is that they embrace the objectives of SDGs. Based on Ibn al-Qayyim's interpretation, Shari'ah is all about goodness, wisdom, mercy, and kindness.

This chapter aims exclusively to examine the concerning relationship between the SDGs Islamic finance and how these two intersected. It discusses some of the working examples which indeed demonstrate the validity of Islamic finance as a key to sustainability development goals. The chapter provides, in terms of the Islamic institutions' challenges in SDGs implementation, useful suggestions.

Research is vital in finding out the exact effects of the implementation of SDGs through Islamic finance. SDGs must finely dissect their suitability to Islamic finance, analyzing how Islamic finance instruments, institutions, and ethics can fulfill the global SDG ambitions.

References

AIBIM. (2023). *Value-based intermediation report 2022: Emerging to engaging* (p. 89). The Association of Islamic Banking and Financial Institutions Malaysia (AIBIM). https://aibim.com/value-based-intermediation/VBI-Report-2022.pdf

Al-Ghazali, A. H. M. (1937). *Al-Mustasfā min Ilm al-Usūl* (Vol. 1). Al-Maktabah al-Tijariyyah.

Al-Roubaie, A., & Sarea, A. M. (2019). Green investment and sustainable development: The case of Islamic finance. *Journal of Islamic Business and Management (JIBM)*, *09*(01). https://doi.org/10.26501/jibm/2019.0901-002

Arner, D. W., Buckley, R. P., Zetzsche, D. A., & Veidt, R. (2020). Sustainability, FinTech and financial inclusion. *European Business Organization Law Review*, *21*(1), 7–35. https://doi.org/10.1007/s40804-020-00183-y

Ascarya, A. (2022). The role of Islamic social finance during Covid-19 pandemic in Indonesia's economic recovery. *International Journal of Islamic and Middle Eastern Finance and Management*, *15*(2), 386–405. https://doi.org/10.1108/IMEFM-07-2020-0351

BNM. (2018). *Value-based intermediation: Strengthening the roles and impact of Islamic finance* (BNM/RH/DP 034–2). Bank Negara Malaysia. https://www.bnm.gov.my/documents/20124/761682/Strategy+Paper+on+VBI.pdf/b299fc38-0728-eca6-40ee-023fc584265e?t=1581907679482#:~:text=Value%2Dbased%20intermediation%20(VBI)%20aims%20to%20deliver%20the%20intended,returns%20and%20long%2Dterm%20interests

Budalamah, L. H., El-Kholei, A. O., & Al-Jayyousi, O. R. (2019). Harnessing value-based financing for achieving SDGs: Social innovation model for Arab municipalities. *Arab Gulf Journal of Scientific Research*, *37*(3), 1–19.

Cuervo-Cazurra, A., Doh, J. P., Giuliani, E., Montiel, I., & Park, J. (2022). The United Nations' sustainable development goals: Pros and cons for managers of multinationals. *AIB Insights*, *22*(1). https://doi.org/10.46697/001c.32530

Dirie, K. A., Alam, Md. M., & Maamor, S. (2023). Islamic social finance for achieving sustainable development goals: A systematic literature review and future research agenda. *International Journal of Ethics and Systems*. https://doi.org/10.1108/IJOES-12-2022-0317

Dusuki, A. W. (2008). Understanding the objectives of Islamic banking: A survey of stakeholders' perspectives. *International Journal of Islamic and Middle Eastern Finance and Management*, *1*(2). Article 2. https://doi.org/10.1108/17538390810880982

Ebrahim, R., Abdulla, Y., & Kumaraswamy, S. (2021). Islamic finance and sustainable development goals in Bahrain. In 2021 International Conference on Sustainable Islamic Business and Finance (pp. 8–13). https://doi.org/10.1109/IEEECONF53626.2021.9686329

Harahap, B., Risfandy, T., & Futri, I. N. (2023). Islamic law, Islamic finance, and sustainable development goals: A systematic literature review. *Sustainability*, *15*(8), 6626. https://doi.org/10.3390/su15086626

Hassan, M. K., Saraç, M., & Alam, A. (2020). Circular economy, sustainable development and the role of Islamic finance. In M. Saraç & M. K. Hassan (Eds.), *Islamic perspective for sustainable financial system* (pp. 1–26). Istanbul University Press. https://doi.org/10.26650/B/SS10.2020.017.01

Herianingrum, S., Supriani, I., Sukmana, R., Effendie, E., Widiastuti, T., Fauzi, Q., & Shofawati, A. (2023). Zakat as an instrument of poverty reduction in Indonesia. *Journal of Islamic Accounting and Business Research*. https://doi.org/10.1108/JIABR-11-2021-0307

How Islamic finance contributes to achieving the sustainable development goal. OECD Development Policy Paper No.30. www.oecdilibrary.org/docserver/acl480caen.pdf?expires=1629477190&id=id&accname=guest&checksum=92110EE3633FC75FAB04B223252ABOC. Accessed on September 27, 2022.

Ismail, A. Y., Musafar Hameed, L. B., Mohamad Suhaimi, A. F., Jamaludin, N. I., & Shahimi, S. (2020). Value based intermediation and interconnection of sustainable development goals in Islamic banking framework. *International Journal of Islamic Economics and Finance Research*, *3*(1), 45–56. https://doi.org/10.53840/ijiefer11

Lawal, I. M., & Ajayi, J. M. A. (2019). The role of Islamic social finance towards alleviating the humanitarian crisis in North-East Nigeria. *Jurnal Perspektif Pembiayaan Dan Pembangunan Daerah*, *6*(5), 545–558. https://doi.org/10.22437/ppd.v6i5.6508

MOF. (2022, September 24). Full redemption of award-winning Sukuk Prihatin, Malaysia's first digital Sukuk. https://www.mof.gov.my/portal/en/news/press-release/full-redemption-sukuk-prihatin-digital-sukuk

Mohammad, M. S., & Abduh, M. (2022). The role of Islamic finance in achieving the SDG number 9: Build resilient infrastructure, promote sustainable industrialization and foster innovation. *IQTISHADIA*, *15*(1), 89. https://doi.org/10.21043/iqtishadia.v15i1.13747

Mohd Nor, S. (2016). Islamic social bank: An adaptation of Islamic banking? *Jurnal Pengurusan*, *46*, 43–51.

Rehman, A. A. (2019, January 23). Islamic finance for social good: Sustainable development in Islamic social finance. *Islamic Finance for Social Good*. https://www.undp.org/blog/islamic-finance-social-good

Smolo, E., & Ismail, A. G. (2011). A theory and contractual framework of Islamic micro-financial institutions' operations. *Journal of Financial Services Marketing*, *15*(4). Article 4. https://doi.org/10.1057/fsm.2010.24

Smolo, E., Seho, M., & Hassan, M. K. (2020). Development of Islamic finance in Bosnia and Herzegovina. *Journal of Economic Cooperation and Development*, *41*(1). Article 1.

Sulaiman Bin Abdulaziz Al Rajhi Charitable Foundation. (2022). *Charities and projects count by administrative regions*. Sulaiman Bin Abdulaziz Al Rajhi Charitable Foundation. https://www.rf.org.sa/en

Tlemsani, I., Zaman, A., Mohamed Hashim, M. A., & Matthews, R. (2023). Digitalization and sustainable development goals in emerging Islamic economies. *Journal of Islamic Accounting and Business Research*. https://doi.org/10.1108/JIABR-03-2023-0092

UNCTAD. (2018). *Achieving the sustainable development goals in the least developed countries a compendium of policy options* (UNCTAD/ALDC/2018/4). United Nations. https://unctad.org/system/files/official-document/aldc2018d4_en.pdf

Yu, Y., & Huang, J. (2021). Poverty reduction of sustainable development goals in the 21st century: A bibliometric analysis. *Frontiers in Communication*, *6*, 754181. https://doi.org/10.3389/fcomm.2021.754181

Zain, N. R. M., Mahadi, N. F., & Noor, A. M. (2019). The potential in reviving waqf through crowdfunding technology: The case study of Thailand. *Al-Shajarah: Journal of the International Institute of Islamic Thought and Civilization (ISTAC)*, (Special Issue), 89–106.

Zauro, N. A., Saad, R. A. J., Ahmi, A., & Mohd Hussin, M. Y. (2020). Integration of Waqf towards enhancing financial inclusion and socio-economic justice in Nigeria. *International Journal of Ethics and Systems*, *36*(4), 491–505. https://doi.org/10.1108/IJOES-04-2020-0054

Chapter 6

Achieving Social Well-Being and Financial Inclusion Through Islamic Microfinance: A Case Study of Akhuwat Islamic Microfinance

Abidullah Khan[a], *Syeda Beena Zaidi*[b], *Abid Mahmood*[b] *and Shabeer Khan*[c]

[a]Sakarya University, Türkiye
[b]Sukkur IBA University, Pakistan
[c]Al Yamamah University, Saudi Arabia

Abstract

The low-income groups in developing nations need microcredits to support their family needs. As banks avoid providing microcredits due to high costs, microfinance institutions are the last resort for this segment of society. The cost of borrowing for the borrowers is indeed high. However, these microfinance institutions play a significant role in financial inclusion. In Muslim countries where financial inclusion takes a hit as a portion of society does not want to indulge in usury transactions, Islamic microfinance institutions play a vital role. In this chapter, the focus is on the Islamic microfinance institutions and their role in achieving the objectives of Shari'ah (maqasid al-Shari'ah) along with the fulfillment of goal of financial inclusion. A case study of Akhuwat Foundation found that the institution offers different interest-free microcredit products along with free healthcare and clothing to the needy segment of society. In this way, not only that the financial inclusion is achieved but also the objectives of Shari'ah are fulfilled. The study provides key facts to the academia and microfinance industry in achieving financial inclusion and fulfilling maqasid al-Shari'ah altogether, in which the banking sector is lacking.

The Future of Islamic Finance, 83–102

doi:10.1108/978-1-83549-906-120241006

Keywords: Islamic microfinance; Maqasid al-Shari'ah; financial inclusion; Akhuwat foundation; Qard Hasan; social wellbeing

Introduction

The notion of microfinance is relatively recent when contrasted with the traditional banking system. Microfinance gained prominence following the success of the microcredit program introduced by Grameen Bank in the 1970s. This initiative targets economically disadvantaged individuals, specifically those with extremely low incomes that are insufficient for their sustenance, as well as an extremely impoverished segment of society characterized by both a lack of income and severe malnutrition. The evolution from a microcredit institution to a comprehensive microfinance institution occurred gradually.

Microfinance comprehends a wider scope than microcredit, whereby microcredit only focuses on providing credit to those excluded by the banking system. On the contrary, microfinance concentrates not only on microcredit but also provides saving account facilities and insurance (Hasan et al., 2022), the same as most commercial banks do. However, banks do not offer microcredit because of the costs associated with screening and monitoring the borrowers. Due to the high cost related to microcredit, the overall returns of the bank can take a hit which could be ultimately transferred to the depositors and shareholders. On the contrary, microfinance institutions emerged to target and include the excluded group in the financial system. Due to the small size and costs associated with microcredit, microfinance institutions could not achieve economies of scale, ultimately translating into higher financing costs (Zamore et al., 2023). Thus, for a borrower, the cost of borrowing is always higher than what the bank could offer.

It is important to recognize that the funding mechanisms of microfinance institutions differs from commercial banks' financing in two fundamental aspects. First, unlike commercial banks, microfinance institutions do not rely heavily on deposits. Second, microfinance institutions' debt financing is usually provided by noncommercial lenders in addition to commercial sources. The noncommercial funds are raised from development agencies, governments, cooperatives, and other microfinance institutions. International funding organizations such as the World Bank are one of the noncommercial entities for microfinance institutions. Noncommercial entities provide funds to microfinance institutions to assist less-developed countries in achieving growth and poverty alleviation. On the other hand, the commercial fund providers are mostly commercial and global banks (Islam et al., 2014).

Information friction significantly influences the debt costs of microfinance institutions. In countries where the regulations are weak and the judiciary is corrupt, adverse selection is more probable, making it expensive for microfinance institutions to raise funds (Garmaise & Natividad, 2010). Since these information frictions are quite prominent in less-developed countries, the cost of borrowing is higher for microfinance institutions.

On the other hand, nonprofit microfinance institutions depend on donor agencies such as nongovernmental organizations (NGOs), government, and private donors. They focus on extremely poor segments of society by providing them with interest-free loans and technical assistance to improve their entrepreneurial skills. The challenge for such institutions is reducing information asymmetry to recover the capital on time. Thus, we can categorize microfinance institutions into for-profit and not for profit institutions where the former functions, to some extent, like a microlevel bank and the latter acts like a social credit institution aimed at reducing poverty with no profit motive.

Despite having such a high cost of finance, microfinance institutions still play an important role in the financial inclusion of the excluded households. Financial inclusion is quite low in developing countries, and governments are trying to achieve optimal financial inclusion through different policies. For instance, in Pakistan, the State Bank of Pakistan introduced the National Financial Inclusion Strategy (NFIS) to include financially excluded households. Consequently, microfinance institutions play a key role in reaching out to rural areas. There are several factors responsible for financial exclusion, and among those is interest-based financing, due to which a significant segment of society does not prefer to deal with conventional financial institutions. The other factors include low literacy rates and deprivation from the basic necessities of life. The connection between well-being and financial inclusion can be seen in Table 6.1, where the countries with better Human Development Index (HDI) have high financial inclusion.

Islamic financial institutions, in this regard, can play an important role in increasing financial inclusion by creating awareness among the masses about its difference from conventional counterparts. As part of the Islamic financial system, Islamic microfinance institutions also target financial inclusion by channeling

Table 6.1. The Comparison of Selected Asian Countries on the Basis of Human Development and Financial Inclusion.

Country	HDI	Financial Inclusion
Japan	19	98.5%
Malaysia	61	88.0%
Thailand	64	95.6%
Iran	77	90.0%
China	82	88.8%
Indonesia	116	51.8%
Bangladesh	128	52.8%
India	130	77.7%
Pakistan	161	21.0%

Source: Human Development Index (2020), Global Financial Inclusion (2021), The World Bank.

funds to those needing microcredit to fulfill their needs. Since Islamic microfinance institutions have the same target customers as conventional microfinance institutions, the key differences exist in their substance and form. In the next section about the overview and principles of Islamic microfinance, we will discuss the difference based on the substance, i.e. achieving social wellbeing and *Shari'ah* compliance. The final section discusses the form by elaborating on a case study of Akhuwat microfinance products.

Overview and Principles of Islamic Microfinance

Islamic microfinance is a component of the Islamic social finance. Khan et al. (2023) categorize Islamic microfinance institutions under two categories of the Islamic social finance spectrum based on revenue and profit objectives. Both types focus on financial inclusion. However, there are key differences between them. Revenue-based are those Islamic financial institutions that focus on providing services to low-income groups without profit motive. These institutions are only focused on achieving break-even such that the overhead expenses are covered. Akhuwat Islamic microfinance is an example of providing loans on the principle of *qard hasan*, where the institution only charges a fixed fee to support its operations. On the other hand, Islamic microfinance institutions with profit motive work on the principle of gaining profits by managing the spread between their borrowing cost and profits earned from financing.

Principles of Islamic Microfinance

Compared with conventional microfinance, Islamic microfinance aims to promote social wellbeing and poverty alleviation through adherence to *Shari'ah's* principles. In other words, Islamic microfinance must raise capital and extend financing through *Shari'ah*-compliant means (Smolo & Ismail, 2011). *Shari'ah* compliance can be achieved by avoiding *riba, gharar*, and *maysir*-based activities, investing in *halal* avenues, backing the transaction by asset(s), and sharing risk pertaining to the transaction (Imran, 2021). These principles of compliance are further explained below:

- *Riba:* The root word "*Riba*" literally means an addition, excess, growth, and increase. The word *Riba* is used for charging markup, interest, or usury (Imran, 2021). In the context of *Shari'ah*, the definition can be derived from the Islamic legal maxim, "Every loan that brings benefit is usury" (*Kullu qarḍ Jarra Manf'atan fahuwa Riba*) (Amanullah, 2018). From this, we can conclude that receiving markup on the principle is *riba* and hence not allowed as the Qur'an, on many occasions, prohibited dealing in *riba* transactions and at one instance considered it as war against Allah and his Messenger (pbuh).[1] Therefore, if an Islamic microfinance institution deals with loans for receiving debt and

[1] Al-Quran 2: 279.

extending financing, it must be *riba*-free, or other modes of Islamic financial contracts may be utilized (see Smolo & Ismail, 2011).

- *Gharar: Gharar* means ambiguity or uncertainty. In Islamic Financial transactions, if the essentials of a contract contain ambiguity, it can lead to deceit where one party takes advantage of the other (Alam et al., 2017). Therefore, any financial transaction that includes excessive *gharar* will invalidate the contract.
- *Maysir: Maysir* means gambling or speculation. In Islamic financial transactions, all Islamic financial institutions must avoid dealing in financial activities involving gambling or speculation, such as investment in financial derivatives, taking short positions in stocks, etc. (Mihajat, 2016).
- *Investment:* An Islamic financial institution must make investment decisions by avoiding *riba, gharar*, and *maysir*. It also needs to invest in *halal* avenues that *Shari'ah* does not prohibit. For example, an Islamic financial institution must not extend financing to a borrower who needs a loan to establish a wine production business.
- *Asset backing (productivity):* The Islamic economic system is against generating wealth through speculative means, i.e. making money from thin air. Instead, it encourages the promotion of real economic activities that lead to increased productivity. In conventional finance, money is treated as an asset, while in Islamic finance, it is considered solely as a medium of exchange. Therefore, dealing in financial instruments backed by debt is prohibited. This means that loan-based transactions with a profit motive are forbidden. Instead, *mushakarah* and *mudarabah*-based financing are highly encouraged. Also, *salam* and *ististna'*-based financing led to the creation of real assets. Thus, if an Islamic microfinance institution has a profit motive, it must deal in asset-backed transactions and avoid loan-based transactions.
- *Risk sharing:* Islam does not promote risk aversion; instead, it embraces the concept of risk sharing. The legal maxim "*Al-ghunm bil ghurm*" – which means "returns are justified by taking risks" – legitimizes profit earning subject to risk sharing. This implies that all parties involved in the contractual agreement must collectively bear the risks associated with ownership or capital. For instance, depositors or donors of Islamic microfinance institutions are not guaranteed their capital. On the liability side, *qard hasan* or *mudarabah* contracts are utilized. In contrast, for financing (the asset side of Islamic microfinance institution), *murabahah, ijarah, salam, istisna', mudarabah, mushakarah,* etc., can be utilized. *Mudarabah* and *musharakah* contracts operate on the principle of risk sharing, while other contracts do contain ownership risk in one way or another.

*The Social Well-Being Perspective (*Maslahah*) of Islamic Microfinance*

Islamic microfinance operates on the principles of social well-being and *Shari'ah*-compliance. As far as social well-being is concerned, Islam emphasizes leading a respectful and peaceful life following the divine guiding principles of *Shari'ah.*

Al-Qarafi (1994) linked *maslahah* and *maqasid* via a "fundamental rule" that: "A purpose (*maqasid*) is not valid unless it leads to the fulfillment of some good (*maslahah*) or the avoidance of some mischief (*mafsadah*)." Therefore, In Islamic law, a "maqasid" embodies the interests of humanity, serving as the core principle aimed at promoting justice, eliminating bias, and alleviating hardship through the principles of compassion and guidance. It promotes cooperation and mutual support within families and society at large. This is manifested in the realization of the term *maslahah*, which means the public interest. *Maslahah*, in Islamic scholars' opinion, is the all-encompassing value and objective of *Shari'ah*, and it is associated with compassion in all its aspects and purposes. *Maslahah* sometimes connotes the same meaning as *maqasid*, and scholars have also used the two terms almost interchangeably (AbdelKader, 2003).

Maqasid al-Shari'ah is an Arabic term combining two words: *Maqasid*, which has several meanings, including objectives, purposes, intents, aspirations, and rationales, and *Shari'ah*, which refers to the religious guidelines in Islam. Thus, the objectives or purposes for the Islamic rulings reflect the meaning of *maqasid al-Shari'ah*. In the contemporary era, Ibn Ashur stands out as the foremost figure in advancing the concept of *maqasid*. *Maqasid al-Shari'ah al-Islamiyyah* represents a pivotal effort in the 20th century aimed at refining the theory of *maqasid*. The term is elaborately defined as follows: "*maqasid al-Shari'ah* (the objectives of *Shari'ah*) encompasses the preservation of order, attainment of benefit, prevention of harm or corruption, establishment of equality among people, fostering reverence, obedience, and effectiveness of the law, and empowering the Ummah (nation) to achieve strength, respect, and confidence" (Ibn Ashur, 1946).

Furthermore, Ibn Ashur categorized the *maqasid al-Shari'ah* into three main groups, namely:

(1) *Maqasid 'ammah* (general objectives).
(2) *Maqasid khassah* (specific objectives).
(3) *Maqasid juz'iyyah* (partial objectives).

General objectives include the goals reflected in all or most facets of religious legislation (Al-Qahtani, 2015). On the other hand, the objectives are concerned with disciplines such as private conduct, family law, and financial transactions (Dusuki & Bouheraoua, 2011). While partial objectives relate to a particular issue or question or to a particular proof that acts as a base for the deduction of the larger purpose of *Shari'ah* (Al-Qahtani, 2015).

Al-Ghazali's widely recognized the depiction of *maqasid al-Shari'ah* asserts that promoting human beings' welfare is Shari'ah's purpose, which indicates that their faith, lives, wealth, prosperity, and intellectuality should be protected. The public interest is ensured and served by these fundamental factors, which are considered to be important (Al-Ghazali, 1356/1937, pp. 139–140). The Muslim scholars unanimously agreed that Islam comes to safeguard these elements and believe that safeguarding these elements are the major *maqasid al-Shari'ah* (Chapra, 2008; Rauf, 2015).

Aspects of Maqasid al-Shari'ah

Numerous eminent scholars have expounded upon diverse facets of *maqasid al-Shari'ah*. For instance, Shaykh Dr. Yusuf Al-Qardhawi outlines five key points of *maqasid al-Shari'ah:* first, to prioritize convenience; second, to uphold justice; third, worship (*ta'abud*); fourth, *da'wah* (propagation of Islam); and fifth, to seek *fitrah* (natural/original constitution) (Ismail, 2021).

The classical economics literature has highlighted different dimensions *of maqasid al-Shari'ah*. These dimensions collectively represent the comprehensive framework of *maqasid al-Shari'ah* as elucidated by prominent Islamic scholars, reflecting the ethical, spiritual, economic, social, and legal objectives of Islamic jurisprudence. Table 6.2 summarizes the diverse facets of *maqasid al-Shari'ah* elucidated by these scholars.

Table 6.2. Summary of *Maqasid-al-Shari'ah* Dimensions.

Dimensions of *Maqasid-al-Shari'ah*	**Definition**
Attainment of success, prosperity, or the well-being *(Falah)*	The primary objective of human life is to attain *falah*, not only in the present life but also in the hereafter. *Shari'ah* serves as the guidance to achieve this ultimate purpose of human existence, as outlined in numerous verses of the Holy Quran.
Protection of life (*Hifz-al-Nafs*)	Ensuring the protection and wellbeing of human life is a fundamental principle. This includes safeguarding individuals from harm, violence, and any threats to their physical wellbeing.
Protection of religion (*Hifz-al-Din*)	Upholding the freedom of religious practice and protecting the core tenets of faith is paramount. This dimension emphasizes safeguarding individuals' right to adhere to and practice their religious beliefs.
Protection of intellect (*Hifz-al-'Aql*)	The preservation of intellectual faculties and mental wellbeing is integral. This involves measures to promote education, critical thinking, and avoiding actions that may harm one's intellectual capacities.

(Continued)

Table 6.2. *(Continued)*

Dimensions of *Maqasid-al-Shari'ah*	Definition
Protection of lineage (*Hifz-al-Nasl*)	This dimension underscores the importance of maintaining family and societal structures that ensure the wellbeing and continuity of future generations. It involves protecting the institution of marriage and the rights of children.
Protection of wealth (*Hifz-al-Mal*)	The safeguarding of property and wealth is a crucial aspect. This includes measures to prevent theft, fraud, and economic exploitation, ensuring fair and ethical economic practices.
Justice and equity (*'Adl and Ihsan*)	Ensuring justice and fairness in all aspects of societal interactions is a foundational principle. This dimension emphasizes the establishment of a just legal system and the equitable distribution of resources.
Promotion of good (*'Amr bil-Ma'ruf*)	Encouraging virtuous actions and fostering a righteous and ethical society is emphasized. This involves promoting positive behaviors and discouraging actions that may lead to harm or corruption.
Prevention of harm (*Nahy 'an al-Munkar*)	Discouraging and preventing harmful actions and behaviors within society is vital. This includes prohibiting actions that may lead to societal degradation or individual harm.
Facilitation of public welfare (*Maslahah*)	Striving for the common good and the welfare of society as a whole is a central objective. This involves considering the wellbeing of the community in legal and ethical decisions.

Source: Developed by Authors through a comprehensive analysis of past literature.

However, the above mentioned *maqasid* are categorized based on the priority of needs and their benefits, delineating three levels of urgency and significance. The first level is *daruriyyat* (necessities), encompassing essential needs critical for sustaining life; their neglect would result in its destruction, causing chaos and disruption in the journey of life (Zaydan, 1989). According to Al-Zarqa (1998), *daruriyyat* refers to actions undertaken to safeguard the five essential needs (*daruriyyat al-khams*): religion, soul, intellect, lineage, and property. The second level comprises of *hajiyyat* (needs), representing necessities beyond basic human requirements. If these needs are unfulfilled, one's life will not be interrupted. However, it will cause hardship and potentially lead to difficulties (Zaydan, 2000). The third level encompasses *tahsiniyyat* (luxuries), regarded as complementary to life. Its absence will not be an inconvenience to human life nor will it cause hardship, but it will be excluded from commendable ethics (Al-Tamimi et al., 1993). According to Raysūnī (2005), *tahsiniyyat* are supplementary needs; their non-fulfillment may reduce the overall comfort of life.

Role of Islamic Microfinance in Achieving Maqasid al-Shari'ah

According to Al-Qaradhawï (2008), *Shari'ah* encompasses several forms of *maqasid* (underlying intents) that are related to wealth (*mal*), including wealth circulation and distribution (Al-Qaradhawï, 2008; Alkhan, 2016). Social scientists generally believe that every culture needs to institutionalize a proper system for the just distribution of resources among all members of society. Islam, another name for peace and justice, has provided comprehensive guidance regarding the fair distribution of resources among all members of society and the just personal distribution of income. Islamic economic system is considered a socio-religiously constructed system that places the well-being of society at the center and achieves human development through fair distribution, social justice, and equity, as proposed by *maqasid al-Shari'ah*. In the wake of attaining these socioeconomic objectives, Islamic financial institutions' main concern is creating and enduring balance between profit motive and social well-being for the betterment of the whole society (Ahmed, 2000; Al-Omar & Abdel-Haq, 1996; Haron, 1995).

Maqasid al-Shari'ah proposes a social value system for the proper functioning of society and a strong framework for alleviating the troubles and hardships of humans and establishing justice. Thus, all aspects of human life – including intellectual, moral, personal, economic, political, and social – should strictly be in line with *maqasid al-Shari'ah* to ensure social well-being in all spheres of life. This can be achieved through the formation of Islamic social finance institutions on a bigger scale. Thus, Islamic microfinance can be a structural solution to cater to the need for a social welfare system based on care and dignity for the poor through mutual help, behavioral reforms, and character building. Nevertheless, microfinance institutions founded on the comprehensive Islamic social finance system using *zakat*, *waqf*, and *qard hasan* tools can significantly uplift the economically suppressed class of society. Thus, the realization of *maqasid al-Shari'ah* is essential to counterbalance the disparity between profit-making and social objectives.

According to Dusuki (2008), the core difference between Islamic financial institutions and their conventional counterparts lies not only in their way of doing business but the value system which guides the overall operations and outlook of Islamic financial institutions. These values should be expressed in the minutiae of their transaction and overall societal role. This demands the internalization of the underlying philosophy of Islamic finance in its true spirit, form, and substance, particularly in its financing patterns. The restricted view of understanding *Shari'ah* by only focusing on the legality forms of a contract must be changed. Instead, the substance that has greater implications for the realization of *maqasid al-Shari'ah* should be equally emphasized especially when structuring a financial product.

Thus, realizing *maqasid al-Shari'ah* is fundamental in the practice of Islamic finance. In other words, performing *Shari'ah*-compliance is not complete by focusing solely on the legalistic and mechanistic elements of *ahkam al-Shari'ah* (the rulings of Islamic law). Rather, the performance should go further to achieve the values and higher intents outlined by the *Shari'ah*. Therefore, claiming any financial practice as Shari'ah-compliant without first considering the *maqasid* or objectives would render it meaningless. Anything that departs from justice to injustice, from mercy to its opposite, from well-being to misery, and from wisdom to frivolous has nothing to do with the *Shari'ah*, even if it is claimed to be very consistent with some interpretations of scholars (Ibn al-Qayyim, 2002).

Islamic finance and economic fundamentals are grounded on economic well-being, justice, universal brotherhood, social welfare, and equitable income distribution. Such an ethical-financial system will be based on two strong pillars, namely financial and religious, which are tied up with the self-evident approach of Islamic moral economy (IME), which explains *maqasid al-Shari'ah* as a source of ultimate wellbeing of mankind (Asutay, 2012). This suggests the essentialness of the Islamic financial institutions' policymakers to devise their operations grounded on the overall welfare and a greater standpoint from the *maqasid al-Shari'ah* framework, not just concentrating on *Shari'ah* compliance.

Despite this appealing theoretical dimension, the Muslim world's reality is far from ideal. According to a recent UN Human Development Report, many Muslim countries have been classified as "near multidimensional poverty" or "in extreme multidimensional poverty" (UNDP, 2016). These countries have also received low scores in many human development indicators, including life expectancy, education, and healthcare. This raises the question: to what extent is the concept of *maqasid al-Shari'ah* workable? In this context, Islamic microfinance appears to embody the true spirit of *maqasid al-Shari'ah* principles. In other words, it aims to improve the wellbeing of rural, underprivileged, and destitute people by encouraging them to engage in profitable enterprises through small-scale *Shari'ah*-compliant funding known as Islamic microfinance. Nonetheless, despite the remarkable development in Islamic finance, the current practices – mostly dominated by banking, *sukuk*, and *takaful* industries – appear to be too comfortable with profit maximization and, as such, disappoint social expectations (Thaidi et al., 2022).

Many critics have argued that Islamic finance does not fulfill *maqasid al-Shari'ah* (Moqbel, 2014). An example of this criticism is displayed below: "One fair criticism of current Islamic finance is that it is delinked from the broader goals or underlying intents (*maqasid*) of Islam. Thus, it is not connecting to and not impacting the real economic challenges, such as economic development in general and poverty, destitution, inequalities, etc., in particular" (Farooq, 2009, p. 46).

Since one of the main objectives behind microfinance is to alleviate or reduce poverty (Morduch, 2000), which in turn enhances the socioeconomic condition of societies, we may conclude that this objective and implication go hand in hand with some (if not all) of the main *maqasid al-Shari'ah* principles, which is to improve the socioeconomic condition of humans, society, and alleviate poverty (Al-Qura-Daghï, 2011; Ash-Shubail, 2015). The empirical data and analysis indicate that Islamic microfinance contributes to serving many key aspects of *maqasid al-Shari'ah*, including: (1) poverty reduction; (2) economic enhancement; (3) enhancing the social condition of society; (4) wealth distribution and circulation; and (5) enhancing intellectual levels of society (AlKhan & Hassan, 2020).

The underlying principle of Islamic microfinance is the application of Islamic values to promote social justice for all and to achieve economic development while building human capability as a center of attention. The impact of Islamic microfinance can be discussed into two areas: economic and social.

The Islamic social finance sector encompasses various components within the Islamic finance industry. Traditional Islamic institutions rooted in philanthropy, such as *zakat*, *sadaqah*, and *waqf*, form a crucial part of this sector. Furthermore, institutions founded on mutual cooperation, like *Qard* and *Kafalah*, contribute to its framework, while contemporary Islamic microfinance institutions continue to enhance this landscape (Khan et al., 2023). According to the Islamic Research and Training Institute (IRTI), as highlighted in the Islamic Social Finance Report (ISFR) of 2020, Islamic social finance primarily comprises *zakat*, *awqaf* (Islamic endowments), and Islamic microfinance (Nur'aini et al., 2022). Furthermore, Mahmud et al. (2015) also delineate three main categories within Islamic social finance. First, traditional Islamic instruments grounded in philanthropy, such as *zakat*, *sadaqat*, and *waqf*, constitute one category. Second, cooperative-based foundations like *Qard* and *Kafalah* represent another category (Islamic Social Finance Report, 2015). Lastly, there are other modern forms of Islamic financial services, including Islamic microfinance, *sukuk*, and *takaful* (Zain & Engku Ali, 2017).

The economic effect of Islamic microfinance presented by an empirical study of IBBL's (Islamic Bank Bangladesh Limited) impact on rural poverty finds that loans contributed considerably to improving household earnings, the output of harvest and cattle, disbursement, and employment (Rahman & Ahmad, 2010). This effect can also be observed from the operations of Akhuwat Microfinance, which aims to improve the lives of the low-income groups by adhering to the social well-being and *Shari'ah*-compliance principles.

Case Study of Successful Islamic Microfinance Initiative

> As a philosophy, Akhuwat cannot fail; if the movement does not succeed, it will not be a failure of the principles and ideals that guide the organization. Failure could only stem from the waning strength of men and the weakness of their resolve but never from

> the lack of strength in the idea of Akhuwat itself. Dr. Amjad Saqib, Founder and Executive Director Akhuwat Pakistan. (Saqib & Malik, 2019)

Several programs and institutions serve the objective of promoting financial inclusion through Islamic microfinance. One notable organization is the Akhuwat foundation, established by Dr. Amjad Saqib in 2001. The approach adheres to the pragmatic framework of poverty alleviation, which is rooted in the fundamental principle of *Mawakhat* (solidarity and brotherhood) within the Islamic context. Through the principle of *Mawakhat*, the focus is not only on eradicating poverty and promoting financial inclusion but also on satisfying the fundamental principles of *maqasid al-Shari'ah*. Therefore, we studied various products offered by Akhuwat to identify the balance of social wellbeing and *Shari'ah* compliance in the operations of Akhuwat Microfinance.

Though various dimensions of *maqasid al-Shari'ah* are explored through various studies and are mentioned before, we specifically highlight the Akhuwat Foundation products concerning the five widely accepted and recognized dimensions of *maqasid al-Shari'ah* associated with Imam Al Ghazali, namely *hifz al-mal* (protection of wealth), *hifz al-'Aql* (protection of intellect), *hifz al-nafs* (protection of life), *hifz al-nasl* (protection of lineage), and *hifz al-din* (protection of religion) and its relation to financial inclusion.

It is observed from Table 6.1 that a better HDI leads to better financial inclusion where HDI includes health, knowledge, and standard of life as parameters. The objective of financial inclusion cannot be achieved unless the basic needs of an individual are fulfilled, such as basic health facilities, education, food, clothing, etc. Only then can an individual opt for a loan. It means that any individual should be transformed from extremely poor to economically poor to be included in the financial system.

The products of Akhuwat are inspired by the same parameters, which focus on health, education, and uplifting the standards through interest-free loans. These products aim to improve the social well-being of individuals through safeguarding the five objectives of *Shari'ah* and ultimately improving financial inclusion. This relationship is shown in Fig. 6.1.

Safeguarding Wealth (Hifz-al-Mal)

An important product offered by Akhuwat is interest-free microfinance, specifically designed to economically empower individuals through principles of fairness and justice in financial transactions. This monetary aid explicitly fulfills the aim of *maqasid al-Shari'ah*, which is to safeguard wealth by guaranteeing individuals access to funds devoid of usury. A notable example in this context is the provision of benevolent loans (*qard hasan*) to entrepreneurs by Akhuwat. These loans empower them to initiate or enhance their enterprises without the burdensome imposition of interest, promoting economic expansion and prosperity in adherence to the *maqasid al-Shari'ah*. Akhuwat has disbursed around

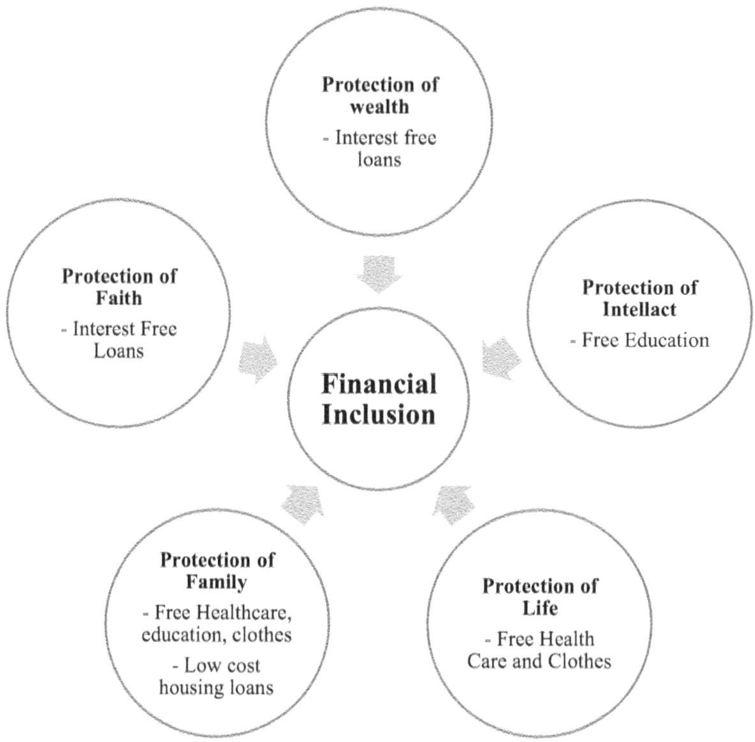

Fig. 6.1. The Relationship Among the Five Objectives of Shari'ah and Financial Inclusion. *Source:* Authors' developed.

USD 794.58 million until February 2024 via individual and group lending with remarkable recovery rate of 99.84% (Akhuwat, 2024). Advancing to 6.13 million beneficiaries is evidence of successful financial inclusion because the loan process is less complex than conventional microfinance institutions. If the process of loan disbursement is observed, one could find a similar loan disbursement process as that of other microfinance institutions where after accepting the loan application, loan appraisal is performed, and guarantees are provided by the borrower (Akhuwat, 2024). However, the unique point about the loan is its disbursement in the *masjid* so that they can bind the debtor to return the amount so that it can be used by the other needy people same as them (Saqib & Malik, 2019).

The loan portfolio of Akhuwat Islamic microfinance loans is not limited only to enterprise loans but also other types of interest-free loans to protect the wealth, family, intellect, human life, and faith. Usually, the loan requirement of the low-income households is not more than PKR 100,000. Therefore, for most of the loan products Akhuwat's loan range varies between PKR 10,000–PKR 100,000 (equivalent to US 36–USD 360) and repayable in 10–36 months. These loans include agriculture microloan which is provided to the farmers to purchase inputs and meet ancillary expenses. Similarly, interest-free liberation loans are provided to those strangled in exploitative loans from loan sharks. Interest-free housing loans are provided for renovation and construction for low-income households. These interest-free loans, along with health, marriage, and emergency loans not only enable the households to support their families economically but also to improve their living standards by protecting their wealth and health. In return, the goal of financial inclusion is also achieved (Akhuwat, 2024).

Safeguarding Intellectual Well-being (Hifz-al-'Aql)

The attainment of *maqsid al-Shari'ah*, namely the safeguarding of intellectual well-being and the advancement of a poverty-free society, necessitates the unrestricted availability of education to the whole populace. The economic well-being of every individual depends on education as it enhances the chances of earning your share eloquently amid fierce competition. According to Akhuwat, the vision of a poverty-free society cannot be achieved if the illiteracy of low-income people is not addressed. In this regard, Fig. 6.2 outlines Akhuwat's Educational Services which provide better opportunities in this regard. They have partnered with the Government of Punjab and restored almost 4,000 primary and secondary schools, established learning hubs for vocational training, and Pakistan's first fee-free residential university is under construction process. Hence, it provides a sustainable way out of poverty's vicious circle by instilling a modern skill set among underprivileged masses. Along with this, education loan that is available for

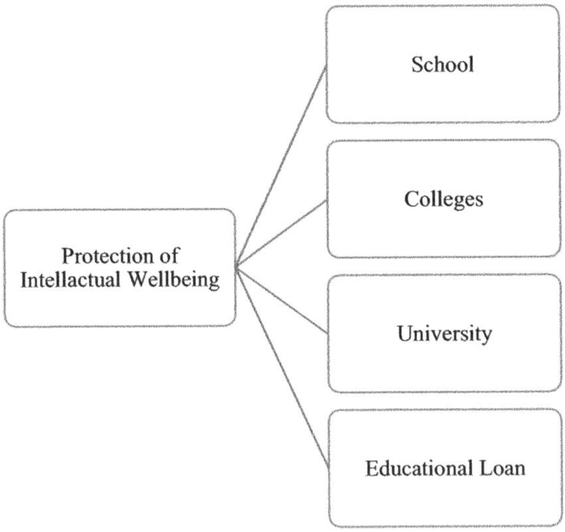

Fig. 6.2. Akhuwat Products/Services for the Protection of Intellectual Well-being. *Source:* Authors' developed.

matriculation up to masters (Akhuwat, 2024), further support the objective of intellectual well-being.

***Protecting Human Life* (Hifz-al-Nafs)**

In low-income nations, reduced life expectancy statistics are mostly attributed to inadequate or malnutrition and limited access to essential seasonal attire, particularly during winter. Safeguarding life is regarded as a crucial aim within the *maqasid al-Shari'ah* framework. It is necessary to acknowledge that the attainment of this goal depends on the provision of basic necessities, such as food, clothing, shelter, and healthcare. The lack of these requirements would make it impossible to achieve this goal. The Akhuwat Clothes Bank has a rigorous protocol for gathering, laundering, and dispensing seasonal garments and other essential items to underprivileged individuals. The clothes bank program has played a significant role in meeting the basic need for clothing among the underprivileged members of society, especially during the winter season when the demand for warm clothing rises substantially. This endeavor has also involved one of the marginalized groups in Pakistani society, namely the transgender community, with the aim of empowering them and improving their social standing. They are entrusted with tasks such as sorting, stitching, altering, and packaging donated clothing to make them useable for distribution among those in need. Through this initiative, they are integrated as active contributors to society. Till 2022, the program benefitted 397,086 families (Akhuwat, 2022). Besides, Akhuwat has supported this community in terms of health benefits, psychological support, and in obtaining identity documentation. Furthermore, the organization provides complimentary medical checkups and subsidized pharmaceuticals, thereby implementing efforts to protect human life in addition to its healthcare services (see Fig. 6.3 for the services offered). Apart from this, their health loan

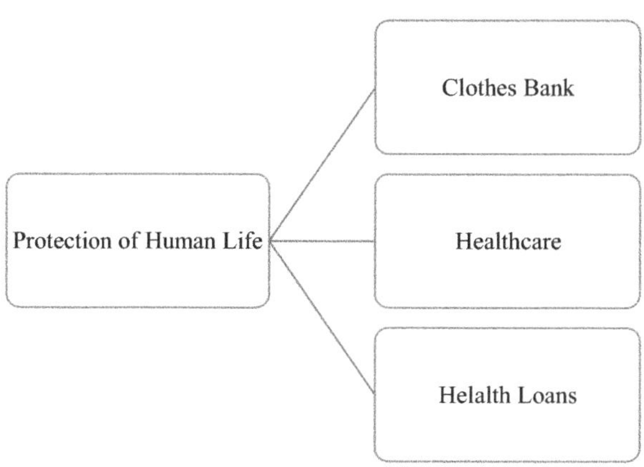

Fig. 6.3. Akhuwats Services for the Protection of Life. *Source:* Authors' developed.

helps the needy get timely treatment, thereby protecting life and stimulating financial inclusion.

***The Protection of Family* (Hifz-al-Nasl)**

The Akhuwat Foundation of Pakistan implements Islamic microfinance based on *Shari'ah* principles to stimulate social development. The organization demonstrates how adhering strictly to Islamic economic principles may efficiently achieve important goals, especially protecting family units. Akhuwat strongly adheres to the core principle of Islamic microfinance, focusing largely on providing interest-free loans to offer financial assistance to families. This steadfast dedication perfectly corresponds with *maqasid al-Shari'ah*, promoting economic stability and the fair allocation of resources, which are fundamental principles in promoting family units.

Akhuwat provides interest-free finance to individuals and also works toward creating strategic business prospects and family support (see Fig. 6.4).

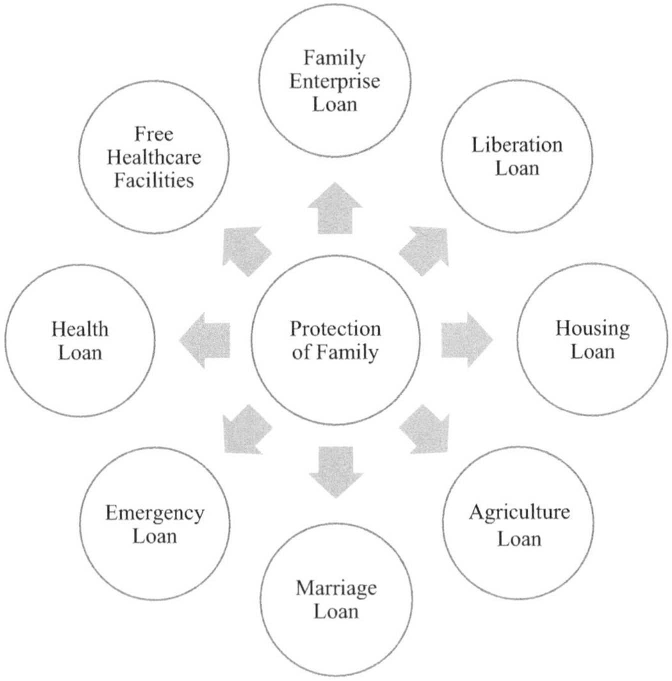

Fig. 6.4. Akhuwat Services for the Protection of Family. *Source:* Authors' developed.

This strategy enables families to achieve self-reliance, guaranteeing a stable economic future. These techniques align with the fundamental *maqasid al-Shari'ah*, particularly in promoting economic fairness and protecting vulnerable populations. Akhuwat's strong commitment to education highlights the connection between Islamic microfinance and the goals mentioned in *shari'ah* principles. The charity actively promotes intellectual growth by supporting children's education within families. Moreover, Akhuwat's strong focus on ethical behaviors aligns with the overarching goals of Shari'ah in fostering ethical conduct. Akhuwat employs a comprehensive strategy encompassing financial services and community development initiatives, vigorously countering predatory lending and protecting families from activities against Islamic teachings.

This comprehensive approach reiterates the mission of *Shari'ah* to protect life and promote wealth. Akhuwat greatly strengthens family structures in society by implementing initiatives that focus on healthcare and essential services. The evident symbiotic connection between Islamic microfinance and the *Shari'ah* objectives, exemplified by the Akhuwat Foundation, is noticeable. Akhuwat plays a crucial role in promoting the well-being of families by providing interest-free financial services, fostering ethical behavior, offering education, and supporting communal development. This helps to achieve the lofty goals of *Shari'ah*.

Protection of Religion (Hifz-al-Din)

Anas ibn Malik reported: The Messenger of Allah, peace and blessings be upon him (pbuh), would say in his supplications,

> O Allah, I seek refuge in You from disability and sloth, cowardice and senility, hardness of heart and negligence, dependence and humiliation and misery. I seek refuge in You from poverty and unbelief, wickedness and discord, hypocrite and fame-seeking and ostentation. I seek refuge in You from deafness and dumbness, insanity and contagion, leprosy and evil ailments. (al-Da'wāt al-Kabīr 348)

The teachings of the Holy Prophet Muhammad (pbuh) emphasize the intrinsic link between poverty and faith. This correlation is also evident in the objectives of organizations like the Akhuwat Organization in Pakistan. The *hadith* highlights that poverty can lead to uncertainty, underlining that poverty is a significant challenge to one's religion. The organization's dedication to Islamic microfinance perfectly corresponds with the Prophet's (pbuh) ideas to tackle this difficulty.

The Akhuwat Islamic Microfinance program offers interest-free loans based on the principle of *qard al-hassan*, aligning with the beliefs of Muslims who refrain from participating in the conventional financial system to avoid usury (*riba*). Moreover, the organization emphasizes ethical conduct in its operational procedures when extending financial services. These ethical principles serve to protect individuals and families, preventing them from engaging in economic practices that contradict Islamic teachings. Additionally, they promote a societal attitude rooted in fairness and respect for religious values.

The Akhuwat Organization's aim aligns fundamentally with the Holy Prophet's (pbuh) teachings on poverty, faith, and social responsibility. Akhuwat aims to establish a connection between economic impact and preserving religious values by implementing Islamic microfinance and community development activities. These efforts are based on the ideals advocated by Prophet Muhammad (pbuh).

Conclusion

The most significant challenge in developing nations is financial inclusion, with a considerable portion of the population still deprived of access to the financial system. Apart from banking, microfinance institutions also play an important role in promoting financial inclusion by reaching out to those needing microcredits. Islamic microfinance institutions are also playing a key role in this regard, where they aim to provide *Shari'ah*-compliant alternatives so that the social wellbeing and financial inclusion goals are met altogether. *Shari'ah*-compliance can be achieved by avoiding *riba, gharar, and maysir* and promoting investment in *halal* avenues, asset-backing, and risk sharing. On the other hand, social well-being is achieved by complying with the objectives of *Shari'ah* (*maqasid al-Shari'ah*). The products offered by Akhuwat Microfinance are analyzed to comprehend the achievement of social well-being and financial inclusion. It is observed that, in addition to providing microcredit facilities, Akhuwat also prioritizes delivering free education, health services, and clothing aligning their operations with the *maqasid al-Shari'ah* principles.

References

AbdelKader, D. (2003). Modernity, the principles of public welfare (Maslaha) and the end goals of Shari'a (Maqasid) in Muslim legal thought. *Islam and Christian-Muslim Relations*, *14*(2), 163–174.

Ahmed, K. (2000). Islamic finance and banking, the challenge and prospects. *Review of Islamic Economics*, *9*(1), 57–82.

Akhuwat. (2022). *Akhuwat progress report 2022*. Akhuwat Foundation. https://akhuwat.org.pk/akhuwat-clothes-bank/

Akhuwat. (2024). *Akhuwat loan process*. https://akhuwat.org.pk/loan-process/

Al-Ghazali, A. H. M. (1356/1937). *Al-Mustasfā min Ilm al-Usūl* (Vol. 1). Al-Maktabah al-Tijariyyah.

Al-Omar, F., & Abdel-Haq, M. (1996). *Islamic banking: Theory, practice, and challenges*. Zed Books.

Al-Qahtani, M. B. A. (2015). *Understanding Maqasid al-Shariah: A contemporary perspective*. International Institute of Islamic Thought.

Al-Qaradhawi, Y. (2008). Maqasid Al-Shari'a Al-Muta'aliqa bil Mal. In *Paper presented at: European council for Fatwa and research*, Dublin, Republic of Ireland, June 2008.

Al-Qarafi, S. (1994). *Al-Dhakheerah* (Vol. 5, p. 478). Dar al-Arab.

Al-Qura-Daghi̇. (2011). Maqasid Al-Shari'a fe - Al-Iqtisad [online]. http://iefpedia.com/arab/wp-content/uploads/2010/11/

Al-Tamimi, I. A. (1993). *Nazarat Fi al-Thaqafah al-Islamiyyah*. Dar ul Furqan.

Al-Zarqa. (1998). *Al-Madkhal al-Fiqhi al-'Am* (Vol. 1, p. 102). Dar al-Qalam.

Alam, N., Gupta, L., & Shanmugam, B. (2017). Prohibition of Riba and Gharar in Islamic banking. In N. Alam, L. Gupta, & B. Shanmugam (Eds.), *Islamic finance: A practical perspective* (pp. 35–53). Palgrave Macmillan. https://doi.org/10.1007/978-3-319-66559-7_3

Alkhan, A. (2016). *A critical analysis of special purpose vehicles in the Islamic banking industry: The Kingdom of Bahrain as a case study*. PhD Thesis, University of Bolton.

Alkhan, A. M., & Hassan, M. K. (2020). Does Islamic microfinance serve maqasid al-shari'a? *Borsa Istanbul Review*, *21–1*(2021), 57–68. http://www.elsevier.com/journals/borsa-istanbul-review/2214-8450

Amanullah, M. (2018). Legal Maxim: "Every loan that brings benefit is usury," its related issues and implementation in pre-Islamic and Malaysian financial transactions (Kaedah Fiqhiyyah: Setiap Pinjaman Beserta Faedah Itu Riba. Isu-Isu Berkaitan dan Perlaksanaannya Sejak Zama). *Journal of Islam in Asia*, *15*(1), 204–227.

Ash-Shubail, Y. (2015). Maqasid ash-Shari'ah (Objectives of Islamic law) [online]. http://islamicstudies.islammessage.com/ResearchPaper.aspx?aid=134

Asutay, M. (2012). Conceptualising and locating the social failure of Islamic finance: Aspirations of Islamic moral economy vs the realities of Islamic finance. *Asian and African Area Studies*, *11*(2), 93–113.

Chapra, M. U. (2008). *The Islamic vision of development in the light of Maqāṣid al-Sharīʿah, the international institute of Islamic thought*. The International of Islamic Thought.

Dusuki, A. W. (2008). Understanding the objectives of Islamic banking: A survey of stakeholders' perspectives. *International Journal of Islamic and Middle Eastern Finance and Management*, *1*, 132–148.

Dusuki, A., & Bouheraoua, S. (2011). The framework of maqasid shariah and its implications for Islamic finance. *Islam and Civilisational Renewal*, *2*, 316–336.

Farooq, M. (2009). The challenge of poverty and mapping out solutions: Requisite paradigm shift for a problem-solving and Islamic perspective. *Journal of Islamic Economics, Banking and Finance*, *5*(2), 45–76.

Garmaise, M. J., & Natividad, G. (2010). Information, the cost of credit, and operational efficiency: An empirical study of microfinance. *Review of Financial Studies*, *23*(6), 2560–2590.

Haron, S. (1995). The framework and concept of Islamic interest-free banking. *Journal of Asian Business*, *11*(1), 26–39.

Hasan, N. Singh, A. K. Agarwal, M. K., & Khushwaha, B. P. (2022). Evaluating the role of microfinance institutions in enhancing the livelihood of urban poor. *Journal of Economic and Administrative Sciences*. https://doi.org/10.1108/JEAS-09-2021-0175

Ibn al-Qayyim. (2002). *Iʿlām al-Muwaqqiʿīn ʿan Rabb al-ʿĀlamīn* (Edited by Abū ʿUbaydah Ālu Salmān and A. ʿUmar Aḥmad). Dār Ibn al-Jawzī.

Ibn Ashur, M. T. (1946). *Maqasid Al-Shari'ah Al-Islamiyah wa Makarimiha* (p. 183). Tunisian printing press, Al-Matba'ah al-Tunisiyyah.

Imran, M. (2021). *Islamic finance 101: Learning through stories*. Liberty.

IRTI (Islamic Development Bank Institute). (2015). *Islamic social finance report*. IRTI.

Islam, Z., Porporato, M., & Waweru, N. (2014). Cost structure and financial sustainability of microfinance institutions: The potential effects of interest rate cap in Bangladesh. *International Journal of Financial Services Management*, *7*(1).

Ismail, N. (2021). *Maqasid Syariah Dalam Ekonomi Islam*. Tazkia Press.

Khan, A., Sukmana, R., & Mahmood, A. (2023). Islamic social finance ecosystem and the role of crowdfunding: A proposed model. *Hamdard Islamicus*, *46*(3), 91–111.

Mahmud, K. T., Hassan, M. K., SOHAG, M., & Alam, F. (2015). Impact of zakat in alleviating rural poverty: A case study of Masjid Council for Community Advancement (MACCA) in Bangladesh. *Access to Finance and Human Development—Essays on Zakah, Awqaf and Microfinance*, *23*.

Mihajat, M. I. S. (2016). Contemporary practice of Ribā, Gharar and Maysir in Islamic banking and finance. *International Journal of Islamic Management and Business*, *2*(2), 1–19.

Moqbel, T. (2014). *Evaluating the shariah compliance and operationalizing Maqasid Al shariah: The case for Islamic project finance contracts*. PhD Thesis, Durham University.

Morduch, J. (2000). The microfinance schism. *World Development*, *28*(4), 617–629.

Nur'aini, Sariah, & Oktaviani, J. (2022). Islamic social finance and Maqashid shariah. *International Journal of Waqf*, *2*(2).

Rahman, M. M., & Ahmad, F. (2010). Impact of microfinance of IBBL on the rural poor's livelihood in Bangladesh: An empirical study. *International Journal of Islamic and Middle Eastern Finance and Management*, *3*(2), 168–190.

Rauf, I. F. A. (2015). *Defining Islamic statehood measuring and indexing contemporary Muslim states*. Palgrave Macmillan.

Raysūnī, A. (2005). *Imam al-Shatibi's theory of the higher objectives and intents of Islamic law*. International Institute of Islamic Thought.

Saqib, M. A., & Malik, A. (2019). *Integral finance – Akhuwat: A case study of the solidarity economy*. Routledge.

Smolo, E., & Ismail, A. G. (2011). A theory and contractual framework of Islamic micro-financial institutions' operations. *Journal of Financial Services Marketing*, *15*(4), 287–295. https://doi.org/10.1057/fsm.2010.24

Thaidi, H. A. A., Ab Rahman, M. F., Ab Rahman, A., & Shamsuri, M. A. F. (2022). The prospects of Islamic microfinance: Maqasid shariah perspective. *TIFBR | Tazkia Islamic Finance and Business Review*, *16*(1), 14–32.

United Nations Development Programme (UNDP). (2016). *Human development report 2016*. United Nations Development Programme.

Zain, M. N. R., & Engku Ali, E. R. A. (2017). An analysis on Islamic social finance for protection and preservation of Maqāṣid al-Sharī'ah. *Journal of Islamic Finance*, *2117*(Special Issue), 133–141.

Zamore, S., Beisland, L. A., & Mersland, R. (2023). Excessive focus on risk? Non-performing loans and efficiency of microfinance institutions. *International Journal of Finance & Economics*, *28*(2), 1290–1307.

Zaydan, A. K. (1989). *Al-Madkhal Lidirasah al-Syari'ah al-Islamiyah* (11th ed., p. 41). Muassasah al-Risalah.

Zaydan, A. K. (2000). *Al-Wajiz fi Usul al-Fiqh* (pp. 379–381). Al-Resalah.

Chapter 7

Sustainable Development: Exploring the Role of Islamic Social Finance in Promoting Sustainable Development and Social Welfare

Ziyaad Mahomed[a] *and Irum Saba*[b]

[a]INCEIF University, Malaysia
[b]Institute of Business Administration (IBA), Pakistan

Abstract

Increasing humanitarian disasters and the need for financial support – specifically within the Organization of Islamic Cooperation (OIC) countries – has forced global humanitarian agencies to consider alternative funding sources. The victims of disaster and those disadvantaged that remain below the poverty line in much of the OIC countries remain concerned about the source of the funding they receive, based on their beliefs. Furthermore, institutions responsible for managing the funding for Sustainable Development Goals (SDGs) targets in their respective countries have also been considering alternative funding. The World Bank and the Islamic Development Bank (IsDB) suggest that the Islamic social finance is largely untapped, with significant potentials for more effective collection and distribution of compulsory alms called zakah and endowments known as *waqf* within the OIC countries. This chapter assesses the current challenges and opportunities for the Islamic social finance and covers some of the successful cases of the Islamic social finance deployment. The authors review approaches where world-renowned institutions have applied interest-free loans for poverty reduction, banking products for agricultural social financing, the utilization of cross-border social funding for socio-economic development and property management using social finance principles. The authors also assess capital market instruments integrated with the Islamic social finance for managing SDG funding gaps.

The Future of Islamic Finance, 103–120

doi:10.1108/978-1-83549-906-120241007

Keywords: Social finance; Sustainable Development Goals; zakah; zakat; *waqf*; *sukuk*; COVID-19

Introduction

Political instability, infrastructural issues, and rising inflation are some of the sources of social issues, while others are related to natural disasters (floods, earthquakes, etc.) and climate change. The United Nations' (UN) SDGs stress the importance of social security, healthcare, and well-being for all human beings (UN SDG 3: Good Health and well-being). The COVID-19 pandemic revealed the shortcomings of healthcare systems in ensuring well-being globally. Many lives were lost in both developed and developing countries due to overcrowded healthcare units, lack of protective equipment, diagnostics, and oxygen. The Secretary General of the UN, António Guterres, said that COVID-19 was just a "dress rehearsal" for future disasters that humanity is clearly not ready for.

The UN launched the SDGs in September 2015 at the UN Sustainable Development Summit (United Nations, 2023). They are a global agenda with a deadline of 2030. Every UN member is expected to achieve 17 (seventeen) goals (that are divided into 169 targets) by 2030. All countries must report their progress to the UN. The SDGs aim to improve the well-being of humans. Based on the human development approach, the SDGs concentrate on people and their well-being and expect that nations aligned with the SDGs will benefit from a unified approach to social and economic issues that have cross-border consequences (Dariah et al., 2016).

The OIC is the world's second-largest intergovernmental organization after the UN, with 57 member states that represent 1.8 billion Muslims globally. It was founded in 1969 by 25 states with the goal of fostering unity among Muslims and advancing the welfare of the worldwide Muslim community (*Ummah*). The Islamic Cooperation Humanitarian Affairs Department (ICHAD) was created by the OIC in 2008 to manage the activities of various humanitarian organizations (non-governmental organizations and bilateral ones) and enable access to assistance during emergencies. For example, the OIC coordinated efforts by over 40 Islamic aid organizations and other civil society organizations to deliver relief supplies across the country when a severe famine struck Somalia in 2011. In addition to its political endeavor to safeguard Muslim communities globally, its financial institution, the IsDB, carries out the actual effort to fund aid.

Both the OIC and IsDB aim to provide access to aid for needy communities by using innovative financing mechanisms for humanitarian and development purposes in their member countries. The increasing trend of the humanitarian funding gap in recent years (OCHA, 2021) indicates the necessity to enhance the efficiency of aid. Islamic social finance instruments can offer a lasting solution during and after crises. Islamic social finance involves offering financial services to the disadvantaged segments of society to attain socioeconomic well-being. It includes institutions based on charity such as *zakah* (obligatory giving), *sadaqah* (voluntary donation), *waqf* (endowment), *qard hasan* (benevolent interest-free loan), and the modern Islamic not-for-profit microfinance (Lawal & Ajayi, 2019).

Crowdfunding is another source of Islamic social financing that has been successful in some OIC countries, such as Indonesia for example. Crowdfunding can leverage a network of contributors to solicit donations for various projects (Hassanuddin et al., 2020). For the OIC countries, Islamic principles and values are a primary patronage factor for customers patronizing Islamic financial intermediation and Islamic social funding. Islamic crowdfunding platforms offer Shari'ah-compliant alternatives for fundraising which appeal to Muslim donors and entrepreneurs based on their beliefs (Hendratmi et al., 2020).

Another instrument in poverty alleviation and socioeconomic development is the social impact *sukuk*. Through the Islamic capital market sector, *sukuk* offer advantages of security, governance, rating and tradability (Mahomed, 2017). *Sukuk* can also incorporate social impact indicators, such as the number of beneficiaries, the quality of service, and the environmental impact, to measure the performance and outcomes of the social projects. Therefore, SDG funding gaps may be reduced considerably with more effective deployment of these instruments as *sukuk* can be used to finance social projects, such as infrastructure, education, health, and environment, that benefit the society and the environment. A combination of traditional Islamic social finance instruments with the stringent structuring requirements of *sukuk* is also expected to provide significant confidence to contributors disillusioned with ineffective economic management of Islamic social funding (Jouti Tahiri, 2019).

This chapter considers solutions to reducing SDG funding gaps in the OIC countries through Islamic social finance solutions. The structure of the chapter includes a review of the traditional Islamic social funding instruments, before delving into the opportunities and challenges of these instruments. We consider the case studies of contemporary social finance applications that may be considered for replication. Finally, we conclude with recommendations for future application.

Primary Islamic Social Finance Instruments – An Overview

Islamic social finance represents a robust array of tools designed to promote wealth redistribution and empower communities. These tools encompass *zakah* (mandatory alms), *sadaqah* (voluntary charity), *waqf* (endowments), *qard hasan* (interest-free, benevolent loans), *takaful* (mutual assistance), *mirath* (inheritance), *wasiyyah* (bequests), and *nafaqah* (financial support), among others, which are strategically employed to mitigate economic disparities. A core tenet of this system is the belief that charitable giving does not result in financial detriment. This is encapsulated in the verse from the Qur'an (35:39) which states: "Indeed, my Lord extends provision for whom He wills of His servants and restricts [it] for him. But whatever thing you spend [in His cause] - He will compensate it; and He is the best of providers." Considering this, the act of charity, whether monetary or in kind, is strongly advocated, with the understanding that the spiritual rewards of aiding others are complemented by potential unexpected material returns. Furthermore, those who engage in charitable acts are believed to receive divine protection from Allah (swt), shielding them from potential calamities.[1] Nonprofit or Islamic social finance instruments have been found effective in supporting the poor, either as individual modes (e.g. Akhuwat in Pakistan) or packaged with other instruments (e.g. Baitul Maal wa Tamwil [BMT] in Indonesia) (Rahmawati & Tanjung, 2015).

The well-established modes of Islamic social finance can be summarized as follows:

Zakah

Zakah is the third of the five pillars of Islam, fundamental tenets that are the basic beliefs and expected practice of those referred to as Muslims. The Qur'an, the primary source of Islamic law mentions *zakah* at least 32 times, 28 of which are in conjunction with the obligatory duty of prayer (*salah*). *Zakah* is a mandatory payment for the wealthy Muslims, as a policy of redistribution of wealth to the less fortunate, vulnerable, or destitute members of the society. The word *zakah* has various meanings in the Arabic language, such as growth, increase, and purity. The term *zakah* also has different implications in the Islamic context: etymological, theological, and legal. Etymologically, *zakah* means purifying or cleansing something from impurities. Theologically, *zakah* implies a spiritual purification that is achieved by giving *zakah*. *Zakah* also signifies growth or increase, which can be interpreted as either a spiritual development by pleasing Allah (swt) or a redistribution of income that can enhance the disposable income of the poor. Legally, *zakah* refers to the obligatory transfer of a specific portion of one's wealth to any of the eligible recipients of *zakah* as prescribed in the Qur'an (9:60). The transfer of *zakah* has a direct impact on the increase of disposable income of the poor, which in turn stimulates the aggregate demand in the economy, leading to more production of goods and services and resulting in economic development and welfare in the overall economy (Bin Lahuri, 2021).

Nisab and Zakatable Assets

Nisab is the minimum amount of wealth that makes a person liable to pay *zakah*. It is a criterion that distinguishes the wealthy from the poor in Islam. *Nisab* has three conditions that must be met (al-Kasani, 1983): (i) *Nisab* must be the excess wealth that remains after meeting one's basic and essential needs, such as one's house, personal vehicle, clothes and furniture; (ii) *Nisab* must be in the possession of the owner for a full lunar year (also known as a "hawl"); and (iii) *Nisab* must be applicable only to those assets that have the potential or actual growth because an item that is not productive or profitable is not *zakatable*.

[1]SWT stands for "Subhanahu wa ta'ala" in Arabic which means "Glory be to Him the Most High."

Zakatable Assets

Zakah is not due on the amount that an individual consumes or intends to consume throughout the year. Rather, it is due only on the net value of an individual's assets that remain at the end of the year. Some of the assets that have *nisab* and are subject to *zakah* are (Abidin & bin Omar, 1870):

- The *nisab* of gold is approximately 85 grams.
- The nisab of silver is approximately 595 grams.
- The nisab of trading goods and cash is calculated using their equivalent value of gold.

If gold and silver do not reach the *nisab* level separately, but their combined value is equal to or more than 595 grams of silver, *zakah* is obligatory on the owner.

The Recipients of Zakah

Zakah is distributed to the eligible individuals who fall under one or more of the eight categories, as specified by the Holy Qur'an in the following verse:

۞إِنَّمَا ٱلصَّدَقَٰتُ لِلْفُقَرَآءِ وَٱلْمَسَٰكِينِ وَٱلْعَٰمِلِينَ عَلَيْهَا وَٱلْمُؤَلَّفَةِ قُلُوبُهُمْ وَفِي ٱلرِّقَابِ وَٱلْغَٰرِمِينَ وَفِي سَبِيلِ ٱللَّهِ وَٱبْنِ ٱلسَّبِيلِ فَرِيضَةً مِّنَ ٱللَّهِ
وَٱللَّهُ عَلِيمٌ حَكِيمٌ

> The alms are only for the poor and the needy, and those who collect them, and those whose hearts are to be reconciled, and to free the captives and the debtors, and for the cause of Allah, and (for) the wayfarer; a duty imposed by Allah. Allah is All Knowing, Wise. (Al-Qur'an, 9:60)

Accordingly, the rightful recipients of *zakah* are divided into eight categories as follows:

(1) The poor (*al-fuqara'*): those who do not have enough income or assets to meet their basic needs.
(2) The needy (*al-masakin*): those who are in difficulty or hardship and need assistance.
(3) The *zakah* administrators (*'amilina 'alayha*): those who collect, distribute, and manage *zakah* funds.
(4) Those whose hearts are to be reconciled (*mu'allafati qulubihim*): those who are new or potential converts to Islam or allies of the Muslim community.
(5) Those in bondage (*ar-riqab*): those who are enslaved or in captivity and need to be freed or ransomed.
(6) Those in debt (*garimin*): those who have incurred debts for a lawful cause and cannot repay them.

(7) Those in the cause of Allah (*fi sabilillah*): those engaged in activities that serve the religion and the community of Islam.
(8) The wayfarers (*ibn al-sabil*): those who are travelers or strangers in need of help or hospitality.

Sadaqah *(Voluntary Charity)*

Sadaqah is different from *zakah* in that it has no limitations and can be given easily. *Sadaqah* means using one's resources and abilities to achieve spiritual purification for a prosperous afterlife, by helping the poor, needy, orphans and the destitute, with the hope of reward from Allah (swt). The Qur'an states

> Indeed, those who believe and do righteous deeds and establish prayer and give zakah will have their reward with their Lord, and there will be no fear concerning them, nor will they grieve. (Al-Qur'an, 2: 277)

Bensaid et al. (2013) argue that the aim of giving charity is not only to purify one's soul and prepare for the afterlife but also to invest in socioeconomic development projects and positive social changes for a better world. Therefore, supporting farmers, funding the education for orphans, providing food, shelter and clothing, paying medical bills is a way of achieving success in this world and the hereafter.

Waqf

Waqf is a perpetual endowment for specific or general beneficiaries. *Waqf* is also defined as a "financial charitable act established by dedicating immovable and movable properties to continuously spend its revenue to fulfill public or family needs, based on the preferences and conditions set by the founder. The *waqf* property becomes inalienable once it is endowed. It belongs to Allah (swt), and the *waqf* property remains intact. Only its generated revenue is allocated to its beneficiaries" (Magda et al., 2016). A founder creates a *waqf* by assigning his properties to the *waqf* that will be managed by trustees according to trust rules. The rules specify how and when the benefit from the *waqf* asset can be distributed and to whom. For the duration of the assets' life, its benefit is assigned to the welfare of the nominated beneficiaries. *Waqf* has a significant historical impact on social transformation and empowerment. *Waqf* institutions are formal structures established through government policy or regulation, which have more impact than individual *waqf* contributions. Çizakça (2000) reports that *waqf* was well established during the Ottoman empire in the 15 and 16th century and replicated in several countries through the 19th century. He notes for example that agricultural *waqf* land comprises 50% of the land in Algeria, 30% in Tunisia (1883), and 12.5% in Egypt (1949). *Waqf* continues to contribute to East and West Africa. For example, the Towfiq Welfare Society (Somalia and Kenya) is a *waqf* center for education and health, supporting 20,000 orphans, students, and instructors, with a total of approximately 400,000 people benefitting. The High Authority of *waqf* (Senegal) is another *waqf* institution supporting 12,500 students in the Qur'anic schools to benefit (IsDB, 2019).

Qard Hasan

Qard hasan is a term for a benevolent loan in Islamic law, given to those who are in need without imposing interest and without demanding the repayment of the principal. The Qur'an has repeatedly urged this mode of lending and has portrayed it as a loan to the Almighty Allah (swt), implying that its reward is with Allah (swt) (see Al-Qur'an, 64:1; 2:245; 5:12; 73:20). *Qard hasan* is motivated by spiritual rather than monetary benefits. Iqbal and Shafiq (2015) argue that *qard hasan* is a feasible alternative to enhance financial inclusion for those who need financing but cannot access conventional microfinance due to lack of credit history or collateral. Successful application of the model can be assessed in practice through Akhuwat and Farz Foundation among others in Pakistan, or the BMT model in Indonesia. As a significant form of the Islamic social finance, these benevolent, interest free loans aim to achieve socioeconomic welfare for the vulnerable and needy segments of society, based on the principles and values of Islam. Therefore, its direct impact on social and economic issues can be substantial, addressing the issues of poverty, inequality, and indebtedness, as well as foster entrepreneurship and innovation.

Takaful

Takaful is a mode of funding that implies mutual support, joint brotherhood and cooperation. *Takaful* is derived from the Arabic verb "*kafala*" which means to guarantee or act as surety for another (Abdul Aziz & Mohamad, 2013). The *takaful* contract entails the parties agreeing to mutually protect each other when faced with events of loss. Contemporary *takaful* is used as an alternative to conventional insurance due to the latter's prohibition in the Islamic law. Therefore, *takaful* is a form of co-operative insurance where participants contribute to a "contingency" fund pool through a contribution known as *tabarru'* in the Islamic law. There are different structures used by *takaful* operators globally like *wakala waqf* model and *mudarabah* model. Contributions are determined based on participant risk and asset value, such that if any participant suffers loss as agreed in the participation contract, then he may claim from the fund. The fund is managed by professional administrators called "Takaful Operators." In practice, the agricultural industry, for example, experiences several disastrous events related to drought due to irregular rainfall, extreme temperatures, flooding, pests, and diseases. These events affect the quality and quantity of the crop production, influencing commodity prices. Therefore, *takaful* reduces the risk of default for farmers in the event of such losses. As a cooperative, the *takaful* will serve as a buffer in the weather events or loss scenarios. *Takaful* serves in the same way for the communities prone to humanitarian disaster. As a contingency against catastrophe, vulnerable communities are able to recover from disruptive events more quickly. In a recent national guide to *takaful* operators in Malaysia called "Value-based intermediation *takaful*" or VBIT, *takaful* is expected to be a contributor to financial resilience of the lower 40% income earners.

Islamic Social Finance: Challenges in Implementation

Zakah

Although *zakah* is considered one of the main classical instruments in the Islamic social finance space, *zakah* institutions confront numerous issues in various aspects of *zakah* management. According to Mahomed (2020), the following are the most significant issues in *zakah* management:

- Legal Issues: Lack of regulation, legal frameworks, or the enforcement of such legislation if they do exist.
- Awareness and knowledge: There is a general ignorance among Muslims about the concept, significance, method of distribution and platforms available for *zakah* distribution in most countries. Although countries like Indonesia, Kuwait and Malaysia are better equipped, most communities consider *zakah* to be limited to *zakah al-fitr*, the charity to be given before the *Eid* celebrations, and is usually only a few dollars.
- Transparency, credibility and traceability: Challenges in the audit of transactions between donor and *zakah* management institution are also evident.
- Low efficiency: In selected jurisdictions *zakah* institutions that are government managed have challenges in achieving quick turnaround times in collection, management and distribution. Mismanagement and corruption in *zakah* institutions is also prevalent due to weak oversight.
- Ambiguity on the identification of deserved recipients
- Difficulty in identifying donors
- Lack of the required skill and expertise (Shari'ah knowledge, fund management and investment and implementation of technological advancement) of *zakah* administrators.

Waqf

The prominence of *waqf* has diminished substantially since the contributions that the instrument made to the social empowerment in the Ottoman period. The contemporary *waqf* application faces several challenges, with only a few countries making some progress in its institutionalization. Even then, many challenges persist. A summary of the key issues in *waqf* management and administration is like *zakah* and can be summarized as follows:

- Regulation: Most countries lack comprehensive legislation and effective legal and regulatory frameworks governing *waqf*.

- Transparency: The transparency of *waqf* management and governance is absent in almost all jurisdictions globally. For countries that have effective regulation for charitable trusts, better governance is achieved. For the remainder, *waqf* is managed informally and often in closed circles of control, susceptible to mismanagement and moral hazards. For regions that manage *waqf* at state or national level, low transparency has led to a deficit of trust in the management of *waqf* (Sharip et al., 2019).
- Legal issues: There are often legal complexities associated with *waqf* management, including the registration and governance of *waqf* properties (Sulistyowati et al., 2022).
- Awareness and knowledge: There is a lack of awareness and understanding about *waqf*, its benefits, and its management among the general public and potential donors (Abd Jalil, 2020).
- Lack of funds: Many *waqf* institutions face financial constraints, which can hinder their operations and the realization of their objectives (Abd Jalil, 2020).
- Idle assets: A significant number of *waqf* assets are idle or underutilized, which means they are not generating any revenue or serving their intended purpose (Mahomed, 2017).
- Management inefficiencies: There are often inefficiencies in the management of *waqf* institutions, which can affect their performance and the delivery of their services (Mahomed, 2022a).
- Incomplete record data: Many *waqf* institutions do not have complete or accurate records of their assets, which can complicate their management (Mahomed et al., 2023).
- Illegal invasion: In some cases, *waqf* properties are illegally occupied, which can prevent them from being used for their intended purpose (Abd Jalil, 2020).
- Limited qualified personnel: There is often a shortage of qualified personnel to manage *waqf* institutions effectively (Mahomed, 2022a).

In addition to these points, it is important to note that the potential of the Islamic social finance and *waqf* is yet to be fully realized. With the right strategies and reforms, these instruments can play a pivotal role in addressing socioeconomic disparities and promoting sustainable development. This underscores the need for continuous research, policy dialog, and stakeholder engagement in this field.

Opportunities for Reform and Impact Maximization

Throughout history, welfare and charity strategies have continually adapted to various contexts, leveraging innovative methods and models to serve communities effectively and efficiently. The SDGs exemplify the development and growth objectives set by the global community.

Islam, through the embodiment of *maqasid al-Shari'ah* (Objectives of the Islamic Law), has consistently pursued impactful, welfare-focused policies that benefit the entire community, utilizing the instruments discussed earlier.

Historical evidence suggests that these policies' successful implementation has led to periods of prosperity in Islamic societies, where *zakah* funds remained unused, not due to mismanagement or inefficiency but because no eligible *zakah* recipients were left. The renowned commentator on the Qur'an, Ibn Kathir (2000), has documented that during the Ummayyad dynasty (661–750 CE), a system was maintained where staff were appointed and salaried to oversee the collection and distribution of *zakah*, which was limited to livestock. Ibrahim (2006) notes that it is challenging to find precise data regarding the amount of *zakah* collected and distributed during the classical Islamic era. Nevertheless, multiple reports indicate that *zakah* played a significant role in eliminating poverty in the region during the reign of Umar ibn Abdulaziz (Ahmed, 2004; Hudayati & Tohirin, 2010).

The opportunities in Islamic social finance are manifold:

(1) Transition from Needs-Based to Asset-Based Policies: Traditional welfare policies, as described by Winnick (1966) in Arefi (2004), focus on redistributing public resources to meet people's needs either directly through subsidies or indirectly through improving living conditions. However, these needs-based policies often lead to a culture of entitlement and over-reliance on external aid, thereby discouraging productivity and perpetuating poverty and income inequality. In contrast, asset-based policies, such as those proposed in the Asset-Based Community Development (ABCD) model, view the community as the greatest asset. By investing in the community's resources, abilities, skills, and experiences, these policies aim to achieve sustainable economic growth and social objectives, aligning with the principles of *waqf* and contributing toward the achievement of the SDGs.

(2) Correcting Misconceptions: There is a common misconception among Muslims today that *waqf* can only be used for the establishment of mosques, schools, or cemeteries. This misunderstanding has contributed to the decline of the *waqf* institution. It is crucial to correct this misperception and highlight that *waqf* is for the benefit of all and can be used to meet various community needs. In the case of *zakah* as well, the understanding of its obligatory nature, calculations and its differentiation from the *zakah* for *Eid* is crucial. Furthermore, the jurisprudence and understanding of Islamic social finance instruments is also evolving. For example, earlier misconceptions of *waqf* being limited to immovable property is changing, and cash *waqf* that is temporary and even revocable is offered by Islamic finance institutions (see Bank Muamalat Malaysia as an example). Productive *zakah* has always been frowned upon due to the limits of its direct ownership. Examples like the Jambi powerplant in Indonesia and Shaukat Khanam hospitals in Pakistan have applied this modality with success.

(3) Fintech opportunities for mobilizing and administering the Islamic social finance are boundless. For example,

- Social media platforms can serve as educational tools to enlighten individuals or groups about the significance of Islamic social finance instruments and their basic conditions, thereby fostering increased societal awareness.

- Blockchain technology, including smart contracts and distributed ledger technology, can offer a unified platform that brings together all stakeholders (i.e. the donors, recipient, government or private institutions and auditors). This technology can enhance the management efficiency and transparency of the instruments, addressing issues of mismanagement and corruption and bolstering the system's credibility. It can facilitate the digitization of *waqf* properties, securing of digital wallets for *zakah* and other charitable payments, ensuring their integrity and enabling usage tracking. Smart contracts can be employed to oversee commercial usage and leasing, as well as monitor long-term litigation.
- Mobile and web technologies can be utilized for cash *waqf* and *zakah* collection, allowing donors to track transactions.
- The adoption of cloud technology can significantly reduce capital expenditure for these institutions.
- Geographical information system (GIS) is one of the distinct features that may be exclusively employed in the context of *waqf* management. GIS is a computer-based tool that analyses, stores, manipulates and visualizes geographic information, usually on a map. GIS can be used to identify and understand the nature of the *waqf* property, which may help to bring about an efficient and economical utilization of the *waqf* properties under its management.

(4) The formation of specialized *waqf* and *zakah* institutions, each focused on a specific and narrow range of assets, could lead to more efficient governance and supervision through decentralization. This shift from a top-down to a bottom-up approach is likely to enhance welfare outcomes and community engagement.

The Case Studies of Islamic Social Finance Practice

Case Study 1: Baitul Maal wa Tamwil (BMT) – Indonesia

The history of BMT in Indonesia can be traced back to 1984 with the establishment of the Teknosa Cooperative at the Salman Mosque of the Bandung Institute of Technology (ITB) (Suseno, 2020). This cooperative provided financing for small businesses in accordance with Shari'ah principles. In 1988, another Shari'ah cooperative, the Ridho Gusti Cooperative, was established in Jakarta.

Two significant events marked the year 1992: the enactment of Law No. 25 on cooperatives, which established the legal standing of BMT, and the introduction of the first BMT, BMT Bina Insan Kamil. In 1995, the All-Indonesia Muslim Scholars Association (ICMI) initiated the establishment of the Center of Micro-Enterprise Incubation (PinBUK) to support the development of small and micro-businesses) (Suseno, 2020).

The development of BMT in the following years was marked by the promulgation of laws and regulations that impacted its operations, such as Law No. 21/2011 on the Financial Services Authority, Law No. 23 of 2011 on *zakat* Management, Law No. 1/2013 on Microfinance Institutions (MFIs), and Ministry of Cooperative and MSME Regulation No. 11 of 2017 on the implementation of Islamic Savings and Financing Cooperatives (KSPPS) by cooperatives.

BMT is considered a unique and holistic form of Islamic microfinance. Unlike Islamic microbanks that exclusively utilize financial intermediation, BMTs use a combination of financial and social intermediation in delivering services to micro, small and medium enterprises (MSMEs) and the poor.

BMT is constituted by two terms: Baitul Mal, which implies the nonprofit motive through managing *zakah*, *infaq*, *sadaqah*, and *waqf* funds, and Baitul Tamwil, which represents the profit motive in saving and financing activities. While Baitul Mal reflects social intermediary/empowerment, Baitul Tamwil is a form of financial intermediary. In addition to these two main roles, BMT also plays another role, that is, *da'wah*, through educating the community to conduct economic activities according to the Shari'ah rules.

As a social organization, BMT is permitted to distribute Islamic social funds received from *zakah*, contributions, and alms payments. In accordance with Article 16 Paragraph (1) of Law No. 23 of 2011 on *zakat* Management, BMT, through its Baitul Mal, can act as the *zakat* Collection Unit (UPZ) of the National Amil *zakat* Agency (BAZNAS), which engages in *zakah* management and assists BAZNAS in general.

Case Study 2: Akhuwat Foundation and the Use of Qard Hasan

The Akhuwat Foundation, a nongovernmental organization established in 2001, serves as a microfinancing initiative aimed at socioeconomic empowerment in Pakistan. The organization operates on principles derived from Islamic commercial law, providing interest-free benevolent loans, or *qard hasan*, to those in need. Funded by donations to an endowment established by the organization, Akhuwat has ensured its sustainability and the success of impoverished entrepreneurs and farmers requiring liquidity.

From its most recent Akhuwat Progress Report (2021), Akhuwat has over 800 branches across the country, has reached more than 5.4 million beneficiaries and disbursed approximately USD 650 million in interest-free microloans. In addition to financial services, the organization provides free education through its network of 301 schools and three colleges, benefiting over 47,000 students. Other areas of focus include healthcare, with nearly 600,000 patients of hepatitis and diabetes receiving treatment free of charge, a cloth bank that has collected over 3.2 million pieces of clothing for distribution, and socioeconomic inclusion initiatives for the Khwajasira or transgender community. Initiated in 2011, the Khwajasira Support Program provides financial assistance, health, and psychological support, among other services, to the community.

Borrowers are expected to pay a nominal administration fee for the loan application process. Loans, which range from PKR 10,000 to PKR 100,000 (approximately USD 35 to USD 350), are used for various purposes, including farming finance, debt repayment, education, marriage, and other emergencies. A notable achievement of Akhuwat is its recovery rate; according to its financial reports, the organization has consistently achieved recovery rates of 99% and higher. This unique approach to microfinance has inspired thousands of volunteers to assist those in need by providing access to Akhuwat financing and ensuring loan recovery.

During recent natural disasters, including floods that displaced millions and the COVID-19 pandemic that strained global healthcare systems, Akhuwat utilized an emergency relief fund to support victims. In addition to providing food hampers and clothing, they offered 34,000 small businesses interest-free loans from the fund, ensuring the basic needs of families were met.

Case Study 3: Malaysian Waqf in Healthcare

Malaysia boasts a robust Islamic social finance structure, driven by both state and federal governments (Hanefah et al., 2015). This structure leverages Islamic blended finance techniques, enabling Malaysian states to utilize Islamic social funding mechanisms to bolster affordable healthcare development within the country.

Several successful healthcare initiatives have been financed and operationalized through *waqf*. These include the An-Nur *Waqf* Clinic managed by Johor Corporation, a Hemodialysis Center, medical equipment for a healthcare center, and the Universiti Sains Islam Malaysia (USIM) Specialist Healthcare Clinic (Klinik Pakar Kesihatan USIM – KPKU), which was approved for operation in 2015 (Jawhar, 2018).

The following Table 7.1 provides an overview of Malaysian healthcare facilities funded through *Waqf* Social Finance:

Table 7.1. Malaysian Healthcare Facilities Funded Through Waqf Social Finance.

Malaysian State	Waqf Administrator	Waqf Management	Healthcare Type	Instrument
Perak	SIRC	Johor corporation	Hemodialysis center	Cash *Waqf*
Kelantan	SIRC	Kelantan SIRC	Medical equipment	Cash *Waqf*
Negeri Sembilan	SIRC	USIM/ KPKU	Specialist healthcare clinic	Cash *Waqf*

Source: Adapted from Ainol-Basirah and Siti-Nabiha (2020).

The primary instrument utilized for funding is the cash *waqf*, which is cash contributed as an endowment for social welfare. As per the requirements of *waqf* assets, cash endowments must be placed in principle-protected investments, with only the returns being distributed to beneficiaries (Mohsin, 2013). Cash *waqf* is regulated by both federal and state rules in Malaysia, as outlined in the Federal Constitution: Schedule Ninth, State List, List II, and falls under the responsibility of the State Islamic Religious Council (SIRC).

Case Study 4: Kenya Red Cross and Farmer Empowerment Through Zakah

In 2017, Kenya experienced one of its most severe droughts, affecting nearly 3 million people. A total of 23 counties out of 47 were affected, and the cost of maize – a staple food - had increased by over 30% (WWA, 2017). A national emergency was declared by the President in February 2017. In response, the International Federation of Red Cross and Red Crescent Societies (IFRC) collaborated with the Zakah Council of the Malaysian State of Perlis (MAIPS) to provide humanitarian assistance to some of those affected. MAIPS agreed to allocate *zakah* funding to support a drought relief program in Kitui County, Kenya, an area severely impacted by the drought.

The program began by identifying the affected area and its communities, ensuring that those in need met the criteria to qualify as *zakah* recipients. The intervention program aimed to use the funding effectively for land rehabilitation and planting, leading to a successful harvest and marketable crops. This empowerment program served as a pilot project to test the application of *zakah* in climate-related disasters.

The MAIPS made a significant contribution of approximately USD 1.2 million in *zakah* funds to a drought relief program. This decision was influenced by the established reputation and proven success of the International Federation of Red Cross and Red Crescent Societies (IFRC) and Kenya Red Cross in executing similar initiatives in the region. In a collaborative effort with the County Government of Kitui, the IFRC and Kenya Red Cross strategically utilized these funds to purchase seeds that were subsequently distributed to 175,000 households within the county. Each of these households received an allocation of approximately 2 kilograms of high-quality green gram seeds. The long-term plan for these seeds involved cultivating them and selling the yield directly to end buyers through a consolidated market, thereby creating a sustainable source of income for these households.

In addition to seed distribution, a portion of the funding was allocated toward the rehabilitation and installation of a total of 30 boreholes. This initiative was crucial in ensuring that these households had consistent access to water for irrigation purposes. This access to water not only facilitated the cultivation of the distributed seeds but also provided a vital resource for the households' daily needs.

Overall, the strategic use of *zakah* funds in this manner played a pivotal role in providing immediate relief to the drought-stricken region while also establishing a foundation for long-term socio-economic improvement.

Case Study 5: Waqf-Linked Sukuk

Historically, *waqf* and *sukuk* have individually played significant roles in promoting welfare within the Muslim community (Çizakça, 2014). Mahomed (2022b) documents how these two instruments have been integrated to form a Case Waqf-linked *sukuk* or CWLS: a financial tool that offers investors features akin to conventional fixed income securities, including potential tradability, rating, and principal guarantee whilst providing social impact.

The CWLS was structured based on a cash endowment provided by the *waqf* founders and stipulated through a *waqf* deed to be used for the expansion of the Ahmad Wardi Eye Hospital in Serang, Indonesia (Musari, 2016). Issued in 2020, the CWLS has profits generated from the utilization of these assets over a predetermined period, that are subsequently distributed to beneficiaries or allocated for welfare initiatives. At maturity, the cash *waqf* is either returned to the *Waqif* or transferred to a group of Trustees for management. The Indonesian Waqf Board (BWI) and Dompet Dhuafa Republika (DDR) were responsible for arranging the cash *waqf*.

This innovative combination of *waqf* and *sukuk* demonstrates the potential of the Islamic social finance to address critical societal needs, such as healthcare, while also offering attractive investment opportunities.

Case Study 6: Sukuk Prihatin Malaysia

Sukuk Prihatin is the first ever digital *sukuk* issued in Malaysia. It was initiated in September 2020 by the Malaysian government during COVID-19 pandemic, to enable Malaysians to participate and contribute to the rebuilding of the nation post-COVID-19. In its National Economic Recovery Plan (PENJANA), the government intended to raise RM500 million (approximately USD 120.2 million) in nominal value from the issuance (The Treasury of Malaysia, 2020).

The proceeds from *sukuk* Prihatin were channeled to the nation's COVID-19 fund (Kumpulan Wang) to finance measures announced in the economic stimulus packages and recovery plan to address the COVID-19 crisis. These measures include:

- Medical expenditure related to COVID-19.
- Supporting research grants for infectious diseases.
- Financing/grants for microenterprises especially women entrepreneurs.
- Enhancing broadband connectivity to schools especially in rural areas which serve as hubs for villages.

To the investors, the *sukuk* presents the opportunity to earn risk-free returns with possible tax incentives and support the nation's rebuilding post-COVID-19.

Concluding Remarks

Sustainable development embodies the concept of fulfilling current needs without jeopardizing the capacity of future generations to meet their own requirements. The realization of this vision is anchored in three core elements: economic growth, social inclusion, and environmental protection. Islamic finance principles align with this vision by promoting activities that are socially inclusive, environmentally conscious, and conducive to development.

As an economic system, Islamic finance champions the principles of risk-sharing, equitable wealth distribution, and fairness and justice in all transactions. Key Islamic social finance instruments such as *zakah, waqf* and *sadaqah* have been utilized extensively to assist the impoverished, at-risk, and destitute populations. These instruments have facilitated access to affordable housing, enhanced living standards, and provided improved healthcare and education opportunities.

It is evident that the fundamental instruments of Islamic finance, ranging from *zakah* and *waqf* donations to *takaful* (Islamic insurance) and *sukuk* (Islamic bonds), can be effectively channeled toward achieving the SDGs. Thus, the principles of Islamic finance, and the instruments through which they are operationalized, can play a pivotal role in realizing the UN SDGs globally. By improving the lives of individuals irrespective of their race, nationality, or faith, these principles and instruments contribute to building a more equitable and sustainable future for all.

References

Abd Jalil, M. I. (2020). Issues and challenges of waqf practice in Malaysia: A review. *Labuan e-Journal of Muamalat and Society*, *14*, 80–86. ISSN 1985-482X.

Abdul Aziz, A. F., & Mohamad, S. (2013). *Fulfillment of Maqasid al-Shariah via Takaful*. https://mpra.ub.uni-muenchen.de/id/eprint/47776

Abidin, I., & bin Omar, M. A. (1870). *Radd al-Mukhtar a'la al-Dur al-Mukhtar*. Dar al-Kutb al-A'ilmiyyah.

Ahmed, H. (2004). *Roles of Zakah and Awqaf in poverty alleviation*. Islamic Development Bank.

Ainol-Basirah, A. W., & Siti-Nabiha, A. K. (2020). The roles of Islamic social finance in the era of post-COVID-19: Possible prospects of waqf institutions for economic revival. *International Journal of Industrial Management*, *7*, 1–8.

Akhuwat Progress Report. (2021). https://akhuwat.edu.pk/year-wise-progress-report/

al-Kasani, A. (1983). *Bada'i al-Sana'i fi Tartib al-Shara'i* (Vol. 1). Dar al-Kutub al-Ilmiyyah.

Arefi, M. (2004). Neighborhood jump-starting: Los Angeles neighborhood initiative. *Cityscape*, 5–22.

Bensaid, B., Grine, F., Nor, M. R. M., & Mohd Yusoff, M. Y. Z. (2013). Ethico-spiritual dimensions of charity: An Islamic perspective. *Middle-East Journal of Scientific Research, 13*(13), 2.

Bin Lahuri, S. (2021). The role of zakat and waqf in sustainable development goals (SDGs). *Al-Bukhary Social Business Journal, 2*(1), 34–41.

Çizakça, M. (2000). *A history of philanthropic foundations: The Islamic world from the seventh century to the present* (pp. 2–10). Boğaziçi University Press.

Çizakça, M. (2014). Can there be innovation in Islamic finance? Case study: Esham. In *Paper to be presented at the 11th IFSB Summit, Knowledge Sharing Partner Session: "New Markets and Frontiers for Islamic Finance: Innovation and the Regulatory Perimeter"*, Mauritius, May 20.

Dariah, A. R., Salleh, M. S., & Shafiai, H. M. (2016). A new approach for sustainable development goals in Islamic perspective. *Procedia-Social and Behavioral Sciences, 219*, 159–166.

Hanefah, H. M. M., Jali, A., Ramli, A. M., Sabri, H., Nawal, N., & Shahwan, S. (2015). *Waqf models in Iskandar Malaysia: An analysis*. https://www.academia.edu/download/36874667/2010-usim-waqf-models-in-iskandar-malaysia-full-paper.pdf

Hassanuddin, H., Aziz, I., Rohana, R., Salwani, S., Arbaiah, A., Hakimin, H., & Afthanorhan, A. (2020). Modeling the social, economic and environmental effects of Pondok Tahfiz. *Management Science Letters, 10*(9), 1915–1922.

Hendratmi, A., Ryandono, M. N. H., & Sukmaningrum, P. S. (2020). Developing Islamic crowdfunding website platform for startup companies in Indonesia. *Journal of Islamic Marketing, 11*(5), 1041–1053.

Hudayati, A., & Tohirin, A. (2010). Management of zakah: Centralised vs decentralised approach. In *Paper presented at Seventh International Conference – The Tawhidi Epistemology: Zakat and Waqf Economy*, Bangi.

Ibn Kathir, I. (2000). *Tafsir al-Qur'an al-Azim* (Vol. 1). Darussalam.

Ibrahim, I. (2006). Zakah memartabatkan kecemerlangan ummah. In *South East Asia Zakah Conference.*

Islamic Development Bank (IsDB). (2019). Annual Report 2019. Islamic Development Bank.

Iqbal, Z., & Shafiq, B. (2015). Islamic finance and the role of Qard-al-Hassan (benevolent loans) in enhancing inclusion: A case study of AKHUWAT. *ACRN Oxford Journal of Finance and Risk Perspectives, 4*(4), 23–40.

Jawhar. (2018). Manual Panduan Pengurusan Wakaf Institut Pendidikan, Jabatan Wakaf Zakat dan Haji (JAWHAR).

Jouti Tahiri, N. (2019). Social finance ecosystem: A conceptual framework. *International Journal of Islamic and Middle Eastern Finance and Management, 12*(5), 696–714.

Lawal, I. M., & Ajayi, J. M. (2019). The role of Islamic social finance towards alleviating the humanitarian crisis in North-East Nigeria. *Jurnal Perspektif Pembiayaan dan Pembangunan Daerah, 6*(5), 545–558.

Magda, M. I., Dafterdar, H., Cizakca, M., Alhabshi, S. O., Razak, S. H., Sadr, S. K., Thamina, A., & Obaidullah, M. (2016). *Financing the development of old waqf properties: Classical principles and innovative practices around the world.* Palgrave Macmillan.

Mahomed, Z. (2017). *The Islamic social finance & investment imperative.* IF HUB, INCEIF University.

Mahomed, Z. (2020). *Islamic social finance module, executive masters in Islamic finance*. INCEIF University.

Mahomed, Z. (2022a). Modelling effective zakat management for the 'stans' of Central Asia and establishing pandemic resilience. In *Towards a post-Covid global financial system: Lessons in social responsibility from Islamic finance* (pp. 143–159). Emerald Publishing Limited.

Mahomed, Z. (2022b). Assessing financing for healthcare infrastructure in Sub-Saharan Africa: Can Islamic finance assist? In *Islamic finance in Africa* (pp. 167–192). Edward Elgar Publishing.

Mahomed, Z., Hamid, B. A., Salim, K., Ali, P., Nor, F. M., Johari, F., & Hassan, W. (2023). Case for a centralized database for waqf administration in Malaysia. *Prseztrzen Spoleczna (Social Space)*. https://www.scopus.com/record/display.uri?eid=2-s2.0-85171572249&origin=resultslist&sort=plf-f&src=s&sid=ccde6fa8ac4094c91a43b971e918ebc6&sot=b&sdt=b&s=TITLE-ABS-KEY%28Case+for+a+Centralized+Database+for+Waqf+Administration+in+Malaysia%29&sl=101&sessionSearchId=ccde6fa8ac4094c91a43b971e918ebc6

Mohsin, M. I. A. (2013). Financing through cash-waqf: a revitalization to finance different needs. *International Journal of Islamic and Middle Eastern finance and management*, *6*(4), 304–321.

Musari, K. (2016). Economic sustainability for Islamic nanofinance through waqf-sukuk linkage program (case study in Indonesia). *International Journal of Islamic Economics and Finance Studies*, *2*(3), 73–94.

OCHA, U. (2021). Content type. World Economic Situation and Prospects, 2021. https://www.un.org/development/desa/dpad/publication/world-economic-situation-and-prospects-2021/

Rahmawati, S., & Tanjung, H. (2015). *Design and determine holistic financial inclusion through Baitul Maal Wa Tamwil* (No. WP/6/2015). https://publication-bi.org/repec/idn/wpaper/WP062015.pdf

Sharip, S. M., Awang, M., & Ismail, R. (2019). Management effectiveness in waqf institutions in Malaysia: A literature review. *International Journal of Academic Research in Business and Social Sciences*, *9*(11), 254–271.

Sulistyowati, Sukmana, R., Ratnasari, R. T., Ascarya, & Widiastuti, T. (2022). Issues and challenges of waqf in providing healthcare resources. *Islamic Economic Studies*, *30*(1), 2–22. https://doi.org/10.1108/IES-09-2021-0034

Suseno, P. (2020). *Baitul Maal Wat Tamwil (BMT): A faith and community-based microfinance. Islamic business cases series*. National Committee of Islamic Economy and Finance (KenKs).

Treasury of Malaysia. (2020). Sukuk Prihatin knowledge pack. https://penjana.treasury.gov.my/pdf/gom-sukuk-prihatin-knowledge-pack.pdf

United Nations. (2023). *The Sustainable Development Report (2023)*. https://unstats.un.org/sdgs/report/2023/The-Sustainable-Development-Goals-Report-2023.pdf. Accessed on March 05, 2024.

World Weather Attribution Report. (2017). https://www.worldweatherattribution.org/kenya-drought-2016/. Accessed on November 12, 2023.

Chapter 8

Promoting Sustainable Development Through Islamic Social Finance

Alija Avdukić[a] *and Edib Smolo*[b]

[a]University of Dundee, UK
[b]Effat University, Saudi Arabia

Abstract

This chapter is about the role Islamic finance has been able to stay on the track of facing social–economical predicaments and on the way to sustainable development with the involvement of social prosperity. When trying to investigate the convergence between social finance and Islamic standards, what is argued is that a need for observing financial operations in the same way as prodevelopment theories arise. It is considered that in a holistic approach, which assumed a social justice as the basic ethic of the Islamic financial system, the final result tends to be more appropriate. One of the main elements that makes Islamic banking stand up in a high grade is maqasid al-Shari'ah due to its responsibility to assess social performance and apply new updated technologies for sustainable growth based on Sustainable Development Goals (SDGs). In addition to that, the situation is critically observed and the gap between ambitions functions and the reality in Islamic banking and finance is also pointed out to find some reconciliation between aspirations and facts. While its ancient foundations did point to the prospect of Islamic banking to serve as a major contributor to the social and economic development, the industry players of today have now been preoccupied with the profit-making objectives and financial performance rather than social banking. This chapter focuses on the role of Islamic finance as a breakthrough force and shows the way that this influence could shape the discussions of financial systems, so that economics follow, and ethical principles and become factors for the national economy to grow more robustness.

The Future of Islamic Finance, 121–139

doi:10.1108/978-1-83549-906-120241008

Keywords: Islamic economics; Islamic social finance; sustainable development; Maqasid al-Shari'ah; objectives of Shari'ah; Sustainable Development Goals (SDGs)

Introduction

With its foundation in ethical principles and incorporation within Islamic tenets, the field of Islamic finance has progressed into a highly auspicious financial model for resolving intricate socioeconomic dilemmas. The purpose of this section is to carry out probings in order to effect that in international development, Islamic finance being key provides a platform that aids sustainability while at the same time poverty reduction. The examination delves deeper into three fundamental components: for instance, the trio; Islamic finance, *takaful* (Islamic insurance), and the capital markets under which falls what is known as "Islamic social finance." It draws a curtain allowing the world to see and experience how firmly a diverse range of tools have been fashioned to answer the call of the everlasting specialized needs of the community, ways that are multifaceted in nature.

The financial mid-managers emerged in the 1990s that gave wings to diminishing economics as thus people from bottom to communal began to have access to funds. An important factor among these is the rise of social finance institutions – Islamic, which serves as a singular entity that collapses to raise community development funds. This principle then seems to be instrumental, which has been a progression with financial entities, based on the development theories that empower the unprivileged through increasing social capital, helping local capacity managed sustainable commercial enterprises and finally bridging the social and financial landscapes. In doing so, these financial entities contribute to the amelioration of individuals' lives, facilitating increased participation in processes propelling economic growth and development. Encompassed within the broader scope of the sustainable development agenda, the World Bank has actively championed this paradigm of microeconomic development. Herein, projects are conceptualized with beneficiaries engaging in decision-making processes and fund management (Mansuri & Rao, 2004; Sairally, 2007). All in all, the anticipation is that these endeavors will fortify social, economic, and environmental progress, concurrently diminishing poverty in developing nations.

In relation to the Islamic financial system, there is no single definition. Islam simply stipulates that any Muslim must live according to the Shari'ah, that is, according to the concepts of equality, social justice, and fairness. In other words, the Shari'ah specifies what is or is not acceptable, in terms of behavior, in Muslim life. This includes, at least partially, economic and commercial activity. The Islamic financial system, according to the ethics of Islam, is based on two principles: the prohibition of earning interest and the social responsibility of investment (Haneef, 1997).

This chapter establishes a nexus between social finance and Islamic principles, particularly delving into the robust emphasis on social development and human well-being within the Islamic worldview. The advent of distinctly Islamic approaches to finance aligned with prodevelopment ideologies and the discourse surrounding the moral economy in Islam accurately mirrors the essence of community development. Unfortunately, instances of practical application in Islamic banking reveal a predilection for financial gains at the expense of community development, underscoring a deficiency in prioritizing the latter. As posited by Asutay (2007, 2012), the ascent of Islamic financial institutions (IFIs) and the evolution of financing methods have failed to exert a discernible impact on the lives of Muslims. El-Gamal (2006) and Asutay (2012) address the most problematical issue characteristic of the existing Islamic financial system, namely, the lack of social justice and the fact that the socio-economic matter is impervious to the substructuring processes. This chapter targets to cautiously distribute the social fund based on Islamic moral economy with the view to superimposing sustainable development credentials formulated by the World Bank. Key aspects are in building connections between Muslim communities and also the enabling of economic development through a study on the social sphere present in the finance industry. The main focus of this task is the examination of the authorizing component of this operation, as it requires to be conducted at the same moment in a harmony balance between the profit and the rules which are deeply inscribed in Islamic values. Consequently, this kind of financial institutions are supposed to balance between the profitability and the ethics of Islamic religion. At the same time, that also lies within the fundamental values of their social mission. Hence, via this synergistic integration of the mentioned fundamental elements, our target is to establish equally sustainable financial architectures that not only manage to stay relevant economic institutions but also profoundly touch the societies' improvement and the implementation of the sustainable development goals.

Islamic Moral Economy and Sustainability

A brick in the fabric of Muslim civilization since its inception in seventh century AD is the concept of moral economy, which equivalates the sensibility of society and notions of the right and the wrong to money gaining. The ethics of Islamic moral economy greatly emphasis on the conduct of oneself, justice, and well-being of all humans which have been the source of sustainable development for the society even ranging far back as the origin of sustainable development.

In line with the Islamic moral economy, commandments regarding the economic affairs and relationships are found in Qur'an and the Hadith, and they give a way how economy should be run. For instance, the Qur'an considers as a sin the charging or payment of interest (*riba*) as well as any endeavor that entails unpredictability (*gharar*). At the same time, we have the Qur'an sanctioning zakat (a sort of religious tax or charity) and consequently the fairness and legitimacy of trade (Mirakhor & Askari, 2010; Smolo, 2013). The era of Prophet Muhammad (pbuh) Arab world is the pursuit of morality in the Muslim world become more marked. This in a nutshell covers the basics of the Islamic paradigm in which ethics are applied as hallmarks in business transactions. Ethical and moral elements of classical Islamic societies gave birth to the emergence of a unique economic system. The *awqaf* (pl. of *waqf*) that was a distinct institution aimed for the use of money and resources for the public good. *Hisbah* (market regulation) was an essential institution in which the market was actively regulated using an ethical approach. The *bayt al-mal* (public treasury) was created to serve the interests of the community by promoting the equitable distribution of wealth. All of this represents an early model of sustainability.

While this can be exemplified via the *waqf* system as this played the pivotal role in attainment of social sustainability through provision of a civic-society welfare system (Ahmad, 2015; Haneef, 2018; Lamido & Haneef, 2021; Qurrata et al., 2021). Social services like health, education, among others were funded by it, as people in the end benefited (Khan, 2015). Interestingly, *waqf* system ensured that economy was fair by providing opportunities for the poor. Also, to *waqf* the social justice was a key premise of sustainability (Abdullah, 2018; Kuanova et al., 2021). As such, Haneef (2018) considers the *waqf* as "the 'third' or voluntary sector of the economy."

The concept of *hisba*, involving market practice regulation and ensuring product quality, furthered economic sustainability. The *muhtasib*, a market inspector, ensured ethical trading practices, prevented exploitation, and upheld consumer rights, fostering a fair and transparent market system (Hussain et al., 2019).

Throughout history, the Islamic moral economy faced numerous challenges, especially with the advent of colonialism and modern capitalism. Nevertheless, the revival of the Islamic finance system in the 20th century highlighted the tendency to reassert the Islamic moral economy. Islamic banking and finance, set according to Shari'ah-originated regulations, has got lots of attention worldwide. On the Islamic finance, some of the significant pillars which include the sharing of risk and also prohibition of interest and also ethical investment fall in line with the financial prudence.

In the recent period, there is a pinpoint rise in the debate on bringing Islamic moral economy type ideas in line with the sustainability goals. One significant aspect is the introduction of the Islamic social finance tools such as *zakat*, *sadaqah* (charity by choice), and *qard hasan* (benevolent loan), which are part of the ongoing modern sustainable efforts like "green *sukuk*" (Islamic bonds for green projects). The "tool" in question has many areas of United Nations (UN) SDGs which gained its extensive use by focusing on issues such as social inclusion, economic growth, and environmental sustainability.

Local resource itself implies that Islamic financial services are the driving agent in this process. It is steadily significant to enhance the area of Islamic finance as about bond and share markets. It can encourage the availability of local resources for the development of the nation. The *sukuk* might be the main fundraising and investing instruments that the market is using (Azman et al., 2022; Marwan et al., 2022; Marwan & Haneef, 2019). A well thought approach to credit facility's aspects in line with Islamic finance creates a leeway that can be used to develop massive public projects with particular focus on infrastructure development. In effect, Islamic finance can be inserted into the business environment by combining it with a pragmatic approach of the fintech solutions of the present day, and in the process, address burning issues of the moment.

In this manner, Islamic banking assures its clients of ethical and socially responsible investments (SRIs), explicitly excluding interest-based loans, deemed usury (*riba*), as well as steering clear of risk (*gharar*), speculation (*maysir*), unethical investments (such as tobacco, weapons, pornography, casinos, and gambling), and those prohibited by Islamic tenets (such as pork and alcohol). Furthermore, the Shari'ah has laid down a framework that precisely delineates legal and contractual relationships in commercial dealings. To align with Islamic legality, both Islamic banks and the Islamic subsidiaries of conventional banks have devised legal-financial mechanisms. These mechanisms hinge on concepts like *mudarabah, musharakah, murabahah, ijarah, sukuk*, and *istisna'*. The auspicious potential of Islamic finance extends beyond the purview of Muslim institutions (Iqbal & Mirakhor, 2007; Smolo, 2013).

Many conventional banks now provide Islamic services and products, with the expectation that the expansion of these services in the future will offer investors, whether Muslim or not, a broader array of options and opportunities. This expansion aims to facilitate financing for commercial and real estate projects. While creating Shari'ah-compliant financial products for Muslim investors, the industry's proponents essentially replace conventional financial terminology with specific terminology. Through adept financial engineering, Islamic banking has successfully identified substitutes in line with Islamic principles for all types of investment instruments, ranging from the safest to the most speculative, effectively rendering *non-halalizable* options *halal* (Smolo & Musa, 2020).

The Islamic financial sector is a lucrative market that uses these techniques to achieve the same performance as traditional banking. However, the services of an Islamic institution are not meant only for Muslims. In this regard, Islamic banking is part of the new trend of ethical investment funds and socially responsible financing. An Islamic bank must not only abide by the secular laws of the country in which it operates but must also conform to the precepts of Islamic law.

Embracing collaborative financial endeavors, Islamic banking institutions, akin to their Western counterparts in venture capital, will facilitate the realization of innovative ventures or those harboring substantial developmental prospects, thereby engendering the creation of myriad employment opportunities. For adherent investors, the SRI methodology aligns with a governance deeply intertwined with religious principles encapsulating its "business ethics," delineating distinctive perspectives (Kuanova et al., 2021).

Microcredits play a crucial role for individuals who are venturing into the business realm. While conventional banks typically remain detached from microfinance, the same is often true for most Islamic banks. Nonetheless, an Islamic enterprise should stand out through its commitment to the social facet of its operations. According to Yunus, showcasing the societal role of Islamic banks involves channeling funds, via microfinance, into endeavors undertaken by the most marginalized, aiming to elevate their income and prosperity, thereby contributing to overall development. Through the financing of micro-enterprises, Islamic banks can diversify their clientele, especially given their surplus liquidity resulting from a scarcity of products adhering to Islamic principles, compounded by competitive forces (Abdul Rahman, 2010; Al Breiki & Nobanee, 2019; Begum et al., 2019).

The Ethical and Socio-economic Foundations of Islamic Finance

The discourse on Islamic economics propels the field's societal aspirations, underscoring socioeconomic objectives encompassing equality, social justice, poverty alleviation, and human well-being. A succinct overview of the socio-economic goals within the Islamic economic system, as delineated by a prominent Islamic economists (Al-Sadr, 1961; Al-Tahawi, 1974; Chapra, 1970; Kahf, 1973; Naqvi, 1978; Qutb, 1953; Siddiqi, 1981), unfolds as follows:

- *The Promotion of Economic Well-being:* Focusing on enhancing the overall economic prosperity.
- *The Attainment of Sufficiency and Peace:* Striving for self-sufficiency, tranquility, and the elimination of hunger and fear within society.
- *Fulfillment of Basic Human Needs:* Ensuring the satisfaction of fundamental human requirements.
- *TheProvision of Ease and Convenience in Life:* Optimizing the utilization of natural resources to facilitate a convenient and comfortable life.
- *The Fulfillment of Spiritual Needs:* Addressing the spiritual dimensions of individuals.
- *Establishment of Economic and Social Justice:* Advocating for justice, equality of opportunity, and collaboration within the economic and social framework.
- *Promotion of Universal Brotherhood and Justice:* Encouraging equitable income distribution, individual freedom, and justice while operating within the framework of social welfare.

Maqasid al-Shari'ah, providing a framework cantered around the concept of human well-being and its progression, is consistently invoked with the intention of realizing specific objectives. It serves as a foundational structure for evaluating the social performance of Islamic banks. Anchored in Islamic finance, *maqasid al-Shari'ah* empowers the sector to play a pivotal role in advancing the SDGs and fostering global economic and social justice. In the contemporary landscape, the successful implementation of sustainable finance aligned with the SDGs and *maqasid al-Shari'ah* critically relies on embracing technology-based solutions. This approach facilitates the targeted allocation of financial resources to high-impact economic segments, enhancing nations' ability to achieve financial inclusion more efficiently and effectively.

Early Islamic economics literature ascribed a socially responsible duty to members of society, emphasizing the collective pursuit of socio-economic goals. Both Muslim individuals and IFIs are obligated to operate in the public interest (*maslahah*) and uphold the common good. In stark contrast to the *homo economicus* principle found in neo-classical literature, where actions are guided by self-interest, individuals guided by Islamic philosophy and morality are expected to exemplify traits such as charity, humanism, and social responsibility. Consequently, they are identified as *homo islamicus* (Arif, 1989; Asutay, 2007; Hanic & Smolo, 2023; Smolo, 2013).

The ethical principles of unity (*tawhid*), equilibrium (*al-adl wa'l-ihsan*), free will (*ikhtiyar*), and responsibility (*fard*), along with philosophical notions regarding human accountability before God and man's role as a vicegerent (*khalifah*) on Earth, are posited as forces that temper self-interested behavior. These principles not only encourage the prudent use of scarce resources but also promote environmental conservation and the fulfillment of social obligations (Ahmad, 1980; Chapra, 1992, 2008; Naqvi, 1978, 1981, 1994).

Moreover, Islamic financial methodologies are touted for their inherent proclivity toward expansion and development. This stems from their facilitation of real and asset-backed transactions, nurturing entrepreneurial endeavors, renouncing interest, speculative practices, and gambling. They actively champion productive businesses that contribute to humanity's welfare and advocate for a culture of prudent risk-taking. These principles play a pivotal role in both positive and negative screening of investments, considering quantitative metrics such as debt levels, the ratio of cash and interest-bearing securities to assets, the proportion of interest-bearing assets generated by a company, and the ratio of accounts receivable to assets. This evaluation extends to the fundamental activities of the business (Sairally, 2007).

Islamic Banking and Finance Between Aspirations and Realities

Within the realms of Islamic economics, banking, and finance literature, the profit and loss sharing mechanisms of *mudarabah* and *musharakah* take center stage, emphasized for their robust economic appeal (Asutay, 2007; Chapra, 1985; Khan, 1989; Mergaliyev et al., 2021; Mirakhor & Smolo, 2012; Siddiqi, 1981, 1985, 2000; Tag El-Din, 2007). As argued by Mirakhor and Smolo (2012, 2014), ideal Islamic finance envisions a comprehensive range of instruments within an Islamic economy, governed by institutional guidelines set by Allah (swt) and operationalized by the Prophet (pbuh), including market behavior rules prescribed by Islam. This spectrum's fundamental purpose is to distribute and allocate risk across market participants, preventing concentration within the borrowing class. Islam introduces three categories of risk-sharing instruments: (i) *mu'amalat* risk-sharing tools in the financial sector; (ii) redistributive risk-sharing instruments employed by the economically more privileged to share risks with the less fortunate; and (iii) inheritance regulations from the Qur'an, guiding the equitable distribution of an individual's wealth among current and future generations of inheritors. Additionally, the foundational concepts of *waqf*, *sadaqah*, and *zakah* are perceived as integral to advancing the well-being of Muslim communities.

In contrast to the literature's endorsement of profit-and-loss sharing arrangements, there has been a notable bias toward *murabahah* and short-term trade-based financing transactions in the portfolios of Islamic banks. Furthermore, it's crucial to highlight that the original Islamic contract modes are bilateral, tied to the real economy. Nonetheless, modern Islamic finance has succeeded in (i) transforming bilateral contracts from the real sector to the finance sector, making them multilateral, and (ii) adapting conventional finance risk transfer instruments to align with Shari'ah principles (Mirakhor & Smolo, 2012, 2014).

This preference has sparked numerous disputes in the realm of Islamic finance. Critics argue that Islamic banks, in certain instances, mimic conventional finance by implementing interest-like fixed return instruments (Warde, 2000, p. 240). They also note the selection of financial products closely resembling conventional counterparts while sidestepping equity standards considered problematic by Islamic jurists (El-Gamal, 2005). Additionally, concerns have been raised about the allocation of financial resources to consumption channels rather than production (Hasan, 2005) and the direction of Islamic finance toward contributing to the growth of money, fostering consumer indebtedness rather than linking financial services to the real and productive sector (Asutay, 2007, 2012).

Dusuki (2005) argues that the overuse of fixed return modes has cast doubt on the Islamic credentials of Islamic banking and finance, viewing it as a mere gimmick since the goods and services provided by IFIs mirror those of their conventional counterparts. Critics assert that, akin to conventional banks, Islamic banks predominantly prioritize profit, raising questions about their social obligation to support the growth of Muslim communities. Moreover, it is suggested that the simple substitution of alternative fixed-return financing options for *riba* indicates an implicit risk aversion, undermining their social identity rather than demonstrating a robust commitment to socioeconomic development.

As for social finance, the prevailing belief is that Islamic finance has veered off course from its initial aspiration to institutionalize a state-of-the-art financial system that would uplift the Islamic world both socially and economically. This deviation is attributed to the failure of Islamic finance to cultivate more risk-sharing mechanisms, instead opting for interest-like fixed return instruments reminiscent of conventional financial models (Asutay, 2012; Warde, 2000). The discrepancy between the pledged objectives and the actual performance, commonly referred to as the "gap between promise and performance" (Warde, 2000), has been extensively discussed by Islamic economists such as Siddiqi (2004), Hasan (2005), El-Gamal (2006), Asutay (2007), and Smolo and Musa (2020). They perceive it as a divergence between the literature on Islamic economics and the practical applications of Islamic finance, representing the operational facet of the Islamic economic system. Siddiqi (2004) and El-Gamal (2006) fortify these arguments by underscoring how Islamic banks have prioritized economic and financial efficiency, or financial engineering, over social engineering and sustainable development, driven by social objectives.

In recent years, critiques of Islamic financial products and services have grown significantly, with some scholars questioning their Islamic authenticity (Mansoori, 2011a, 2011b). Critics argue that these products often prioritize form over substance, citing examples like *bay' bithaman ajil* (BBA – differed payment sale) and *tawarruq munazzam* (organized monetization) as instances rooted in *hilah*, a technique to avoid direct involvement in usurious transactions. This approach seems to be more of a camouflage for usury than a lawful alternative (Smolo & Musa, 2020). Ahmed (2011), addressing this controversy in relation to the theory of *maqasid al-Shari'ah* (objerctives of Islamic law), categorizes Islamic banking products into three groups: (i) pseudo-Islamic products using *hilah*; (ii) Shari'ah-compliant products meeting both form and substance criteria but neglecting social interests (*maslahah*); and (iii) Shari'ah-based products meeting all requirements, including form, substance, and public interests.

The initial stage of establishing Islamic banks (Warde, 2000), the intricate operational environment where their survival hinges on effective competition with conventional banks (Haron & Kamaruddin, 2005), and the myriad challenges they face related to legal and regulatory frameworks, political and economic conditions, and insufficient human resources are commonly cited reasons for Islamic banks tending to neglect socioeconomic concerns. Hasan (2004) specifically points out numerous misconceptions surrounding Islamic banks and their insufficient operational structure. He contends that Islamic banks have predominantly emulated commercial banks but lack the necessary framework, capability, environment, and staff to meet expectations. Finally, it depends on whether they can handle the funding of opportunities, come up with enduring ventures that involve uncertainties, and meet the community demands of better socioeconomic development.

As a result, the implication between Islamic banks and conventional commercial banks remains clearer by the comparison of the two banking modes of the Islamic banks and their commercial counterpart Asutay (2007). In the view puts Asutay a practical stance toward the Islamic finance which he terms as managing direct response to variety of financial markets. In the marketplaces, financial products are becoming diversified. Most of the time, the products subordinate values with the economic incentives penalizing people who have religious beliefs as the behavioral norms. Within this context, Islamic banks are, in a sense, forced to adopt what Asutay defines as the "second-best solution." This strategic compromise is a must for their survival and their firm integration into the global financial system which is not at all stiff. Facing this level of challenge, Islamic banks, however, are very smart as the comply Islamic principles and at the same time fulfill the demand of the market which forces them to redesign their structures in such a manner that they are now of the same models or structures as those of commercial banks. This adjustment is a response to the actual environment where the banking institutions face the challenging task to do the right thing and the globally harmonious integration.

First and foremost, as part of the list of articles dealing with Islamic economics, some authors assign IFIs the role of carrying out socially responsible activities, recommending for them to be universal banks that help to foster socioeconomic development of the entire society (Al-Zuhayli, 2003; Asutay, 2007, 2012; Chapra, 1985; Hasan, 2004; Mergaliyev et al., 2021; Siddiqi, 1983; Warde, 2000). Many within the Muslim community perceive Islamic banking and finance as inherently a social business, with the expectation that Islamic banks actively contribute to growth in a socially conscientious manner (Yusuf & Bahari, 2015). The historical roots of Islamic banking and finance trace back to the 1960s, showcasing its early experiments and foreshadowing its pivotal role in socioeconomic growth (Kahf, 2007).

For instance, Tabung Haji Malaysia commenced operations in 1962, with a dual mission of aiding Muslims in Malaysia in saving for the *hajj* pilgrimage and offering opportunities for active participation in high-profile investment activities across industries, services, plantations, real estate, and property. This groundbreaking initiative not only highlighted the moral and traditional facets of Islamic banking and finance but also proposed a community banking model, showcasing its potential to fortify regional economies and benefit local populations. The establishment of Mit Ghamr savings houses (1963–1967) in Egypt, modeled after the German Savings and Loans system but grounded in Islamic principles, further solidified the notion of social and communal banking (Lewis & Algaoud, 2001).

In 1971, the Nasser Social Bank emerged as a social lending organization, providing support to the underprivileged and destitute, while simultaneously funding students and small-business owners – a noteworthy advancement in the sector's development. The pivotal establishment of the Islamic Development Bank (IsDB) in 1973 marked another significant milestone, playing a pivotal role in assisting member nations within the Organization of Islamic Cooperation (OIC) with funding development projects.

Despite Islamic banking's early practices and Islamic economic theory's emphasis on economic growth, the prevailing consensus is that Islamic banks should be more involved in community development. It is argued that the modeling of Islamic banking and finance has shifted the focus from social banking to profit-and-loss sharing and profit motivation. This shift is observed in the prioritization of tasks such as financial engineering, efficiency building, product creation, viability, and profitability. If a social function is supported, it is often relegated to the periphery of the institution's broader operations.

From an Idea to a Global Trend

The financial industry is multicultural. If, in the West, we could speak of ethical banking as the "third way," the Muslim world has found a way to develop a financial system in accordance with their beliefs and based on the governing principles of their religion. Perhaps the name "Islamic finance" is a misnomer. Kahf (2003) critically examines various definitions of Islamic economics and finance. He attempts to establish a connection between these definitions while expressing concern about the excessive use of the prefix "Islamic," as seen in terms like "Islamic economics" or "Islamic finance." Kahf argues that such usage goes against the universal message of Islam and restricts the scope of scientific endeavors. As a positive example, he highlights Ibn-Khaldun's definition of *"'ilm al-'umran al-bashari wa-l-ijtima' al-insani,"* the science of mankind's civilization and human socialization. Notably, Ibn-Khaldun refrains from using the prefix "Islamic" to avoid limiting this science solely to Islamic society and Muslims. In doing so, Ibn-Khaldun aims to prevent this science from being considered non-Islamic. In contrast, modern writers frequently add the "Islamic" prefix, a practice that, according to Kahf, falls short of capturing the true Islamic essence as demonstrated by Ibn-Khaldun (Kahf, 2003, pp. 12–13).

Consequently, talking about "Islamic ethics in economics" would be convenient because it is ethics that is concerned in the first place. However, the ethical approach to investments, which is currently lacking, is not exclusive to religion. The sense of equity, the redistribution of wealth (principle of *zakat* in Islam) and enrichment through productive capital exclusively drawn from legitimate trade are universal ethical principles before being Islamic.

These principles permeate through all religious and humanist traditions, serving as a potential wellspring of inspiration for the financial realm. The thriving Islamic financial sector holds immense potential in fostering the establishment of an equitable economic system that upholds environmental values and actively engages in social development. This aside, perhaps there is an extra challenge with complexity, yet without doubt, we should not allow the heavy shadows of the aforesaid to obscure the real, concrete issues.

The Islamic financial administrative area, which is commonly inadequately understood when compared with the conventional counterpart, has been consolidating its territory extensively in the last few decades. However, its maintain position of an outsider, taking a very small percentage of the world finance market, it is the last several years are characterized by its dramatic growth. Leaving behind the limited finds in designated geographical zones and a restricted range of items specifically for Muslim practicing, this sector went into a journey that was great in scope, very unlike any before. This learning includes acquiring new instruments through the principle of financial innovations recently-made. In Islam, tangible demarcation of religion from citizens' existent and secular lives is not traceable. Intertwining with the faith values, the economy becomes an underlying force shaping people's behavior in terms of a savvy way of expenditure. With the growing population of Muslims worldwide in an incomparable manner, it is the increase in the products' demand. They simply require the items that comply with their persona (Atıf et al., 2021; DinarStandard, 2023; IFSB, 2023).

Islamic financial which is demonstrated that a new financial system which relies on noninterest revenue is viable in economics but it has a real and practical significance in a sense that it offers an alternative for conventional financial as operational model. This paradigm shift, therefore, puts into question the current prevailing concepts on profitability in the financial industry that embodies ethical finance and Islamic banking. Through its expansion, Islamic finance recognizes itself as the solution of sustainable and efficient financial operations which by indicate not only the feasible ability of the system with zero interest as the main revenue stream, but it also turns out to be quite desirable substitute that works effectively, likable and ethically. This will have an impact on debates around financial systems, enabling people to see that the system is not merely a tool that meets economic ends. However, it can be a guide to ensure financial sustainability alongside ethical principles. This modernization project provides Islamic finance with a chance of becoming an innovative example for reassessing old concepts and redefining accepted rules, which then sets the beginning of a new era for the main financial sector.

Major sectors, playing decisive roles, are vital to the mobile path followed by the financial sector developed in Islamic tradition. A kind of banking and *sukuk* market controling in the Middle East, Southeast Asia and the United Kingdom have replaced their traditional market. The expansion of these places, plus take volumes in investment funds and insurance companies, promises the estate of long-lasting development not only in their traditional base but also in western nations (DinarStandard, 2023; IFSB, 2023). The Islamic banking founded on the Shari'ah principles operates as a financial system that runs in tune with ethical values sought by the whole world's assortment of people who value sincerity. Simultaneously, the market of *sukuk* (Islamic securitization bonds) has come to the spotlight as one of the supportive roles in ethical investment and debt rearrangement. The expansion of these financial products into the West testifies that historically, these financial instruments are considered adequate tools for a multifaceted portfolio construction. However, the development of financial products, namely the funds and insurance, is also important. As these segments develop and reach full maturity, not only will their impact enhance the cult's overall resilience but will also open up opportunities for its expansion in the West as well. In addition to the ethical choices that are created as a result of the diversification of Islamic financial instruments, financial inclusion which is one of the established principles of this model of finance is a critical factor for the extension of its global reach. Consequently, the development and expansion of Islamic finance will be heavily dependent on these leading sectors and the strategic significance of their performance in the process improving or making the impact more relevant at the global level.

While there is still a considerable distance to cover, it is not unexpected that this financial business model will soon penetrate Latin America. Achieving these goals is crucial for the development of international regulations that provide security through universally accepted standards. These standards should serve as a guide for all market operators, indicating the next steps to foster the growth of this sector. Thus, Islamic finance is poised to reach a comparable standing with its Western counterparts in the latter half of this century. Regulatory authorities and global financial markets increasingly accommodate this model, taking measures to avoid exclusion from the tangible and potential benefits that Islamic philosophy, applied to banking, can bring to the financial industry model. It is indisputable that Islam is one of the major religions globally. Unfortunately, some of the worst atrocities are wrongly committed in its name. Setting aside fanatical-criminal episodes related to finances, Islam encompasses a set of distinct principles (Kuanova et al., 2021).

The Tools of Islamic Sustainable Development

Islamic finance and sustainable investment both share the objective of creating a positive social and environmental impact through financial activities. The principles guiding sustainable finance stem from the Qur'an, where Allah allegedly forbids usury (*riba*) enrichment, emphasizing the legitimacy of *halal* investments that exclude controversial sectors like weapons, drugs, and gambling. In Islamic finance, sustainable investments are assessed for their risk absence (*gharar*) and must serve a recognizable practical purpose, such as financing public works. These principles, along with the rejection of speculation and betting in traditional "shadow finance" based on the Islamic principle of *maysir*, form a holistic approach. Islamic finance further aligns with the concept of almsgiving (*zakat*), with a percentage of annual profits devoted to charity.

Sukuk serves as a tangible embodiment of these principles, functioning as participation certificates representing undivided ownership shares in a total asset comprised tangible assets – commonly referred to as "asset-backed securities." *Sukuk*, essentially targeted financing securities for specific projects, facilitate the attraction of capital from Islamic countries to Western financial shores. This convergence aims to unite development and sustainability by applying Islamic finance principles to projects with significant ESG impact, such as those in renewable energies, social housing, sustainable infrastructures, and digitization. Notably, investments in these areas often originate from countries like Malaysia and the United Arab Emirates.

Islamic finance has the potential to catalyze novel and profound economic relations, positioning Rome as a hub in the Mediterranean, toward North Africa, strengthening ties with the Gulf, and looking toward deep Asia, including the ex-Soviet Muslim republics eager to align with global trends. Uniquely, the synergy between sustainability and finance can also adopt an Islamic version, steering clear of controversial figures in countries where Islam is prevalent.

As stated by Atıf et al. (2021), the Islamic perspective on sustainable development is deeply ingrained in the fundamental teachings of the religion. Islamic principles uphold an environmental ethics that designates humans as stewards (*khalifah*) of the Earth, entrusted with its care and preservation. The Holy Qur'an (6:165) underscores this role, proclaiming, "*It is He who has appointed you khalifah on the Earth,*" forming the basis for a distinctive approach to sustainable development within Islamic thought (Biancone & Radwan, 2019).

Central to the Islamic worldview is the concept of *tawhid*, emphasizing the unity of God and recognizing the interconnectedness of all elements of creation. This principle by nature provides the opportunity of a generalized approach to the concept of sustainable development in the light of a balance between the pursuits of individual, community and environment's well-being. Therefore, it becomes one of the spiritual forces for environmental/social conscience that goes beyond economic and material views (Alkaabi & Nobanee, 2019; Hanic & Smolo, 2023; Naqvi, 1978).

Moreover, the Islamic ideas of *maslahah* (public interest) and *israf* (wastefulness) and *mufsid* (corruption) are exemplary of the rest of sustainable development. Sustainability ideology in these traditional cultures is based on the principles of resource conservation and mutual benefits, and the above system models are built on the principle of coexistence of man and nature (Chang et al., 2019).

The *maqasid al-Shari'ah* show the ethical framework for the sustainable Islamic developments through maintenance of religion, life, intellect, lineage, and property which are all encompassing for the existence of a sustainable society. Therefore, further economic measures and policies, that fall under this approach, have an obligation to protect these basic human requirements (Khan, 2019).

Thus, according to these principles, some barriers impede implementation of Islamic sustainable development in Muslim-populated countries. The principles are frequently transmitted via culture, socioeconomics and politics and this can see to the delay in putting these ideals into policies. Therefore, putting in place sustainable policies, governance, education and awareness are required to be moved toward the realization of the principles of Islamic sustainable development (Harahap et al., 2023).

Muslim-minority countries' level of case studies serve as the evidence of possibly tremendous influences of Islamic sustainable development. For instance, in Malaysia, the *waqf* (endowment) principle as Islam divides this to protect nature and biodiversity reserves. Indonesia too has introduced game changer "green *sukuk*" or Islamic bonds for ecosystem friendly projects helped by two sides of a coin of Islamic finance and sustainability.

Consequently, Islamic sustainable development means a combination substantially different in nature from the traditional Western secular concepts which present as a superior model of sustainable development. Through an intricate web it embraces the spiritual, environmental, social and economic aspects of sustainability, making a case for a comprehensive treatment that is imbedded in a holistic perception. Although providing the Islamic sustainable development with the full scale and application is not an easy task, especially in educational, building awareness, and governance entrapment within Islamic countries, it is feasible to apply it to all aspects of the life if there is a will. Through harmonizing these ancient ethical principles with the modern sustainable development techniques, this power which obviously can maintain our planet and create prosperity for coming generations (Nawaz et al., 2019).

Conclusion

Looking back at the Islamic finance and its early days where the roots are analyzed as well as challenges and opportunities of the present times, we come to the vast picture. The moral principles of the Islamic economy show a historical determination toward economic justice, corporate social responsibility, and economic growth under a green vision. In the face of barriers that being conscious of these Islamic finance ethics in the present-day economy may present, the story of how these finance practices rebounded and have started adopting the modern economic trends is a promising sign. The preceding holistic assessment which demonstrates that Islamic societies can leverage their strong moral economic heritage by the mutual action of the principles of Islamic moral Economy and the modern ethical objectives, set the path for a far more inclusive, equal, and sustainable future.

Islamic hermetic financing's role in community development as well as pursuit of socioeconomic justice and contributing to the achievement of SDGs are the aspects of both success stories and gaps. This chapter by making balance between negative criticism such as range between ambition and reality especially in the implementation of Islamic banking as well as positive aspect of Islamic finance as part of the economy globally is the message to be concluded with. The main accent on technical, ethical and social justice solutions rather than on the money and capital itself that are characteristic to Islamic finance, enable it to get the role of a dynamic agent to remodel the financial systems and contribute to the economic development of the world. Essentially, the idea of the historical principles envisaging the future of Islamic finance is the one that merges the ancient values of the past with the current demands of the present in order to mold the Islamic finance of tomorrow as it is not only capable of preserving its constituent roots but it also can become an important factor in creating a fairer and more environmentally sustainable global economic system.

References

Abdul Rahman, A. R. (2010). Islamic microfinance: An ethical alternative to poverty alleviation. *Humanomics*, *26*(4). Article 4.

Abdullah, M. (2018). Waqf, sustainable development goals (SDGs) and maqasid al-shariah. *International Journal of Social Economics*, *45*(1), 158–172. https://doi.org/10.1108/IJSE-10-2016-0295

Ahmad, K. (1980). Economic development in an Islamic framework. In K. Ahmad (Ed.), *Studies in Islamic economics* (pp. 5–22). The Islamic Foundation.

Ahmad, M. (2015). Role of waqf in sustainable economic development and poverty alleviation: Bangladesh perspective. *Journal of Law, Policy and Globalization*, *42*. https://core.ac.uk/download/pdf/234650379.pdf

Ahmed, H. (2011). Maqaṣid al-Shariah and Islamic financial products: A framework for assessment. *ISRA International Journal of Islamic Finance*, *3*(1). Article 1.

Al Breiki, M., & Nobanee, H. (2019). The role of financial management in promoting sustainable business practices and development. *SSRN Electronic Journal*. https://doi.org/10.2139/ssrn.3472404

Al-Sadr, M. B. (1961). *Iqtisaduna*. Dar al Fikr.

Al-Tahawi, I. (1974). *Al-Iqtisad al-Islami Madhaban wa Nizaman Wa Dirasah Muqaranah (Islamic economics: A school of thought and a system)*. Majma'al Buhuth al-Islamiyyah.

Al-Zuhayli, W. (2003). *Financial transactions in Islamic jurisprudence* (M. A. El-Gamal, Trans., Vol. 1). Dar al-Fikr.

Alkaabi, H., & Nobanee, H. (2019). A study on financial management in promoting sustainable business practices & development. *SSRN Electronic Journal*. https://doi.org/10.2139/ssrn.3472415

Arif, M. (1989). Towards establishing the microfoundations of Islamic economics: The basis of the basics. In A. Ghazali & S. Omar (Eds.), *Readings in the concept and methodology of Islamic economics*. Pelanduk Publications.

Asutay, M. (2007). A political economy approach to Islamic economics: Systemic understanding for an alternative economic system. *Kyoto Bulletin of Islamic Area Studies, 1*(2). Article 2.

Asutay, M. (2012). Conceptualising and locating the social failure of Islamic finance: Aspirations of Islamic moral economy *vs* the realities of Islamic finance. *Asian and African Area Studies, 11*(2). Article 2. https://doi.org/10.14956/asafas.11.93

Atıf, M., Hassan, M. K., Rabbani, M. R., & Khan, S. (2021). Islamic FinTech: The digital transformation bringing sustainability to Islamic finance. In M. K. Hassan, A. Muneeza, & A. M. Sarea (Eds.), *COVID-19 and Islamic social finance* (1st ed., pp. 91–103). Routledge. https://doi.org/10.4324/9781003121718

Azman, S. M. M. S., Ismail, S., Haneef, M. A., & Engku Ali, E. R. A. (2022). An empirical comparison of sustainable and responsible investment *ṣukūk*, social impact bonds and conventional bonds. *ISRA International Journal of Islamic Finance, 14*(3), 256–273. https://doi.org/10.1108/IJIF-04-2021-0074

Begum, H., Alam, A. S. A. F., Mia, M. A., Bhuiyan, F., & Ghani, A. B. A. (2019). Development of Islamic microfinance: A sustainable poverty reduction approach. *Journal of Economic and Administrative Sciences, 35*(3), 143–157. https://doi.org/10.1108/JEAS-01-2018-0007

Biancone, P. P., & Radwan, M. (2019). Social finance and financing social enterprises: An Islamic finance prospective. *European Journal of Islamic Finance.* Special Issue Islamic and Social Finance: Comparing Policies and Solutions for Funding Public Infrastructures and Social Services at Global Level. https://doi.org/10.13135/2421-2172/3176

Chang, W. F., Amran, A., Iranmanesh, M., & Foroughi, B. (2019). Drivers of sustainability reporting quality: Financial institution perspective. *International Journal of Ethics and Systems, 35*(4), 632–650. https://doi.org/10.1108/IJOES-01-2019-0006

Chapra, M. U. (1970). The economic system of Islam. *Islamic Quarterly, 14*(4). Article 1.

Chapra, M. U. (1985). *Towards a just monetary system: A discussion of money, banking and monetary policy in the light of Islamic teaching*. The Islamic Foundation.

Chapra, M. U. (1992). *Islam and the economic challenge*. Islamic Foundation; International Institute of Islamic Thought.

Chapra, M. U. (2008). *The Islamic vision of development in the light of the Maqasid Al-Shariah*. The International Institute of Islamic Thought (IIIT). Occasional papers series 15.

DinarStandard. (2023). *State of the global Islamic economy report 2023/2024*. DinarStandard with the support of Dubai's Department of Economy and Tourism (DET). https://www.dinarstandard.com/post/state-of-the-global-islamic-economy-report-2023

Dusuki, A. W. (2005). Corporate social responsibility of Islamic banks in Malaysia: A synthesis of Islamic and stakeholders' perspectives [PhD]. In *The American journal of Islamic social sciences: Vol. PhD thesis*. Loughborough University.

El-Gamal, M. A. (2005). *A basic guide to contemporary banking and finance*. http://www.nubank.com/islamic/primer.pdf

El-Gamal, M. A. (2006). *Islamic finance: Law, economics, and practice*. Cambridge University Press.

Haneef, M. A. (1997). Islam, the Islamic worldview, and Islamic economics. *IIUM Journal of Economics and Management*, 5(1). Article 1.

Haneef, M. A. (2018). Waqf as a socio-economic institution. *Journal of King Abdulaziz University Islamic Economics*, *31*(2), 71–78. https://doi.org/10.4197/Islec.31-2.5

Hanic, A., & Smolo, E. (2023). Islamic approach to corporate social responsibility: An international model for Islamic banks. *International Journal of Islamic and Middle Eastern Finance and Management*, *16*(1). Article 1. https://doi.org/10.1108/IMEFM-07-2021-0284

Harahap, B., Risfandy, T., & Futri, I. N. (2023). Islamic law, Islamic finance, and sustainable development goals: A systematic literature review. *Sustainability*, *15*(8), 6626. https://doi.org/10.3390/su15086626

Haron, S., & Kamaruddin, B. H. (2005). Wealth mobilisation by Islamic banks: The Malaysian case. In M. Iqbal & R. Wilson (Eds.), *Islamic perspectives on wealth creation*. Edinburgh University Press. https://doi.org/10.3366/edinburgh/9780748621002.001.0001

Hasan, Z. (2004). Measuring the efficiency of Islamic banks: Criteria, methods and social priorities. *Review of Islamic Economics*, *8*(2). Article 2.

Hasan, Z. (2005). Islamic banking at the crossroads: Theory versus practice. In R. Wilson & M. Iqbal (Eds.), *Islamic perspectives on wealth creation* (pp. 11–25). Edinbourgh University Press. http://mpra.ub.uni-muenchen.de/2821/

Hussain, H. I., Grabara, J., Razimi, M. S. A., & Sharif, S. P. (2019). Sustainability of leverage levels in response to shocks in equity prices: Islamic finance as a socially responsible investment. *Sustainability*, *11*(12), 3260. https://doi.org/10.3390/su11123260

IFSB. (2023). *Islamic financial services industry stability report 2023*. Islamic Financial Services Board (IFSB).

Iqbal, Z., & Mirakhor, A. (2007). *An introduction to Islamic finance: Theory and practice*. John Willey & Sons.

Kahf, M. (Ed.). (1973). *Challenges confronting the Islamic economist*. University of Utah.

Kahf, M. (2003). Islamic economics: Notes on definition and methodology. *Review of Islamic Economics*, *13*. Article 13.

Kahf, M. (2007). Success factors of Islamic banks: An empirical study. In S. S. Ali & A. Ahmad (Eds.), *Islamic banking and finance: Fundamentals and contemporary issues* (pp. 121–168). IRTI.

Khan, W. M. (1989). Towards an interest-free Islamic economic system. *Journal of King Abdulaziz University: Islamic Economics*, *1*, 3–38.

Khan, M. T. (2015). Historical role of Islamic waqf in poverty reduction in Muslim society. *Pakistan Development Review*, *54*(4), 979–996.

Khan, T. (2019). Reforming Islamic finance for achieving sustainable development goals. *Journal of King Abdulaziz University Islamic Economics*, *32*(1), 3–21. https://doi.org/10.4197/Islec.32-1.1

Kuanova, L. A., Sagiyeva, R., & Shirazi, N. S. (2021). Islamic social finance: A literature review and future research directions. *Journal of Islamic Accounting and Business Research*, *12*(5), 707–728. https://doi.org/10.1108/JIABR-11-2020-0356

Lamido, A. A., & Haneef, M. A. (2021). Shifting the paradigms in *waqf* economics: Towards renewed focus on socioeconomic development. *Islamic Economic Studies*, *29*(1), 18–32. https://doi.org/10.1108/IES-04-2021-0014

Lewis, M. K., & Algaoud, L. M. (2001). *Islamic banking*. Edward Elgar Publication.

Mansoori, M. T. (2011a). Is "Islamic banking" Islamic? Analysis of current debate on Sharī'ah legitimacy of Islamic banking and finance. *Islamic Studies*, *50*(3/4). Article 3/4.

Mansoori, M. T. (2011b). Use of Hiyal in Islamic finance and its Shari'ah legitimacy. *Journal of Islamic Business and Management*, *1*(1). Article 1.

Mansuri, G., & Rao, V. (2004). Community-based and-driven development: A critical review. *The World Bank Research Observer*, *19*(1), 1–39.

Marwan, S., & Haneef, M. A. (2019). Does doing good pay off?: Social impact bonds and lessons for Islamic finance to serve the real economy. *Islamic Economic Studies*, *27*(1), 23–37. https://doi.org/10.1108/IES-05-2019-0001

Marwan, S., Ismail, S., Haneef, M. A., & Engku Ali, E. R. A. (2022). Critical success factors of implementing sustainable and responsible investment (SRI) Sukuk for economic recovery from COVID-19 pandemic. *Journal of Economic and Administrative Sciences*. https://doi.org/10.1108/JEAS-08-2021-0160

Mergaliyev, A., Asutay, M., Avdukic, A., & Karbhari, Y. (2021). Higher ethical objective (Maqasid al-Shari'ah) augmented framework for Islamic banks: Assessing ethical performance and exploring its determinants. *Journal of Business Ethics*, *170*(4). Article 4. https://doi.org/10/gkq8v5

Mirakhor, A., & Askari, H. (2010). *Islam and the path to human and economic development*. Palgrave Macmillan.

Mirakhor, A., & Smolo, E. (2012). Discovering the roots of conventional and Islamic finance. In H. Dar (Ed.), *Global Islamic finance report (GIFR) 2012* (pp. 148–153). Edbiz Consulting Limited.

Mirakhor, A., & Smolo, E. (2014). Epistemological foundation of finance: Islamic and conventional. *Islamic Banking and Finance Review*, *1*(1). Article 1. https://doi.org/10.32350/ibfr.2014.01.01

Naqvi, S. N. H. (1978). Ethical foundation of Islamic economics. *Islamic Studies*, *17*(2). Article 2.

Naqvi, S. N. H. (1981). *Ethics and economics: An Islamic synthesis*. Islamic Foundation.

Naqvi, S. N. H. (1994). *Islam, economics, and society*. Kegan Paul International; Distributed by Routledge.

Nawaz, H., Abrar, M., Salman, A., & Bukhari, S. M. H. (2019). Beyond finance: Impact of Islamic finance on economic growth in Pakistan. *Economic Journal of Emerging Markets*, *11*(1). Article 1. https://doi.org/10.20885/ejem.vol11.iss1.art2

Qurrata, V. A., Yusida, E., Hussain, N. E., Merlinda, S., Purnamasari, V., & Seprillina, L. (2021). Effectiveness of cash waqf management in improving community welfare: Challenges and opportunities. *Review of Integrative Business and Economics Research*, *10*(SI-1), 342–359.

Qutb, S. (1953). *Social justice in Islam* (J. B. Hardie, Trans.; Repr). Islamic Publications International.

Sairally, S. (2007). Community development financial institutions: Lessons in social banking for the Islamic financial Industry. *Kyoto Bulletin of Islamic Area Studies*, *1*(2), 19–37. https://doi.org/10.14989/70893

Siddiqi, M. N. (1981). *Muslim economic thinking: A survey of contemporary literature*. Islamic Foundation.

Siddiqi, M. N. (1983). *Banking without interest*. The Islamic Foundation.

Siddiqi, M. N. (1985). *Partnership and profit-sharing in Islamic law*. The Islamic Foundation.

Siddiqi, M. N. (2000). Islamic banks: Concept, precept and prospects. *Review of Islamic Economics*, *9*, 21–35.

Siddiqi, M. N. (2004). *Riba, bank interest and the rationale of its prohibition*. Islamic Economics Research Center. Visiting Scholars' Research Series No. 2.

Smolo, E. (2013). *Uvod u islamsku ekonomiju i finansije: Teorija i praksa*. Dobra knjiga.

Smolo, E., & Musa, A. M. (2020). The (mis)use of al-Hilah (legal trick) and al-Makhraj (legal exit) in Islamic finance. *Journal of Islamic Accounting and Business Research*, *11*(9). Article 9. https://doi.org/10.1108/JIABR-01-2020-0009

Tag El-Din, S. I. (2007). Capital and money markets of Muslims: The emerging experience in theory and practice. *Kyoto Bulletin of Islamic Area Studies*, *1*(2), 54–71.

Warde, I. (2000). *Islamic finance in the global economy*. Edinburgh University Press.

Yusuf, M. Y., & Bahari, Z. B. (2015). Islamic corporate social responsibility in Islamic banking: Towards poverty alleviation. In H. A. El-Karanshawy, A. Omar, T. Khan, S. S. Ali, H. Izhar, W. Tariqullah, K. Ginena, & B. Al-Quradaghi (Eds.), *Ethics, governance and regulation in Islamic finance* (Vol. 4, pp. 73–90). Bloomsbury Qatar Foundation.

Chapter 9

Sustainable Synergy: The Ethical Imperative of Islamic Banking in Shaping a Responsible Financial Future

Hazik Mohamed

Stellar Consulting Group, Singapore

Abstract

In this chapter, the author look at the symbiotic relationship between Islamic banking and sustainability and how it affects environmental, social, and governance (ESG) practices. It explains the tenets of sustainable Islamic banking by looking at the relationship between banks and ESG and climate-related factors. This study examines corporate finance mechanisms via commercial Islamic banking, highlighting noninterest-based loans with a focus on sustainability, social responsibility, and the environment as cutting-edge financial instruments. Among the topics examined are green corporate deposits, syndicated financing, project finance, and sustainable trade finance, as well as instruments like sustainable shipping letters of credit.

As part of its aim to boost responsible financial practices and ethical investments, the chapter highlights how sustainability principles can be integrated into Islamic banking. The contribution of Islamic banking to corporate financing offers a range of environmentally friendly and sustainable financial products that are in line with moral values as determined by the Shari'ah. This covers consequences linked to sustainability as well as effects on the environment and society. This study goes into the field of investment banking and demonstrates how moral and responsible investment choices can be made by applying the principles of Islamic finance.

The chapter concludes by emphasizing the crucial role Islamic banking plays in maintaining financial stability and resilience. It presents arguments that Islamic banking can be a catalyst for positive change, by aligning financial practices with ethical principles so that global banking becomes more sustainable and responsible.

The Future of Islamic Finance, 141–153

Published under exclusive licence by Emerald Publishing Limited
doi:10.1108/978-1-83549-906-120241009

Keywords: Islamic banking; sustainable finance; environmental, social, and governance (ESG); green financial products; ethical investment

Banks, ESG and Climate-Related Factors

Asset prices and/or borrower defaults may be more volatile for banks that have significant exposure to carbon-intensive industries or companies. In many economies, banks are the largest financial institutions, so managing the risk associated with the transition to a more sustainable world is crucial not only for financial stability but also for social and environmental wellbeing. Not only does this help banks to mitigate climate-related and other risks but it also presents a substantial commercial opportunity for financial institutions too.

Alongside risk management and commercial opportunities, there is a growing consensus that banks should increase their green and sustainable finance activities for ethical and societal reasons. Some US$3.8 trillion of financing had been provided by 60 global banks to fossil fuel companies between 2015 and 2020, significantly outweighing their flows of finance to emissions reduction and other sustainable objectives (ShareAction, 2020). On a positive note, however, the ShareAction report found that it was possible for a bank to drastically improve its performance in this area in a relatively short period of time as, for example, Lloyds Banking Group has done.

A strategy reset which aligned capital with sustainable goals was needed to drive meaningful action. Some examples of how this can be done include through the growth of sustainability-linked loans and transition bonds.

Green and sustainable banking practices are at different stages of evolution internationally, reflecting variation in financial and economic circumstances, and different regulatory priorities. While progress has been slower in some countries than others, the sustainable banking sector has grown to encompass a wide range of strategies and activities. Evolving green and sustainable banking practices across G20 countries can be grouped into two broad categories:

(1) Implementing sustainable practices across the bank's strategy, governance, risk management functions, culture, and skills. Actions such as these are frequently part of a broader trend to promote sustainable banking practices, which take into account both environmental and social factors. Leading banks are now striving to make positive impacts across all areas of their activities rather than focusing on financial losses, reputational risk, and social and environmental harm.
(2) Providing loans and credit, retail savings products, and capital market activities to mobilize private capital for green investments.

Some of the main ways in which banks are incorporating green and sustainable practices are summarized in the Table 9.1 below:

Table 9.1. Incorporating Green and Sustainable Practices in Islamic Banks.

Function	Concept	Implementation
Credit and financing	• Ensuring environmental due diligence in credit decisions • Assessing financing portfolios for emerging environmental risks • Enhancing the positive performance	• Extending green credit to key sectors, such as energy-efficient housing • Extending green credit to a broadening range of commercial sectors, such as clean energy, clean transport, green buildings, water and sanitation
Capital markets	• Integrating climate and environmental risks into investment research	• Raising capital through equity placements and IPOs • Raising capital through debt market underwriting of green *sukuk*
Savings	• Reducing environmental impacts of banking operations • Offering green savings products to retail customers	• Offering green savings products to retail customers
Investments	• Offering green investments products to retail customers	• Offering green investments products to retail customers

Source: Adapted from UNEP Green Banking System: Taking Stock of G20 Green Banking Market Practice (2016).

The Principles of Sustainable Islamic Banking

The Islamic Finance industry should concretize its principles that can be reflected as responsible banking in the form of Principles of Sustainable Islamic Banking (PSIB). The PSIB are aligned with sustainability goals and address ESG issues while maintaining Islamic ethical values. By ensuring that financial activities align with standards of ethical conduct, social justice, and environmental stewardship, sustainable Islamic banking promotes long-term prosperity and well-being for society. These universal values can be formally recognized as the industry's view of professional banking upheld by customer focus, resolute leadership, novel management and ethical professionalism.

The PSIB can provide a framework, supporting tools and a supportive peer network to help Islamic banks incorporate the Shari'ah stewardship into green and sustainable finance principles to guide their strategies and activities and link their business plans to societal goals, as also echoed in the UN Sustainable Development Goals (SDGs) and the Paris Agreement.

The PSIB can be expressed in the UN Principles of Responsible Banking (PRB) format (see Table 9.2).

In the implementation of the principles, the banks are required to conduct an initial impact analysis to identify their significance on the economies, environments, and societies where they operate, and develop plans to increase the positive and reduce negative impacts.

Signatories should then set and publish a minimum of two (but ideally more) targets that seek to increase the positive and reduce negative impacts and that are aligned with the SDGs.

Table 9.2. The Principles of Sustainable Islamic Banking (PSIB), Modified From the UN Principles of Responsible Banking (PRB).

Principle 1: Consensus-Driven
To align the bank's business strategy to be consistent with and contribute to individuals' needs and society's goals, as expressed in the Sustainable Development Goals (SDGs), the Paris Climate Agreement and relevant national and regional frameworks.
Principle 2: Impact and Target Setting
To continuously increase the bank's positive impacts while reducing the negative impacts on, and managing the risks to, people and environment resulting from its activities, products and services. To this end, targets will be set and published where they have the most significant impacts.
Principle 3: Clients and Customers
To work responsibly with our clients and our customers to encourage sustainable practices and enable economic activities that create shared prosperity for current and future generations.
Principle 4: Stakeholder Engagement
To consult, engage and partner with relevant stakeholders to achieve society's goals proactively and responsibly.
Principle 5: Shari'ah Governance
To implement our commitment to the Shari'ah principles through effective governance and a culture of responsible banking.
Principle 6: Transparency and Accountability
To periodically review our individual and collective implementation of the Shari'ah principles and be transparent about and accountable for our positive and negative impacts and our contribution to society's goals.

Source: Adapted from UNEP FI (2019) Principles for Responsible Banking. https://www.unepfi.org/wordpress/wpcontent/uploads/2019/07/FINAL-PRB-Signature-Document-2-Interactive-22-07-19.pdf.

Islamic banks could also join the Collective Commitment to Climate Action (CCCA) which can help to fast-track the implementation of PRB. The CCCA banks have committed to

- Take decisive action from the moment of signing, focusing on the most carbon-intensive and climate-vulnerable sectors within their portfolios.
- Within three years of signing, set and publish sector-specific targets for aligning their portfolios with a well below 2° and striving for 1.5 °C trajectory, based on scientific climate scenarios.
- Drive and facilitate the necessary transition in the real economy through their client relationships, products and services.

Each CCCA bank reports annually on its progress in implementing the commitment and achieving set targets. Every two years, the banks report on their collective progress.

For the PSIB to drive and support a culture of responsible, sustainable banking, an alignment driven by consensus is needed at the industry as well as the institutional levels but more profoundly at the individual level.

Sustainability-linked Islamic banks can play a pivotal role in helping to shape the future of Islamic finance, drive positive social change, and contribute to global efforts for achieving sustainability and inclusive economic growth by incorporating these principles into their operations. Islamic Finance professionals and Shari'ah Advisory committees need to acquire relevant knowledge and skills to be able to develop and deploy financial products, services and tools that will mobilize capital to support that transition, address climate-related and societal risks, and help customers and communities with direct investment in green and sustainable finance opportunities.

Commercial Islamic Banking

Corporations and large enterprises usually have more complex financing needs than small firms. Green Islamic commercial banking is based on Islamic finance principles and includes asset-backed financing, risk-sharing, and ethical behavior while considering environmental impacts in its business operations. They are in line with sustainability's more general goals, which include encouraging sustainable development and responsible banking practices.

Islamic banks provide green financing options like green deposits, green *sukuk* (Islamic bonds), green trade finance, and green investment banking to fund ecologically friendly projects and initiatives. These products not only promote energy efficiency and renewable energy sources, but they are also made to help environmentally conscious projects like sustainable infrastructure.

Islamic banks carry out due diligence to evaluate the social and environmental effects of projects funded by green Islamic commercial banking. This process includes evaluating possible risks and opportunities, making sure that legal requirements and industry standards are followed, and involving stakeholders in the decision-making process.

Islamic banks should engage customers, investors, regulators, and communities as stakeholders in green banking initiatives to foster transparency, accountability, and stakeholder participation. It is necessary to share information about green financing initiatives, solicit feedback from stakeholders, and disclose information about green financing practices in order to build long-lasting partnerships with NGOs, government agencies, and other stakeholders.

However, customers, investors, and bankers are less aware of such sustainable financial tools and practices, which is one of the key challenges facing green Islamic commercial banking. Both companies seeking to develop new, sustainable business models and technologies as well as those engaged in environmentally harmful activities both rely on wholesale and investment banks to provide their financing needs.

Whilst many banks maintained or increased financing to fossil fuel companies during the period some, including Deutsche Bank, China Construction Bank and BPCE/Natixis, substantially reduced funding to the fossil fuel sector. Overall, however, fossil fuel financing from the largest banks increased from approximately US$640 billion in 2016 to US$1.27 trillion total climate finance worldwide (Climate Policy Initiative, 2022) detracting from rather than supporting the transition to a sustainable, low-carbon world.

Green Corporate Financing

Environmentally sustainable businesses and projects are supported by green corporate financing. The principles of Islamic finance underpin the use of green corporate financing, including ethical behavior, risk sharing, and asset backed financing, along with a strong emphasis on environmental stewardship and social accountability. Energy efficiency projects, renewable energy initiatives, waste management, and sustainable agriculture are targeted for investments. As financial activities are aligned with environmental sustainability goals and Islamic ethical principles, green corporate financing is crucial to shaping the future of Islamic finance.

Apple issued its third green bond in February 2021, totaling US$2.8 billion. Proceeds from the bonds will be used to support renewable energy initiatives, energy efficiency improvements, and green building initiatives. Apple's commitment to sustainability is reinforced by this issuance, which aligns with its 2030 goal of becoming carbon neutral throughout its supply chain.

Similarly, Toyota issued its first green bond in September 2021, raising US$2.5 billion for environmentally sustainable projects. Proceeds from the bonds will fund investments in electric vehicles, hydrogen fuel cell technology, renewable energy, and energy-efficient manufacturing processes. As a leading innovator in the automotive industry, Toyota's green bond offering demonstrates its commitment to sustainable mobility. In these examples, companies are gaining access to green financing to finance sustainability initiatives, reduce their environmental impact, and align their climate goals. Corporate green finance is essential for accelerating the transition to a low-carbon economy and promoting environmental stewardship.

In recent years, most major international banks across the G20 have developed methodologies and implemented procedures to integrate environmental, climate-related, and other sustainability risk factors into credit risk management systems. These include ensuring environmental due diligence in credit decisions and assessing loan portfolios for climate-related and other sustainability risks, and their impact on other risks. In relation to residential mortgage financing, monitoring and reporting the environmental impact of commercial and corporate lending is also important for banks, regulators and others to track alignment with the objectives of the Paris Agreement.

In October 2021, the Islamic Development Bank announced its Sustainable Finance Framework, which includes provisions for issuing green, social, and sustainability *sukuk*. The framework aims to mobilize Islamic finance resources to address environmental and social challenges, in addition to social development, investment in renewable energy, and mitigation of climate change. Based on the IsDB's Sustainable Finance Framework, multilateral sustainable finance operations can be incorporated into Islamic finance operations.

Green, Social and Sustainability-Linked Loans

Innovative financing instruments such as sustainability-linked loans, social loans, and green loans, are designed to integrate ESG considerations into Islamic finance. By providing these loans in Shari'ah terms, Islamic finance will be able to fortify sustainable and ethical investments further in future ESG financial undertaking.[1]

It is rooted in the principles of Islamic finance that green, social, and sustainable loans are made in accordance with the principles of ethical conduct, social responsibility, and sustainability. In addition to adhering to Shari'ah guidelines, these (*riba*-free) loans are intended to finance projects and initiatives that have a positive impact on the environment and society, whilst sharing its risks equitably. It is important to note that the sustainability criteria also underlying these loans are in alignment with Islamic finance's broader objectives, including the promotion of economic prosperity, social justice, and environmental responsibility.

A green loan is intended to provide financial support for environmental initiatives, such as the installation of renewable energy sources, the construction of

---

[1]Shari'ah terms provide a framework for providing financing in accordance with Islamic principles, ensuring that financial transactions are conducted in a manner that is ethical, just, transparent, and compliant with Islamic law. The objectives (maqasid) of the Shari'ah goes beyond the forms in the protection of deen (religion), nafs (life), aql (thought/mind), nasl (progeny), mal (wealth) alone as simplified by Al-Ghazali, but to a broader substantial purpose in ensuring accountability (musa'alah), balance (mizan), justice (adl), trustworthiness (amanah) and stewardship (khilafah).

energy-efficient buildings, the implementation of sustainable agriculture, and the disposal of environmental waste. Green loans are available to projects that meet specific environmental criteria and help mitigate climate change and reduce environmental impact.

Social loans provide low-cost housing, education, and healthcare facilities, as well as poverty alleviation initiatives to marginalized communities. Investments made under the social loan program are focused on reducing social inequalities, promoting inclusion, and enhancing societal well-being.

Sustainability-linked loans are aligned with sustainability targets, and their performance indicators are based on sustainability criteria. Borrowers are encouraged to achieve sustainability goals by tying loan terms to their performance in sustainability areas, such as reducing carbon emissions, improving energy efficiency, or enhancing social impact. In the event a borrower achieves or exceeds these targets, preferential terms may be offered to him or her, such as reduced interest rates or a longer repayment period.

Considering that green, social, and sustainability-based loans are becoming increasingly common, Islamic financial institutions should consider these loans important for the future of Islamic finance since they allow them to align their financing activities with ESG principles and support sustainable development initiatives. By offering these asset-backed loans with risk-sharing terms, Islamic banks have an opportunity to distinguish themselves from their usurious competitors, to attract socially responsible investors, and to contribute to the well-being of society and the environment. Furthermore, integrating ESG considerations into lending practices can improve Islamic financial institutions' long-term financial performance and enhance stakeholder trust.

The Loan Market Association (LMA) have published Guidance to support the application of the Green Loan Principles, to clarify definitions and to harmonize approaches to the use of the Principles.[2]

Green Syndicated Financing

A syndicated loan is a loan offered by a group of lenders (referred to as a syndicate) that work together to provide funds for a single borrower. The borrower could be a corporation, a large project, or a country. Loan syndication most often occurs in situations where a borrower requires a large sum of capital that may be too much for a single lender to provide or outside the scope of a lender's risk exposure levels. Thus, multiple lenders work together to provide the borrower with the capital needed. Recently, syndicated loans have been used to raise substantial amounts of capital to finance major green and sustainable projects.

Islamic banks can facilitate large-scale environmentally sustainable projects by pooling resources with other financial institutions. Syndicated loans enable Islamic banks to allocate capital more efficiently and diversify their exposure to green investments, contributing to their sustainability objectives.

[2]For more information, please see: https://www.lma.eu.com/sustainable-lending.

Multiple lenders, including Islamic banks, share the risk of green projects through syndicated financing. It guarantees the stability and resilience of Islamic banks' balance sheets by mitigating the potential financial risks associated with large-scale infrastructure and renewable energy projects.

As a result of participating in green syndicated financing, Islamic banks gain access to a broader network of expertise, knowledge, and networks in the sustainable finance sector. The collaboration between Islamic banks and other financial institutions, development banks, and investors can help Islamic banks to leverage best practices, share insights, and identify new investment opportunities.

In June 2017, the Spanish Bank BBVA arranged a £265 million green syndicated term loan with Tradebe, the Spanish waste reclamation and recycling firm.[3] The transaction was supported by 11 national and foreign financial institutions and was the world's first green syndicated loan. The loan is Tradebe's main source of corporate funding and provides the company with the ability to comfortably fund general corporate needs, together with its future mid-term growth plan, combining organic growth with selective acquisitions.

In June 2021, ING Turkey, a part of ING Group, declared the conclusion of its first sustainability linked syndicated loan.[4] The proceeds of the ESG-linked US$37 million and US$321 million term loan facilities will be used by the bank for general trade finance purposes.

In October 2021, Egypt's finance ministry launched its first US$2 billion syndicated sustainable term loan and Islamic term financing facility with a three-year tenor.[5]

Green Project Finance

Project finance – which is also known as non-recourse finance – refers to loans offered in wholesale banking to fund large infrastructure projects. A project financing structure involves a number of equity investors, known as "sponsors", and a "syndicate" of banks or other financing institutions that provide loans to the operation.

Green project finance enables Islamic banks to fund renewable energy projects such as solar, wind, hydro, and geothermal power plants. By financing these projects, Islamic banks contribute to the development of clean and sustainable energy sources, which aligns with global efforts to mitigate climate change and reduce carbon emissions. Green project finance can also support the development of sustainable infrastructure projects such as green buildings, public transportation systems, and waste management facilities. Islamic banks can provide

[3]BBVA (2017) leads the world's first green syndicated financing in term loan format: https://www.bbva.com/en/bbva-leads-worlds-first-syndicated-financing-scheme-loan-format/.

[4]ING Bank signs €300m equivalent ESG-Linked Term Loan Facilities: https://www.khaleejtimes.com/banking-and-finance/ing-bank-signs-e300m-equivalent-esg-linked-term-loan-facilities.

[5]Bank Consortium Arranges US$2bn Debut Hybrid Murabaha/Conventional Financing Facility for Egypt: https://www.ddcap.com/news-in-brief-16/.

funding for infrastructure projects that incorporate energy-efficient technologies, reduce environmental impact, and enhance resilience to climate change.

As of 2021, the ESG tranche of the Egyptian finance ministry's US$2 billion syndicated sustainable term loan and Islamic term financing facility will be used to fund green projects as per Egypt's Green Financing Framework, which was implemented in September 2020.[6] The total portfolio of eligible green projects comprises approximately 16% is renewable energy, 19% clean transportation, 26% sustainable water and wastewater management and 39% pollution prevention and control (UNFCCC, 2022).

More recently, Cenergi RE (the renewable energy arm of Cenergi SEA) secured a dual-tranche green club financing facility to fund the acquisition and development of biogas power plants in Malaysia.[7] In addition to producing electricity and methane gas, these biogas projects reduce carbon dioxide emissions and improve wastewater quality. As a result of the green club financing facility, proceeds from the loan will be used for financing several biogas projects have been developed in Malaysia in an effort to increase its renewable energy usage to 20% by the year 2025. This facility will allow Cenergi RE and the project companies to leverage a single facility to fund a variety of projects simultaneously. With the assistance of the 2% rebate on profits provided by Credit Guarantee Corporation Malaysia (CGC), Cenergi RE will be able to save on financing costs for these projects according to the Malaysia's Green Technology Financing Scheme. The CGC will also provide 60% guarantee on the financing amount, which will enhance the financial security position of financiers significantly. By investing in green projects, Islamic banks can play a pivotal role in advancing sustainability goals, addressing climate change, and fostering a more equitable and resilient future for all.

Sustainable Trade Finance

In addition to facilitating environmentally sustainable trade transactions, green trade finance facilitates the import and export of green goods and services. Islamic banks contribute to environmental sustainability and responsible business practices by supporting sustainable supply chain activities such as renewable energy, energy-efficient technologies, and eco-friendly products.

Islamic banks can provide funding for a variety of renewable energy initiatives, such as the importation of solar panels, wind turbines, and other energy-related machinery. Islamic banks help mitigate the effects of climate change and reduce emissions by endorsing clean and sustainable energy sources in addition to supporting the trade in renewable energy.

---

[6]Egypt launches its debut US$ 2 Billion ESG Term Loan and Islamic Term Financing Facility: https://www.emiratesnbd.com/en/media-centre/media-centre-info/?mcid_en=974.

[7]Cenergi RE secures green club financing facility to develop biogas power plants: https://islamicsustainable.com/cenergi-re-secures-green-club-financing-facility-to-develop-biogas-power-plants/.

Businesses may be encouraged to invest in environmentally friendly practices and technologies by offering financing for green trade transactions. By offering trade finance facilities supporting green initiatives favorable terms and conditions, companies can be encouraged to adopt sustainable business models and contribute to environmental conservation.

In order to ensure compliance with sustainability standards and regulations, green trade finance involves thorough environmental due diligence. A key component of Islamic banks' trade finance process is the environmental risk assessment criteria. By incorporating these criteria into their lending practices, they can promote responsible lending practices and mitigate the environmental risks of their transactions.

A major element of international trade is the buying and selling of products across countries with different legal systems, cultural differences, and business environments. As a result, export financing tends to be riskier and more complicated than domestic financing. Customers and suppliers often do not understand one another across different countries, they have to transact in foreign currencies, and they must wait longer for physical trade to take place. There is often a cashflow issue for exporters, as they cannot sell to customers who will pay in advance, causing them to require interim financing.

Because of the risks associated with international trade, the World Trade Organisation estimates that between 80 and 90% of world trade relies on some kind of trade finance.[8] One recent innovative example is the sustainable shipment letter of credit (SSLC).

The Sustainable Shipment Letter of Credit

The SSLC is a tool that helps banks reduce the costs associated with exporting certified sustainable palm oil to emerging economies (CISL, 2014).[9] There is a key issue in the palm oil supply chain that producers are faced with, that is, major emerging market importers do not favor sustainable methods of production, often as a result of the anticipated premium prices, resulting in a mixed signal for producers.

Letters of credit for sustainable shipments typically require exporters to provide documentation that the shipment has been produced and transported in an environmentally responsible and socially responsible manner. Should the shipment be made with renewable energy or a reduction in greenhouse gas emissions, the exporter might need to provide proof of adhering to specific environmental regulations. In addition, it is probable that the exporter will have to furnish proof of equitable labor practices and compensation for individuals engaged in the manufacturing and delivery of the merchandize.

---

[8]WTO on the challenges of trade financing: https://www.wto.org/english/thewto_e/coher_e/challenges_e.htm.

[9]The Banking Environment Initiative or BEI's Sustainable Shipment LC: A financing innovation to incentivize sustainable commodity trade (CISL, 2014).

A SSLC compels businesses to follow sustainability standards and encourages them to employ more environmentally friendly production and shipping procedures. Furthermore, in order to encourage accountability and transparency in supply chains, businesses may be obliged to submit documentation of their sustainability initiatives.

Conclusion

We have explored the multifaceted world of Islamic green finance, emphasizing Islamic banking's pivotal role in the global financial landscape. A dichotomy exists between bank's impact on society and environment, recognizing both its potential for positive change as well as its risks. It is evident that Islamic principles provide a robust framework to successfully navigate the complex contemporary financial landscape, as evidenced by the symbiosis between Islamic banking and sustainable finance. The integration of ESG considerations into Islamic banking practices not only aligns with ethical principles but also positions Islamic banks as pioneers in fostering sustainability within the industry.

Throughout the chapter, we have examined the PSIB, traversing the realms of commercial banking, corporate financing, and investment banking. The emergence of innovative financial products, such as green, social, and sustainability-linked loans, highlights the adaptability of Islamic banking to meet the evolving demands for ethical and sustainable financial solutions.

Crucially, the incorporation of sustainability principles extends beyond individual financial products, permeating the core of Islamic banking operations. From green corporate deposits to syndicated financing, project finance, and sustainable trade finance, Islamic banking demonstrates a holistic commitment to ethical financial practices that address ESG considerations.

Identifying actionable steps to align finance with international commitments, such as focusing on the Paris Agreement and broader sustainability objectives, is essential as financial institutions navigate the dynamic sustainability landscape. Islamic banks can significantly contribute to environmental conservation through their involvement in sustainable business practices and models, thus encouraging a shared commitment to protecting the environment.

We found that the Shari'ah principles for responsible banking are consistent with international sustainability frameworks such as the Paris Agreement and the SDGs, based on the moral framework of Islamic finance. Financial organizations can enhance their ability to incorporate environmental and social concerns into their core offerings by investigating green and sustainable banking products and services.

The significance of Islamic banking in creating a financial ecosystem that puts responsible and sustainable finance practices first must be recognized when analyzing the nuances of this synergy. To attain a more moral and sustainable financial sector, we will need to work together, be innovative, and have a common dedication to values that go beyond financial gains.

Because of this, the main purpose of this chapter is to act as a general guide for financial institutions looking to become more sustainable in their operations by navigating Islamic green finance. It is much more likely that a more just and sustainable global financial system will be achieved when these institutions align their operations with international sustainability goals, Shari'ah principles, as well as adopt green banking practices. In this manner, they will not only enhance their own resilience, but also contribute to a more sustainable and equitable world financial system. The global economy is at a crossroads between the financial sector and the environment, and the principles and practices outlined here envision a more sustainable and greener future for financial services as we square off at the intersection between financial innovation and environmental responsibility.

References

BBVA. (2017). BBVA leads the world's first green syndicated financing in term loan format. https://www.bbva.com/en/bbva-leads-worlds-first-syndicated-financing-scheme-loan-format/

Cambridge Institute for Sustainability Leadership. (2014). Sustainable shipment letter of credit: A financing solution to incentivise sustainable commodity trade. https://www.cisl.cam.ac.uk/resources/sustainable-finance-publications/sustainable-shipment-letter-of-credit

Climate Policy Initiative. (2022). Global landscape of climate finance: A decade of data. https://www.climatepolicyinitiative.org/publication/global-landscape-of-climate-finance-a-decade-of-data/

ShareAction. (2020). Banking on a low carbon future. https://shareaction.org/wp-content/uploads/2020/04/ShareAction-Banking-Report-2020.pdf

UNEP FI. (2016). Guide to banking and sustainability - Edition 2. https://www.unepfi.org/fileadmin/documents/guide_banking_statements.pdf

UNEP FI. (2019). Principles for responsible banking. https://www.unepfi.org/wordpress/wp-content/uploads/2019/07/FINAL-PRB-Signature-Document-2-Interactive-22-07-19.pdf

UNFCCC Standing Committee on Finance [SCF]. (2022). Report of the standing committee on finance. https://unfccc.int/sites/default/files/resource/cp2022_8_cma2022_7_adv.pdf

Chapter 10

Sustainable Agriculture and Islamic Finance: Cultivating Prosperity and Values

Nor Razinah Mohd. Zain[a], *Oumaima Tounchibine*[a] *and Houda Lechheb*[b]

[a]IIUM Institute of Islamic Banking and Finance (IIUM), Malaysia
[b]Ibnu Tofail University, Morocco

Abstract

Agriculture is one of the oldest socio-economic activities. It involves growing valuable plants and animals for human existence. Sustainable agriculture should be understood in light of the global sustainable development movement, which emphasizes balancing environment, society and economics. With the ongoing effects of the COVID-19 pandemic and the recent war between Russia and Ukraine, sustainable agriculture can help eliminate food insecurity caused by food shortages and agricultural sector disruptions. Recently, investors, practitioners, academicians, researchers, regulators and financiers are increasingly interested in using Islamic financing products and qualified Shari'ah-compliance contracts to promote sustainable agriculture. Many Organization of Islamic Cooperation (OIC) states still rely on agriculture for socioeconomic growth. These countries are major contributors to Islamic financial growth. This study assesses Islamic finance's role in promoting sustainable agriculture in selected OIC countries. The researchers use qualitative methods and meta-analysis data to determine the constraints and benefits of implementing Islamic financial products for sustainable agriculture. This study suggests that OIC state governments should promote sustainable agriculture. OIC member states have different achievements relating to their sustainable agriculture. Based on socio-economic factors, agriculture policies or plans, leadership and political will, Islamic finance products and Shari'ah-compliance contracts are found underutilized in meeting sustainable agriculture and sector stakeholders' needs. A solid Islamic financial framework for sustainable agriculture, good governance and improved agriculture policy are needed.

The Future of Islamic Finance, 155–173

doi:10.1108/978-1-83549-906-120241010

Keywords: Sustainability; sustainable development goals; sustainable agriculture; Islamic finance; ESG; OIC countries

Introduction

The emergence of agriculture was a transformative milestone in human history, involving the cultivation of plants and the rearing of animals for various essential purposes, such as sustenance, textiles, and medicinal plants. This shift marked the departure from the nomadic lifestyle of hunting and gathering to a more settled way of existence. Before agriculture, human communities were small and constantly on the move in search of food and resources. The introduction of agriculture led to the establishment of permanent communities, laying the groundwork for the development of social structures and larger societies (Mazoyer & Roudart, 2006; Viana et al., 2022). The transition to settled living through agriculture not only altered the physical landscape but also provided a stable environment for cultural development. At the core of this agricultural revolution stood the domestication of animals and the cultivation of foodstuffs, both of which were emphasized as pivotal elements in reshaping the fundamental tapestry of human existence. In addition to altering the means of livelihood, these practices had far-reaching consequences that affected many different aspects of human existence, such as it enabled the creativity of ancient agricultural techniques (Homburg et al., 2023). This suggests that agricultural practices were highly developed during this period of transition, demonstrating the ingenuity and flexibility of ancient civilizations (Brevik et al., 2018). Agriculture has profound impacts on cultural practices, economic systems and societal structures which contribute to the intricate of human history. With a more predictable food supply, individuals had time for activities beyond basic survival needs, leading to the flourishing of art, music, religion and language evolution. Economically, agriculture catalyzes a significant shift in human societies by fostering the development of trade, specialization, and more complex economic systems, including the rise of markets, division of labor and accumulation of wealth.

Looking ahead to 2025, the advancement of agriculture remains crucial for society. However, it is important to note that excessive agricultural development often brings adverse consequences. These include deforestation, where forests and natural habitats are converted into farmland, leading to biodiversity loss, habitat destruction and increased greenhouse gas emissions (Carreira et al., 2024; Ritchie, 2021). Unsustainable agricultural practices such as monoculture farming, excessive tillage and improper use of agrochemicals can also degrade soil quality over time, resulting in issues like soil erosion, nutrient depletion, compaction and salinization (David Raj et al., 2024). Additionally, the excessive use of fertilizers, pesticides and herbicides can contaminate water sources through runoff and leaching, causing water pollution and contributing to problems like eutrophication and algal blooms (Kumari et al., 2024). Moreover, the expansion of agricultural land often encroaches upon natural habitats, further endangering biodiversity and disrupting ecosystems (Li et al., 2024). These practices not only pose health risks to individuals living near agricultural areas (Adepoju et al., 2024), they also contribute significantly to greenhouse gas emissions, exacerbating climate change and impacting agricultural productivity and food security (Malaisamy, 2024).

With the introduction of Sustainable Development Goals (SDGs) by the United Nations (UN), agricultural development has become of the utmost importance in the pursuit of achieving such goals. These goals include an all-encompassing appeal to eradicate poverty, protect the environment, and guarantee universal prosperity and peace by the year 2030. Agriculture is intricately connected to a number of the SDGs, and the growth of agriculture is essential to the achievement of a number of these goals. Here are a few of these relevant goals with agriculture development: No Poverty (SDG1), Zero Hunger (SDG2), Good Health and Well-being (SDG3), Decent Work and Economic Growth (SDG8) and Industry, Innovation and Infrastructure (SDG9). The reduction of poverty can be achieved through agricultural development, which has the potential to generate incomes, enhance livelihoods, and generate employment opportunities, especially in rural regions where poverty is frequently concentrated (Zhang et al., 2024). Undeniably, agricultural plays a critical role in attaining food security and eradicating starvation, which is reflected in SDG2. Critical to achieving this goal are boosting agricultural productivity, promoting sustainable farming practices, allowing market accesses to the farmers, and bolstering their resilience to climate change (Ghimire et al., 2024). It is also vital to have access to nutritious and safe sustenance to promote health. Agricultural development plays a pivotal role in achieving this goal through its provision of a wide array of nourishing food products. Employment opportunities can be created throughout the entire value chain of agriculture, including cultivation, processing, and marketing (Miar et al., 2024). It can also encourage investment in rural areas, entrepreneurship and innovation, thereby stimulating economic development. In order to increase productivity, strengthen resilience to climate change, and promote sustainable land management practices, agricultural research and innovation are indispensable (Madamombe et al., 2024). Additionally, the development of market linkages, roads and storage facilities are rural infrastructure investments that are indispensable for the expansion of agricultural value chains (Verma & Bibhakar, 2024).

While the importance of agriculture and its linkage with SDGs is presented here, the adverse effects of unsustainable agriculture practices require a careful strategic treatment. Thus, this gives raise to the concept of sustainable agriculture in the modern discourse. Looking closely to the finance market globally, Islamic finance receives a gradual increase of interests among stakeholders such as investors, practitioners, academicians, researchers, regulators, financiers, etc. (Alhammadi, 2024), in utilizing Islamic finance products in empowering sustainable agriculture (Parveen, 2022). Currently, there is still a lack of discussions that address the intersection of Islamic finance with sustainable agriculture.

Moreover, with the continuous impacts from the aftermath of the COVID-19 pandemic and the recent war between Russia and Ukraine, sustainable agriculture can be the key to eliminate food insecurity that occurs due to the shortage of food supplies and the disturbance that happened in agriculture sectors in the involved countries (Aljounaidi et al., 2024). Thus, this study aims to evaluate the practices from Islamic finance in promoting sustainable agriculture among the selected countries from the OIC. There are many of the OIC countries that still depend on their agriculture sector for their socioeconomic development (SESRIC, 2020). These countries are also among the biggest contributors to the growth of Islamic finance globally. By adopting qualitative research methodology and meta-analysis evaluation, the rest of the chapter is organized as follows: The following section provides an overview of sustainable agriculture. Subsequently, the discussion continues with the alignment of Islamic finance with sustainable agriculture by looking at the possible opportunities and challenges. Next, the study discusses practices of Islamic finance in promoting sustainable agriculture in the selected OIC countries. Finally, before conclusion remarks, the study suggests strategies in promoting and advancing sustainable agriculture through Islamic finance's practices.

Understanding Sustainable Agriculture: Principles and Practices

In relation to sustainability, sustainable agriculture can be considered an approach to farming or agriculture that aims to meet the needs of the present without compromising the ability of future generations to meet their own needs (Smit & Smithers, 1993). Basically, it involves integrating three main dimensions, which are (i) environmental stewardship; (ii) social equity; and (iii) economic viability. According to Velten et al. (2015), there is no definite definition for sustainable agriculture; instead, there are emerging definitions to describe the concept of sustainable agriculture. Without undermining other emerging definitions, in defining sustainable agriculture, there are two clear definitions suggested by Velten et al. (2015), which are taken from US Congress (1990) and MacRae et al. (1989). The first definition describes sustainable agriculture as an integrated system of plant and animal production practices which is intended to achieve the following long-term benefits: (a) meet the nutritional and fibre requirements of human beings; (b) improve environmental conditions; (c) optimize the utilization of natural biological cycles and controls while conserving non-renewable and on-farm resources; (d) ensure the economic sustainability of agricultural operations; and (e) enhance the standard of living for farmers and society at large (US Congress, 1990; Velten et al., 2015). According to the second definition, sustainable agriculture covers management practices that utilize natural processes to preserve resources, reduce waste and environmental effect, avert issues, and enhance agroecosystem resilience, self-regulation, evolution, and sustained production for the sustenance and well-being of all (MacRae et al., 1989; Velten et al., 2015). From these definitions, an observation can be made. Sustainable agriculture has certain objectives that should be fulfilled, such as the enhancement of productivity, the maintenance of natural resources' quality, the reduction of soil erosion and the disappearance of plant nutrients, and the enhancement of farm profitability (Smit & Smithers, 1993). These objectives should be considered in achieving sustainable agriculture. Failure to do so may bring imbalances between environment, social and economy as components of sustainable development.

Sustainable agriculture stands out with specific principles (Trigo et al., 2021), which promote the balance of environmental stewardship, social equity and economic viability. Based on the collected literature, there are six important principles of sustainable agriculture. Here, they are summarized as the followings:

(1) Ecological integrity concerns with the aim of sustainable agriculture to balance the use of ecosystems that are similar to those that are found in nature by fostering biodiversity, soil health and ecosystem resilience. It places an emphasis on the use of agroecological strategies such as crop rotation, polyculture, agroforestry and integrated pest management in order to preserve ecological balance and reduce reliance on external inputs. According to Robertson and Swinton (2005), environmental integrity poses as the greatest challenge for sustainable agriculture, which requires close inspection of each stage of farming or agriculture.

(2) Resource efficiency concerns with the aim of sustainable agriculture to increase effectiveness of resource utilization by minimizing waste, saving water, and lowering energy use (Obaisi et al., 2022; Pisante et al., 2023). This initiative encourages the implementation of methods such as conservation tillage, water-saving irrigation systems, and the utilization of renewable energy sources to improve resource productivity and resistance to climate change.

(3) Healthy condition of soil or maintaining healthy soils is essential to the practice of sustainable agriculture since they facilitate the growth of plants, the cycling of nutrients, and the retention of water (M. Tahat et al., 2020; Powlson et al., 2011). There are several sustainable soil management strategies that attempt to increase soil structure, fertility, and microbial variety while simultaneously minimizing erosion and pollution. Some examples of these activities include organic farming, cover cropping, composting, and crop residue retention (Turmel et al., 2015).

(4) Water management concerns with the preservation of freshwater resources, safeguard of water ecosystems, and guarantee of equal access to water for agricultural and domestic purposes in sustainable agriculture. It is imperative that responsible water management and methods should be implemented, especially to avoid wastage and maximizing its utilization (Nalluri & Karri, 2024; Majumdar et al., 2024).

(5) Biodiversity conservation in sustainable agriculture can be traced from its role in ensuring the resilience of ecosystems, pollination, biodiversity and pest management (Karaca & Ince, 2019). It fosters the preservation of natural habitats, the rehabilitation of degraded landscapes and the promotion of crop diversification to improve the resilience and flexibility of agroecosystems to changing environmental conditions (Yanagi, 2024).

(6) Climate resilience is also one of important principles of sustainable agriculture (El Chami et al., 2020), where it helps in combatting climate change by encouraging methods that reduce greenhouse gas emissions, store carbon and improve the ability to withstand climate challenges. It encompasses agroecological methods, including agroforestry, conservation agriculture, and livestock management techniques that decrease emissions, improve carbon storage and establish climate-resilient food systems (Deguine et al., 2023).

In accomplishing abovementioned objectives as suggested by Smit and Smithers (1993), sustainable methods of farming or agriculture require the use of a wide variety of approaches or practices, which may include both conventional and modern methods. Agroecology, organic farming, permaculture, regenerative agriculture and community-supported agriculture (CSA) are among practices of sustainable agriculture that can be considered (Oberč & Arroyo Schnell, 2020). Agroecology applies ecological principles to agricultural systems. It prioritizes the incorporation of traditional knowledge, biological processes, and biodiversity in the development of sustainable and resilient agricultural systems (Ewert et al., 2023). Intercropping, crop rotation, biological pest management, and soil conservation are all agroecological practices. Suitable with nature, organic farming does not utilize synthetic pesticides, fertilisers and genetically modified organisms (GMOs) (Gore et al., 2023). Natural inputs, including compost, cover crops, and crop rotations, are utilized to sustain soil fertility, regulate insect populations, and foster ecological equilibrium. Thus, it protects animal welfare, biodiversity preservation, and soil health. Another sustainable agriculture practice is permaculture (Yadav et al., 2023). It aims to produce sustainable human environments by emulating natural patterns and processes. It combines ecological, agricultural and sustainable design principles to build productive and resilient systems with minimal inputs and upkeep. Food forests, swales, keyline design and water harvesting techniques are all examples of permaculture practices (Ferraro-Fanning, 2023).

Consistent with sustainable agriculture, regenerative agriculture aims to rehabilitate damaged ecosystems, raise soil quality and improve ecosystem functions (Schreefel et al., 2020). The goal is on restoring soil organic matter, boosting biodiversity and improving water retention capacity to establish robust and efficient agricultural systems. Regenerative agriculture approaches may cover no-till farming, rotational grazing and holistic land management (Khangura et al., 2023). There are also farming models that can be used for sustainable agriculture practice. One of this farming models is CSA. CSA promotes direct connections between farmers and consumers, typically through subscription-based memberships or cooperative agreements (Sulistyowati et al., 2023). It encourages local food production, short supply chains and customer involvement in food production decisions. CSA improves food security, fosters social cohesiveness and advocates for sustainable farming practices (Parot et al., 2023). Significantly, sustainable agriculture is critical to tackling the complex issues such as environmental degradation, climate change and social injustice. By embracing principles such as ecological integrity, resource efficiency and biodiversity conservation, as well as implementing practices such as agroecology, organic farming and regenerative agriculture, a proper agriculture development can be considered which directly or indirectly supports sustainable food systems that will feed people for generations.

Sustainable Agriculture From the Islamic Perspective

Sustainable agriculture in Islam is based on the teachings of Qur'an, the practices of Prophet Muhammad (pbuh – peace and blessings be upon him) and the rules of Islamic jurisprudence (*Fiqh*). Although classical Islamic literature does not contain a specific term for sustainable agriculture, the principles and ideals of Islam offer a foundation for encouraging environmentally-conscious and socially-responsible farming methods (Borhan & Aziz, 2009; Finnegan, 2011; Aziz, 2012). Moreover, Islam considers the agriculture sector a societal obligation known as *fardu kifayah*. From an Islamic standpoint, engaging in agriculture is considered a noble pursuit. A person engaged in agriculture sector is responsible not only for their own well-being but also for the community. This is similar to the concept of donation (*sadaqah*) in Islam. Referring to agriculture, the Almighty Allah (swt) the exalted mentioned regarding agriculture in Surah Al-Baqarah of Al-Quran, verse 261:[1]

> The likeness of those who spend their wealth in Allah's way is as the likeness of a grain which groweth seven ears, in every ear a hundred grains. Allah giveth increase manifold to whom He will. Allah is All-Embracing, All-Knowing. (Al-Quran, 2:261)

Farmers or those who are involved in agriculture are bound to consistently strive to obtain Allah's bounties and dedicate the proceeds from their agricultural pursuits to charitable endeavors. It is a part of etiquettes of agriculture in Islam (Mustafa et al., 2017). This is done by aiding those in need, expressing gratitude and praising Allah (swt). However, farmers who only have the intention on amassing wealth but decline to worship Allah (swt) are considered transgressors (Al-Qurtubi, 2006). The excessive use of resources, even for the purpose of agriculture, that brings destruction on the surface of the Earth is counted as sins. This can be observed from the following verse:

> He it is Who produceth gardens trellised and untrellised, and the date-palm, and crops of divers flavour, and the olive and the pomegranate, like and unlike. Eat ye of the fruit thereof when it

---

[1]SWT stands for '*Subhanahu wa ta'ala*' in Arabic which means 'Glory be to Him the Most High.'

fruiteth, and pay the due thereof upon the harvest day, and be not prodigal. Lo! Allah loveth not the prodigals. (Al-Quran 6:161)

Aligning Islamic Finance With Sustainable Agriculture: Potentials and Challenges

Islamic finance is founded on the principles of Shari'ah, the Islamic legal system, which prioritizes socially and ethically responsible investing and financing practices. Sustainable agriculture, on the other hand, seeks to develop environmentally-friendly farming practices, while also promoting social fairness and economic viability. The combination of sustainable agriculture and Islamic financing provides significant opportunities for supporting agriculture programmes or projects which address global concerns such as food security, climate change and poverty reduction. Moreover, participating in agricultural sector is viewed as a virtuous profession. There is a clear potential for fostering prosperity through the adoption of ethical financing principles from Islamic finance in sustainable agriculture initiatives. By enhancing shared values present in both sectors, there are opportunities for growth. Undeniably, there are also challenges that must be carefully addressed. Consequently, there is a need to unlock the full potential of Islamic finance in supporting sustainable agriculture. These potentials can be seen from their ethical alignments, long-term investment strategy, socio-economic benefits for the society, environmental sustainability approach and considerations from market demands.

Ethical alignment is one of the most obvious benefits of integrating sustainable agriculture and Islamic finance. In accordance with the tenets of Islamic finance, ethical investing, risk-sharing and equitable wealth distribution are emphasized. Simultaneously, these ethical values are well-aligned with sustainable agriculture, which emphasizes on social justice, economic empowerment and environmental stewardship. This alignment may be utilized by Islamic financial institutions or IFIs to attract investors who are in search for socially and ethically responsible investments. Such ethical alignment can be considered virtuous and significantly important to reach success (*al-falah*) and prosperity (Anggara et al., 2024). Sustainable agriculture initiatives occasionally demand expenditures that are made for over an extended period of time. Such situation happens because of the amount of time that is required to execute sustainable agriculture practices such as soil regeneration, agroforestry and ecosystem restoration. By incorporating Islamic financing or investment products, which prioritize risk-sharing and profit-sharing models, consistent capital can be provided for such initiatives. This aligns with the inherent long-term vision of sustainable agriculture. Furthermore, the absence of interest (*riba*) ensures that farmers and those engaged in the agriculture sector are shielded from additional charges on their financing, which could occur with conventional loans dependent on fluctuating interest rates. This directly or indirectly fosters a layer of security, enabling them to proceed with their work confidently (Khattak & Ali, 2024).

Additionally, as highlighted by Ikerd (1998), sustainable agriculture projects have the potential to generate significant social impact by creating employment opportunities, improving livelihoods and empowering local communities, particularly in rural areas. It also has the ability to push forwards efforts in achieving sustainable development agendas. IFIs can prioritize investments in sustainable agriculture projects that contribute to social welfare, poverty alleviation and inclusive economic development. This way, they are fulfilling their mandate of promoting social justice and equity. It is also important to maintain food security for the focused segment of the society. As a requirement of the Islamic wealth management, Islamic finance principles also prioritize the conservation and sustainable utilization of natural resources, such as land, water and biodiversity. Thus, IFIs can aid in the mitigation of climate change and environmental sustainability by providing financial support for sustainable agriculture initiatives that prioritize water management, biodiversity preservation and soil conservation (Muhmad et al., 2021). There is a growing market demand for sustainably produced food products among consumers, retailers and investors worldwide (Petro, 2022). Hence, IFIs can tap into this market demand by financing sustainable agriculture projects that adhere to eco-friendly practices, ethical standards, and permissible (*halal*) activities, thereby fostering economic growth and market expansion.

Aligning Islamic finance with sustainable agriculture is not free from challenges. These challenges may vary from one country to another. Some of the challenges are lack of awareness, complexity of transactions, regulatory limitations, popularity of sustainable agriculture and assessment of Islamic finance impacts on sustainable agriculture.

Many practitioners from IFIs may have limited understanding of sustainable agriculture concepts, practices, and investment opportunities. This lack of awareness needs to be addressed by bridging the knowledge gap and raising their awareness about the potential synergies between the Islamic finance sector and sustainable agriculture. This is essential to unlock investment potentials for both sectors. Moreover, sustainable agriculture projects often involve complex transactions, such as land acquisition, water rights, carbon credits, and ecosystem services. Structuring Islamic finance instruments to accommodate these complexities while ensuring compliance with Shari'ah principles can be challenging and may require specialized expertise and innovative financial solutions. It is also important to note that Islamic finance operates within a regulatory framework governed by Shari'ah, which may impose certain restrictions on investment activities, financial transactions and business practices. Thus, it may serve as regulatory limitations which need to be navigated through the existing legal system of the country. The regulatory limitations can also be a challenging constraint which requires careful consideration from legal, ethical and financial aspects. Finally, financing or investment products from Islamic finance must remain Shari'ah-compliant at all time, which may require certain adjustments to a country's laws.

Besides these challenges, there is an increasing interest in sustainable agriculture financing within the Islamic finance sector (Setyaningsih & Jayaprawira,

2020). However, the level of investments is still relatively small when compared to conventional finance at the global scale. To achieve scalability and integrate sustainable agriculture into Islamic finance, it is essential to focus on attracting larger investments, establishing scalable business models and fostering supportive governmental settings through inclusion of environmental policies. This situation is impacted by the popularity of sustainable agriculture among IFIs. At the same time, the assessment of Islamic finance impacts toward sustainable agriculture requires urgent consideration. Assessing the social, environmental and economic impact of sustainable agriculture investments can be challenging, particularly within the context of Islamic finance, which places a strong emphasis on ethical values and social justice. Developing standardized metrics and methodologies for measuring the impact of Islamic finance investments on sustainable agriculture is essential for transparency, accountability and informed decision-making. As for now, such assessment is still absence. This indicates that continuous efforts should be carried out in aligning Islamic finance with sustainable agriculture.

The Practices of Islamic Finance in Promoting Sustainable Agriculture in Selected OIC Member States

Many countries within the OIC rely heavily on agriculture for their economies, livelihoods and food security. These countries often possess extensive agricultural sectors, with a significant proportion of their populace involved in agricultural pursuits. Thus, sustainable agriculture is important to be considered by their relevant stakeholders, especially policy makers and regulators. For examples, agriculture plays a crucial role in Indonesia's economy, where a significant portion of Indonesian population is involved in the sector. Indonesia is a major producer of rice, palm oil, rubber, cocoa and coffee (Morley et al., 2019). At the same time, Malaysia is well known as the second-largest producer of palm oil in the world (Hassan et al., 2023). Natural rubber, cash crops and rice are also highly produced in Malaysia as their valuable agricultural commodities (Takahashi, 2024). Pakistan and Bangladesh also depend on their agricultural products in boosting their economy (Tasneem & Khan, 2024). Pakistan is popular for their wheat, rice, sugarcane, cotton and fresh fruits. Meanwhile, Bangladesh is a major producer of rice, jute, tea, and fisheries (Parvin et al., 2024). Egypt is famous throughout history as the prominent economic driver of agriculture, where this country produces beneficial crops such as wheat, maize, rice, cotton and vegetables with an advantageous from the Nile River's fertile delta areas (Lago-Olveira et al., 2023). Significantly, rural areas of Turkey depend on agriculture where they have their local grains, fruits, vegetables, livestock and dairy products (Keskin & Güneş, 2023). Iran produces a wide range of agricultural products, including wheat, barley, rice, fruits, vegetables and livestock (Amiraslani & Dragovich, 2023). Morocco is known for its production of cereals, citrus fruits, olives and vegetables, which is supported by irrigation systems and favorable climate conditions (Amachraa, 2023). Nigeria is a major producer of crops such as cassava, yams, maize, millet, sorghum and cocoa, with agriculture serving as a source of income for millions of smallholder farmers (Akanwa et al., 2023). Majority of these countries also actively participate in the global market of Islamic finance.

There are several practices of Islamic finance which can be utilized in promoting sustainable agriculture across OIC countries. It is found that these practices may be traced from the existing financing or investment products that are applied by IFIs. They are not only Shari'ah-compliance, but also promote ethical and environmentally friendly principles consistent with Shari'ah and can be used to achieve SDGs. These Islamic finance practices are related to (i) profit-and-loss sharing (PLS) contracts (*mudarabah* & *musharakah*); (ii) *murabahah* and *salam* contracts; (iii) *ijarah* and *istisna'* contracts; (iv) *takaful* (Islamic insurance); (v) Islamic microfinance; (vi) *sukuk* (Islamic bonds); and (vii) environmental and social responsibility screening. It is noted by the researchers here that the practices should not be limited to the list as provided here, which warrant comprehensive future research.

Islamic finance prioritizes equity-based financing via PLS arrangements like *mudarabah* and *musharakah* (Ibrahim et al., 2023). Within agriculture, these types of contracts enable IFIs to collaborate with farmers or *agripreneurs* (agriculture entrepreneurs) by offering funding in return for a portion of the earnings. This fosters risk-sharing and supports sustainable agriculture practices by ensuring that all parties are committed to the success of the project. Meanwhile, *murabahah* contracts entail the sale of commodities at an agreed-upon marked-up price between the customer and seller. IFIs can utilize *murabahah* contracts to fund the acquisition of agricultural products, equipment or machinery for farmers or agripreneurs in the agricultural sector (Habriyanto et al., 2023). *Salam* contract enables the pre-purchase of agricultural goods, offering farmers funds for production and guaranteeing a reasonable price (Parveen, 2022). Also, Islamic leasing (*ijarah*) and manufacturing (*istisna*) contracts can be used to fund agricultural infrastructure like irrigation systems, greenhouses, or processing facilities (Majid, 2024; Saqib & Roberts, 2017). IFIs may use these contracts to facilitate the leasing of assets or the construction of customized agricultural equipment or infrastructure, enabling farmers to access necessary resources and encouraging efficiency and sustainability.

Nowadays, *takaful* is innovatively used by farmers to get a protection against agricultural risks, such as crop failure, livestock diseases or natural disasters (Sulaiman et al., 2023). As a means of bolstering agricultural resilience and sustainability, IFIs can provide farmers with *takaful* products, which are designed to meet their unique needs, protecting them financially from possible hazards that are inherent in the sector. Furthermore, to promote financial inclusion and alleviate poverty, Islamic microfinance institutions may provide smallholder farmers and rural entrepreneurs with financial services that are Shari'ah-compliant in nature. Islamic microfinance institutions have the potential to offer innovative investment schemes for sustainable agricultural activities, including crop production, livestock rearing and agro-processing (Budiyoko et al., 2024). This could help underprivileged communities to improve their livelihoods through sustainable agriculture.

Alternatively, *sukuk* are designed to yield returns from Shari'ah-compliant enterprises or tangible assets. IFIs may issue *sukuk* to finance agribusiness ventures, rural infrastructure initiatives or sustainable agricultural development projects, such as irrigation schemes. *Sukuk* may offer investors the opportunity to contribute to sustainable agriculture initiatives, while simultaneously earning returns that are permissible or halal (Taqwiem & Rachmadi, 2023). At the same time, IFIs frequently integrate criteria related to environmental and social responsibility when making investment determinations and carrying out financing operations. This may involve the exclusion of investments that are associated with agricultural practices that are detrimental to the environment or society, such as labor exploitation, land exploitation or deforestation. It is also known as environmental and social responsibility screening (Agustin et al., 2023). Conversely, IFIs may assign greater importance to investments that advocate for equitable trade practices, sustainable agriculture and the preservation of biodiversity. Simultaneously, this is also in parallel with the principles of *maqasid al-Shari'ah* (objectives of the Islamic law).

Strategies in Promoting Sustainable Agriculture via Islamic Finance

As mentioned in previous sections, sustainable agriculture is crucial to tackle issues like food security, climate change and environmental degradation. Islamic finance, with its emphasis on ethical investing, risk-sharing and social responsibility, can play a critical role in advancing sustainable agriculture efforts. While efforts to align Islamic finance with sustainable agriculture are important, it is also important to look at the leadership and commitment of OIC countries, their polices on adoption of sustainable agriculture, potential constraints and their regional differences. From the researchers' observation here, there are certain OIC countries that are committed in their leaderships to enforce sustainable agriculture through introducing policies, national plans, strategies and changes of laws (Sales, 2023). This can be seen in Malaysia, Indonesia, Turkey, Morocco and Egypt. Even though the achievement in adopting sustainable agriculture is different from one OIC country to another, sustainable agriculture practices can be traced such as conservation agriculture, organic farming, agroforestry, integrated pest management and water-efficient irrigation techniques.

Depending on the socio-political scenario of the OIC countries and economic achievements, their constraints remain different from each other which require certain degree of collaborations with countries that face similar issues in sustainable agriculture. Such constraints are evident in water shortages, soil degradation, climate change effects, restricted financial and technological access, insufficient institutional capacity and inadequate infrastructure and market connections. Similarly, significant disparities exist among OIC countries regarding the status of sustainable agriculture, with different degrees of progress among them. Southeast Asian and North African countries such as Malaysia, Indonesia and Morocco, demonstrate committed leaderships for their sustainable agriculture policies. On the contrary, sub-Saharan African and Middle Eastern countries encounter more tough obstacles due to water scarcity, land degradation, conflict and poverty which may hinder the implementation of sustainable agricultural practices.

By looking at the development of Islamic finance, recommended strategies are presented here in promoting sustainable agriculture across OIC countries. IFIs of these countries may participate through their innovative financing and investment products and ethical practices. IFIs have the capacity to create investment and financing products that adhere to Shari'ah principles and are specifically designed to cater to the requirements of agricultural stakeholders. These products should be able to address the unique challenges faced by the agricultural sector, such as seasonality, weather-related risks and input costs. Unfortunately, Islamic finance solutions and Shari'ah-compliance contracts are not being fully utilized to satisfy the needs of sustainable agriculture and sector players. An established Islamic finance structure is required for sustainable agriculture, effective governance and enhanced agricultural policies. IFIs may invest in initiatives for sustainable agriculture, which concurrently foster social equity, economic development and environmental conservation. Community-based agricultural cooperatives, organic farming initiatives, agroecological practices and renewable energy programmes for agriculture are a few examples of such initiatives. IFIs can promote sustainable agriculture initiatives, thereby generating financial gains and contributing to positive social and environmental outcomes.

In order to finance sustainable agriculture initiatives that contribute to the mitigation of climate change, conservation of biodiversity and management of natural resources, green *sukuk* (Islamic bonds) may be issued. These *sukuk* could raise capital for environmentally sustainable agricultural practices, including agroforestry, soil conservation and water management, in accordance with Shar'ah principles. Green *sukuk* issuance has the potential to mobilize capital for sustainable agriculture initiatives and attract environmentally conscious investors. To promote sustainable agriculture initiatives, IFIs may form partnerships with international development organizations, government agencies and non-profit organizations. These alliances have the potential to streamline the process of exchanging knowledge, mobilizing resources and executing projects in critical domains including rural development, environmental conservation and food security. Through capitalizing on the knowledge and connections of development organizations, IFIs have the potential to enhance their influence in the realm of sustainable agriculture. It is crucial that IFIs integrate environmental, social and governance (ESG) criteria into their investment decision-making processes in order to guarantee that their holdings are in line with sustainable development objectives. This may entail performing due diligence on environmental and social risks, screening investments according to ESG factors and monitoring the influence of investments on sustainability outcomes. Sustainable investment in the agricultural sector can be encouraged by IFIs through the incorporation of ESG criteria into their investment strategies.

Conclusion

Advancing sustainable agriculture through Islamic finance necessitates a comprehensive strategy that combines Shari'ah principles, financial creativity and stakeholder involvement. IFIs can contribute by investing in sustainable agriculture projects, building resilient and inclusive agri-food systems, developing Shari'ah-compliant financing and investment products, involving in issuance of green *sukuk*, providing capacity-building support, fostering partnerships and integrating ESG criteria to ensure sustainable agriculture, food security, protect environment sustainability and promote social welfare. By working together and implementing well-planned projects, Islamic finance in OIC countries may play a key role in promoting sustainable agriculture development, leading to beneficial impacts on agricultural communities and progress toward global sustainability objectives.

References

Adepoju, A. O., Femi-Adepoju, A., Jalloh, A., & Faeflen, S. (2024). Soil pollution and management practices. In R. Frazer-Williams, M. B. Ogundiran, & E. I. Unuabonah (Eds.), *Environmental pollution and public health* (pp. 187–236). Elsevier.

Agustin, F., Muhtadi, R., & Sahal, S. (2023). The importance of implementing environment, social and government (ESG) and Maqasid Shariah-based Islamic finance in Islamic bank. *Journal of Islamic Economic Laws*, *6*(2), 133–158.

Akanwa, A. O., Banerjee, A., Jhariya, M. K., Muoghalu, L. N., Okonkwo, A. U., Ikegbunam, F. I., Ezeomedo, I. C., Okeke, S. O., Igwe, P. U., Arah, V. C., Anukwonke, C. C., Obidiegwu, M. C., & Madukasi, E. I. (2023). Climate-induced conflicts between rural farmers and cattle herders: Implications on sustainable agriculture and food security in Nigeria. *Ecorestoration for Sustainability*, 373–416.

Al-Qurtubi, Abi Abdullah Muhammad Ibn Ahmad Ibn Abi Bakr. (2006). *al-Jami' li Ahkam al-Quran wa al-Mubayyinu Lima Tadammanahu min al-Sunnah wa al-Furqan* (Vol. 10). Mua'assah al-Risalah.

Alhammadi, S. (2024). Islamic finance as a driver for enhancing economic sustainability and innovation in the GCC. *Journal of Science and Technology Policy Management*. https://doi.org/10.1108/JSTPM-11-2023-0206

Aljounaidi, A., Ali, M., & Shabbir, S. (2024). Economic impacts of the Russia-Ukraine conflict on developing countries: A focus on agriculture, industry, and food security. *Research Journal of Social Sciences and Economics Review*, *5*(1), 1–15.

Amachraa, A. (2023). Navigating Morocco's agricultural policy: Unraveling the nexus of water, food security, and trade tensions in global value chains. *Preprints*, *2023*, 2023070604. https://doi.org/10.20944/preprints202307.0604.v1

Amiraslani, F., & Dragovich, D. (2023). Food-energy-water nexus in Iran over the last two centuries: A food secure future? *Energy Nexus*, 100189.

Anggara, W., Harahap, I., & Nawawi, Z. M. (2024). Systematic literature review: The paradigm of developing nations oriented towards falah. *International Journal of Science, Technology & Management*, *5*(1), 163–175.

Aziz, M. R. A. (2012). *Agriculture in Islam: From the perspective of economics, banking & finance*. Penerbit UTM Press.

Borhan, J. T., & Aziz, M. R. A. (2009). Agriculture and its contribution from the Islamic economics perspective. *Sains Humanika, 50*(1).

Brevik, E. C., Homburg, J. A., & Sandor, J. A. (2018). Soils, climate, and ancient civilizations. *Developments in Soil Science, 35*, 1–28. Elsevier.

Budiyoko, B., Wati, D. R., Prayoga, A., & Berliana, D. (2024). Islamic financial literacy and moral hazards in the utilization of Islamic microfinance by traditional rice farmers in Central Lampung, Indonesia. *SSRN*. https://ssrn.com/abstract=4689593 or http://doi.org/10.2139/ssrn.4689593

Carreira, I., Costa, F., & Pessoa, J. P. (2024). The deforestation effects of trade and agricultural productivity in Brazil. *Journal of Development Economics, 167*.

David Raj, A., Kumar, S., Kalambukattu, J. G., & Chatterjee, U. (2024). Land degradation and its relation to climate change and sustainability. In A. D. Raj, S. Kumar, J. G. Kalambukattu, & U. Chatterjee (Eds.), *Climate crisis: Adaptive approaches and sustainability* (pp. 121–135). Springer Nature Switzerland.

Deguine, J. P., Aubertot, J. N., Bellon, S., Côte, F., Lauri, P. E., Lescourret, F., Ratnadass, A., Scopel, E., Andrieu, N., Bàrberi, P., Becker, N., Bouyer, J., Brévault, T., Cerdan, C., Cortesero, M., Dangles, O., Delatte, H., Phuong, T. Y. D., Dreyer, H., . . . & Lamichhane, J. R. (2023). Agroecological crop protection for sustainable agriculture. *Advances in Agronomy, 178*, 1–59.

El Chami, D., Daccache, A., & El Moujabber, M. (2020). How can sustainable agriculture increase climate resilience? A systematic review. *Sustainability, 12*(8), 3119.

Ewert, F., Baatz, R., & Finger, R. (2023). Agroecology for a sustainable agriculture and food system: From local solutions to large-scale adoption. *Annual Review of Resource Economics, 15*, 351–381.

Ferraro-Fanning, A. (2023). *The sustainable homestead: Create a thriving permaculture ecosystem with your garden, animals, and land.* Cool Springs Press.

Finnegan, E. (2011). Cultivating faith: The relationship between Islam and sustainable agriculture in rural communities of American Muslims. *Global Food Insecurity: Rethinking Agricultural and Rural Development Paradigm and Policy*, 53–62.

Ghimire, M., Khanal, A., Bhatt, D., Dahal, D., & Giri, S. (2024). Agroforestry systems in Nepal: Enhancing food security and rural livelihoods–A comprehensive review. *Food and Energy Security, 13*(1), e524.

Gore, V. B., Ghumde, S. A., Narale, S. B., & Sidam, P. D. (2023). Biotechnology and organic farming. *Advances in Biotechnology, 248*.

Habriyanto, H., Sucipto, S., & Pratiwi, R. (2023, April). Analysis of implementation of murabahah contract in agricultural financing at Indonesian Sharia Bank Branch Office Jambi (hybrid contract model as alternative solution). In T. D. Warninda, F. E. A. Azra, & D. P. Nugraha (Eds.), *Proceedings of the 3rd International Conference of Islamic Finance and Business, ICIFEB 2022*, Jakarta, Indonesia, July 19–20, 2022.

Hassan, N. A. M., Zakaria, K., Salleh, K. M., & Ahmed, S. M. (2023). An empirical analysis of Malaysian palm oil export to world major palm oil importing countries. *Operations Research and Decisions, 33*(1), 61–73.

Homburg, J., Grunwald, S., & Brevik, E. C. (2023). From native American tradition to modern-day America: Native origin legends that involve soil and Earth. In N. Patzel, S. Grunwald, E. C. Brevik, & C. Feller (Eds.), *Cultural understanding of soils: The importance of cultural diversity and of the inner world* (pp. 181–207). Springer. https://link.springer.com/book/10.1007/978-3-031-13169-1

Ibrahim, E., Akbar, W., Mujiburohman, M., & Rahima, D. (2023). Mudharabah contract as economic strengthening in Indonesia (literature study on Islamic financial institutions and community economic activities). *Jurnal Al-Qardh*, *8*(1), 52–63.

Ikerd, J. (1998). Sustainable agriculture, rural economic development, and large-scale swine production. *Pigs, Profits, and Rural Communities*, 157–169.

Khattak, Z. R., & Ali, R. F. (2024). Impact of riba based transactions on the socio-economic system of Pakistan. *Pakistan Research Journal of Social Sciences*, *3*(1).

Karaca, M., & Ince, A. G. (2019). Conservation of biodiversity and genetic resources for sustainable agriculture. *Innovations in Sustainable Agriculture*, 363–410.

Keskin, B., & Güneş, E. (2023). The European green deal: Implications for Turkey. *Mediterranean Politics*, 1–13.

Khangura, R., Ferris, D., Wagg, C., & Bowyer, J. (2023). Regenerative agriculture—A literature review on the practices and mechanisms used to improve soil health. *Sustainability*, *15*(3), 2338.

Kumari, D., Thakur, A., Tiwari, A. K., & Singh, R. (2024). Types and sources of agricultural pollution: Identifying the different pollutants generated by farming practices and their origins. In A. Kumar, D. Kumar, J. Singh, & R. Kumar (Eds.), *A comprehensive exploration of soil, water, and air pollution in agriculture* (pp. 71–85). BFC Publications.

Lago-Olveira, S., El-Areed, S. R., Moreira, M. T., & González-García, S. (2023). Improving environmental sustainability of agriculture in Egypt through a life-cycle perspective. *Science of the Total Environment*, *890*, 164335.

Li, F., Wu, S., Liu, H., & Yan, D. (2024). Biodiversity loss through cropland displacement for urban expansion in China. *Science of the Total Environment*, *907*.

MacRae, R. J., Hill, S. B., Henning, J., & Mehuys, G. R. (1989). Agricultural science and sustainable agriculture: A review of the existing scientific barriers to sustainable food production and potential solutions. *Biological Agriculture & Horticulture*, *6*(3), 173–219.

Madamombe, S. M., Karanja Ng'ang'a, S., Öborn, I., Nyamadzawo, G., Ngonidzashe, C., Kihara, J., & Nkurunziza, L. (2024). Climate change awareness and adaptation strategies by smallholder farmers in semi-arid areas of Zimbabwe. *International Journal of Agricultural Sustainability*, *22*(1), 2293588.

Majid, R. (2024). Empirical analysis and financing of agricultural sector in East Java. *Migration Letters*, *21*(S3), 804–823.

Majumdar, A., Upadhyay, M. K., Giri, B., Yadav, P., Moulick, D., Sarkar, S., Thakur, B. K., Sahu, K., Srivastava, A. K., Buck, M., Tibbett, M., Jaiswal, M. K., & Roychowdhury, T. (2024). Sustainable water management in rice cultivation reduces arsenic contamination, increases productivity, microbial molecular response, and profitability. *Journal of Hazardous Materials*, 133610.

Malaisamy, A. (2024). Climatic shifts and agricultural strategies: A thorough review on impact of climate change on food security and crop productivity. *International Journal of Environment and Climate Change*, *14*(1), 817–831.

Mazoyer, M., & Roudart, L. (2006). *A history of world agriculture: From the neolithic age to the current crisis*. NYU Press.

Miar, M., Rizani, A., Pardede, R., & Basrowi, B. (2024). Analysis of the effects of capital expenditure and supply chain on economic growth and their implications on the community welfare of districts and cities in central Kalimantan province. *Uncertain Supply Chain Management*, *12*(1), 489–504.

Morley, S., Kennedy, A., Pradesha, A., & Hadiwidjaja, G. (2019). *The role of agriculture in the structural transformation of Indonesia* (Vol. 1838). International Food Policy Research Institute.

Muhmad, S. N., Muhamad, R., & Sulong, F. (2021). Sustainable development goals and Islamic finance: An integrated approach for Islamic financial institutions. *Indonesian Journal of Sustainability Accounting and Management*, *5*(1), 123â–136.

Mustafa, Z., Tasir, S. F., Junoh, N., & Zakaria, N. H. (2017). The etiquettes of agriculture in Islam. *Journal of Contemporary Social Science Research*, *2*(1), 28.

Nalluri, N., & Karri, V. R. (2024). Superior effect of nature-based solutions in soil and water management for sustainable agriculture. *Plant Science Today*, *11*(1), 06–20.

Obaisi, A. I., Adegbeye, M. J., Elghandour, M. M., Barbabosa-Pliego, A., & Salem, A. Z. M. (2022). Natural resource management and sustainable agriculture. In M. Lackner, B. Sajjadi, & W. Y. Chen (Eds.), *Handbook of climate change mitigation and adaptation* (pp. 2577–2613). Springer International Publishing.

Oberč, B. P., & Arroyo Schnell, A. (2020). Approaches to sustainable agriculture. *Exploring the Pathways, 486*.

Parot, J., Wahlen, S., Schryro, J., & Weckenbrock, P. (2023). Food justice in community supported agriculture–Differentiating charitable and emancipatory social support actions. *Agriculture and Human Values*, 1–15.

Parveen, Z. (2022). Agriculture financing through Bay Salam in Islamic banking institutions: Theory and practice. *Al-Qamar*, 107–138.

Parvin, R., Bari, M. S., & Muhammad, N. (2024). Impacts of climate change on Teesta river basin char lands: A study of livelihood and ecosystem dynamics in Bangladesh. *International Journal of Environment and Climate Change*, *14*(2), 407–422.

Petro, G. (2022). Consumers demand sustainable products and shopping formats. *Forbes*. https://www.forbes.com/sites/gregpetro/2022/03/11/consumers-demand-sustainable-products-and-shopping-formats/

Pisante, M., Gogoi, N., & Farooq, M. (2023). Sustainability, sustainable agriculture, and the environment. In M. Farooq, N. Gogoi, & M. Pisante (Eds.), *Sustainable agriculture and the environment* (pp. 3–24). Academic Press.

Powlson, D. S., Gregory, P. J., Whalley, W. R., Quinton, J. N., Hopkins, D. W., Whitmore, A. P., Hirsch, P. R., & Goulding, K. W. (2011). Soil management in relation to sustainable agriculture and ecosystem services. *Food Policy*, *36*, S72–S87.

Ritchie, H. (2021, February 4). *Drivers of deforestation*. Our World in Data. https://ourworldindata.org/drivers-of-deforestation?utm_medium=email&utm_source=govdelivery

Robertson, G. P., & Swinton, S. M. (2005). Reconciling agricultural productivity and environmental integrity: A grand challenge for agriculture. *Frontiers in Ecology and the Environment*, *3*(1), 38–46.

Sales, A. P. (2023). Agricultural frontiers and environment: A systematic literature review and research agenda for emerging countries. *Environment, Development and Sustainability*, 1–26.

Saqib, L., & Roberts, K. W. (2017). Istisnā'- A realistic approach to the concept in Islamic finance and its application to the agricultural sector in Pakistan. *Al-Idah*, *34*(1), 18–39.

Schreefel, L., Schulte, R. P. O., De Boer, I. J. M., Schrijver, A. P., & Van Zanten, H. H. E. (2020). Regenerative agriculture–The soil is the base. *Global Food Security*, *26*, 100404.

Setyaningsih, P., & Jayaprawira, A. R. (2020). Strengthening agricultural investment through sustainable Islamic banking. *International Journal of Business Studies*, *4*(2), 82–103.

Smit, B., & Smithers, J. (1993). Sustainable agriculture: Interpretations, analyses and prospects. *Canadian Journal of Regional Science*, *16*(3), 499–524.

Statistical, Economic and Social Research and Training Centre for Islamic Countries (SESRIC). (2020). *Agriculture and food security in OIC member countries*. Organization of Islamic Cooperation (OIC). https://sesricdiag.blob.core.windows.net/sesric-site-blob/files/article/748.pdf

Sulaiman, S. M., Bunu, M. A., & Alkassim, J. L. (2023). Acceptance of agricultural takaful among crop farmers in Yobe State, Nigeria. *Journal of Islamic Business and Management*, *13*(1).

Sulistyowati, C. A., Afiff, S. A., Baiquni, M., & Siscawati, M. (2023). Challenges and potential solutions in developing community supported agriculture: A literature review. *Agroecology and Sustainable Food Systems*, *47*(6), 834–856.

Tahat, M. M., Alananbeh, K. M., Othman, A. Y., & Leskovar, D. I. (2020). Soil health and sustainable agriculture. *Sustainability*, *12*(12), 4859.

Takahashi, A. (2024). Agriculture and rural villages in the national economy. In A. Takahashi (Ed.), *Regime changes and socio-economic history of rural Myanmar, 1986-2019* (pp. 41–64). Springer Nature Singapore.

Taqwiem, A., & Rachmadi, K. R. (2023). Cash waqf linked Sukuk financing in the development of sustainable agriculture from the Maqashid Syari'ah perspective. *Jurnal Ilmiah Ekonomi Islam*, *9*(2), 1745–1754.

Tasneem, F., & Khan, M. A. (2024). Growth and structural transformation–Options for Pakistan. *Research in Globalization*, *8*, 100190.

Trigo, A., Marta-Costa, A., & Fragoso, R. (2021). Principles of sustainable agriculture: Defining standardized reference points. *Sustainability*, *13*(8), 4086.

Turmel, M. S., Speratti, A., Baudron, F., Verhulst, N., & Govaerts, B. (2015). Crop residue management and soil health: A systems analysis. *Agricultural Systems*, *134*, 6–16.

U.S. Congress. (1990, November 28). *Food, agriculture, conservation, and trade act of 1990. Public law 101–624*. U.S. Farm Bill. https://www.govinfo.gov/content/pkg/COMPS-10649/pdf/COMPS-10649.pdf

Velten, S., Leventon, J., Jager, N., & Newig, J. (2015). What is sustainable agriculture? A systematic review. *Sustainability*, *7*(6), 7833–7865.

Verma, P., & Bibhakar, P. (2024). Challenges and solutions in the agricultural sector of India. In M. A. Khan, R. Khan, & P. Praveen (Eds.), *Infrastructure possibilities and human-centered approaches with industry 5.0* (pp. 125–141). IGI Global.

Viana, C. M., Freire, D., Abrantes, P., Rocha, J., & Pereira, P. (2022). Agricultural land systems importance for supporting food security and sustainable development goals: A systematic review. *Science of the Total Environment, 806*.

Yadav, S. P. S., Lahutiya, V., Ghimire, N. P., Yadav, B., & Paudel, P. (2023). Exploring innovation for sustainable agriculture: A systematic case study of permaculture in Nepal. *Heliyon, 9*(5).

Yanagi, M. (2024). Understanding the ecological significance of wheat: Roles, climate change impacts, and biodiversity conservation strategies. *Geographical Research Bulletin, 3*, 6–9.

Zhang, C., Zhou, Z., Zhu, C., Chen, Q., Feng, Q., Zhu, M., Tang, F., Wu, X., Zou, Y., Zhang, F., Zheng, J., & Yu, T. (2024). Analysis of the evolvement of livelihood patterns of farm households relocated for poverty alleviation programs in ethnic minority areas of China. *Agriculture, 14*(1), 94.

Chapter 11

Fintech and Islamic Finance: Opportunities and Challenges

Issa Hamadou[a] *and Umer Suleman*[b]

[a]Universitas Islam Internasional Indonesia (UIII), Indonesia
[b]Wahed, UK

Abstract

After the financial crisis of 2007–2008, the financial service industry realized that the world's worst financial catastrophe had been caused by an age of easy money and lax monitoring. This realization led to pressure on regulators to overhaul the financial system during the Great Depression. Banks were required to make sure they implemented a variety of endogenous risk-minimization mechanisms and assume accountability for verifying the stability of the financial scheme. Innovative financial technology (fintech) solutions arose in this more regulated environment to address – or, as one would argue, avoid – risks that arose during the financial crisis. The goal of this chapter is to examine the possible challenges and opportunities of incorporating fintech into Islamic finance. Four services are provided by Islamic fintech: finance, payments, advisory, and compliance. The traditional financial system is being recolonized by Islamic fintech. Fintech adoption in Islamic finance could lead to greater financial inclusion, the solution to emergencies like COVID-19, and the achievement of Sustainable Development Goals (SDGs) for a sustainable national economy. However, there could be obstacles associated with this acceptance in the form of risk, investment, and regulatory issues. In order for fintech companies to be innovative and address social issues that conventional financial institutions fail to address, authorities must provide a market whereby these companies can thrive without having to be acquired by major banks or focus their innovation solely on meeting the demands of these banks. Furthermore, they need to be explicit about the regulations' applicability to fintech companies, especially with regard to how to strike a balance between being a technology company and a financial institution.

The Future of Islamic Finance, 175–188

doi:10.1108/978-1-83549-906-120241011

Keywords: Challenges; financial inclusion; Fintech; Islamic finance; Islamic fintech; opportunities; poverty alleviation

Introduction

The financial crisis of 2007–2008 changed how the financial services industry operated, realizing the era of easy money, and weak oversight had led to the nastiest worldwide financial crisis; subsequently, during the Great Depression, regulators were under pressure to reform the financial system. Banks had to ensure they applied various measures endogenously to minimize risks and take responsibility for confirming the solidity of the financial scheme. In this more regulated environment, innovative fintech products emerged to address (or circumvent, one could say) risks that occurred during the financial crisis. Yin et al. (2022) argued that fintech development greatly impacted the financial outreach of the banks after the financial crisis. Fintech startups involved in, for example, P2P (peer-to-peer) lending and online payment services have shown noticeable growth since the financial crisis. Implementing digital infrastructure enabled banks to reduce risks and better serve the financial markets. Furthermore, fintech promotes financial inclusion by reducing costs and increasing accessibility to banking services by transmitting digital infrastructure (mobile phones, internet, etc.) to unbanked communities.

Integrating Islamic finance within the general fintech architecture allows the industry to spread in scope and influence. Islamic finance aims to create an equitable and inclusive financial system guided by ethical and moral considerations. Over the years, this niche sector has gained prominence, offering an alternative approach to banking and investment that aligns with Islamic principles. Now, at the crossroads of tradition and technology, Islamic fintech is carving out its own space in the financial realm. The convergence of Islamic finance with blockchain technology, artificial intelligence (AI), and digital payments is paving the way for a new era of financial services that cater to the unique needs of Muslim consumers and investors. Accordingly, Islamic fintech has emerged in the last decade with considerable potential growth. Thus, why did Islamic fintech exist, and what could be its potential opportunities and challenges? This question will be answered throughout this chapter. The remaining parts of this chapter are organized as follows. Section 2 shows an overview of fintech. Section 3 examines the challenges and opportunities of integrating fintech in Islamic finance. Finally, the last section provides a brief conclusion of the chapter.

An Overview of Fintech: Evolution, Ecosystem and Business Models

The Evolution of Fintech

A developing sector of the global finance business is fintech. It indicates the application of technology to deliver minor or significant adjustments to financial services (Alshater and Othman, 2020). Fintech, according to the Financial Stability Board, is defined as financial innovation made possible by technology that could eventually result in the development of innovative business models, applications, processes, or products that have a significant impact on financial markets, institutions and the offer of banking services (Alshater et al., 2022).

According to Alshater et al. (2022), the evolution of fintech started as early as 1866. Its progress can be summarized into three stages. The first stage was manifested by telegraphs and trans-Atlantic cables, which were used as intermediation to communicate in financial industries.

The second phase of the fintech evolution was characterized by the introduction of automated teller machines (ATMs) and virtual banking between 1967 and 2008. Technology was employed during this time to design financial services and products. Adopting cutting-edge technologies like blockchain, AI, and cloud computing signaled the start of the third stage in 2008. Fintech is hailed as a disruptive innovation that will change the game and upend established financial systems (Lee & Shin, 2018). As of 2023, the size of the global fintech market was estimated to be $226.76 billion. Throughout the forecast period, 2024–2032, it is expected to grow at a Compound Annual Growth Rate (CAGR) of 16.8%, reaching USD 917.17 billion by 2032 (Global et al. and Forecast 2024–2032, 2023).

Fintech Stakeholders

Researchers frequently break down the fintech players into components of essential players to study organizational transformation and relationships between organizations. However, there is ongoing debate over the appropriate level of analysis needed to comprehend and study the fintech ecosystem (Migozzi et al., 2023). According to Lee and Shin (2018), five parties are involved in fintech: government, traditional financial institutions, fintech start-ups, software developers, and financial clients (see Fig. 11.1).

The software developers provide necessary technologies such as cloud computing, big data analytics, social networks, AI, and digital platforms. These technologies are relevant for market analysis and financial product design. Conventional banking institutions work together with fintech start-ups for funding provisions and to get quicker access to new technologies. Fintechs benefit from access to funding, and ultimately, they both serve the same consumer base.

Fintech revenue is deemed to be generated by both individual consumers and small and medium enterprises (SMEs). According to recent research, 25% of unbanked and 16% of underbanked clients in the Association of Southeast Asian Nations (ASEAN) use digital financial services, indicating a solid diffusion of any fintech segment in the area (Aduba et al., 2023). Krupa and Buszko (2023) discovered that young clients are more interested in fintech than adults, with criteria such as male gender, family size, and financial decision-making influencing their experience. Fintech is used more by those under 30 than adults, while individuals over 30 may utilize it if they properly inspect it.

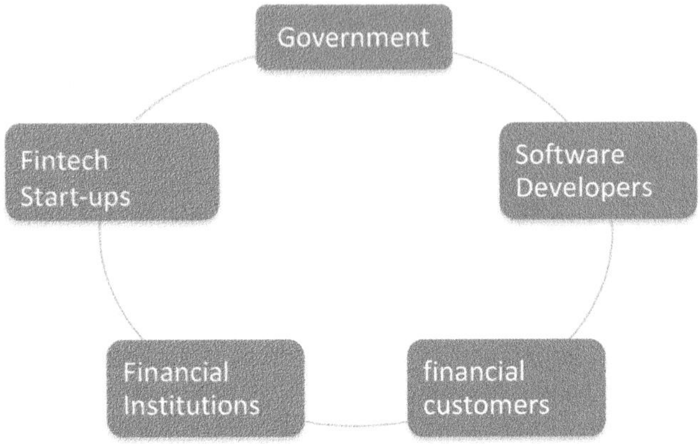

Fig. 11.1. Fintech Stakeholders. *Source:* Adapted from Lee and Shin (2018).

The government provides regulatory support for the development of new products to facilitate their adoption. For example, Singapore provided a new regulation for digital payment systems to give customers maximum convenience and confidence while making online payments (Reuters, 2016). As fintech changes the global financial system, the government must uphold and strengthen its privacy and cyber security control.

Fintech Applications

Over the last 10 years, fintechs have raised over $500 billion in funding, with cryptocurrency contributing more than $50 billion in 2021 and 2022. When fintechs reached their zenith in 2021, their public valuations had reached $1.3 trillion, accounting for around 9% of all financial sector valuations worldwide. The $12.5 trillion global financial services market is split relatively evenly between banking and insurance and centered in North America and Asia-Pacific (APAC) (Goyal et al., 2023). With yearly fintech sales expected to increase more than sixfold from 2021 to 2030 to reach $1.5 trillion, fintechs are predicted to play a significant and growing role in this boom. By 2030, it is anticipated that the revenues of banking fintechs will account for one-fourth of worldwide banking valuations, rising from 4 to 13% of banking revenue pools.

Insuretechs are anticipated to increase from 0.3 to 2% of insurance income pools in the industry.[1] Over the next 20 years, this expansion will take on distinct forms depending on geography and the affected segments. This will result in varying degrees of maturity, which variations will mainly influence funding

[1]The application of technology innovations meant to wring efficiency and cost savings out of the current insurance business model is referred to as "insurtech." Conceived from the term fintech, insurtech is a mashup of the terms "insurance" and "technology."

sources, talent pools, local regulatory stances, and technological acceptance. Every area is in a distinct stage of the broader fintech development, with different stakeholders looking to adapt and apply strategies that have worked well elsewhere or to develop unique solutions to particular problems in their respective fields (Goyal et al., 2023).

Insurance solutions, fundraising, payments, financing, financial planning, and capital markets are among the roughly six fintech application models (Lee & Shin, 2018; Suryono et al., 2020). One of the fintech models that is expanding the fastest is the payment model. Fintech businesses focusing on payments may quickly and cheaply expand their customer base. Popular technologies like barcodes and QR codes are used in the most current advancements in fintech mobile payments (Li, 2016). The most widely used mobile payment apps are Google Wallet, Apple Pay, and Samsung Pay. According to Maybray (2023), wealth management involves utilizing technology to enhance and mechanize several areas of wealth management. One of the popular fintech business models for wealth management is the automated wealth manager or "robo-advisor." It provides financial assistance for a small portion of the cost of a real-life consultant (Lee & Shin, 2018). Fintech crowdfunding allows networks of people to direct the development of new media, goods, and concepts while also collecting money for venture capital or charitable causes.

Three parties are involved in crowdfunding: the entrepreneur or project initiator who requires financing, potential contributors who could be engaged in assisting the project or cause, and an intermediary organization that helps to arrange communication between the participants and the initiator. Contributors can obtain information about various programs and financing options for product/service development from the moderating organization. The three most common types of crowdfunding business models are reward-based, donation-based, and equity-based.

Another significant fintech development is P2P lending for consumers and businesses. Fintech P2P lending enables individuals and companies to lend and borrow from one another. Fintech is utilized in the capital markets to offer practical and affordable goods and services for trading, foreign exchange, capital investment, risk management, and research. Trading is one potential application of capital market fintech. Trading fintech enables traders and investors to communicate, exchange information, place orders to purchase and sell stocks and commodities and keep a real-time eye on hazards.

Fintech aims to facilitate a closer connection between the customer and the insurer in insurance fintech operations. Utilizing data analytics, they compute and correlate risk. When the clientele grows, they present products that cater to their requirements (auto, life, health, or liability insurance, for example). Fig. 11.2 below represents a fintech application summarizing the above explanation. It shows the different ways in which technology can be leveraged to provide better financial services.

A High-Level Overview of Islamic Fintech

Islamic Fintech Moving Beyond Existing Islamic Finance Products

Islamic fintech refers to the application of technology to offer financial services that comply with Shari'ah to clients of Islamic financial institutions and banks

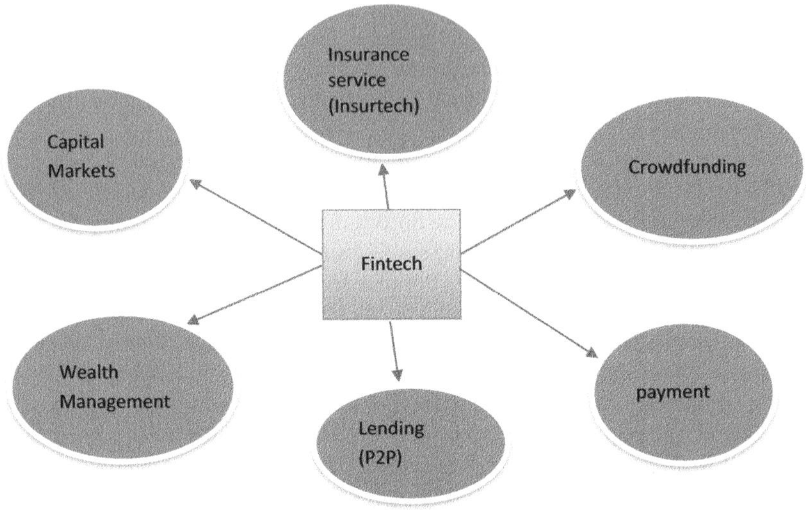

Fig. 11.2. Fintech Application. *Source:* Authors' own conception.

(Hassan et al., 2020). With a focus on goods that comply with Islamic law, Islamic fintech is similar to conventional fintech (Alshater and Othman, 2020). According to Baber (2019), an Islamic fintech offers four different services: finance, advising, payments, and compliance. The influx of start-ups offering innovative methods of generating capital has led to a tremendous surge in crowdfunding platforms. Islamic fintech encourages Shari'ah-compliant goods and expands Muslim investors' and customers' access to finance (Dawood et al., 2022).

Can the fundamental problems with the traditional financial system be resolved by incorporating Islamic Banking Principles into Fintech? Haneef and Smolo (2013) contend that the worldwide financial crisis presents a chance to improve conditions and that the Islamic banking industry should take the lead in achieving this. However, this has to be viewed with skepticism, considering that Islamic finance missed a great chance to take on the traditional banking system during the most recent global recession. Even though the crisis had a limited impact on Islamic Financial Institutions, the fundamental flaws in the capitalist economic system are relevant to their development (Haneef & Smolo, 2013; Smolo & Mirakhor, 2010). This is because, when mishandled, Islamic finance can become just another instrument for generating profits, with no regard for these goods' broader effects on society. Many products, even those with seemingly Shari'ah-compliant structures, fall short of the results the Shari'ah is supposed to deliver. Regardless of economic strength, Islamic finance's fundamental *maqasid* (objectives) are the fair and equal allocation of resources, which upholds rights and guarantees the transparent fulfillment of commitments.

Fintech will only uphold the status quo and fall short of realizing its full promise as a tool to broaden the availability of financial services if the same businesses deliver the exact products faster and more effectively. Nevertheless, fintech has already demonstrated its ability to be a viable option for investors and people needing money. The expansion of crowdfunding, a market with a global yearly growth rate of 167%, perfectly illustrates this. Global crowdfunding volume hit $16.2 billion in 2014, and the trend continues to rise.

Although a large portion of this expansion has come from lending-based platforms, which typically do not adhere to Islamic ethical standards, we are witnessing a revolution in ethical investing favoring equity-based platforms. This equity-based approach satisfies individual ethical or religious requirements while outperforming the industry overall and boasting a startling expansion rate of 182% that complies with Shari'ah.

In 2021, $79 billion was the total value of Islamic fintech transactions in all the countries that comprise the Organization of Islamic Cooperation (OIC). Although this only makes up 0.7% of the global fintech volume of transactions, Islamic fintechs are predicted to grow at a 17.9% CAGR to reach $179 billion by 2026. This growth forecast is higher than conventional fintechs, which are projected to grow at a 15% CAGR over the same period. Congested fintech categories include payments, deposit and lending, and fundraising even though they continue to proliferate and offer investors easy targets (GIFR, 2022). The Islamic fintech market size is concentrated in nations with a substantial Muslim population. It demonstrates that Islamic fintech is widely recognized and applied in most Muslim countries. Based on the anticipated transaction volume, Saudi Arabia, Iran, Malaysia, Indonesia, and the United Arab Emirates are the top countries. Thus, it shows an essential concentration of marketplace activity among the principal jurisdictions (GIFR, 2022).

Islamic Fintech Opportunities

According to Rabbani et al. (2020), Islamic fintech is showing interesting developments in Muslim countries. The advancement of mobile and smartphone technology has cleared the path for the expansion of fintech in these countries. Suleman (2019) highlighted that fintech has already shown promising results in providing an option to investors and individuals needing funding. Crowdfunding, an industry with a global yearly growth rate of 167%, is a perfect example. The global crowdfunding volume hit $16.2 billion in 2014, continuously growing. There is potential for co-integrating fintech into Islamic finance to benefit the unbanked and small-to-medium-sized businesses. Adopting fintech in Islamic finance could help improve financial inclusion, overcome financial crises such as COVID-19, and achieve SDGs for a sustainable nation (Alshater et al., 2022).

Islamic fintech is a great source of financing for the younger generation. Firmansyah and Ramdani (2018) surveyed young graduates in Indonesia and discovered that Islamic fintech companies can significantly assist entrepreneurs. It will be a significant accelerator for young graduates to finance their entrepreneurship ideas successfully. They also claimed that about 84% of early adopters are content to shop while performing *sadaqah*. By inventing a new technology and business model, Islamic fintech start-ups significantly promote financial access and reduce social problems in Indonesia. Once again, fintech innovations have brought numerous benefits to the financial sector, like cost savings, more excellent quality services, and client satisfaction. Integrating fintech in Islamic finance can help achieve Islamic social finance objectives by targeting people experiencing poverty. Rabbani et al. (2022) presented an AI-powered Islamic fintech approach to assist the destitute and underprivileged afflicted by COVID-19. The approach employs an AI and NLP (natural language processing) powered fintech platform to collect and allocate zakat funds to needy, underprivileged, COVID-19 victims, and vulnerable. They argued that integrating fintech into Islamic financial services can give people opportunities to get financial assistance and receive zakat and *sadaqah* in a short time. Consequently, fintech enables the objective and application of Islamic social finance by targeting low-income people, which can lead to financial inclusion. In addition, considering that Islamic fintech offers a more affordable option for financial services, its development holds great promise for developing countries. Simultaneously, it tests the competence of regulatory bodies to preserve stability and protect investors and institutions from dishonest trading activities (Saba et al., 2019). Fintech supports businesses in gaining a competitive advantage and increasing efficacy (Kou et al., 2021; Zouari & Abdelhedi, 2021). Shaikh (2020) underscored the significance of monetary and environmental sustainability outreach, adaptability, and the synergy of non-monetary factors, including dedication, payback inducements, and the impact of multipliers on skill development.

From a global perspective, fintech is a significant driver for financial institutions in attaining balanced development (Arner et al., 2020). The entire potential of fintech to serve the SDGs may be realized through a gradual method of creating fundamental infrastructure for the digital financial revolution. For example, Demir et al. (2020) investigated the impact of fintech on income inequality across 140 countries. They argued that fintech improves income equality through financial inclusion. Furthermore, the findings suggested that increased financial inclusion, aided by digital access, considerably decreases income inequality across all quantiles, particularly in higher-income countries. The study by Kanga et al. (2021) suggested that in the long run, fintech's implications on financial inclusion and gross domestic product (GDP) per capita outweigh its short-term impact. Their findings concluded that improving financial sector performance and promoting fintech adoption are desirable policy objectives.

Islamic Fintech Challenges

Islamic fintech solutions are also facing numerous challenges. Dawood et al. (2022) state that the main challenges of Islamic fintech are investment management, risk management, and regulation challenges.

Regulation Challenges

Fintech policies impact the financial stability of banks in a number of ways. According to Khan et al. (2023), these include initiatives by the regulatory environment to guarantee effective risk management, safeguard consumers, deal with cybersecurity and data protection, promote innovation through regulatory sandboxes, create interoperability standards, enforce capital and prudential requirements, and offer regulatory guidance. As per the findings of Alshater et al. (2022), the primary obstacles to the advancement of fintech in Islamic finance are the absence of legal regulations and inadequate financial knowledge. Another study by Nastiti and Kasri (2019) discovered that fintech-related legislation was ineffective in achieving the goal, at least in the medium term. This was assumed to be due to the limited number of Islamic banks. Perhaps, since Islamic fintech is still in the progression of development, testing, and the discussion of results and experiences, the regulatory challenges for this business are seen as among the most critical issues highlighted and explored in the selected research (Dawood et al., 2022). Although it is occasionally claimed that equity crowdfunding is generally Shari'ah-compliant, a closer look at the models shows how important it is to create unique Shari'ah-compliant equity crowdfunding to have a sustainable halal market (Abdullah & Oseni, 2017). In jurisdictions where the regulator is agnostic to faith, such as the Financial Conduct Authority (FCA) in the UK, there is an additional challenge to ensure that Shari'ah-compliant is presented to the regulator in a form the regulator will understand, e.g. debt structures. An example of this is Murabaha arrangements for Home Purchase Plans (HPP), which will still be recognized as mortgages.[2]

The government should provide legal compliance, regulation, licensing, and socializing issues related to crowdfunding to ensure legitimacy for the nation (Hendratmi et al., 2019). According to a thorough examination of the literature, Shari'ah compliance has emerged as one of the biggest obstacles to the development of Islamic fintech. Moreover, it is plausible that Islamic fintech could pose challenges for Islamic financial institutions concerning operational efficacy, customer retention, accountability, and transparency. Expanding and diversifying Islamic business activities and transactions could be possible by developing Islamic fintech applications and procedures that adhere to Shari'ah principles (Çakmak, 2023).

There is not a single globally recognized regulatory body that oversees Islamic fintech. This is not surprising considering that national regulations govern Islamic financial institutions, including Islamic fintech companies, just like traditional financial services laws. Because of this, many leading authorities tasked with creating guidelines and the legal foundation for Islamic fintech are in densely populated places. These regulatory bodies comprise, among others, the Central Bank of Saudi Arabia, the Financial Services Authority of Indonesia, the Bank Negara Malaysia & Securities Commission of Malaysia, and regulators in Western markets like the FCA of the UK, which permits Islamic fintechs to function within their conventional regulatory framework (GIFR, 2022).

---

[2]https://www.handbook.fca.org.uk/handbook/PERG/14/4.html.

Risk Management Challenges

A central risk associated with fintech is the increased exposure to cybersecurity threats. As fintech relies heavily on digital platforms and the processing of vast amounts of sensitive data, the potential for cyberattacks and data breaches is heightened. Additionally, the fast pace of technological advancements in the FinTech sector often outpaces the development of robust regulatory frameworks, leaving consumers vulnerable to potential fraud and scams. Moreover, fintech operations are not immune to system glitches, technical malfunctions, or operational failures, which can disrupt financial operations and lead to financial losses for consumers and companies (PWC, 2018). Therefore, regulators, policymakers, and industry players must prioritize establishing comprehensive cybersecurity measures, proactive regulatory frameworks, and contingency plans to mitigate the risks associated with fintech. The more specific risks relating to Islamic fintechs, referenced in The State of the Global Islamic Economy Report 2023/24 (SGIER), also highlight the marketing risk "actually targeting Muslims in Muslim minority countries since early 2022 on meta platforms such as Facebook and Instagram. Now, even Google or TikTok have started removing targeting options related to Muslim interests." This severely restricts the ability of Islamic fintech from Muslim minority markets to promote their product to their desired user base. Connected to this is the ability to secure capital for Islamic fintech start-ups since marketing measurability is a key driver of investment.

Investment Management Challenge

Using an Islamic crowdfunding platform, Ishak and Rahman (2021) looked into using *mudarabah* (silent partnership) as an investment mechanism. According to their findings, *mudarabah* itself is not an entirely appropriate instrument, especially for equity-based Islamic crowdfunding, despite the possibility of Islamic crowdfunding using fintech as an effective platform. This is because of the high associated risks, which include fraudulent enterprises, insufficient restrictions to protect investors' money and complex share structures that dilute influence on the partnership. Some risks can be mitigated by implementing fintech solutions, such as tight project monitoring, enhanced regulatory measures to safeguard investment funds, improved *mudarabah* procedures, and increased awareness of the *mudarabah* idea among all stakeholders.

The challenges of Islamic fintech are also attached to founder Incompetence, fraud, and project risk (Agrawal et al., 2014). According to Rahman et al. (2020), because P2P lending and equity crowdfunding have proliferated in Malaysia, it is widely believed that crowdfunding remains beneficial for business owners there. It cannot, however, sway their choice to employ crowdsourcing. It suggests that some business owners are hesitant to share their ideas online. This opinion is in line with feedback from Malaysian operators of crowdfunding platforms, who have stated that some entrepreneurs are reluctant to engage in crowdfunding, especially those who lack computer technology and information skills (Rahman et al., 2016). This study highlights the difficulties in investment management. Some business owners lack the managerial abilities to oversee Islamic fintech firms.

Conclusion

To sum up, the primary aim of this chapter was to analyze the potential advantages and difficulties associated with incorporating fintech into Islamic finance. One may argue that the integration of fintech into Islamic finance offers a plethora of potential concerning social values, economic values, and environmental conservation – all of which can contribute to accomplishing the SDGs. These prospects will not come without challenges, however. The most significant obstacle to the growth of Islamic fintech is the absence of regulatory frameworks and low financial knowledge. Therefore, the government must enact laws that permit innovation while safeguarding consumers; educational institutions must invest in specialized research units and human capital must be drawn from within to establish an environment conducive to the growth of Islamic fintech in a nation.

The plethora of financial service industries where fintech can be connected, including cryptocurrencies, blockchain, cross-border payments, etc., is critical to Islamic fintech's success. Islamic fintech needs to keep up with the rapid development of the conventional finance industry to achieve this. Because the fundamental idea of fintech-shared money complies with Shari'ah laws, the potential for Islamic finance exceeds that of traditional finance. Again, university students should start awareness campaigns among tech users to guarantee that Islamic fintech expands and thrives sustainably.

Fintech needs to be inventive if it is to be relevant in the long run because Islamic financial institution's use of technology impacts not just the Muslim community but also non-Muslims and the global finance sector. If fintech is appropriately handled and has the appropriate people leading it, there is a chance to address global inequity. It is already creating chances for online banking services and opening doors for individuals to enter industries previously inaccessible to large players like asset managers and hedge funds. Rather than capitalizing on outdated greed, fintech should be a tool for democratizing financial power and resolving real-world issues.

Fintech offers a key solution to the main issue facing existing Islamic finance institutions: they were forced to operate within an existing financial services framework, making it challenging to implement a comprehensive application of Shari'ah and limiting their freedom to be creative. There is no simple answer to how to do this, but regulators have a role to play. They need to create a market in which fintech companies do not need to be acquired by large banks to be viable or devote their innovation to serving the banks' needs. In addition, regulators must be clear about how rules apply to fintech businesses, particularly the balance between being a financial institution and a technology company.

Because fintech is inherently disruptive, it presents a chance for the market to be creative and develop more Shari'ah-compliant goods that are more spirit-aligned than merely form-based, democratizing business prospects. Looking back, fintech technology seems to provide chances for financial integration and liberalization that will benefit the more developed economies. However, better solutions from a Shari'ah perspective that are presented as more people-centric are desperately needed if Islamic fintech is to be an effective remedy to financial inequality and global inequity worldwide.

References

Agrawal, A., Catalini, C., & Goldfarb, A. (2014). Some simple economics of crowdfunding. *Innovation Policy and the Economy*, *14*, 63–97. https://doi.org/10.1086/674021

Abdullah, S., & Oseni, U. A. (2017). Towards a sharī'ah compliant equity-based crowdfunding for the halal industry in Malaysia. *International Journal of Business and Society*, *18*(1), 223–240. https://www.researchgate.net/publication/320863564_Towards_a_shari%27ah_compliant_equity-based_crowdfunding_for_the_halal_industry_in_Malaysia

Aduba, J. J., Asgari, B., & Izawa, H. (2023). Does FinTech penetration drive financial development? Evidence from panel analysis of emerging and developing economies. *Borsa Istanbul Review*, *23*(5), 1078–1097. https://doi.org/10.1016/j.bir.2023.06.001

Alshater, M. M., & Othman, A. H. A. (2020). Financial technology developments and their effect on Islamic finance education (تطورات التقنية المالية وتأثيرها على التعليم المالي الإسلامي). https://ideas.repec.org/a/abd/kauiea/v33y2020i3no9p161-187.html

Alshater, M. M., Saba, I., Supriani, I., & Rabbani, M. R. (2022). FinTech in Islamic finance literature: A review. *Heliyon*, *8*(9), e10385. https://doi.org/10.1016/j.heliyon.2022.e10385

Arner, D. W., Buckley, R. P., Zetzsche, D. A., & Veidt, R. (2020). Sustainability, FinTech, and financial inclusion. *European Business Organization Law Review*, *21*(1), 7–35. https://doi.org/10.1007/s40804-020-00183-y

Baber, H. (2019). FinTech, crowdfunding and customer retention in Islamic Banks. *Vision*, *24*(3), 260–268. https://doi.org/10.1177/0972262919869765

Çakmak, C. (2023). *Islamic FinTech* (pp. 1–6). Springer eBooks. https://doi.org/10.1007/978-3-030-93703-4_160-1

Dawood, H. M., Zadjali, F. A., Rawahi, M. A., Karim, S., & Mohamed, H. (2022). Business trends & and challenges in Islamic FinTech: A systematic literature review. *F1000Research*, *11*, 329. https://doi.org/10.12688/f1000research.109400.1

Demir, A., Pesqué-Cela, V., Altunbaş, Y., & Murinde, V. (2020). FinTech, financial inclusion, and income inequality: A quantile regression approach. *The European Journal of Finance*, *28*(1), 86–107. https://doi.org/10.1080/1351847x.2020.1772335

Firmansyah, H. B., & Ramdani, A. L. (2018). The role of Islamic financial technology (FinTech) start-up in improving financial inclusion in Indonesia case: Angsur. *Social Science Research Network*. https://doi.org/10.2139/ssrn.3194546

GIFR. (2022). *Global Islamic FinTech report 2022 | Salaam gateway - Global Islamic economy gateway*. https://salaamgateway.com/specialcoverage/islamic-FinTech-2022.

Global FinTech Market Report and Forecast 2024-2032. (2023). Expert market research. https://www.expertmarketresearch.com/reports/FinTech-market

Goyal, D., Varma, R., Rada, F., Pande, A., Jauregui, J., Corelli, P., Tripathi, S., Sénant, Y., Dab, S., Erande, Y., Choi, J., Koserski, J., Carrubba, J., Morris, N., Rotman, F., Risley, M., & Suri, S. (2023, May 25). *Global FinTech (2023). Reimagining the future of finance*. BCG Global. https://www.bcg.com/publications/2023/future-of-FinTech-and-banking

Haneef, R., & Smolo, E. (2013). Reshaping the Islamic finance industry: Applying the lessons learned from the global financial crisis. In H. Ahmed, M. Asutay, & R. Wilson (Eds.), *Islamic banking and financial crisis: Reputation, stability and risks* (pp. 21–39). Edinburgh University Press. https://doi.org/10.3366/edinburgh/9780748647613.003.0002

Hassan, M. K., Rabbani, M. R., & Ali, M. a. M. (2020). Challenges for Islamic finance and banking in the post-COVID era and the role of FinTech. *ResearchGate*. https://www.researchgate.net/publication/349138882_Challenges_for_the_Islamic_Finance_and_banking_in_post_COVID_era_and_the_role_of_FinTech

Hendratmi, A., Ryandono, M. N. H., & Sukmaningrum, P. S. (2019). Developing an Islamic crowdfunding website platform for startup companies in Indonesia. *Journal of Islamic Marketing*, *11*(5), 1041–1053. https://doi.org/10.1108/jima-02-2019-0022

Ishak, M. S. I., & Rahman, M. H. (2021). Equity-based Islamic crowdfunding in Malaysia: A potential application for mudharabah. *Qualitative Research in Financial Markets*, *13*(2), 183–198. https://doi.org/10.1108/qrfm-03-2020-0024

Kanga, D., Oughton, C., Harris, L., & Murinde, V. (2021). The diffusion of FinTech, financial inclusion, and income per capita. *The European Journal of Finance*, *28*(1), 108–136. https://doi.org/10.1080/1351847x.2021.1945646

Khan, H. H., Khan, S., & Ghafoor, A. (2023). FinTech adoption, the regulatory environment, and bank stability: An empirical investigation from GCC economies. *Borsa Istanbul Review*, *23*(6), 1263–1281. https://doi.org/10.1016/j.bir.2023.10.010

Kou, G., Akdeniz, Ö. O., Dinçer, H., & Yüksel, S. (2021). Fintech investments in European banks: a hybrid IT2 fuzzy multidimensional decision-making approach. *Financial Innovation*, *7*(1). https://doi.org/10.1186/s40854-021-00256-y

Krupa, D., & Buszko, M. (2023). Age-dependent differences in using FinTech products and services—Young customers versus other adults. *PLoS One*, *18*(10), e0293470. https://doi.org/10.1371/journal.pone.0293470

Lee, I., & Shin, Y. J. (2018). FinTech: Ecosystem, business models, investment decisions, and challenges. *Business Horizons*, *61*(1), 35–46. https://doi.org/10.1016/j.bushor.2017.09.003

Li, P. (2016). Current and future years of E-commerce. In *Encyclopedia of E-commerce development, implementation, and management* (pp. 1031–1044). IGI Global eBooks. https://doi.org/10.4018/978-1-4666-9787-4.ch073

Maybray, B. (2023, September 8). FinTech wealth management: How wealth advisors can stay resilient. https://blog.hubspot.com/. https://blog.hubspot.com/the-hustle/wealth-management-FinTech

Migozzi, J., Urban, M., & Wójcik, D. (2023). "You should do what India does": FinTech ecosystems in India reshaping the geography of finance. *Geoforum*, 103720. https://doi.org/10.1016/j.geoforum.2023.103720

Nastiti, N. D., & Kasri, R. A. (2019). The role of banking regulation in developing Islamic banking financing in Indonesia. *International Journal of Islamic and Middle Eastern Finance and Management*, *12*(5), 643–662. https://doi.org/10.1108/imefm-10-2018-0365

PWC. (2018). Managing operational risk inherent to FinTech adoption: Observations and recommendations. www.pwc.co.uk. https://www.pwc.co.uk/financial-services/assets/pdf/operational-risk-meets-operational-resilience.pdf

Rabbani, M. R., Hassan, M. K., Khan, S., & Muneeza, A. (2022). *A FinTech-based Zakat model using artificial intelligence* (pp. 49–63). Springer eBooks. https://doi.org/10.1007/978-3-031-14941-2_3

Rabbani, M. R., Khan, S., & Thalassinos, E. (2020). FinTech, blockchain, and Islamic finance: An extensive literature review. *International Journal of Economics and Business Administration*, *VIII*(2), 65–86. https://doi.org/10.35808/ijeba/444

Rahman, M. P., Duasa, J., Kamil, M., & Kamil, N. (2016). Factors contributing to the success of crowdfunding: The Malaysian case. https://www.semanticscholar.org/paper/Factors-contributing-to-the-success-of-the-case-Rahman-Duasa/55cf6c41d6bdc527ef7dfa9860c8a955c3a1bc23

Rahman, M. P., Thaker, M. A. M. T., & Duasa, J. (2020). Developing a Sharīʿah-compliant equity-based crowdfunding framework for entrepreneurship development in Malaysia. *ISRA International Journal of Islamic Finance*, *12*(2), 239–252. https://doi.org/10.1108/ijif-07-2018-0085

Reuters. (2016). Singapore will update electronic payment regulations in the FinTech drive. https://www.reuters.com/article/singapore-cenbank-FinTech-idUSL3N1B01II/

Saba, I., Kouser, R., & Chaudhry, I. S. (2019). FinTech and Islamic finance-challenges and opportunities. *Review of Economics and Development Studies*, *5*(4), 581–590. https://doi.org/10.26710/reads.v5i4.887

Shaikh, S. A. (2020). Using FinTech in scaling up Islamic microfinance. *Journal of Islamic Accounting and Business Research*, *12*(2), 186–203. https://doi.org/10.1108/jiabr-10-2019-0198

Smolo, E., & Mirakhor, A. (2010). The global financial crisis and its implications for the Islamic financial industry. *International Journal of Islamic and Middle Eastern Finance and Management*, *3*(4), 372–385. https://doi.org/10.1108/17538391011093306

Suleman, U. (2019, September 1). *Islamic FinTech: More virtual than reality? - Islam21c*. Islam21c. https://www.islam21c.com/islamic-thought/islamic-FinTech-more-virtual-than-reality/

Suryono, R. R., Budi, I., & Purwandari, B. (2020). Challenges and trends of financial technology (FinTech): A systematic literature review. *Information*, *11*(12), 590. https://doi.org/10.3390/info11120590

Yin, F., Jiao, X., Zhou, J., Yin, X., Ibeke, E., Iwendi, M., & Biamba, C. (2022). FinTech application on banking stability using Big Data of an emerging economy. *Journal of Cloud Computing*, *11*(1). https://doi.org/10.1186/s13677-022-00320-7

Zouari, G., & Abdelhedi, M. (2021). Customer satisfaction in the digital era: evidence from Islamic banking. *Journal of Innovation and Entrepreneurship*, *10*(1). https://doi.org/10.1186/s13731-021-00151-x

Chapter 12

Digital Currencies and Their Compatibility in the Islamic Finance Industry

Edib Smolo[a] *and Ziyaad Mahomed*[b]

[a]Effat University, Saudi Arabia
[b]INCEIF University, Malaysia

Abstract

The chapter is devoted to the in-depth analysis of the compliance between the Shari'ah rules and digital currency within the context of Islamic finance. The emergent trend of digital currencies, especially virtual based as in the case of Bitcoin, has raised questions on the issue of their compatibility with ethical and legal moral rights. The paper covers core issues like Shari'ah implementation, the utilization of tangible assets, crypto as a medium of exchange and some obstacles in merging crypto into Islamic banking. Besides that, the paper outlines workable solutions for overcoming these difficulties, including the introduction of Shari'ah-compliant cryptocurrencies, the development of a regulatory framework and the need for enlightenment and collaboration. Furthermore, the manuscript will exhibit some Islamic-centric digital currencies, e.g. the Islamic Coin and OneGram, to illustrate that a successful integration into Islamic finance is possible. Furthermore, future estimations consider the implications of central bank digital currencies (CBDCs) in Islamic finance which brings up both opportunities and challenges. The conclusion calls for ongoing research and innovation spanning traditional as well as digital (cryptocurrencies) in order to achieve Shari'ah harmonization and eventual evolution of the Islamic finance sector.

Keywords: Digital currency; Islamic finance; Shari'ah-compliant; CBDCs; artificial intelligence; cryptocurrency; blockchain

The Future of Islamic Finance, 189–206

doi:10.1108/978-1-83549-906-120241012

Introduction

The term digital currencies cover the various types of virtual or electronic forms of currency offered which are secured and confirmed by cryptographic technologies that commonly are called cryptocurrencies. As is known, the most important thing about these digital currencies is their autonomy and absence of regulation by any centralized authority or government, which makes them different from common fiat currencies.

It is undeniable that the digital currencies hold the potential to exert different kinds of influence on the field of Islamic finance. A listing of potential effects of digital currencies in the realm of Islamic finance includes the answering of concerns about compliance with Shari'ah principles, their role as medium of exchange, the development of transparency and accountability, the enhancement of charity and fairness, the expansion of financial inclusion, and the incorporation of digital currencies into Islamic financial services. Thereby, the implementation of digital currencies in Islamic finance is expected to ensure the speed, precision and accuracy of the transactions besides safeguarding transparency and good governance and working toward the enhancement of financial inclusion and risk mitigation, while at the same time being in the judiciary harmony with established Islamic financial creations and products. Collectively, virtual currencies are a promising future that might radically change the nature of Islamic finance.

The Implications of Digital Currencies on Global Finance

Digital currencies have the potential to revolutionize global finance by reshaping cross-border transactions and ushering in a new era of borderless economic interactions. This innovative form of currency is reshaping monetary systems and international trade relations, both at the national and global levels, representing the third category of currency that evolves alongside privately issued digital assets and central bank-issued digital currencies (Tan, 2023). The persistent embrace of digital currencies, particularly CBDCs, poses a peril to the dominion and sway wielded by central banks over conventional currencies (Martin, 2021). As digital assets become more deeply ingrained in the fiscal framework, central banks may witness a waning influence on interest rates, inflation rates, and economic equilibrium. Such dynamic could even revolutionize the world monetary system, demanding as careful examination.

Due to the decentralized nature of digital currencies like cryptocurrencies, financial stability and consumer protection face a wealth of risks. Market turbulence, loose regulatory frameworks, and shaping such domains for illicit undertakings or cyberattacks constitute a serious risk. In the wake of growing adoption of digital currencies, the regulators will need to address these problems to maintain the stability of the economy. The ascension of digital currencies, especially Bitcoin, disrupts the orthodox financial infrastructure by obviating the necessity for intermediaries such as financial institutions and credit card corporations (Proettel, 2019). This disruption carries the potential to augment efficiency, yet concurrently prompts questions of regulatory oversight and structural considerations. Hence, striking a harmonious equilibrium between innovation and stability becomes imperative.

Additionally, the development of sovereign digital currencies (SDCs) can exert a momentous influence on the fiscal framework and the government's capacity to enact monetary policies. It also casts a shadow on privacy and data security (Houser & Baker, 2022). Consequently, this will reshape the financial currents within the global fiscal milieu, necessitating regulatory adaptations and novel approaches to managing digital currencies. For instance, the integration of digital currencies necessitates the resolution of concerns pertaining to transparency and stability, especially regarding cross-border transactions. In a parallel vein, the legitimization of cryptocurrencies for foreign debt obligations, coupled with the absence of asset coverage, could engender a sort of financial bubble that imperils global fiscal steadiness.

Furthermore, artificial intelligence (AI) is making profound inroads into international trade. AI development is rewriting the global trade scenario, affecting the direction of trade flows as well as the revival of manufacturing, where AI is expected to augment global trade by about 2% annually until 2030 (Wu, 2023). Likewise, the launching of CBDCs could drastically modify the monetary regulations as well as the financial landscape, shifting the role and position of financial intermediaries in the financial markets, consequently affecting international trade and the relations between economy and other countries. However, there seemingly arises a problem, namely the menace posed to existing currencies, particularly under extremely high interest rates, and the disruptive of monetary policy channeling. The ramifications and traits of retail digital currencies are still a research study in progress; hence, there is an urge for a comprehensive knowledge of the power structure ahead of their introduction in international trade and economies.

As far as Internet finance is concerned, the widespread use of cryptocurrencies is seamlessly transforming the manner in which we conduct trade and are involved in financial activities. This evolution could affect traditional commercial banks (Prasad, 2022) and change the trade paradigm in the global arena by affecting the transmission mechanism, the structure of monetary issues and monetary circulation, and the role of national currencies as global means of payment (Kuznetsova & Larina, 2023). This is in essence strengthened by the fact that the shift of mainstream money may usher new ways for running the monetary system from the central governments, with doubtless outcomes for companies and economies.

Further, the ongoing conflict between Russia and Ukraine undoubtedly influenced the world's economy, which becomes an obvious reason for more stable and transparent supply chains (Goreczky, 2022). This in turn has given rise to an acceleration in the integration of digital technologies in distribution and manufacturing that has subsequently impacted international trade. In addition, this shock might act as a propellant for the adoption of CDBCs at a faster rate, especially in states that want to replace the dollar-dominated international financial system with one of their own, thus the image of the international monetary system is rapidly changing.

Despite this, the advantages of blockchain-based digital currencies are adequately demonstrated. They provided more transparency and traceability than ever before giving standing to the transaction integrity, decreasing fraud, and establishing a trust among the parties signed under the same transaction (Brammertz & Mendelowitz, 2018). Moreover, digital currencies may well help in advancing so-called financial inclusion, especially for individuals and businesses by way of embracing them in international economic activities to a larger extent than ever before, cutting currency conversion costs, and making easy cross-border trade transactions (Foster et al., 2021; Kamdzhalov, 2020).

Moreover, capitalizing on digital currencies will bring many positives for the economic system of the countries that have an advanced strategy of implementing national digital currencies (Claeys & Demertzis, 2019; Edwards, 2021). Thus, a country should strive to occupy the strategic vantage point in the fast-changing terrain of digital money services. This transformation is poised to disrupt the financial sector. Newer players and fresh market entrants are shining with the new innovations in the financial sector, playing key role in disruption of the traditional financial institutions. Such transformations point to the future of finance being at a crucial point with only change being possible (Mnohoghitnei et al., 2022).

Modern articles highlight the fact that the cryptocurrency trend is not an unchanging but rather a dynamically evolving territory. Moreover, their influence is not limited to small things or only certain aspects of life. They represent the historical background as well as the accounting complexities permeating all cryptocurrencies, arguing for the development of international accounting standards specialized for cryptocurrencies where the sector becomes increasingly connected to the global trade, monetary, and payments systems(Arner et al., 2022; Lilkov & Drea, 2022; Owolabi & Osanyinbi, 2023; Sigurðsson et al., 2023).

Consequently, digital assets which involve nation digital currencies will open up a number of opportunities for the global financial ecosystem available in tandem with its challenges. Among the challenges are loss of central bank authority, problems intertwined with decentralization, the disruption of the old system of financial infrastructure, challenges to the adoption of a system, and the impact on the long run financial system. These changes ask for the immediate action from regulatory institutions, international collaboration, and the mindful evaluation of fiscal landscape as it evolves all the time. Governments, industry leaders, and researchers need to carefully explore these changes in order to make sure that world financial system is still stable and efficient while taking into consideration the multifaceted challenges and opportunities these new technologies bring.

The Potential Impacts of Digital Currencies on Islamic Finance

Digital currencies are capable of impacting Islamic finance in a number of ways. With time, their issuance into the Islamic finance infrastructure become a matter of great importance. Despite the fact that this integration brings about benefits, it is clear that a series of risks follows and should be taken into consideration.

The most important drawback is that digital currency can be very prone to fraud and scams. The decentralization and lack of legal framework of these currencies make them susceptible to fraudulent activities. Additionally, digital currencies having the elements which are similar to anonymity and easy transactions could be useful to the money launderer. Anonymity of the Internet and the possibility of hiding the user identity complicate the process of finding the origin of transactions. Their presence on the international stage as well as its offshore nature makes cryptocurrencies ideal for financing terrorist activities, drugs trafficking and other illegal dealings. This threat highlights the importance of constant monitoring (Abozaid, 2022; Foster et al., 2021).

Likewise, failing to comprehend the distinction between Blockchain technology and digital currencies may eventually lead to improper utilization and inappropriate application of this new wave of technology. Therefore, the continuing digital transformation of Islamic finance calls for the adjustments of financial literacy curricula to address the educational needs of today. The newness of digital tools and products in an areas like Islamic finance market makes the adoption process more difficult; it poses great challenges for the users and fundraisers. With this in mind, the strategy of overcoming the challenges will be through strategic planning and understanding of the market. In this case, financial literacy training becomes vital for individuals to benefit from these digital financial channels (Karim et al., 2022). Tagging digital currencies as "currency" may cause misunderstandings and lead to inappropriate use. Hence, making clear the difference of the two roles as well as their functions is a vital step before any adoption.

The utilization of digital currencies within Islamic finance has also raised ethical concerns that necessitate careful consideration. In general, they do not contradict the doctrines of Islam and can be used in Islamic finance, as they align with the common goals of transparency, investing for social benefit, protecting wealth and the environment, and minimizing friction in terms of money, labor, and time (ISRA, 2016; Smolo, 2013). The use of digital currencies based on the blockchain technology can improve the efficiency of both retail and wholesale, regional and international payments. In addition, it can facilitate harmonization of Shari'ah-compliant products across the globe (Dahdal et al., 2022; Kamdzhalov, 2020). Nevertheless, the Shari'ah permissibility of cryptocurrencies is still debatable. This is due to the fact that these currencies are not backed by any real assets or regulated and supervised by any authorities, state or financial (Abozaid, 2022; Kunhibava et al., 2021). To address various ethical concerns, including stability and intrinsic value, there is a growing need for a central bank-issued digital coin with real intrinsic value and underlying assets (Glavina & Asmiatullin, 2023). The concept of a central bank-issued digital coin with real intrinsic value and underlying asset could solve many issues related to the use of cryptocurrencies in Islamic finance. The advent of the digital currencies by the banks of central bank can lower down the role of commercial banks in a country's financial network and have more transparency. Following that, digital currencies can be used within the Muslim community, most especially for cross-border transactions.

On that note, as the cryptocurrencies like the Bitcoin are credited for its fixed supply, they touch upon the concern of *gharar* (discernment, deception) that exists in the inflow of the money. This has been one of the concerns highlighted by the Islamic finance (Muedini, 2018). Also, smart contracts, which is a key digital infrastructure, need elements that can ensure enforceability, data protection, and dispute resolution to guarantee ethical use. Moreover, when embedded with AI and fintech technologies, the utilization of blockchain technology and smart contracts in Islamic finance leads to transparency, sustainability, accountability, and good governance of financial transactions. These functions are of the essence as they support the ideas of Islamic banking (Chong, 2021; Elamin, 2023; Glavina & Asmiatullin, 2023).

Although digital money could have a positive impact on the Islamic financial sector in the future, there are still several theoretical projections and actual challenges to be addressed. In order to successfully tackle these issues in Islamic finance, it is very essential for Islamic financial institutes to create the regulating policies and laws that put security and compliance in the first place. Moreover, education and awareness with the technologies involved must be the campaign strategies so that the industry are able to completely understand the technologies. Through dealing with these concerns Islamic finance will be able to realize the potential of digital currencies while protecting against these potential risks. At last, cryptocurrencies can be a means for propelling Islamic society into several dimensions, strengthening the general prosperity of this community. Additionally, along with digital currency popularity, the online finance sector may experience a dramatic shift as well. With the crypto gradually becoming a part of our everyday lives, it will bring about some displacement of the trading culture, albeit not entirely.

The Compatibility of Digital Currencies with Shari'ah Law

Given the expansion of cryptocurrencies network in the current financial system of the world, questions on their alignment with Islamic law arise. The clash between the financial innovation and the spirit of religiousness gave rise to a series of ethical dilemmas and legal challenges on the one hand and to the opportunities for growth on the other hand.

Digital currencies or cryptocurrencies have completely changed the manner in which financial transactions and particularly, assets are managed by empowering users with new, nonconventional methods of transactions. However, the digital assets generate debates about their compatibility with Shari'ah law at this same time. Digital currencies including Bitcoin based on the decentralization concept surpass borders and the jurisdiction of authorities of traditional banking institutions. This ultimately puts them in a different category than the ordinary tools for savings and investment and allows them to challenge the prevailing legal and ethical principles.

Meanwhile, Islamic financing which is Shari'ah law-based has principles that are formulated fairly to promote ethical and equal economic practices. This principle also includes the mutual sharing of resources and prohibiting usurious practices (*riba* or interest) and the banning of questionable trading (*gharar*), and complete dedication to balanced economy, social justice and fairness. The alignment of financial tools with these standards is, therefore, in fact a primary concern of the Islamic finance sector.

Shari'ah-Compliance and Maqasid Al-Shari'ah

It must be noted that the basic feature of guaranteeing the compliance with Shari'ah in digital currency deals is entailing Islamic contractual law principles and carrying into effect the achievement of maqasid al-Shari'ah. One can deduce from this maxim that all commercial undertakings should be in compliance with the ethical teaching of Islam to promulgate notions such as equality and not to violate the Islamic principles of justice and prevention of the possible harms (Kunhibava et al., 2021; Muedini, 2018).

Tangible Assets and the Absence of Usury

As per Shari'ah law, the financial affairs should be based on the true (tangible) assets without any traces of usury (*riba*) in it. Digital currencies inherently correspond with this principle since they are devoid of means of usurious practices and could represent something real. It is noteworthy to mention that adherence to Shari'ah principles is a core issue which deals with the acceptability of cryptocurrencies in Islamic banking and finance (Muedini, 2018).

Cryptocurrency as a Medium of Exchange

The Islamic viewpoint regards cryptocurrency as having intrinsic value since it acts as a medium by which other values are exchanged which is a core concept of Islamic finance. The property supports the point that crypto is able to adapt to the conditions of modern Islamic finance, since they occupy the same positions as money (Abubakar et al., 2019).

Gharar and Riba in Cryptocurrency

Contrary to the traditional type of financial instruments, in the case of cryptocurrency risk, the *gharar* (deception) does not derive from the informational asymmetry, but rather is connected to the current market conditions. In addition, cryptocurrency transaction does not include *riba*, thus they are consistent with Shari'ah principles. This differentiation is vital to understanding the ethical principles on which digital currencies are based (Abubakar et al., 2019).

Prohibited Transactions

Shari'ah Law has an express ban on all trades using products, services, or labor that are infringing on Islamic law. As a result, maintaining this principle is one of the most relevant criteria of cryptocurrency transactions. Unveiling the actual scope of these bans and the precise suitability of such bans in the case of digital currencies is intrinsically one of the determining points for their Shari'ah-compliance (Abubakar et al., 2019).

Bitcoin and Digital Currencies in Islamic Finance

Bitcoin and other virtual currencies with a fixed supply cease the risk of deception (*gharar*) and inflation. This characteristic blends perfectly with the cornerstone principle of Shari'ah law, which, in turn, helps eliminate basic ethical issues neglected by traditional financial systems. Bitcoin, as a particular one, offers a perspective of solving some of these challenges through the use of a transparent and decentralized medium for exchange (Muedini, 2018).

Legal Authorities and Government Regulation

Whilst financing using digital currencies represents a compatible proposition with Islamic finance, Imam Al-Ghazali had relegated the issuance and regulation of currency to the government. The Shari'ah law may not allow the usage of cryptocurrency if the government considers the transaction illegal. The status of legal authorities and government regulations in respect to the *halalness* (permissibility) of digital currencies within Islamic financial system is a controversial topic widely discussed and debated these days (Muedini, 2018).

Decentralization and Examination under Shari'ah Law

The concept of decentralization that is central to virtual currencies hence gets peculiar challenge for Shari'ah compliance that calls for a thorough scrutiny in order to check the compatibility of such currencies. Digital currencies are not anchored to the traditional financial system in the absence of the need of financial intermediaries. This could be either considered an advantage or a source of uncertainty for the Islamic finance. This element of decentralization definitely requires a comprehensive study from Islamic point of view (Abubakar et al., 2019).

The Challenges of Digital Currency Integration in Islamic Finance

Issues concerning the integration of digital currencies into the sphere of the Islamic finance involve a lot of challenges and require in-depth deliberations; therefore, their thoughtful consideration is very important for their seamless inclusion to this field.

The Novelties and Scale of the Islamic Finance Market

The digitization of the Islamic finance found to be constrained by its relatively low market size and the ethical factors it is built on that create difficulties for adopting the digital tools and products. The current central banking system which is going through a period of transition characterized by the increase in adoption of cryptocurrency and blockchain technology is operating on a wider scale. However, due to the small size of the Islamic banking industry, the infiltration of CBDC would be a complex process. The combination of technological financial instruments with their sophistication and unconventional nature results in the creation of a hurdle that is a rather significant barrier in the industry of this specialized business.

The Permissibility of Cryptocurrencies

The digital currencies adaptation to the Islamic procedures is a sensitive aspect due to the fact that Shari'ah law categorizes these cryptos as either halal or haram (Kamdzhalov, 2020). This matter is a complex one whose very essence and facts remain debated. Some argue that cryptocurrencies comply with the traditional precepts of Islamic finance while others are skeptical (Adam, 2017). The speculative nature and intrinsic volatility that characterize most cryptocurrencies raise some reasonable questions relating to their conformity to the concepts of Islamic finance. It is then necessary to lay down a clear system for assessing the acceptability of digital currencies based on the Islamic Law. This is very important (Laldin & Djafri, 2021).

Shari'ah-Compliance in Blockchain Transactions

Blockchain technology, the foundation for cryptocurrency operation, combines the two key principles of confidentiality and trust through the digital transactions. However, this raises a considerably difficult Shari'ah compliance matter (Chong, 2021). In a nutshell, the Islamic finance transactions should be strictly regulated by Shari'ah law at all steps of the business operations. The retrospective feature of blockchain, built-in capabilities for Shari'ah-compliance monitoring post-execution, may create a loophole for providing an environment for non-compliant transactions that may have ultimately negative outcomes for the society. Hence, the use of on-the-fly mechanisms to supervise the Shari'ah-compliance of blockchain-enabled financial systems becomes an issue of supreme priority.

Algorithmic Protocols and Maqasid Al-Shari'ah Discrepancy

Smart contracts ranging from the smart *sukuk* to electronic wallets became the cornerstone of the digital finance revolution (Chong, 2021). The contracts made here will have to comply with the principles of *maqasid al-Shari'ah* (Kamdzhalov, 2020). However, the algorithmic protocols that are used for the verification of these contracts are often not in complete harmony with them. Certain smart contracts may end up involving speculative or immoral ventures in which case they will contradict the main objectives of Islamic finance. Striking a balance between the design of algorithmic protocols governing these contracts and the objectives of promoting *maqasid al-Shari'ah* is a fundamental objective which must be achieved.

The Need for Shari'ah Scholars' Profundity

The integration of digital currencies into Islamic finance requires Shari'ah scholars to have immense knowledge of sophisticated financial instruments (Chong, 2021). For this to come true, they must have deep understanding of blockchain technology, cryptocurrency transactions as well as smart contracts intricacies. Through such deep understanding of the principles of Shari'ah, Shari'ah scholars are therefore equipped to apply the relevant principles that will ensure that digital financial products comply to the Islamic principles (Laldin & Djafri, 2021). Thus, financial technologists together with Shari'ah experts constitute the crucial mediator between technical inventions and the respect of Islamic laws.

The Inertia of Islamic Banks

Many Islamic banks lack the agility to adopt to the constantly changing customer decision-making journey and the use of new technologies which reflects in the prototyping of new, technologically driven products and services. This is a significant obstacle, which is a major factor holding back the implementation of digital strategies and the adoption of digital currencies in Islamic finance. The solution of this problem comes with the change in culture within Islamic financial organizations that provides a milieu in which innovation is welcomed and where an agile approach to technology adoption is in the forefront. In short, the introduction of digital currency in the Islamic finance system poses a range of fair challenges which would warrant careful consideration and innovative solutions. These challenges include the modest size of the Islamic finance industry, the complex process of determining the level of permissibility of the crypto, the necessity of Shari'ah-compliant transactions in the blockchain, the alignment with *maqasid al-Shari'ah* principles, the extensive knowledge of the Shari'ah scholars, and the need to overcome the resistance of Islamic banking institutions to change. With the continuous changes in digital finance, Islamic finance sector must be able to keep up while still upholding its fundamental principles to pave the way for a sustainable and compliant future.

Combating the Obstacles in the Way of Adoption of Digital Currencies in Islamic Finance

To make the digital currency applicable in the world of Islamic economics is a real test which deeply roots in the pure postulates of Islamic law that absolutely reject the involvement of *riba* (interest), *gharar* (ambiguity) and *maysir* (games of chance). Nevertheless, it is clear that some of the bottlenecks will remain although they do not diminish the value of through in-depth research and expert investigators finding a solution.

- *Shari'ah-Compliant Cryptocurrencies* – One of the brilliant solutions is the development of Shari'ah-compliant digital coins. These crash assets may conform to Islamic rules of jurisprudence by making their values secure using commodities like gold thus bypassing the ban of ex nihilo fiat currency creation. The uniformity of design and circulation of digital tokens in accordance with Shari'ah principles provide an avenue to comply with the precepts of Islamic finance.
- *The Establishment of Well-Defined Regulatory Framework* – A regulatory framework with sufficient definition has to be implemented as the first move in a war against all the challenges that cryptocurrency and Islamic finance is facing nowadays. Such comprehensive legislation guarantees that the intricacies of the Islamic laws and their application by users and service providers are clear-cut and consonant with Islamic principles.
- *Educational and Awareness Advocacy* – The primary pillar to getting past these challenges is probably the advocacy of knowledge and awareness in the digital currencies sector. This entails Islamic scholars' knowledge of the very technologies underlying digital currencies and their compliance with Islamic dictates. In addition to this, user education also plays a very important role which allow people to handle digital assets in compliance with Shari'ah law. The spread of knowledge about the benefits of these currencies within the Islamic finance jurisdiction is mandatory to increase adoption.
- *Collaboration* – Having collaborative initiatives from Islamic financial institutions, fintech enterprises and regulatory bodies emerge as compulsory. The cooperation may result in innovative and Shari'ah-compliant solutions by rearranging and adapting the current financial products and services in line with Islamic finance principles. At the end of the day, these entities can create unique but harmonized strategies that can help people uptake compliant digital financial services and also revolutionalize the way the services are rendered (Kamdzhalov, 2020)
- *Transparency* – One of the key approaches to overcoming the challenge of obscurity in cryptocurrency transactions is offering transparency. The application of blockchain in transaction validation builds up a transparent, unalterable ledger of all transactions. In doing so, it raises the trust level of users and they can safely conclude their transactions on the basis of Islamic laws, since they can be visibly ascertained.
- *Risk Management* – One of the most important strategies in managing risk should include the development of strong risk management techniques so as to eliminate challenges of gambling or games of chance in digital currency operations. Establishing firm rules around digital currencies, such as their operation and use coupled with technology monitoring and risk management

can be a tool to govern the usage of digital currencies within the boundary of Islamic finance. It also protects traders from unjustified speculations and maintains the Shari'ah principles of risk sharing in Islamic finance.
- *Fatwa and Guidance* – Seeking of fatwas and guidance from Islamic scholars and experts in the topic is vital for the compliance of digital currencies with Islamic law.[1] These legal judgments can become illumination and leading the way, both for users and service providers, toward an appropriate application of digital finance products within the domain of Islamic banking.

On the whole, imparting these possible solutions to the implication of digital currencies on the Islamic finance system is a way of finding a balance between adhering to the Islamic principles while at the same time integrating technology innovation and cultivating financial inclusion.

Opportunities Offered by Digital Currencies in Islamic Finance

The integration of digital currencies in Islamic financial systems has been often tested in many studies with successful outcomes. For example, digital currencies were found to be in line with such principles as transparency, preservation of wealth, and social benefits (Glavina & Asmiatullin, 2023).

Desky and Maulina (2022) targeted on the Islamic banking digital transformation and claimed that, with the help of digital technologies like mobile and digital wallets, banks have improved their competitiveness, achieved operational efficiency and increased customer satisfaction. Furthermore, the inclusion of digital currencies in Shari'ah-compliant portfolios had the benefit of enhanced returns, as well as observing reduced total risk (El Alaoui et al., 2021). Besides, there has been a call for blockchain application in Islamic financial institutions with observed successes in the banking and financial sector (Aysan & Al-Ansari, 2022).

Although this type of research yields useful findings, yet, more comprehensive studies should be conducted to better navigate the path for digital currencies with Islamic finance.

CBDCs and Islamic Finance

Digital currencies are expected to be widely used in the future markets as they offer fast, secure, and streamlined transactions to gain competitiveness (Narayanan, 2020). Financial intermediation is expected to be disrupted with the introduction of CBDCs as more central banks decide to go digital. The future of CBDCs in Islamic finance is promising, with significant potential for higher levels of security, potential for growth and innovation (Alam & Ali, 2021). CBDCs also serve as an entry point to the broader formal financial system. Since they are not limited physically, those living in remote areas can have safe and easy access to digital cash issued by governments on

---

[1]In Islam, *fatwa* refers to a formal ruling or interpretation on a point of Islamic law given by a qualified legal scholar (Shari'ah scholar known as a *mufti*).

their mobile phones. This increases financial inclusion and potentially lowers the cost of transactions with more seamless transactional capabilities. For those that abhor interest, CBDCs can be used as a medium of transacting through Islamic banks, providing access to financing and investment through digital platforms.

However, the benefits of CBDCs for Islamic finance will have to overcome its criticisms. Some critics state that CBDCs could lead to a threat of central banks losing independence. "If fiscal transfers were made through CBDC, there is a risk of blurring the separation between monetary and fiscal policy and a potential reduction in the independence of monetary policy" (BIS, 2020, p. 7). Others state that if cash disappears, CBDCs may cause a policy of negative interest rates (Bordo, 2021). Since Islamic finance is reliant on profit mark-ups primarily from sale/lease financing, the impact of benchmarked negative mark-ups would be disastrous to *mudarabah* (silent partnership) investment-holders and shareholders alike. Other criticisms include oligopoly power through money centralization and the threat of cybersecurity breaches that could result in significant losses for holders in a matter of seconds.

Case Studies: The Integration of Digital Currencies in Islamic Finance

The use Islamic digital currency in Islamic finance is rare. By the end of 2023, only one significantly sized Islamic-based coin was available (Islamic Coin), with several others having either launched and failed or not managing to launch after white paper releases. Two categories of digital currency can usher in the crypto experience for Islamic finance: (i) Crypto that are Shari'ah-based, with the objective of promoting only Shari'ah-compliant transactions and built for the Muslim community; (ii) Conventional crypto that has been screened and deemed Shari'ah-compliant by a Shari'ah certifying body or a Shari'ah scholar. Both categories have a role to play in Islamic finance.

Islamic Coin

Islamic Coin is a cryptocurrency of the HAQQ ecosystem, a scalable and interoperable blockchain built on Proof-of-Stake (PoS) and ethical finance principles. The HAQQ native coin was launched in 2021 and by the end of 2023, has raised a total of US$400 million over two rounds of funding, led by ABO Digital. The HAQQ ecosystem is a blockchain which claims to comply with Islamic jurisprudence. This has been attested by renowned Shari'ah scholars including Shaikh Nizam Yaquby. The *fatwa* states that the HAQQ blockchain platform uses a Proof of Ownership consensus mechanism, where users stake their coins to participate in mining and governance. A portion of Islamic Coin is reserved for a select group of buyers with 10% of the coins minted on the HAQQ Chain to go to the Evergreen DAO Endowment Fund, a charitable fund that supports Islamic projects and is controlled by the miners of HAQQ Chain.

The basis of the Shari'ah approval was on the following conditions.

- Islamic Coin is a financial instrument that can be bought and sold and exchanged for lawful goods and services and is regarded as the property of its holders that cannot be confiscated, and *Zakah* must be given by its holders after acquisition or after mining and owning it according to the *Zakah* rules and standards.
- To verify the software code used to develop the "HAQQ chain" platform at a certified software audit company, to ensure the reliability of the platform and its ability to safeguard the money of its clients.
- To assign an Authority committee for the Evergreen DAO Endowment Fund to ensure the soundness of the Fund's operations.

The approval also states that compliance is based on the whitepaper and did not cover the products to be created via the platform. The approval did not give an opinion on any legal aspects, economic viability, or regulation.

One of the main uses of the coin is its integration with the commodity broker, DDCAP Group, that is linked to more than 300 Islamic banks. DDCAP facilitates commodity trades for institutions on the basis of *tawarruq* (monetization) or *commodity murabahah*. Although the whitepaper did not state how the coin will be used on the platform, the use of digital currency for the purchase of commodities on the metals exchange is the most likely use. Metals or other commodities are purchased through platforms like *Bursa Suq al-Sila'* in Malaysia or DDCAP through traditional fund transfers and involve several transactions represented by digital documents passing from broker to agent/buyer, then back to the market for cash. The documents represent the ownership of the commodities as they change hands. The use of cryptocurrency to facilitate the trade may provide quicker transactional conclusion times and more cost-effective trades. It may also allow for easier cross-border exchange as the crypto becomes the native coin for commodity trades.

OneGram

OneGram is a digital asset that combines the stability of physical gold with blockchain technology. Each OneGram Coin (OGC) is backed by at least one gram of gold, ensuring a stable floor price for the cryptocurrency. This unique feature sets OneGram apart from other cryptocurrencies and provides investors with the benefit of owning a tangible asset.

A portion of the transactional charges on OneGram are used to purchase more gold, thereby increasing the value of OneGram over time. The coin has been certified by Shari'ah scholars, and the OneGram team claims that they prioritize environmental sustainability as well. The coin adopts a delegated PoS approach, resulting in a lower energy consumption compared to traditional proof of work (PoW) protocols.

Islamic finance usage is apparent, as gold ownership is facilitated through the purchase of the coin. However, the trade of gold has specific rules in Islamic law, including the requirement of the trade at spot. In addition, the OneGram team has established a OneGram foundation funded by 2.5% of the transaction fee (or a total of 1%).

Concluding Remarks

With quickly evolving technology and the global trade of data, blockchain-based digital currencies offer significant benefits. Some advantages include increased transparency and traceability in international trade transactions, enhanced integrity and fraud reduction thereby increasing trust between parties. Digital currencies are also expected to contribute to financial inclusion by simplifying global economic participation, reducing currency conversion costs, and enabling seamless cross-border transactions.

In the context of Islamic finance, these developments could be leveraged to further enhance the principles of risk-sharing, prohibition of *riba*, and ethical investing. The integration of digital currencies, particularly blockchain technology, aligns with the Islamic finance principles of honesty and accountability, and its smart contracts can automate compliance with Islamic law. Nevertheless, the development and implementation of digital currencies in Islamic finance require careful consideration and robust regulatory frameworks.

In fact, there remains a significant gap in the development of Islamic digital currencies from conventional, with only a handful being launched since Bitcoin. Use cases are limited although Islamic finance institutions are currently developing digital ecosystems for digital currencies to exist. Metaverse application, for example, is still nascent but holds potential for a crypto usage that is Shari'ah-compliant.

However, there are challenges in implementation, especially in the consideration of Shari'ah-compliance. For instance, blockchain transactions are reviewed for Shari'ah-compliance after the transaction, whereas the current Shari'ah review often takes place ex-ante and then during the transaction. This could allow for non-compliant transactions to occur and potentially make remediation complicated due to the nature of the technology. A solution would be to develop real-time solutions that ensure Shari'ah-compliance within blockchain-based financial systems or else the integrity of Islamic finance transactions will remain below par.

Overall, the limited use cases of digital currencies in the Islamic finance market prompt the urgent need for new research and prototype building. Much of the digital currency research focuses on the Shari'ah-compliance of the major cryptocurrencies rather than the development of purpose-built, Shari'ah-based solutions. Innovation in the digital space will need to be more focused if any significant change in Islamic finance market share is envisaged.

References

Abozaid, A. (2022). Does Sharia recognize the price of encrypted digital currencies? *ISRA International Journal of Islamic Finance (Arabic)*, *9*(2), 79–113. https://doi.org/10.55188/ijifarabic.v9i2.263

Abubakar, M., Hassan, M. K., & Haruna, M. A. (2019). Cryptocurrency tide and Islamic finance development: Any issue? In J. J. Choi & B. Ozkan (Eds.), *International finance review* (pp. 189–200). Emerald Publishing Limited. https://doi.org/10.1108/S1569-376720190000020019

Adam, M. F. (2017). *Bitcoin: Shariah compliant?* Amanah Finance Consultancy Ltd. https://afinanceorg.files.wordpress.com/2017/08/research-paper-on-bitcoin-mufti-faraz-adam.pdf

Alam, N., & Ali, S. N. (Eds.). (2021). *Fintech, digital currency and the future of Islamic finance: Strategic regulatory and adoption issues in the Gulf Cooperation Council.* Palgrave Macmillan. https://doi.org/10.1007/978-3-030-49248-9

Arner, D. W., Buckley, R. P., Didenko, A. N., & Zetzsche, D. A. (2022). *Ukraine, sanctions and central bank digital currencies: The weaponization of digital finance and the end of global monetary hegemony?* Asia Global Papers No. 7. Asia Global Institute. https://doi.org/10.2139/ssrn.4133531

Aysan, A. F., & Al-Ansari, K. A. (2022). Central bank digital currencies, internet of things, and Islamic finance: Blockchain prospects and challenges. *SSRN Electronic Journal.* https://doi.org/10.2139/ssrn.4128096

BIS. (2020). *Central bank digital currencies foundational principles and core features.* Bank for International Settlements. https://www.bis.org/publ/othp33.pdf

Bordo, M. (2021). *Central bank digital currency in historical perspective: Another crossroad in monetary history* (p. w29171). National Bureau of Economic Research. https://doi.org/10.3386/w29171

Brammertz, W., & Mendelowitz, A. I. (2018). From digital currencies to digital finance: The case for a smart financial contract standard. *The Journal of Risk Finance*, *19*(1), 76–92. https://doi.org/10.1108/JRF-02-2017-0025

Chong, F. H. L. (2021). Enhancing trust through digital Islamic finance and blockchain technology. *Qualitative Research in Financial Markets*, *13*(3), 328–341. https://doi.org/10.1108/QRFM-05-2020-0076

Claeys, G., & Demertzis, M. (2019). *The next generation of digital currencies: In search of stability* (Issue No. 15; Policy Contribution, pp. 1–12). Bruegel. http://aei.pitt.edu/102352/

Dahdal, A., Truby, J., & Ismailov, O. (2022). The role and potential of blockchain technology in Islamic finance. *European Business Law Review*, *33*(2), 175–192. https://doi.org/10.54648/EULR2022005

Desky, H., & Maulina, I. (2022). Digital transformation in Islamic banking. *International Journal of Multidisciplinary Research and Analysis*, *5*(12), 3616–3622. https://doi.org/10.47191/ijmra/v5-i12-42

Edwards, S. (2021). Central bank digital currencies and the emerging markets: The currency substitution challenge. *Challenge*, *64*(5–6), 413–424. https://doi.org/10.1080/05775132.2021.2004738

El Alaoui, A. O., Dchieche, A., & Asutay, M. (2021). Combining Islamic equity portfolios and digital currencies: Evidence from portfolio diversification. In N. Alam & S. Nazim Ali (Eds.), *Fintech, digital currency and the future of Islamic finance* (pp. 31–48). Springer International Publishing. https://doi.org/10.1007/978-3-030-49248-9_3

Elamin, M. O. (2023). Advancing ethical and sustainable economy: Islamic finance solutions for environmental, social, & economic challenges in the digital age. *International Journal of Membrane Science and Technology*, *10*(5), 408–429. https://doi.org/10.15379/ijmst.v10i5.2515

Foster, K., Blakstad, S., Gazi, S., & Bos, M. (2021). *Digital currencies and CBDC impacts on least developed countries (LDCs)*. Technical Paper 1.2; Dialogue on Global Digital Finance Governance. UNDP. https://www.ssrn.com/abstract=3871301

Glavina, S. G., & Asmiatullin, R. R. (2023). Digital currencies: Opportunities in Islamic finance. *Scientific and Educational Areas Under Modern Challenges*, 128–135. https://doi.org/10.21661/r-560136

Goreczky, P. (2022). *The Impact of the Russia-Ukraine War on the major transformation trends of the global economy*. (KKI Elemzések) [KKI policy brief]. Institute for Foreign Affairs and Trade. https://doi.org/10.47683/KKIElemzesek.KE-2022.28

Houser, K. A., & Baker, C. (2022). Sovereign digital currencies: Parachute pants or the continuing evolution of money. *NYU Journal of Law & Business*, *18*(2), 527–597.

ISRA. (2016). *Islamic financial system: Principles and operations* (2nd ed.). International Shari'ah Research Academy for Islamic Finance (ISRA).

Kamdzhalov, M. (2020). Islamic finance and the new technology challenges. *European Journal of Islamic Finance*, First Special Issue for EJIF Workshop. https://doi.org/10.13135/2421-2172/3813

Karim, S., Rabbani, M. R., & Bawazir, H. (2022). Applications of blockchain technology in the finance and banking industry beyond digital currencies. In S. Khan, M. H. Syed, R. Hammad, & A. F. Bushager (Eds.), *Blockchain technology and computational excellence for society 5.0* (pp. 216–238). IGI Global. https://doi.org/10.4018/978-1-7998-8382-1.ch011

Kunhibava, S., Mustapha, Z., Muneeza, A., Sa'ad, A. A., & Karim, M. E. (2021). *Ṣukūk* on blockchain: A legal, regulatory and Sharī'ah review. *ISRA International Journal of Islamic Finance*, *13*(1), 118–135. https://doi.org/10.1108/IJIF-06-2020-0120

Kuznetsova, V. V., & Larina, O. I. (2023). Implications of the introduction of retail digital currencies by central banks for international economic relations. *International Trade and Trade Policy*, *9*(2), 85–99. https://doi.org/10.21686/2410-7395-2023-2-85-99

Lilkov, D., & Drea, E. (2022). *Regulating the digital future: A centre–right approach to crypto assets and digital currencies*. Asia Global Papers No. 7. The Wilfried Martens Centre for European Studies.

Laldin, M. A., & Djafri, F. (2021). The role of Islamic finance in achieving sustainable development goals (SDGs). In M. K. Hassan, M. Saraç, & A. Khan (Eds.), *Islamic finance and sustainable development: A sustainable economic framework for Muslim and non-Muslim countries* (pp. 107–126). Springer International Publishing. https://doi.org/10.1007/978-3-030-76016-8_6

Martin, V. (2021). Central bank digital currencies. *Bankarstvo*, *50*(3), 109–139. https://doi.org/10.5937/bankarstvo2103109M

Mnohoghitnei, I., Horobeţ, A., & Belaşcu, L. (2022). Bitcoin is so last decade – How decentralized finance (DeFi) could shape the digital economy. *European Journal of Interdisciplinary Studies*, *14*(1), 87–99. https://doi.org/10.24818/ejis.2022.06

Muedini, F. (2018). The compatibility of cryptocurrencies and Islamic finance. *European Journal of Islamic Finance*, *10*, 2018. https://doi.org/10.13135/2421-2172/2569

Narayanan, H. (2020). Is future a rule of digital currency? *International Journal of Research -GRANTHAALAYAH*, *8*(8), 96–106. https://doi.org/10.29121/granthaalayah.v8.i8.2020.935

Owolabi, S. A., & Osanyinbi, T. G. (2023). The historical evolution, developments and accounting implications of cryptocurrency operations. *European Journal of Accounting, Auditing and Finance Research*, *11*(10), 55–72. https://doi.org/10.37745/ejaafr.2013/vol11n105572

Prasad, E. S. (2022). *The future of money: How the digital revolution is transforming currencies and finance* (Reprinted). The Belknap Press of Harvard University Press.

Proettel, T. (2019). *International digital currencies and their impact on monetary policy: An exploration of implications and vulnerability*. No 11-2019; Hohenheim Discussion Papers in Business, Economics and Social Sciences, Issues 11–2019. University of Hohenheim, Faculty of Business, Economics and Social Sciences. http://hdl.handle.net/10419/206404

Sigurðsson, K., Þór Eyþórsson, G., & Kristjánsdóttir, H. (2023). Digital currencies, SWOT analysis. *Baltic Journal of Economic Studies*, *9*(3), 1–9. https://doi.org/10.30525/2256-0742/2023-9-3-1-9

Smolo, E. (2013). *Uvod u islamsku ekonomiju i finansije: Teorija i praksa*. Dobra knjiga.

Tan, B. J. (2023). *Central bank digital currency adoption: A two-sided model*. WP/23/127; IMF Working Papers (p. 53). International Monetary Fund. https://www.imf.org/en/Publications/WP/Issues/2023/06/16/Central-Bank-Digital-Currency-Adoption-A-Two-Sided-Model-534325

Wu, L. (2023). The application and impact of artificial intelligence technology in international trade. In *2023 6th International Conference on Computer Network, Electronic and Automation (ICCNEA)* (pp. 228–232). https://doi.org/10.1109/ICCNEA60107.2023.00056

Chapter 13

Islamic Banking and the Fourth Industrial Revolution: The Current Application, Adoption, and Future Challenges of Artificial Intelligence

Syaima Adznan[a], *Soliha Sanusi*[a], *Hafizah Omar Zaki*[a], *Mohamed Mahees Raheem*[b] *and Edib Smolo*[b]

[a]Universiti Kebangsaan Malaysia (UKM), Malaysia
[b]Effat University, Saudi Arabia

Abstract

Digital transformation has made enormous changes in the banking domain, where financial technology (fintech) is the salient driving force inside it. For Islamic banking, artificial intelligence (AI) is one of the most innovative technologies that has shifted banks into the entire virtual environment. In this context, the main objectives of this chapter are to discuss the current application of AI in the Islamic banking industry, to identify the challenges faced by the banks in adapting AI while ensuring Shari'ah compliant in their operations, and to shed light on the future of banking and how it will influence Islamic banks in this digital era. This chapter also provides several examples of the application of several Shari'ah robo-advisors used by Islamic banks. Robo advisors are mainly an advanced AI tool involved in investment and portfolio management. The unique value of AI for Islamic banks lies within its own-Shari'ah AI framework that is used to fulfill Shari'ah-related matters, which requires active collaboration between Shari'ah scholars, regulatory bodies, and Islamic banks. Despite all the challenges, AI holds immense potential for Islamic banking to improve efficiency, accessibility, and risk management. Finally, the chapter paves the way for further discussion on building a responsible and innovative Islamic financial system in the era of AI.

The Future of Islamic Finance, 207–219

doi:10.1108/978-1-83549-906-120241013

Keywords: Artificial intelligence; Islamic banking; Shari'ah; Shari'ah AI; fintech; banking industry

Introduction

Islamic banks play a significant role in promoting financial inclusion and stability in the global economy. They have sustained a market growth momentum of 15.3% and were estimated to be worth US$8.06 trillion in 2026 (IFSB, 2023). Islamic fintech also demonstrated a steady market growth of an estimated US$49 billion, representing 0.7% of the global fintech transaction volume, and this growth is expected to increase to over US$179 billion by 2026. The emergence of technology systems and applications is showing signals of maturity and has forced many industries, including Islamic banks, to develop more innovative financial products and provide speedy, timely, reliable, and effective financial solutions (Adznan et al., 2023b; Manoj, 2023). While the technology solution must comply with Shari'ah , it should also uphold moral integrity and protect the sociopolitical environment as the optimal objective of Islamic banks (Adznan et al., 2022, 2023b). The unique value proposition of Islamic banks has increased the challenge for management, especially the Shari'ah committee (Adznan et al., 2023a), in ensuring that all the products and businesses comply with Shari'ah.

Digital transformation in the banking industry creates opportunities to change the business model and achieve economic growth. It refers to the continuous changes in society and businesses due to digital technologies that improve businesses and customer experience and generate novel business models (Vedapradha & Ravi, 2021). Transformational solutions provided by digital banking are based on three building blocks: widespread digital infrastructure, dynamic banking services markets, and advanced digital products (Um et al., 2023). As far as the digital infrastructure and digital products in digital transformation are concerned, fintech stands predominant. It is simply the fusion of financial services with technological advancements. Due to the unstoppable product and process innovation and transformation, fintech is continuously emerging (Li et al., 2023). The development of fintech has created a vital influence on banking applications and, in turn, is an essential theme for previous scholars in the same domain. Hence, many tools, platforms, and technologies have been integrated into the banking digital transformation strategy in the modern world (Adznan et al., 2023b; Lada et al., 2023). That includes but is not limited to AI-integrated platforms such as blockchain and AI. Many works on the adoption of fintech tools highlight that it enhances financial inclusion and brings a sustainable competitive advantage (Adznan et al., 2023b). Furthermore, it facilitates the most common banking tasks, such as organizing transactions, account keeping, investment, and portfolio management, while reducing the information asymmetry in the marketplace (Dewasiri et al., 2023).

The Role of Artificial Intelligence in Islamic Banking

Along with growing digital economies and rapidly evolving customer preferences, the Islamic banking industry needs to embrace and enhance its technological and people capabilities to provide competitive solutions. In this manner, AI enables a secure and seamless end-to-end banking experience is now an integral part of the industry. The potential influence that AI could bring to the Islamic banking industry cannot be denied. AI is one of the most transformational technologies driving the fourth industrial revolution (4IR). The global market revenue for AI software from 2018 to 2023 indicated that the trend is increasing yearly, indicating a positive vibe to AI in the future (Dewasiri et al., 2023). The various roles of AI from an Islamic banking perspective will be explored here:

Increased Productivity and Efficiency

Automation that is powered by AI has the ability to significantly streamline manual processes within Islamic banks, thereby freeing up human resources to concentrate on operations that are more strategic (Fernandez et al., 2023). Many bankers use chatbots as their frontline to deal with customers. During busy days, it helps the customers a lot because sometimes human resources cannot entertain them immediately, and customers do not prefer to be on hold on the phone for long hours. Because of this situation, there is the potential for a substantial improvement in operational efficiency, a reduction in expenses, and a speedier turnaround time. It will ultimately contribute to an increase in productivity and profitability. Imagine a world in which workers can engage in more in-depth contact with customers and offer novel financial solutions such as automated account opening, verification of customer documents, and loan processing (Fernandez & Aman, 2021).

Financial Inclusion

Promoting financial inclusion is one of the fundamental principles of Islamic banking. This principle ensures that all individuals have access to financial services that are in accordance with Shari'ah law and ethical standards. Fintech solutions that are powered by AI, such as mobile banking applications and robo-advisors, have the potential to bridge the gap and reach populations that are not banked or underserved, particularly in geographically remote places. This situation has the potential to enable individuals to participate more actively in the financial system, contributing to the expansion of the economy and enhancing their general well-being (Vedapradha & Ravi, 2021). This condition will be discussed under social Islamic finance or social crowdfunding, which can help the needy or businesses from micro- or small enterprises (Sanusi & Shafiai, 2015). Currently, there are varieties of non-bank institutions that provide solutions to customers without a requirement to open an official account with bank institutions. Neobanks that run virtually assist laborers who live far away from banks or have problems with bank institutions transferring money overseas or doing any transactions online. Examples of neobanks are Bigpay and Wise. Hence, the neobank resembles the bank institution but in the virtual transactions with chatbot facilities provided. Islamic Bank shall take this opportunity to serve needy customers since the coverage is broader.

Risk Management and Shari'ah Compliance

Islamic banks can identify and evaluate financial risks with more precision due to the capabilities of AI algorithms, which can analyze large volumes of data with remarkable speed and accuracy. Consequently, this situation makes it possible to improve risk management, implement proactive mitigation methods, and create a financial climate that is more secure and stable (Abdullah et al., 2022). Additionally, AI can be applied to screen investments for Shari'ah compliance, which ensures adherence to Islamic values and ethical rules, thereby encouraging trust and confidence among clients.

Transparency and Traceability

Blockchain technology, another revolutionary technology of the fourth industrial revolution, can be combined with AI to improve the transparency and traceability of Islamic banking systems. The establishment of confidence among clients, the strengthening of relationships with stakeholders, and the guarantee that all financial activities comply with Islamic principles and ethical norms are all outcomes of this. Imagine an environment for the financial sector that is both open and safe, where every transaction is recorded and easily available, and which encourages responsibility and responsible financial practices (Manoj, 2023; Muslichah & Sanusi, 2019). Blockchain, on the other hand, helps Islamic banks be more transparent and reliable. Ji and Tia (2021) conducted a substantial study that revealed that the distinctive advantage of blockchain technology is that it has the capacity to disrupt the traditional business intelligence offerings of financial institutions. This potential encompasses smart contracts, digital payments, database management, and records; however, cryptocurrencies are the most frequently referenced output. Blockchain-based cryptocurrencies impact bank services in three ways: as a means of payment, as a token to redeem benefits, and as a guarantee. In turn, the following three functions of a bank are impacted by blockchain technology: account opening, message transmission (including the transmission of encrypted messages), and authentication.

Innovation and Personalized Financial Solutions

AI opens a new frontier for innovation in Islamic banking, making it possible to create novel financial products and services in accordance with Shari'ah law and designed to meet the ever-changing requirements and preferences of a wide range of customers.

Banks can serve customers through intelligent application programming interfaces (APIs) tailored to be compatible with their customers' goals, risk profiles, and ethical values. The data-driven AI, on the other hand, can help assess clients individually and give valuable insights into their profiles. In this regard, client participation and loyalty can be enhanced, leading to the growth of an inclusive and responsive financial system (Sangwan et al., 2020; Um et al., 2023). Table 13.1 highlights the cases of AI applications in the operational sphere of Islamic banking.

Challenges and Opportunities in Implementing AI in Islamic Banking

Due to the exponential advancements in AI, the shape of industries is transforming across the world, and human–machine interaction is continuously being reinvented extensively (Um et al., 2023; Vedapradha & Ravi, 2021). The Islamic banking industry, too, is not spared. The Islamic Banking industry, having its

Table 13.1. An Example of AI Application in Islamic Banking Operations.

- BIMB Investment Management Berhad (BIMB Investment), a wholly owned subsidiary of Bank Islam Malaysia Berhad has launched the a, a Shari'ah-compliant equity growth fund that aims to provide investment returns to investors through investment in Shari'ah-compliant global technology equities. The Fund capitalises on strong technology market trends using the latest AI research and technology by Arabesque AI, the artificial intelligence business unit of the Arabesque Group.
- Wahed Invest is an international robo-advisor that follows Shari'ah principles and provides a range of investment options tailored to various requirements and risk tolerances.
- Ethis Robo is a UK-based robo-advisor that follows Shari'ah principles and provides various ethical investment choices.
- AYMEN is a Shari'ah-compliant robo-advisor located in Malaysia, providing investment plans for individuals and institutions.
- Jarir is a Shari'ah-compliant robo-advisor based in the UAE that provides a range of investment opportunities, such as *sukuk* and real estate.
- An Innovative Lab developed by Bahrain Islamic Bank (BisB) is a dedicated in-house facility that offers automated investment recommendations to clients according to their financial targets and risk tolerance. The Bank invested in Shari'ah Robo to offer automated investment guidance to clients according to their financial objectives and risk tolerance.

foundations based on tradition and ethical principles, also faces the same challenges and prospects brought about by AI. Integrating AI within the daily operations of Islamic banks can help augment performance by automating and streamlining tasks and improving customer services and risk management techniques (Litimi et al., 2023). On the flip side, the implementation of AI can also present numerous other obstacles and challenges.

Navigating the Shari'ah Compliance Landscape: A Central Challenge

In essence, AI algorithms are required to comply strictly with the Shari'ah parameters. Interest-based transactions are prohibited, and AI algorithms must be programmed in a way to negate them wherever they may arise. Moreover, intricate details and requirements of Shari'ah law may be included, and this might differ across various Islamic schools of thought. Thus, it is vital to take measures to keep the fundamental Islamic banking principles in place within artificially intelligent systems while developing, implementing (or conceiving) those systems. The development of comprehensive and quality oversight mechanisms that can track as well as detect either non-compliance or ethical issues in algorithms as well as apps is a must (Adzinan et al., 2023b; Lada et al., 2023; Manoj, 2023). Banks must come up with a comprehensive AI framework that is custom-tailored for their own conditions and based on the knowledge of experts in Islamic Finance and state-of-the-art AI algorithms. As AI advances rapidly and is increasingly interlinked with our society, Shari'ah-compliance of AI should leverage AI technology and simultaneously comply with Islamic principles and values. The *maqasid al-Shari'ah* (objectives of Shari'ah), namely the protection of religion, life, posterity, intellect, and property, should be safeguarded to ensure societal benefit and prevention of harm.

However, ensuring the incorporation of ethics in a Shari'ah AI framework also facilitates advancement in sustainable technologies. Algorithms can unintentionally reflect biases and social disparities, raising questions about their accountability and independence (Fernandez et al., 2023).

The Shari'ah AI framework can guarantee transparency in algorithms and promote accuracy in data. It is necessary to place human monitoring and intervention safeguards to ensure and confirm that AI output and decisions do not violate Islamic principles. A recent example is the creation of AI-powered robo-advisors, designed to analyze investments for Shari'ah compliance and to guarantee ethical financial decision-making. Personalized AI-driven applications can cater to one's specific financial requirements and strategies based on their own savings and investment objectives (Manoj, 2023).

Though the perceived benefits are multifold, developing functional and universally accepted Shari'ah AI frameworks come with their own difficulties. Conflicting interpretations of various principles, maxims and texts may lead to disagreements, hence the need for the AI framework to be agile enough to accommodate various contexts and technological needs. This requires close collaboration between AI experts, Shari'ah scholars, and experts with a joint understanding of Islamic finance principles and AI algorithms to ensure that the end product satisfies both technological requirements and Shari'ah constraints.

To this end, it is posited that Islamic banks form dedicated committees comprising qualified and accredited Shari'ah scholars and AI experts (Adznan et al., 2022), who will be ultimately responsible for the evaluation and approval of AI applications and models. The custom Shari'ah-AI framework developed by the bank should be used for the development and application of AI solutions, with supervision from AI specialists, Shari'ah scholars, and related governing authorities. Periodic risk assessments should be conducted internally and externally to ensure transparency and proper interpretation, implementation, and compliance with Shari'ah parameters within AI. Robust procedures and checks and balances should be established to ensure AI systems can operate autonomously in responsible decision-making. This can ultimately enable Islamic banks and financial institutions to leverage on AI to offer innovative financial services to their customers. (Vedapradha & Ravi, 2021).

Transparency and Identifiability: Establishing Trust in the "Invisibility" of AI

One of the challenges of Islamic banks is that they cannot visualize and see AI modalities. Shari'ah regulations mandate that business dealings should be open to public scrutiny, in addition to certain ethical standards and should avoid interest, which is deemed *haram* (forbidden). Sophisticated AI algorithms might pose challenges to regulators and consumers in understanding the logic of the decision-making process. The lack of transparency and possible comprehension can result in trust erosion and the related problem with the spread of the algorithmic models. To get a positive opinion from the public toward AI-based projects, the banks must be absolutely clear in terms of reliability and accessibility. Islamic banks need to exhaust every means to educate the public on AI algorithm creation and how their decisions are made. It creates a bond in which the clients can rely on the information given to them, allowing them to make positive financial decisions. The identification of AI is deemed an effective tool for such purposes where AI may be capable of interpreting its modeling approach in an understandable manner to the user. Through this, they will be able to know the purposes of the financial decisions, approvals of credits, product recommendations and all other outputs provided by AI as essential parts of unbiased actions concerning transparency and trust. (Dewasiri et al., 2023; Fernandez et al., 2023).

Effective and efficient communication with clients must be implemented so they understand how AI can be used in day-to-day operations and that the involvement of AI algorithms will not cause any stress or worry. Effective communication in this context would encompass the sharing and the information that would be useful in addressing the wrong assumptions and unrealistic anxiety around AI.

Last but not least, putting in place systems and processes that ensure data governance is imperative. Islamic banks have to create and implement clear policies and regulations governing the acquisition, usage, and storage of data and ensure Shari'ah-compliance and nondisclosure of such information. Through the adoption of good practices in data warehousing with a keen eye on the source and the lineage of the data, it is possible to trace and minimize bias. Introducing AI ethical frameworks based on Shari'ah law will guarantee the fair usage of the technology with the establishment of measures to eliminate bias, promote equity and strive for diversity. AI-enabled financial services can expand financial inclusion and make it easier for marginalized individuals and the community to participate in the economy. Nevertheless, the accessibility problem is a major constraint for Islamic financial institutions. To this end, banks should plan ahead of time to prevent the technology backlash in industries where access to digital communication infrastructures and literacy are limited. This may deny some people, as well as society itself, the opportunity to benefit from AI-enabled services. Islamic banks have the potential to remove this obstacle via the establishment of educational and advisory programs where people are encouraged to have confidence and interact with AI-powered services in a smart and easy manner that each and every person, regardless of their level in life, can understand. Through the allocation of budget and development of educational programs on financial and digital literacy, it is possible to bring out the benefits of AI, which will build trust, engage more people in the financial ecosystem, and form communities that would be able to make income and find jobs with the help of AI. To achieve this, we need to join hands with Islamic banks, technology developers, Shari'ah experts, and regulators in order to ensure the transparency and capability of AI solutions that don't breach Shari'ah.

Data Security and Privacy: Protecting Sensitive Information

The parading of AI in Islamic banking implies a more significant transformation, but at the same time, it requires the task of protecting valuable customer data. The incorporation of AI poses an enticing opportunity for thieves, which requires the management of Islamic banks to prioritize strong security and privacy protections. Ensuring data security necessitates a comprehensive strategy that includes the implementation of sophisticated encryption techniques, safe access controls, and resilient network security systems as crucial first measures. Consistently allocating resources to enhance infrastructure and conduct vulnerability assessments is essential to proactively address ever-changing cyber threats (Zaki & Fernandez, 2023). It is crucial to establish explicit protocols for the gathering, utilization, and retention of data. Adherence to data reduction standards entails collecting solely the essential information required for legitimate objectives. Conducting regular data audits and providing employee training on data security protocols are also crucial. Islamic banks are required to comply with rigorous data privacy standards. These rules are the cornerstone of the collection, storage, and use of data that take the user's privacy rights into account. The security rules sometimes may require sensitive data, and it is thus crucial to consider these difficulties that may arise during the process of harmonizing the Shari'ah laws with the security practices. Moreover, it is critical to summon Shari'ah experts when making decisions related to data processing and establishing rules and regulations that will be applied to secure collected data. This approach becomes more of a norm for the implementation of Islamic ethics, the establishment of trust among people, and the creation of a suitable environment in the digital world. In addition, observance of these principles ensures the representation of Islamic values and proper conduct in online interactions.

As pointed out by Adznan et al. (2023a), privacy and trust are key factors in the Islamic banking system. Customers' explicit consent regarding the way their data is used and/or their ability to create their own individual privacy limitation parameters should be a must. Opt-out procedures should be visible at a glance, and questions about data access should be answered right away to create transparency and confidence. Islamic banks should work in alliance with information technology service providers, regulators, and cyber security agencies to form a strong digital security strategy that is consistent with Islamic jurisprudence. The implementation of a security protocol that is a fusion of technological features with data-centricity can be used to provide privacy protection and data-driven analysis on the one hand and ensure privacy protection on the other hand.

To deal with the digital barriers that Islamic banks may face, they need to be very specific about the data governance legal framework, as well as continue to use state-of-the-art cybersecurity and infrastructure technologies and establish a safe and reliable environment for their customers. This kind of strategy requires the bank players to transform their perceptions toward a problem-solving mindset, as well as build privacy-enhancing tools for sensitive data protection.

Ethical Considerations: Ensuring Fairness and Inclusivity

Islamic financial institutions can improve customer experience through the delivery of customized and state-of-the-art products and services using instant reach and effectively integrating the advancements of AI technologies into the banking industry. On the one hand, it is possible to believe that this could be the kind of fuel to keep the biased or unfair societies going, while on the other hand, it could be a barrier that interferes with the process of social progress. It is key that AI use in Islamic banks maintains high ethical standards that actively emphasize reduction or, if possible, elimination of discriminatory practices that may be based on factors such as ethnicity, gender, or race. Adequate audits have to be prepared in the proper manner and conducted from time to time, so as to enable AI algorithms to fit properly with the management controls and safeguards. These have to be well managed and approved in order to find any possible bias that exists. The inclusion of diversity promotion criteria avoids bias risk and achieves fairness and inclusivity for all customers. Therefore, the establishment of ethical principles and security measures pertaining to AI can be the foundation of the credibility of the products as they promote equity and fairness, thus making the banking system just.

Bridging the Talent Gap: Building a Skilled Workforce

AI use in the banking area is freshly developed, and in the case of Islamic banks, there is a shortage of people with sufficient knowledge to deal with such advanced technology. Limited access to specialists in the fields of AI and Islamic banking constitutes a significant obstacle impeding the implementation of AI technology within Islamic banks (Adznan et al., 2023; Lada et al., 2023; Zaki et al., 2023). Thus, the merging of AI and Islamic banking requires the backing of experts whose knowledge is adequately deep in both fields. The professionals will have their distinct technical backgrounds at hand that easily help them combine technical proficiencies with Shari'ah requirements. As a result, they will be able to design solutions that satisfy the Shari'ah requirements. This absence of expertise in AI and digital technologies necessitates that Islamic banks and other financial institutions invest in training and employee development for the purpose of precipitating an environment conducive to knowledge transformation and innovation. Employees need to be given the skills and space to try out new ideas and technologies and build on this base to develop original AI solutions. Creating such a learning atmosphere is one of the most needed conditions to accomplish the recruitment and retention of staff with sufficient knowledge of AI and Islamic banking.

With the speed of growth we are witnessing in the digital space, the reluctance of people to be trained and educated in AI may be a reason those won't accept this technology. It could be intensified by a shortage of experienced instructors and learners not only in AI but also in Islamic finance as well. They require collaborative actions with agreed-upon strategic partnerships between Islamic banking institutions, technologically updated universities, and colleges to provide talent related to skills or that kind of ability. Educational institutions also need to recognize the needs of the sector and incorporate AI and other necessary digital skills within the curriculum to ensure that their graduates have the edge over others in the employment arena. Consequently, the growing requirement for AI know-how at all levels poses a serious challenge to Islamic banks to have the capacity to attract and retain skillful personnel. The technological advancement of a skilled workforce at the grassroots level will ensure the successful implementation of AI solutions in Islamic banking institutions. Today, the technology and the solutions are endless and multi-faceted. Therefore, Islamic banks shouldn't go behind and lose touch with this innovation in order to keep current and attract future customers. Furthermore, Islamic banks need to provide a safe and open ecosystem where all staff are incorporated, and diversity, inclusion, and other ideas are incorporated and respected.

Beyond the Challenges: Embracing the Opportunities of AI for the Future

The AI transformation is unlike anything that has happened before, and the advantages that it brings can be seen across all industries (Zaki et al., 2023). Through AI, Islamic banks can make significant progress in terms of efficiency, stimulate innovation, provide personalized customer services, and favor a diverse and inclusive financial system. AI can equip Islamic banks with the capabilities to launch advanced financial products and services that meet the distinct requirements of their clients, especially those from the Muslim community. Chances are everywhere, for instance, through microfinance for micro, small, and medium enterprises or ethical investment opportunities that comply with Shari'ah rules for investors and entrepreneurs. Also noteworthy are the services through AI-driven mobile banks in regions with no or insufficient banking infrastructure.

At the institutional level, AI assists in automating tasks such as account opening, KYC verification, and transaction processing, which relieves human resources to concentrate on more essential projects (Fernandez & Aman, 2021). AI can be effectively integrated into the processes of boosting operational performance, which in turn contributes to cost minimization and an increase in overall productivity. Customers will have no problem creating an account and doing transactions within minutes, while the AI will take the opportunity to carry out the processes that used to take a long time in just a few seconds. Moreover, Islamic banks can use AI as a tool to ensure proper compliance with the strict rules of Shari'ah law because Shari'ah-compliance inspections can be automated by verifying transactions that comply with Islamic ethics and by detecting possible violations. Thus, through identifying pros and cons, Islamic banks can use AI opportunities to create a future-oriented, ethical, accessible, sustainable, and reliable financial environment.

Conclusions

AI will fundamentally change the path of Islamic finance, providing its unique opportunities and advantages. AI can be used strategically to the benefit of Islamic banks by providing resources that help with R&D and implementation of their systems. This can lead to the ushering of a new age in banking that is driven by innovation and oriented toward social impact. What is fast becoming glaring is the topping up of expertise on AI and its implications on Islamic banking and finance. It is thus becoming indispensable to set up the expertise to develop AI solutions as respecter and upholder of the Islamic principles. Partnering with AI experts and sharing advanced technologies and competencies around, Islamic banks will speed up the process of AI integration and incorporation into their daily workflow. To immensely harness human capital base, AI specific courses must be developed for professionals and students concurrently involving academia, business and technical training institutions to impart knowledge and skill sets which will empower the individuals for AI Islamic banking. In conclusion, Islamic financial institutions can employ AI to attain financial success and fulfill their social responsibility, thereby contributing toward a more equitable yet prosperous future for society.

References

Adznan, S., Sori, Z. M., & Mohd, S. M. R. (2022). Intellectual capital disclosure and corporate governance: Empirical evidence from a cross country that offering Islamic bank services. *Asian Journal of Accounting and Governance*, *18*, 47–164.

Adznan, S., Muhamad Sori, Z. B., & Mohamad, S. (2023a). Intellectual capital disclosure (ICD) in Islamic banks: Does the diversity of Shariah committee matters? *International Journal of Islamic and Middle Eastern Finance and Management*, *16*(6), 1269–1286. https://doi.org/10.1108/IMEFM-02-2023-0055

Adznan, S. B., Muhamad Sori, Z. B., & Mohamad, S. (2023b). Intellectual capital disclosures (ICD) of Islamic banks under IFRS versus AAOIFI regimes: An international evidence. *Journal of Islamic Accounting and Business Research*. Vol. ahead-of-print No. ahead-of-print. https://doi.org/10.1108/JIABR-10-2022-0284

Dewasiri, N. J., Karunarathne, K. S. S. N., Menon, S., Jayarathne, P. G. S. A., & Rathnasiri, M. S. H. (2023). Fusion of artificial intelligence and blockchain in the banking industry: Current application, adoption, and future challenges. In *Transformation for sustainable business and management practices: Exploring the spectrum of industry 5.0* (pp. 293–307). Emerald Publishing Limited.

Fernandez, D., & Aman, A. (2021). The challenges of implementing robotic process automation in global business services. *International Journal of Business and Society*, *22*(3), 1269–1282.

Fernandez, D., Dastane, O., Omar Zaki, H., & Aman, A. (2023). Robotic process automation: Bibliometric reflection and future opportunities. *European Journal of Innovation Management*, *27*(2). https://www.emerald.com/insight/content/doi/10.1108/EJIM-10-2022-0570/full/html

Islamic Financial Services Board (IFSB). (2023). *Islamic financial services industry stability report*. https://www.ifsb.org. Retrieved on 'February 15, 2024.

Ji, F., & Tia, A. (2022). The effect of blockchain on business intelligence efficiency of banks. *Kybernetes*, *51*(8), 2652–2668. https://doi.org/10.1108/K-10-2020-0668

Lada, S., Chekima, B., Karim, M. R. A., Fabeil, N. F., Ayub, M. S., Amirul, S. M., … & Zaki, H. O. (2023). Determining factors related to artificial intelligence (AI) adoption among Malaysia's small and medium-sized businesses. *Journal of Open Innovation: Technology, Market, and Complexity*, *9*(4), 100144.

Li, T., Zahari, A. I., & Sanusi, S. (2023). The sustainability of technological innovation in China: From the perspective of network relationships. *Sustainability*, *15*(5), 4242.

Litimi, H., BenSaïda, A., & Raheem, M. M. (2023). Impact of FinTech growth on bank performance in GCC region. *Journal of Emerging Market Finance*, https://doi.org/10.1177/09726527231218423

Manoj, S. (2023). A study: How AI is incorporated in the middle east banking. *Journal for Research in Applied Sciences and Biotechnology*. https://doi.org/10.55544/jrasb.2.3.27

Muslichah, I., & Sanusi, S. (2019). The effect of religiosity and financial literacy on intention to use Islamic banking products. *Asian Journal of Islamic Management (AJIM)*, 85–92.

Nik Abdullah, N. H., Sanusi, S., & Savitri, E. (2022). The role and implications of big data on strategic management accounting practices: A case study in a Malaysian manufacturing company. *Management & Accounting Review (MAR)*, *21*(1), 41–60.

Shaikh, S. A., Ismail, M. A., Shafiai, M. H. M., Ismail, A. G., & Shahimi, S. (2017). Role of Islamic banking in financial inclusion: Prospects and performance. https://doi.org/10.1007/978-3-319-45910-3_3

Sangwan, V., Prakash, P., & Singh, S. (2020). Financial technology: A review of extant literature. *Studies in Economics and Finance*, *37*(1), 71–88. https://doi.org/10.1108/SEF07-2019-0270

Sanusi, S., & Shafiai, M. H. M. (2015). The management of cash waqf: Toward socio-economic development of Muslims in Malaysia. *Jurnal Pengurusan*, *43*.

Um, N., Attayah, S., Zaheer, A., & Muhammad, A. (2023). Banking 4.0: Artificial intelligence (AI) in banking industry & consumer's perspective. *Sustainability*. https://doi.org/10.3390/su15043682

Vedapradha, R., & Ravi, H. (2021). Innovation in banking: Fusion of artificial intelligence and blockchain. *Asia Pacific Journal of Innovation and Entrepreneurship*, *15*(1), 51–61. https://doi.org/10.1108/APJIE-09-2020-0142

Zaki, H. O., & Fernandez, D. (2023). Automation in digital marketing. In O. Dastane, A. Aman, & N. Safie Bin Mohd Satar (Eds.), *Digital natives as a disruptive force in Asian businesses and societies* (pp. 241–251). IGI Global.

Zaki, H. O., Fernandez, D., Dastane, O., Aman, A., & Sanusi, S. (2023). Virtual reality in digital marketing: Research agenda based on bibliometric reflection. *Marketing Intelligence & Planning*, *41*(4), 505–524.

Chapter 14

The Future of Islamic Finance

Sutan Emir Hidayat[a], *Khairunnisa Musari*[b], *Siti Masrohatin*[b] *and Edib Smolo*[c]

[a]National Committee for Islamic Economy and Finance (KNEKS), Indonesia
[b]Kiai Haji Achmad Siddiq State Islamic University (UIN KHAS), Indonesia
[c]Effat University, Saudi Arabia

Abstract

In this chapter, the integration of diverse discussions from preceding chapters converges into a comprehensive exploration of four pivotal challenges facing Islamic finance both presently and in the future. The chapter systematically addresses these challenges, commencing with a focused analysis on augmenting the role of Islamic finance in fostering financial inclusion. It scrutinizes innovative strategies to broaden access to financial services. Moving forward, the narrative navigates the intricate intersection of Islamic finance and sustainability, unraveling the potential synergy between these two domains and their collective contribution to Sustainable Development Goals (SDGs). The exploration extends to the realm of digitalization, probing how modern technologies such as artificial intelligence and blockchain can serve as catalysts for the progression of Islamic finance. Finally, the chapter delves into the imperative of harmonizing the Islamic financial industry (IFI), tackling challenges and proposing solutions to enhance uniformity and coherence in practices. These nuanced discussions not only address contemporary challenges but also underscore their critical role in achieving the SDGs and aligning with the targets of the Paris Agreement by 2030, providing valuable insights for scholars, practitioners, and policymakers in the field of Islamic finance.

Keywords: Financial inclusion; sustainability; sustainable finance; Islamic finance; Islamic sustainable finance; inclusive finance; digitalization; financial technology (fintech); harmonization; standardization

The Future of Islamic Finance, 221–242

doi:10.1108/978-1-83549-906-120241014

Introduction

Islamic finance has been a global presence for over six decades, dating back to the establishment of the Egyptian Mit Ghamr Saving Bank in 1963. Over the years, the industry has witnessed substantial progress, transcending religious, ethnic, national, and state boundaries. Notably, countries with predominantly non-Muslim populations have articulated their aspirations to emerge as global Islamic financial hubs. This trend not only underscores the industry's widespread appeal but also instills optimism that the Islamic economy and finance are poised to evolve into integral components of the mainstream economic and financial systems in the future.

Nevertheless, a series of unforeseen crises have unfolded in recent years, including the ongoing COVID-19 pandemic, the conflicts in Russia and Ukraine, and instances of droughts, floods, and heat waves attributable to climate change. These crises have dealt a significant blow to endeavors to realize the 17 targets outlined in the SDGs and adhere to the Paris Agreement's commitments. The repercussions of these global challenges not only impact broader sustainability initiatives but pose a distinctive challenge for the IFI, necessitating a thoughtful reassessment of strategies and resilience in the face of evolving global circumstances. Overall, there are at least four main challenges that are currently faced by the IFI, and they might hinder the development of the industry in the future. First, financial inclusion is at the very low level, which means that many people still don't have access to financial services. This is especially the case of Muslim majority countries. Second, there is a lack of integration of sustainability practices into Islamic financial institutions (IFIs). Third, digitalization within the IFI is lagging behind its conventional counterpart. Fourth, the issue of standardization, although not new, still represents a significant obstacle to the future growth of the IFI. In other words, the differences in Shari'ah opinions that are reflected in the IFI's practices may hinder its growth potentials (Smolo, 2009a, 2009b; Smolo & Habibovic, 2012).

Based on the above background, this chapter aims to elaborate and scrutinize the above four issues as follows: (1) Islamic finance and financial inclusion; (2) Islamic finance and sustainability; (3) Islamic finance and digitalization; and (4) Islamic finance and the issue of standardization. These issues are very relevant and very important to be tackled in order ensure the achievement of the SDGs and the Paris Agreement in 2030. It is very important to really understand those issues in order for the regulators and authorities to come out with policies and regulations that will tackle those issues.

Islamic Finance and Financial Inclusion

Financial inclusion is all about inclusiveness in the provision of affordable formal financial services to all individuals and businesses. Financial inclusion ensures that people and firms have access to basic and affordable financial services in the formal financial sector. Today, financial inclusion is a global agenda which aims to help achieve the SDGs. In many countries, particularly in the emerging countries, financial inclusion is considered an important part of their strategies to achieve inclusive growth and equitable economic development. Therefore, they emphasize on the promotion of financial literacy among the public (ADBI, 2014; Musari, 2022; Ozili, 2018, 2022; Sapovadia, 2018).

Given the above situation, Islamic finance should play a significant role in enhancing financial inclusion especially in Muslim majority countries, particularly through Islamic microfinance (Jouti, 2018). Rooted in Shari'ah values, Islamic microfinance can boost financial inclusion in various regions with a significant Muslim population, such as in the Maghreb region, Central Asia, South East Asia and the Gulf Cooperation Council (GCC) (Musari & Sayah, 2023). However, the financial inclusion level driven by Islamic microfinance in the Maghreb region is still far behind the Southeast Asian region (Aaminou, 2022). This implies that the stakeholders in the Maghreb region have not yet captured the full potential of the Islamic microfinance industry in driving socio-economic impacts for people within the bottom of the pyramid (BoP).

In order to obtain an overview of the level of financial inclusion in Muslim majority countries, Table 14.1 shows the account ownership percentage of adults with an account, women with an account, and poor adults with an account in several member states of the Organization of the Islamic Cooperation (OIC). However, low levels of financial inclusion do not imply low scores on the Human Development Index (HDI) as countries characterized by low levels of financial inclusion are evident across various HDI categories (high, medium, and low levels of development). Notably, there are countries where financial inclusion remains below 30%, as evidenced by the percentage of adults holding bank accounts falling within the range of 19–21% and, in some cases, as low as 10%. This underscores a significant observation that HDI does not consistently correlate with the level of financial inclusion, indicating a nuanced and varied relationship between human development and access to financial services.

One of the major causes of this anomaly is the existence of usury (*riba*) based financial system (Arzayeva & Dochshanova, 2016). No doubt, implementing usury based financial system on the underprivileged society is not significantly helping them out of poverty. This is one of the main reasons for the need for the Islamic financial system. Therefore, Rahman (2020) encouraged policymakers in Muslim countries that have concerns on financial inclusion to explore the potential of Islamic financial instruments. By doing so, they can achieve financial inclusion goals and focus on improving the regulatory and financial infrastructure that will enable environment for the system to flourish. One of the important steps that need to be taken by those countries is to explicitly insert Islamic finance into their national development plans (long, medium, and short terms). This will ensure a bright future for Islamic finance.

In a recent exploration by Karlan et al. (2021), a sense of optimism regarding the prospective trajectory of Islamic finance emerges. The investigation unfolds a heightened demand for Shari'ah-compliant financial services in specific Muslim-majority regions, surpassing the interest in their conventional counterparts. Significantly, the research provides compelling evidence, indicating a preference for these financial products and a willingness to incur a premium for them despite closely

Table 14.1. HDI and Account Ownership, by Economy, 2021, in OIC Member States.

Country	HDI Rank	HDI 2021	Adults With an Account (%)	Women With an Account (%)	Poor Adults With an Account (%)
Very High Human Development					
United Arab Emirates	26	0.911	86	87	83
Saudi Arabia	35	0.875	74	63	67
Türkiye	48	0.838	74	63	61
Kazakhstan	56	0.811	81	84	82
Malaysia	62	0.803	88	88	83
High Human Development					
Albania	67	0.796	44	46	27
Iran, Islamic Rep.	76	0.774	90	85	87
Algeria	91	0.745	44	31	32
Egypt	97	0.731	27	24	20
Tunisia	97	0.731	37	29	32
Uzbekistan	101	0.727	44	39	41
Jordan	102	0.720	47	34	37
Gabon	112	0.706	66	61	59
Lebanon	112	0.706	21	17	13
Indonesia	114	0.705	52	52	47
Medium Human Development					
Kyrgyzstan	118	0.692	45	44	44
Iraq	121	0.686	19	15	14
Tajikistan	122	0.685	39	39	38
Morocco	123	0.683	44	33	34
Bangladesh	129	0.661	53	43	49
Cameroon	151	0.576	52	49	34
Low Human Development					
Pakistan	161	0.544	21	13	18
Togo	162	0.539	50	44	39
Nigeria	163	0.535	45	35	33
Benin	166	0.525	49	40	41
Uganda	166	0.525	66	65	51

Table 14.1. *(Continued)*

Country	HDI Rank	HDI 2021	Adults With an Account (%)	Women With an Account (%)	Poor Adults With an Account (%)
Senegal	170	0.511	56	50	48
Afghanistan	180	0.478	10	5	6
Sierra Leone	181	0.477	29	25	21
Guinea	182	0.465	30	24	24
Burkina Faso	184	0.449	36	31	25
Mozambique	185	0.446	49	39	34
Mali	186	0.428	44	41	38

Source: UNDP (2022), Demirgüç-Kunt et al. (2022).

aligning with the financial characteristics of conventional options. This revelation accentuates a promising path for advancing and accepting Islamic finance within the financial realm.

Islamic Finance and Sustainability

In contemporary times, numerous nations worldwide have incorporated environmental concerns into their national visions. Nonetheless, a delicate equilibrium unfolds within sustainable development, juggling ecological and environmental resilience against economic and human development, even after achieving SDGs (Musari & Khan, 2023). Undoubtedly, the intricate interplay between economic development and environmental sustainability has been a focal point for fervent debate over the years (ElMassah & Hassanein, 2023). To this end, we need to rely more on sustainable finance. In general, sustainable finance entails incorporating ESG considerations into investment decisions within the financial sector. This approach aims to foster long-term investments in sustainable economic activities and projects, reflecting a commitment to responsible and impactful financial practices.

A palpable illustration of this discourse materializes in the discernment that a heightened HDI appears to coincide with a mounting Ecological Footprint (Khan, 2022, 2023). Table 14.2 shows the level of HDI, SDGs Index (SDGi) achievements, and Ecological Footprint produced by the member states of the OIC. The table shows that countries that fall into the very high human development category and have relatively higher SDGi achievements also produce higher ecological footprints than other countries. This also means that there is a strong possibility of positive correlation between human development and ecological footprints. In other words, a better human development agenda has higher ecological footprints consequence.

William Rees and his former doctoral student, Mathis Wackernagel, are frequently associated with ecological footprints. The term "Ecological Footprint"

Table 14.2. HDI, SDGi, and Ecological Footprint in OIC Member Countries.

No.	Country	HDI Rank	HDI 2021	SDGi	Ecological Footprint (Number of Earths Required)
Very High Human Development					
1	United Arab Emirates	26	0.911	68.8	5.8
2	Bahrain	35	0.875	64.3	5.4
3	Saudi Arabia	35	0.875	66.6	3.8
4	Qatar	42	0.855	66.8	8.7
5	Türkiye	48	0.838	70.4	2.2
6	Kuwait	50	0.831	64.5	5.7
7	Brunei Darussalam	51	0.829	67.1	5.2
8	Oman	54	0.816	69.2	4.8
9	Kazakhstan	56	0.811	71.1	2.8
10	Malaysia	62	0.803	70.4	2.8
High Human Development					
11	Albania	67	0.796	71.6	1.4
12	Iran	76	0.774	68.6	2.2
13	Maldives	90	0.747	n.a	n.a
14	Algeria	91	0.745	71.5	1.5
15	Azerbaijan	91	0.745	73.5	1.6
16	Turkmenistan	91	0.745	66.1	2.6
17	Egypt	97	0.731	68.7	1.0
18	Tunisia	97	0.731	70.7	0.9
19	Suriname	99	0.730	71.6	2.1
20	Uzbekistan	101	0.727	69.9	1.4
21	Jordan	102	0.720	69.4	0.9
22	Libya	104	0.718	n.a	n.a
23	Palestine	106	0.715	n.a	n.a
24	Guyana	108	0.714	63.9	2.2
25	Gabon	112	0.706	62.8	1.4
26	Lebanon	112	0.706	66.3	2.1
27	Indonesia	114	0.705	69.2	1.1

Table 14.2. *(Continued)*

No.	Country	HDI		SDGi	Ecological Footprint (Number of Earths Required)
		Rank	2021		
Medium Human Development					
28	Kyrgyzstan	118	0.692	73.7	1.0
29	Iraq	121	0.686	62.3	1.1
30	Tajikistan	122	0.685	69.7	0.7
31	Morocco	123	0.683	69.0	1.0
32	Bangladesh	129	0.661	64.2	0.4
33	Cameroon	151	0.576	55.5	0.7
34	Comoros	156	0.558	n.a	1.3
35	Mauritania	158	0.556	55.8	1.5
36	Côte d'Ivoire	159	0.550	n.a	0.6
Low Human Development					
37	Pakistan	161	0.544	59.3	0.5
38	Togo	162	0.539	n.a	0.6
39	Nigeria	163	0.535	54.2	0.5
40	Benin	166	0.525	51.2	0.7
41	Uganda	166	0.525	54.9	0.6
42	Senegal	170	0.511	58.7	0.8
43	Djibouti	171	0.509	50.3	1.6
44	Sudan	172	0.508	49.6	0.8
45	Gambia	174	0.500	60.2	0.6
46	Guinea-Bissau	177	0.483	n.a	0.8
47	Afghanistan	180	0.478	52.5	0.5
48	Sierra Leone	181	0.477	53.0	0.7
49	Guinea	182	0.465	51.3	1.0
50	Yemen	183	0.455	52.1	0.4
51	Burkina Faso	184	0.449	54.5	0.6
52	Mozambique	185	0.446	53.6	0.5
53	Mali	186	0.428	54.1	0.7
54	Niger	189	0.400	52.2	0.9
55	Chad	190	0.394	41.3	0.9

Source: UNDP (2022), Global Footprint Network (2022).

gained prominence when Rees challenged the prevailing economic resource utilization model, emphasizing the need for heightened focus on the land required to sustain urban areas (Collins & Flynn, 2015). This Ecological Footprint concept represents an innovative environmental accounting approach. It evaluates the impact of human activities on the biosphere by contrasting it with the biosphere's inherent regenerative capacity (Wackernagel & Galli, 2007). Previously, the terminology of the ecological footprint was called a regional capsule (Rees, 1986) and appropriated carrying capacity (Rees, 1992). Now, the ecological footprint is known as a comprehensive measure for assessing environmental sustainability and human activity effect (Rees & Wackernagel, 1996); an accounting system that documents the ecological performance; a highly aggregated measure of people's use of nature (Wackernagel & Beyers, 2019); and a measure of how much of the Earth's biologically productive land and water area is needed to support a population's consumption and waste production (Musari & Khan, 2023).

Therefore, the Ecological Footprint emphasizes the need for OIC countries, especially those in the Very High Human Development category, to tackle ecological and natural capital challenges. This involves transitioning their economies towards more restorative, sustainable, regenerative, and equitably intergenerational economic models (Musari & Khan, 2023). Then, by implementing a circular economy, (Islamic) Smart Cities in the GCC region have a crucial part in reducing Ecological Footprint and can be an engine for creating ecological and environmental resilience to achieve sustainable well-being (Musari, 2024), at once as best practices for other OIC countries.

The growth and depth of Islamic finance, measured by the rise in total assets, asset quality, profitability, and efficiency of Islamic banks, might lead to a nonlinear increase in CO_2 emissions with a U-shaped relationship. Other findings suggest that increasing Islamic social responsibility, consumer education, and awareness about Islamic banking could mitigate the positive effects of energy consumption on greenhouse gas emissions (Frontiers Editorial Office, 2023).

Islamic Finance and Digitalization

According to the *State of the Global Islamic Economy Report 2022*, digital connectivity and the rise of m-commerce and e-commerce became the driver of the Islamic economy. In 2020, several OIC countries from Southeast Asia and the Middle East and North Africa (MENA) had a higher internet penetration than the global average of 59%, whereas the GCC countries had a penetration of almost 99%. Besides, the Internet penetration for the African region grew by nearly 21% more than in pre-COVID-19 years, which is also the highest growth globally.

At the same time, Malaysia, Indonesia, and Saudi Arabia are among the OIC countries which became the adopter of the highest global m-commerce and e-commerce, more than each global average of 55.4% and 76.8% as of December 2020. In the post-COVID-19 era, the trend is also applied in most Muslim-majority countries and is expected to support the growth of the virtual business (DinarStandard, 2022).

The Global Islamic Fintech (GIFT) Index 2022 indicates that the transaction volume of the Islamic financial technology (fintech) within OIC countries reached US$79 billion in 2021 and will grow to US$179 billion at the compound annual growth rate of 17.9% in 2026. This growth forecast is higher than the growth forecast of conventional fintech for the same period at a rate of 13.5%. GIFT is a composite index consisting of 32 indicators with five categories, namely regulation, capital, talent, infrastructure, and Islamic fintech market and ecosystem. Even though OIC countries master the 10 highest scores, the fast ecosystems come from non-OIC countries (DinarStandard and Elipses, 2022). The country index of the 60 Islamic fintech markets within the GIFT Index is shown in Table 14.3 below. Malaysia, Saudi Arabia, and Indonesia are the leading countries in the Islamic fintech ecosystem in 2022.

Achieving long-term sustainable economic development requires preserving wealth and safeguarding property rights. These measures guide innovations that foster a fair distribution of income and wealth. Additionally, adopting modern

Table 14.3. The GIFT Index.

Rank	Countries	Rank	Countries	Rank	Countries
1	Malaysia	21	Switzerland	41	Cameroon
2	Saudi Arabia	22	Canada	42	Afghanistan
3	Indonesia	23	Luxembourg	43	Thailand
4	U.A.E.	24	Kazakhstan	44	Maldives
5	U.K.	25	Germany	45	Algeria
6	Bahrain	26	China	46	Mauritania
7	Kuwait	27	France	47	Morocco
8	Singapore	28	Japan	48	Palestine
9	Qatar	29	Egypt	49	Iraq
10	Hong Kong	30	Sri Lanka	50	Philippines
11	Pakistan	31	Russia	51	Kyrgyzstan
12	Iran	32	Spain	52	Azerbaijan
13	USA	33	India	53	Albania
14	Bangladesh	34	Tunisia	54	Syria
15	Jordan	35	Lebanon	55	Uzbekistan
16	Turkiye	36	Kenya	56	Burkino Faso
17	Oman	37	Bosnia & Herzegovina	57	Senegal
18	Australia	38	South Africa	58	Libya
19	Nigeria	39	Tajikistan	59	Ivory Coast
20	Brunei	40	Sudan	60	Mali

Source: DinarStandard and Elipses (2022).

technologies and innovations plays a crucial role in boosting productivity and, consequently, promoting economic growth among OIC member states (Askari et al., 2010; Moro-Visconti, 2021).

Hence, aligning with the universal principles of Islam, innovations in Islamic fintech should be broadened to benefit all segments of society, especially the underprivileged and underserved populations in regions or countries experiencing a rise in Muslim populations or substantial growth in Islamic finance. This inclusivity also extends to rural areas where individuals have abstained from conventional banking services due to religious or ethical considerations (Gulrez, 2021). It's important to note that Islamic finance fintech should be broadly understood, encompassing more than just banking services (Oseni & Ali, 2019).

Islamic Finance and Standardization

As Islamic finance has been practiced worldwide and covered almost all spectrums of financial services, there are several differences in the practices of Islamic finance across jurisdictions. These differences create confusion among the public and result in inefficiency for multinational financial institutions that have operations globally. The differences in the Shari'ah scholars's opinions also hamper cross border transactional activities among IFIs. In other words, the lack of standardization or at least harmonization in the practices of Islamic finance is one of the ongoing and unresolved issues that need to be urgently tackled (COMCEC, 2022; Smolo, 2009a, 2009b, 2011; Smolo & Habibovic, 2012; Smolo & Smajic, 2011).

The efforts of tackling the issue have been undertaken by the establishment of several Islamic financial standard setting organizations (SSOs) such as the Accounting and Auditing Organization for Islamic Financial Institutions (AAOIFI) and the Islamic Financial Services Board (IFSB). However, not all countries that have Islamic finance adopt the standards issued by those SSOs. Local Shari'ah, accounting and auditing standards are still used by many countries with significant Islamic finance proportion such as Malaysia and Indonesia (Smolo & Habibovic, 2012). Therefore, in order to move forward the issue needs to be solved as soon as possible. This does not mean that we need an absolute standardization, i.e. one-size-fits-all solution. Rather, it means that SSOs – such as AAOIFI – could provide a comprehensive list of acceptable financial instruments (taking into consideration different schools of thoughts and jurisdictions). This would be beneficial on a few fronts. First, it would facilitate financial literacy among IFIs' clients. Second, IFIs within a given jurisdiction could have the same contract structure that would promote uniformity and reduce ambiguity. Third, this would help overall understanding of practices and services provided by IFIs, leaving less room for potential disputes.

Islamic Finance in the Future

Islamic finance is a way to put Islamic principles into financial system. Attempts to develop a specific Islamic type of economy, based upon Islamic religious law, the Shari'ah, can be seen as a manifestation of the wish harbored by Muslims to retain, or regain, their own identity vis-à-vis the capitalist West and, until the fall of communism, the socialist East (Visser, 2013). The main goals of Islamic finance are to offer an alternative medium to the conventional financial system that fosters economic growth and development through profit and loss sharing finance; to promote social well-being by eliminating activities that are considered immoral or harmful; to emphasize on equity participation and ownership principles in financial transactions; and to distribute wealth more evenly and support productive sectors of the economy (Hassan et al., 2019).

Toward More Inclusive Islamic Finance

Philosophically, financial inclusion brings a message for delivering an affordable cost of financial services to a segment of disadvantaged and low-income segments of society (Sapovadia, 2018). Digital technology contributes to impetus financial inclusion, embracing economic innovation, competition, growth in the world, and finally for achieving the SDGs (ADB, 2017; Klapper, 2016; Moro-Visconti, 2021; Yang & Zhang, 2020). Now, technology encourages the creation of digital financial inclusion (Musari, 2022). Naturally, incumbent financial services institutions are being threatened by financial start-ups with innovative financial products and services, including IFIs (Alam & Ali, 2021).

The global community has leveraged experiences and opportunities in utilizing mobile and digital technology as a tool for financial inclusion in various countries. These experiences demonstrate the potential of mobile technology in expanding access to financial services and promoting financial inclusion (Sapovadia, 2018). In the GCC, especially in the micro-*takaful* subsector, general challenges in digital financial inclusion include: lack of awareness; fraud/scams; Shari'ah concerns; technological risk; focusing needs; multiparty involvement; inexperienced customers; and consumer protection (Ashfaq & Zada, 2021).

In Indonesia, a survey of Islamic fintech literacy for Generation Z was conducted to determine what challenges – faced by them in the digital era – are in line with religious values and may accelerate financial inclusion. The survey by Musari & Hidayat (2022) found that Generation Z in Indonesia avoids debt as much as possible, most of them have a habit of doing charity, saving, and have started investing. The majority of them has accessed to digital payment applications but evade access to digital loan services. They are tech-savvy and have religious awareness. They are the social capital for strengthening Islamic inclusive development in Indonesia in the future. Similarly, finance-savvy Muslim youth worldwide who are well-versed in modern technology and big data are eager to contribute to new ventures grounded in Islamic principles (De Anca, 2019).

To reach financial inclusion, a study by Sapovadia (2018) suggested to focus on four primary areas: delivering the services; reducing barriers to access; designing the product; and encouraging take-up. In addition, the variables include trust of users, affordability of services, and convenience which are equally important to encourage wider population to utilize digital and mobile services for financial transactions.

No doubt, financial inclusion functions is an enabler of inclusive economic growth and other developmental goals in the SDGs. Therefore, in the world that is going through the digital revolution, the SDGs may be reached through the digital financial inclusion (UNSGSA, Better Than Cash Alliance, UNCDF & World Bank, 2018). It enables the coverage toward excluded and underserved, unbanked and underbanked, BoP, and micro, small and medium enterprise (MSME) markets that result in an end-to-end impact toward society (Musari, 2022). It provides the access to financial services for 1.6 billion people in developing countries, with more than half of them being women (Saraç & Hassan, 2020).

In order to accelerate digital access of the excluded and underserved populations, there are three key components of the digital financial inclusion namely: a digital transactional platform, retail agents, and the use by customers and agents of a device to transact through the platform (Lyman & Lauer, 2015). No doubt, the digital financial inclusion manifests huge potential by providing opportunities to the previously excluded and underserved people to save, make payments, access financing, insurance, etc. The digital financial inclusion provides opportunities to allow them to manage an irregular income stream, plan for the future, protect them financially from natural disasters and economic shocks as well as find new pathways to survive and obtain a living (Musari & Hidayat, 2022).

In addition, P2P lending and philanthropy platforms, which are low-cost funds, can drive economic growth through increasing financial inclusion through digitalization (Musari, 2022). Similarly, Macchiavello (2018) emphasizes the importance of integrating microfinance with a social business structure and technology, particularly through fintech. This integration, adaptable to local traditions, involves financial cooperatives, savings banks, and Islamic banking. Musari & Sayah (2023) and Hidayat & Musari (2023) advocate for the Islamic Quadruple Helix, a partnership model rooted in Islamic social finance. This model, coupled with ICT, aims to boost productive activities in the real economy, fostering higher and equitable economic growth. The Islamic Quadruple Helix also envisions the development of an innovative system supporting pico-nano-micro-entrepreneurship for socio-economic advancement.

However, although widespread adoption and use of digital finance could increase the financial inclusion, there are several threats and constraints that need to be addressed, such as limited access to smart devices, the need for high-speed internet connectivity, account hacking risks, and digital literacy gaps (Saraç & Hassan, 2020). Yet, for the advancement of financial inclusion policies through digital technology, it is imperative to establish a digital financial inclusion ecosystem. This involves recognizing key stakeholders and regulatory standards and understanding the essential elements needed for the continual development of the ecosystem. The objective is to guide regulators in addressing data governance and customer protection (Oliver Wyman, MicroSave, & ADB, 2017).

Toward More Islamic Sustainable Finance

Climate change, a global concern, has risen to prominence on the development agenda due to its escalating impact, demanding concerted efforts for mitigation. Addressing anthropogenic climate change necessitates a sustainable approach, which, in turn, requires adequate funding. The mobilization of these funds relies on financing, with sustainable finance emerging as a crucial pillar in the sustainable approach. In parallel, Islamic sustainable finance seeks to promote and bolster sustainable development through adherence to Islamic principles.

According to the Securities Commission (SC) Malaysia & the World Bank Group (2019), Islamic finance can attract untapped funding sources not fully utilized by green finance. This underlines the significance of incorporating Islamic finance to harness its potential in incorporating green elements within its financing strategies.

There are a number of terminologies used to describe a financial system that cares about the environment, particularly regarding its sustainability. Given its various derivatives and developments, here are the main ones: including green finance, environmental finance, climate finance, low-carbon finance, renewable energy finance, net zero finance, carbon neutral finance, climate neutral finance, zero carbon finance, negative emissions finance, etc. All of these terminologies are actually part of sustainable finance as defined earlier.

Furthermore, the development of sustainable finance includes an increasing interest in green and sustainable investments, driven by public and private market attention, awareness of environmental, social and corporate governance (ESG) risks on financial performance, and policy support and commitments from the financial industry. However, despite the growing demand, current green investments are still far from being sufficient to achieve the transition to a sustainable economy, potentially resulting in amplified risks in the future (Sommer, 2020).

Indeed, the challenges in mainstreaming sustainable finance include the need to align the financial system with broader societal objectives, engage the private sector in sustainability discussions, and pursue risk reduction and stable long-term returns. These challenges impact the integration of ESG principles into the financial system by requiring a shift in mindset and practices. It involves overcoming obstacles such as pricing risk accurately, internalizing the costs of delaying mitigation measures, incentivizing technological change toward sustainability, and promoting financial innovation. Additionally, there is a need for a resilient ecosystem and strong financial governance reform to ensure that sustainable finance becomes the norm rather than the exception (Serrate, 2019).

Looking from an Islamic economics perspective, Islamic sustainable finance is one form of activity in realizing the sustainable eligible sectors. Based on the degree of need, these sustainable eligible sectors are divided into three priority levels, namely *dharuriyyat* (primary/essentials), *hajiyyat* (secondary/complementaries), as well as *tahsiniyyat* (desirables) which can be distributed into tertiary, quaternary, quinary, and senary levels (Musari, 2023). In principle, sustainability implementation at the *tahsiniyyat* stage will be realized if the concept of sustainability at the *dharuriyyat* and *hajiyyat* levels have been fulfilled.

Toward More Islamic Digital Finance

The fourth Industrial Revolution-driven technologies exponentially enhanced and/or disrupted Shari'ah-compliant financial services, operations, business models, and customer engagement in the 20th century (DinarStandard & Elipses, 2021). However, it is important to utilize Islamic fintech to solve the challenges facing the Islamic economy (Djani, 2022). Although there is no compelling confirmation so far that fintech will replace traditional finance, it has undoubtedly impacted the finance industry, improved access to finance, attracted new categories of investors, and opened up chances for new varieties of projects (Bollaert et al., 2021).

To have more of the Islamic digital finance, an Islamic digital financial service ecosystem is needed. An overview of the Islamic digital financial service ecosystem is shown in Table 14.4. Referring to the *Global Islamic Fintech Report 2021*, the landscape of the Islamic Fintech Framework includes five pillars, namely Islamic Fintech (iFintech) Services, iFintech Operations, Customers, Ecosystem Enablers, and Enabling Technologies. Meanwhile, according to the International Telecommunication Union Telecommunication Standardization Sector (ITU-T, 2016), the digital financial services ecosystem consists of several key players,

Table 14.4. The Global Islamic Fintech Ecosystem.

Pillars	**Components**		
iFintech services	Give and protect	Social finance	*Waqf*, *zakat*, *sadaqah*
		Insurance	InsureTech, TakaTech
	Save and invest	Wealth management	Robo-advisory, pensions, portland financial management (PFM), asset management
		Deposits and lending	Challenger banking, open banking, mortgages, personal finance, student finance
	Finance	Raising funds	P2P, crowdfunding
		Payments	Payments, remittances, foreign exchange
		Capital markets	Investment, trading, *sukuk*
		Digital assets	Platforms and exchanges, wallets and custodians, token issuers
		Alternative finance	Alternative finance, SME finance, trade finance

Table 14.4. *(Continued)*

Pillars	Components	
iFintech operations	Back office	Information technology (IT), human resource (HR), compliance, accounting
	Middle office	Risk, treasury, supply chain, customer service or onboarding
	Business intelligence	Dashboards, decision making tools, market research
Customers	Consumers (e.g. high-net-worth individual (HNWI), mass affluent, low income)	
	Businesses/organizations	
	Financial institutions	
Ecosystem enablers	Legal and regulatory enablers	Global: Multilateral institutions National: Financial regulators
	Advisory	Lawyers, Shari'ah scholars, consultants
	Financial institutions	Venture capital firms, Islamic banks, sovereign wealth funds
	Technology firms	Incumbent "big tech" large technology firms
	Supporting institutions	Research institutions, education and training institutes, fintech associations, accelerators
Enabling technologies	Artificial intelligence	Machine learning, data and analytics, big data
	Distributed ledger technology	Crypto, blockchain, tokenization
	Security	Biometrics; cybersecurity; identify verification
	Cloud	Cloud, software as a service (SaaS)

Source: DinarStandard & Elipses (2021).

namely: (i) the users – consumers, businesses, government agencies, and non-profit groups which have needs for digital and interoperable financial products and services; (ii) the providers – banks, other licensed financial institutions, and non-banks which supply those products and services through digital means; (iii) the financial, technical, and other infrastructures that make them possible; and (iv) the governmental policies, laws, and regulations which enable them to be delivered in an accessible, affordable, and safe manner.

Certainly, the imperative of establishing the Islamic digital financial service ecosystem today is crucial, given the dynamic environment and the need to confront future challenges. Apart from upholding a robust and independent risk management function that primarily addresses core financial risks in Islamic finance institutions, comprehensive oversight of operational and reputational risks becomes pivotal. Presently, cybersecurity demands heightened attention due to the increased exposure of customer data to potential risks associated with emerging technologies, as noted by Mohamed & Ali, 2019.

It is evident that regulations and supervision serve as the foundational pillars for ensuring stability in the Islamic financial sector. Consequently, there is a pressing need to establish a harmonized and standardized IFI. This not only bolsters regulatory frameworks but also contributes to the overall stability and resilience of the Islamic financial landscape.

Toward More Harmonized/Standardized Islamic Financial Industry

In order to ensure sustainable growth of Islamic finance, pushing the harmonization agenda is very crucial. Higher adoption of Shari'ah, accounting, auditing, prudential, and other standards issued by SSOs is the key for a bright future of the global IFI. Therefore, there should be more involvement of representatives of all jurisdictions sitting in the boards of the SSO. For example, there should be more representatives from South East Asian Countries in the AAOIFI. Similarly, there should be more representatives from the Middle East in the standards boards of the IFSB.

Undoubtedly, the journey toward a more inclusive Islamic finance, coupled with an emphasis on Islamic sustainable finance and digital finance, presents challenges for various stakeholders, including Islamic scholars, platform developers, jurists, regulators, investors, and others. Ensuring the Shari'ah compliance of digital-based financial transactions is paramount and should align with the same standards applied to any other financial transactions. Consequently, there is a need for specific regulations, Shari'ah principles, and Shari'ah-governance standards tailored to digital-based services (Yasini & Yasini, 2019). This recognition underscores the importance of establishing a regulatory framework and governance standards specifically designed for the evolving landscape of digital Islamic finance.

Hence, achieving Shari'ah-compliant outcomes necessitates the establishment of a more harmonized and standardized IFI. Adopting such a framework is anticipated to enhance efficiency and yield more advantages than drawbacks for the industry. While the concept is not novel (Smolo, 2009a, 2009b, 2011; Smolo & Habibovic, 2012; Smolo & Smajic, 2011), it remains imperative for all stakeholders in IFIs to revisit and prioritize this initiative earnestly (COMCEC, 2022). Bringing this matter to the forefront and implementing it soon is crucial for the continued evolution and prosperity of the Islamic financial landscape.

Conclusion

In recent years, the IFI has encountered several unforeseen crises, each presenting its impacts and challenges. Notably, four key challenges loom over the industry presently and in the future: financial inclusion, sustainability, digitalization, and the standardization of the Islamic financial sector. These challenges persist as significant concerns for all stakeholders within IFIs until the SDGs and the objectives outlined in the Paris Agreement are achieved by 2030. Addressing these issues is paramount for IFIs' collective well-being and success.

Financial inclusion is a global agenda in order to reach SDGs. Most countries, particularly in emerging countries, are embracing financial inclusion as a necessary policy to achieve inclusive growth and equitable economic development. Digital financial inclusion can also drive inclusive growth for Islamic finance. Through digital financial inclusion, Islamic finance can serve the underserved, unbankable, and the base of the pyramid segments.

Sustainability emerges as a critical concern as nations worldwide grapple with the challenges posed by climate change. In a broader context, sustainability is the amalgamation of economic, social, and environmental facets. It encompasses the preservation of economic growth, the pursuit of intergenerational equity, and the safeguarding of the current environmental quality. Notably, a natural alignment exists between sustainability and Islamic finance. Through Islamic sustainable finance, it stands poised to channel funds toward the financing of sustainable sectors, adhering to principles that ensure compatibility with Islamic values. This convergence presents an opportunity for Islamic finance to play a pivotal role in supporting sustainability initiatives.

Digitalization can act as a disruptor to the current financial ecosystem. However, digitalization can also act as enabler of financial inclusion and sustainability in achieving the SDGs and also for financing the eligible green sectors to achieve the targets of the Paris Agreement. Thus, Islamic finance move toward digitalization by embracing technology-based Islamic financial services. The Shari'ah-compliance of digital-based financial transactions shall not differ from the Shari'ah-compliance of any other financial transactions. Hence, digital-based financial services need their own regulations and their own Shari'ah-compliance and Shari'ah-governance standards.

Ultimately, standardization, or at the very least harmonization, stands out as another crucial issue demanding resolution for the growth of the IFI. The implementation of standardized practices holds the potential to yield numerous benefits for the entire Islamic financial sector. Tailored standards are indispensable, encompassing debt and equity-based technology platforms and extending across systems, risk management, controls, and other pertinent domains. Addressing these aspects will enhance operational efficiency and contribute to the overall robustness and advancement of the IFI.

Recommendations

Based on the previous facts about the level of financial inclusion, HDI, SDGi, and Ecological Footprint in Muslim majority countries, this study comes out with four recommendations:

First, developing the taxonomy of Islamic finance as a set of criteria that provides the basis for an evaluation of Islamic financial inclusion and Islamic sustainable finance, including for creating the scheme of Islamic blended finance which integrates the Islamic commercial finance and Islamic social finance. This taxonomy can be used as the basis for the development of incentive and disincentive policy of various inclusive and sustainable programs or projects; become guidelines for information openness, risk management, and development of innovative Islamic financial inclusion and Islamic sustainable finance products and/or services; guidance for developing investment instruments that meet the principles of Islamic financial inclusion and Islamic sustainable finance, then the long-term implications are expected to be able to achieve Islamic fiscal sustainability.

Second, doing financial inclusion and green transition with partnerships and collaboration with government, technical, operational, academic, business, industry, social societies, civil society, and entrepreneurs worldwide to grow financial inclusion and green ecosystems in any fields. Public and private collaboration is crucial in converting challenges into opportunities at a national, regional, and global level. All must act together, collaborate, and led by example. Institutional arrangement through Islamic N-Tuple Helix which can be adopted by emerging countries with Muslim-majority populations to manage Islamic social finance for supporting the financial inclusion as well as the inclusive and sustainable Islamic finance.

Third, embracing the digitization, digitalization, and then digital transformation as enabler to open the Islamic finance ecosystem. They generally will cause disruption, but they can facilitate the green transition to a sustainable future. Digitization, digitalization, and digital transformation phenomenon are bringing unprecedented disruptions for all traditional business models and hastening the need for a redesign and digitalize many activities. However, they present opportunities to create new value and economic growth for Islamic finance industry.

Fourth, pushing the standardization or at least harmonization agenda by involving more parties in the standards board of the SSOs that represent wider jurisdictions of Islamic finance.

References

Aaminou, M. W. (2022). *Towards a better financial inclusion in Maghreb countries: Insights on the role of Islamic microfinance and fintech.* Research Report No. 22. Research Center for Islamic Economics (IKAM).

ADB. (2017, January). *Financial inclusion in the digital economy.* ADB Briefs no. 75. Asian Development Bank (ADB).

ADBI. (2014). *Financial inclusion in Asia: Country surveys.* Asian Development Bank Institute (ADBI).

Alam, N., & Ali, S. N. (2021). Introduction: Fintech and Islamic finance in the Gulf Cooperation Council (GCC). In N. Alam & S. N. Ali (Eds.), *Fintech, digital currency and the future of Islamic finance strategic, regulatory and adoption issues in the gulf cooperation council* (pp. 1–8). Palgrave Macmillan.

Arzayeva, M., & Dochshanova, A. (2016). Problems of development of Islamic financing in Kazakhstan: Financial and legal aspects. *Indian Journal of Science and Technology*, *9*(S1), 1–5. https://doi.org/10.17485/ijst/2016/v9iS1/99524

Ashfaq, M., & Zada, N. (2021). The application of fintech in microtakaful as a means of digital financial inclusion: Insights from the GCC. In N. Alam & S. N. Ali (Eds.), *Fintech, digital currency and the future of Islamic finance strategic, regulatory and adoption issues in the gulf cooperation council* (pp. 77–106). Palgrave Macmillan.

Askari, H., Iqbal, Z., Krichene, N., & Mirakhor, A. (2010). *The stability of Islamic finance: Creating a resilient financial environment for a secure future*. John Wiley & Sons (Asia) Pte. Ltd.

Bollaert, H., Lopez-de-Silanes, F., & Schwienbacher, A. (2021). Fintech and access to finance. *Journal of Corporate Finance*, *68*, 101941. https://doi.org/10.1016/j.jcorpfin.2021.101941

Collins, A., & Flynn, A. (2015). *The ecological footprint: New developments in policy and practice*. Edward Elgar Publishing.

COMCEC. (2022). *Standardization efforts in Islamic finance*. COMCEC Coordination Office. http://ebook.comcec.org/Kutuphane/Icerik/a5231a21-a35d-42fb-afbf-f29b4ec4e1e2.pdf

De Anca, C. (2019). Fintech in Islamic finance: From collaborative finance to community-based finance. In U. A. Oseni & S. N. Ali (Eds.), *Fintech in Islamic finance* (pp. 47–63). Routledge.

Demirgüç-Kunt, A., Klapper, L., Singer, D., & Ansar, S. (2022). *The global Findex database 2021: Financial inclusion, digital payments, and resilience in the age of COVID-19*. International Bank for Reconstruction and Development (IBRD)/The World Bank.

DinarStandard. (2022). *State of the global Islamic economy report 2022*. DinarStandard, Dubai Islamic Economic Development Center, and Salaam Gateway.

DinarStandard and Elipses. (2022). *Global Islamic fintech report 2022*. DinarStandard, Elipses, and Saalam Gateway.

DinarStandard, & Elipses. (2021). *Global islamic fintech report 2021*. DinarStandard, Elipses, and Salam Gateway.

Djani, D. (2022). Importance of utilising Islamic fintech to solve the challenges facing the Islamic economy. In DinarStandard And Elipses (Ed.), *Global Islamic fintech report 2022* (p. 22). DinarStandard, Elipses, and Saalam Gateway.

ElMassah, S., & Hassanein, E. A. (2023). Economic development and environmental sustainability in the GCC countries: New insights based on the economic complexity. *Sustainability*, *15*, 7987. https://doi.org/10.3390/su15107987

Frontiers Editorial Office. (2023). Retraction: Effect of Islamic financial development on carbon emissions: A spatial econometric analysis. *Frontiers in Environmental Science*, *11*, 1349896. https://doi.org/10.3389/fenvs.2023.1349896

Global Footprint Network. (2022). *National footprint and biocapacity accounts 2023 edition*. https://www.footprintnetwork.org/licenses/public-data-package-free/

Gulrez, T. (2021). Strategic assessment of Islamic fintech in GCC countries. In N. Alam & S. N. Ali (Eds.), *Fintech, digital currency and the future of Islamic finance strategic, regulatory and adoption issues in the gulf cooperation council* (pp. 223–242). Palgrave Macmillan.

Hassan, M. K., Aliyu, S., & Hussain, M. (2019). A contemporary review of Islamic finance and accounting literature. *The Singapore Economic Review*. https://doi.org/10.1142/s0217590819420013

Hidayat, S. E., & Musari, K. (2023). Towards the global halal MSMEs hub through the digitally-enabled society: An institutional arrangement with Islamic n-tuple helix. In A. Rafiki (Ed.), *Digitalization in halal management. Contributions to environmental sciences & innovative business technology* (pp. 15–28). Springer. https://doi.org/10.1007/978-981-99-5146-8_2

ITU, T. (2016, May). *The digital financial services ecosystem*. International Telecommunication Union Telecommunication Standardization Sector (ITU-T) Focus Group Digital Financial Services.

Jouti, A. T. (2018). Islamic finance: Financial inclusion or migration? *ISRA International Journal of Islamic Finance*, *10*(2), 277–288. https://doi.org/10.1108/IJIF-07-2018-0074

Karlan, D., Osman, A., & Shammout, N. (2021). Increasing financial inclusion in the Muslim world: Evidence from an Islamic finance marketing experiment. *The World Bank Economic Review*, 1–22. https://doi.org/10.1093/wber/lhaa010

Khan, T. (2022). *Rethinking economics in the anthropogenic era. A presentation material for Guest Lecture at Quaid-i-Azam University*, Islamabad, October 13.

Khan, T. (2023). Externalities management from Islamic economic perspective: Rethinking economics and finance in the anthropogenic era. *A presentation material for Kulliyyah of Economics & Management Sciences (KENMS) of International Islamic University Malaysia (IIUM) Distinguished Intellectual Discourse Series, A Prelude to Key Themes in the 15th International Conference on Islamic Economics & Finance (ICIEF) 2023 Conference*, May 26.

Klapper, L. (2016, August 11). *Financial inclusion has a big role to play in reaching the SDGs*. The Consultative Group to Assist the Poor (CGAP). Blog. https://www.cgap.org/blog/financial-inclusion-has-big-role-play-reaching-sdgs

Lyman, T., & Lauer, K. (2015, March 10). *What is digital financial inclusion and why does it matter?* Consultative Group to Assist the Poor (CGAP). Blog. https://www.cgap.org/blog/what-digital-financial-inclusion-and-why-does-it-matter

Macchiavello, E. (2018). *Microfinance and financial inclusion: The challenge of regulating alternative forms of finance*. Routledge.

Mohamed, H., & Ali, H. (2019). *Blockchain, fintech, and Islamic finance. Building the future in the new Islamic digital economy*. Walter de Gruyter Inc.

Moro-Visconti, R. (2021). *Microfintech: Expanding financial inclusion with cost-cutting innovation*. Palgrave Macmillan.

Musari, K. (2022). P2P lending & philanthropy platform: A new face of Asian digital financial inclusion (evidence from Indonesia). In M. N. Almunawar, Z. Islam, & P. Ordóñez de Pablos (Eds.), *Digital transformation management: Challenges and futures in the Asian digital economy* (pp. 185–206). Routledge. https://doi.org/10.4324/9781003224532

Musari, K. (2023). A proposed taxonomy of Islamic green financing to address the sustainable eligible sector. *A paper was presented at the 11th Islamic Economics Workshop "Islamic Economics and Environment" held by Research Center for Islamic Economics (IKAM) in Collaboration with the Turkish Entrepreneurship and Business Ethics Association (İGİAD) and Istanbul 29 Mayis University Economic and Financial Systems Application and Research Center (EFSAM)*, Istanbul, Turkiye, October 13–15.

Musari, K. (2024). Transforming ecological footprint through circular economy innovation towards sustainable well-being in the development of (Islamic) smart cities in GCC countries. In M. D. Lytras, A. Alkhaldi, & S. Malik (Eds.), *The emerald handbook of smart cities in the gulf region: Innovation, development, transformation, and prosperity for vision 2040*. Emerald Publishing Limited.

Musari, K., & Hidayat, S. E. (2022). Digital financial knowledge and behavior of generation Z in Indonesia: A survey of Islamic fintech literacy toward digital financial inclusion. In M. Anshari, M. N. Almunawar, & M. Masri (Eds.), *Fintech development for financial inclusiveness* (pp. 96–117). IGI Global. https://doi.org/10.4018/978-1-7998-8447-7.ch007

Musari, K., & Khan, T. (2023). Sustainable development and circular economy in the GCC countries. *A paper was presented at the Workshop "Circular Economy and Sustainable Development Model: It's Role in the GCC States' National Visions" held by Gulf Research Centre Cambridge (GRCC), University of Cambridge*, Cambridge, United Kingdom, July 11–13.

Musari, K., & Sayah, F. (2023). Islamic quadruple helix, social finance partnership for developing digital financial inclusion in Maghreb region. In A. Rafiki, A. G. Pananjung, & M. D. T. P. Nasution (Eds.), *Strategies and applications of Islamic entrepreneurship* (pp. 67–82). IGI Global. https://doi.org/10.4018/978-1-6684-7519-5.ch005

Oliver Wyman, MicroSave, & ADB. (2017). *Accelerating financial inclusion in South-East Asia with digital finance*. Asian Development Bank (PDB).

Oseni, U. A, & Ali, S. N. (Eds.). (2019). *Fintech in islamic finance*. Routledge.

Ozili, P. K. (2018). Impact of digital finance on financial inclusion and stability. *Borsa Istanbul Review*, *18*(4), 329–340. https://doi.org/10.1016/j.bir.2017.12.003

Ozili, P. K. (2022). Financial inclusion and sustainable development: An empirical association. *Journal of Money and Business*, *2*(2), 186–198. https://doi.org/10.1108/JMB-03-2022-0019

Rahman, M. M. (2020). Financial inclusion for poverty alleviation: The role of Islamic finance in Bangladesh. In A. E. S. Ali, K. M. Ali, & M. H. Azrag (Eds.), *Enhancing financial inclusion through Islamic finance, volume II. Palgrave studies in islamic banking, finance, and economics*. Palgrave Macmillan.

Rees, W. (1986). *The regional capsule concept: An heuristic model for thinking about regional development and environmental policy*. Concept Note, School of Community and Regional Planning, University of British Columbia.

Rees, W. (1992). Ecological footprints and appropriated carrying capacity: What urban economics leaves out. *Environment and Urbanization*, *4*(2), 121–130.

Rees, W., & Wackernagel, M. (1996). Urban ecological footprints: Why cities cannot be sustainable —And why they are a key to sustainability. *Environmental Impact Assessment Review*, *16*(4–6), 223–248. https://doi.org/10.1016/S0195-9255(96)00022-4

Sapovadia, V. (2018). Financial inclusion, digital currency, and mobile technology. In D. L. K. Chuen & R. Deng (Eds.), *Handbook of blockchain, digital finance, and inclusion, volume 2: Chinatech, mobile security, distributed ledger, and blockchain* (pp. 361–385). Academic Press. https://doi.org/10.1016/b978-0-12-812282-2.00014-0

Saraç, M., & Hassan, M. K. (2020). *Islamic perspective for sustainable financial system*. Istanbul University Press.

SC Malaysia & World Bank Group. (2019). *Islamic green finance: Development, ecosystem and prospects*. Securities Commission (SC) Malaysia and the World Bank Group.

Serrate, J. S. (2019, March 31). Turning sustainable finance into mainstream finance. *Social Science Research Network (SSRN)*. https://doi.org/10.2139/ssrn.340280831

Smolo, E. (2009a, October–December). Sustaining the growth of Islamic financial industry: What needs to be done? *Islamic Finance Bulletin (RAM)*, *26*, Article 26.

Smolo, E. (2009b, December 10). Sustainable growth of Islamic financial industry (IFI): Some unresolved issues. In *Curtin International business Conference, school of business, Curtin University of technology*, Sarawak, Malaysia, December 10–12.

Smolo, E. (2011, February). *Standard procedure: The future of Islamic finance industry lies in its consistency* (pp. 47–49). Business Islamica.

Smolo, E., & Habibovic, E. (2012). Barriers to growth of Islamic finance: Issue of standardization. In A. Trakic & H. H. A. Tajuddin (Eds.), *Islamic banking and finance: Principles, instruments and operations* (pp. 715–737). The Malaysian Current Law Journal.

Smolo, E., & Smajic, M. (2011, January 12). A road ahead for Islamic finance industry: A need for standardization. *Islamic Finance News*, *8*(1), 18–19.

Sommer, S. (2020). *Sustainable finance: An overview*. Deutsche Gesellschaft für Internationale Zusammenarbeit (GIZ) GmbH.

UNDP. (2022). *Human development report 2021/2022*. United Nations Development Programme (UNDP). http://hdr.undp.org/en/data

UNSGSA, Better Than Cash Alliance, UNCDF, and World Bank. (2018). *Igniting SDG progress through digital financial inclusion*. United Nations Secretary-General's Special Advocate for Inclusive Finance for Development (UNSGSA).

Visser, H. (2013). *Islamic finance: Principles and practice* (2nd ed.). Edward Elgar Publishing Limited.

Wackernagel, M., & Beyers, B. (2019). *Ecological footprint: Managing our biocapacity budget*. New Society Publishers.

Wackernagel, M., & Galli, A. (2007). An overview on ecological footprint and sustainable development: A chat with Mathis Wackernagel. *International Journal of Ecodynamics*, *2*(1), 1–9. https://doi.org/10.2495/ECO-V2-N1-1-9

Yang, L., & Zhang, Y. (2020). Digital financial inclusion and sustainable growth of small and micro enterprises —Evidence based on China's new third board market listed companies. *Sustainability*, *12*(9), 3733, 1-21. https://doi.org/10.3390/su12093733

Yasini, S., & Yasini, M. (2019). Current trends and future impacts of fintech in Islamic finance. In U. A. Oseni & S. N. Ali (Eds.), *Fintech in islamic finance* (pp. 327–336). Routledge.

Chapter 15

Conclusion: Beyond the Horizon

Mohamed Mahees Raheem and Edib Smolo

Effat University, Saudi Arabia

Abstract

This chapter delves into the complex yet fascinating arena of Islamic finance, looking at its historical foundations and dealing with today's complexities. There is a huge struggle in Islamic economics in meeting the contemporary needs while practising moderate framework, observing the difference between strictly abiding by the rules and achieving the ethical goals beyond the profit. It urges for a value-driven approach within institutions and the implementation of the *zakat*, *sadaqah* and *waqf* systems to fill the Sustainable Development Goal (SDG) financing gap. Seizing the opportunities, the chapter promotes the necessity of Islamic *fiqh* experts with current Shari'ah body of knowledge in considering the ethical and legal aspects alongside fintech. This is essentially to ensure that the implementation of Islamic finance enables the sustainable economic development. Looking toward the Industry 5.0, it expects a combination of artificial intelligence (AI) with Islamic finance and identifies Islamic social finance as a powerful socially-driven tool. In the end, the chapter lays out Islamic finance as the powerful tool to work together to achieve an ethical, equitable, and sustainable financial system.

Keywords: Islamic finance; Islamic banking; Islamic financial institutions; Shari'ah-compliant; Islamic law; maqasid al-Shari'ah; Islamic social finance

With each passing page of this book that opens up new Islamic finance points of view, it becomes evident that the business is at the crossroads of choosing between the old and the new norms. From a meager beginning in the marketplace of Medina to world stage today, Islamic finance has traversed an extraordinary journey. Along these lines, the driving force of this philosophical concept entails the development of perennial values like justice, fairness and social awareness that

The Future of Islamic Finance, 243–249

doi:10.1108/978-1-83549-906-120241015

culminates in appropriate social responses to global challenges of the modern times.

As a major matter, an emerging paradigm of economic thought in Islam was raised, and this brought a breath of fresh air to the economic issues we witness today. In the light of the Islamic principles, the model includes the ideas of equitable distribution, ethical business practices and a stronger emphasis on the social welfare. The Islamic economics is fundamentally derived from the doctrines of *maqasid al-Shari'ah* in the way that it seeks to achieve the objectives of safeguarding of life, health, religion, dignity and property (Lamido, 2016). The Islamic economics framework paves way for systematic and comprehensive solution to deal with the issues such as income inequality, unsustainable economic demand and environmental degradation where the human welfare is given priority beyond mere profit-making (Jan & Asutay, 2019). However, as ideal as it may seem, there is no consensus or universal agreement among scholars and practitioners on the principles and practices of Islamic economics. More often than not, scholars in the field build upon the theoretical framework of modern economic systems, "islamizing" elements that lie within and inculcating Islamic principles where needed (El Maghrebi et al., 2023; Haneef & Furqani, 2009; Nasr, 1991). This can be considered a major challenge toward it becoming reality.

The Islamic financial industry has evolved through stages that has previously focused on mere transactional form toward embedding more stringent criteria toward its substance. For Muslims, one of their actions that they will be held accountable for is on how they earned their wealth and how they spent it (Murtuza, 2002). Wealth, in all its forms, is an *Amanah* (trust) from God, and it has to be treated with utmost responsibility and care. In this regard, merely focusing on ensuring a Shari'ah-compliant form of transaction, without taking into account the source and use of funds, will not be adequate to ensure the true promotion of welfare and ultimately the realization of a bona fide Islamic economic system (Kuran, 1995). Questions pop up where large-scale transactions are structured in a Shari'ah-compliant manner for projects that might ultimately cause harm to any life, health, society and environment. Though transactions may be deemed Shari'ah-compliant on the micro-level, do they translate into maximizing Islamic well-being on the macrolevel?

The hypothesis remains that a true Islamic economy can only be attained if everyone within the economy seeks complete Shari'ah-compliance in all their affairs even if it comes at the cost of conventional profit-maximization objectives. Can the industry move toward *barakah-maximization* (Anwar & Suryani, 2022) or *falah-maximization* (Ibrahim & Chek, 2020) in its economic and business objectives? The Islamic finance industry has long grappled with this debate on form versus substance, and with growing awareness and education on Shari'ah-compliant finance and ethical finance, the industry can be seen moving in a more inclusive and responsible direction.

Among the teething problems faced by the Islamic finance industry is the harmonization of Shari'ah standards across different countries and jurisdictions. There is an immediate need to establish a unified juristic frame of reference for fatwas issued by Shari'ah supervisory boards. This framework should be based on credible fatwas that have been passed through multiple endorsements and standards issued by organizations such as the Accounting and Auditing Organization for Islamic Financial Institutions (AAOIFI). The Harmonization of Shari'ah standards that can be endorsed and applied across jurisdictions will help boost credibility of Islamic financial products, boosting their acceptance and marketability within the global economy (COMCEC, 2022; Smolo, 2009a, 2009b, 2011; Smolo & Habibovic, 2012; Smolo & Smajic, 2011). Shari'ah scholars, jurists and auditors should be able to adopt a unified methodology toward assessing Shari'ah compliance in product development, assessment, operations, governance and financial reporting.

Another important aspect of the future trajectory of Islamic finance is its alignment with the SDGs. Integrating sustainability principles in investment and financing processes by Islamic financial institutions can result in the achievement of the SDG goals and consequently, an inclusive and sustainable global economy.

The process does not only cover shifting the investment principles but also restructuring the internal organizational policies to eventually push the environmental, social and governance (ESG) considerations. Adopting the standards of "Shari'ah-compliance" from a narrow perspective of screening and legal issues toward ethical, societal and environmental aspects poses a number of difficulties.

A mindset shift is also required to move from firm's prioritizing shareholders to empowering stakeholders, ultimately redefining and delivering value that actually considers the interest of the community and environment at large. Islamic banks and financial institutions have come under recent scrutiny for their lack of investment in ESG-friendly initiatives, highlighting the need for more awareness and proactiveness in this regard. In addition, innovative financing models utilizing *zakat*, *sadaqah* and *waqf* can prove to be instrumental in funding the financing gap currently impeding the attainment of SDGs using conventional financing methods. As a source of innovation, one can cite many interesting solutions that Islamic finance may provide to the current issues. Unique solutions such as using *waqf* to provide funds for universal basic income (Raheem, 2021), financing of affordable housing using solar energy and *musharakah mutanaqisah* (diminishing partnership) contracts (Meera et al., 2022) as well as the credit circuit system utilizing trade credit for the working capital management of micro, small and medium enterprises (Raheem et al., 2021) are but some examples.

Similarly, the synergy between the digital economy and sustainable development raises unknown limits, thereby paving room for Islamic finance toward global action oriented to environmental conservation and social equilibrium. Islam teaches its followers to behave righteously and keep the order of nature and the society, even in the most severe situation such as war. According to the historical accounts, a decree by Abu Bakr al-Siddiq, who was the leader at the time, emphasized the need to be mindful of one's actions so that the environment is not affected negatively. He said,

> Stop, O people, that I may give you ten rules for your guidance in the battlefield. Do not commit treachery or deviate from the right path. You must not mutilate dead bodies. Neither kill a child, nor

> a woman, nor an aged man. Bring no harm to the trees, nor burn them with fire, especially those which are fruitful. Slay not any of the enemy's flock, save for your food. You are likely to pass by people who have devoted their lives to monastic services; leave them alone (as cited in Aboul-Enein and Zuhur, 2004).

It is essential for Muslims to realize that these words are of great importance, and they should take this fact into account while consuming the nature either for personal health or for the economic profit. The example given above is a proof that protection and safeguarding of the environment and its various elements is a duty of all Muslims, which must be taken into account in any human interaction. Green finance schemes such as Islamic Green Bonds and Sustainable Investment Funds can facilitate the flow of capital toward environmentally conscious projects and businesses (Wang et al., 2022). Emerging concepts such as circular economy and inclusive wealth are also being used as metrics to determine the "Islamicity" of business practices and financing, with the underlying hypothesis that their adoption and application will ultimately result in a proper attainment of the *maqasid al-Shari'ah* (Hassan et al., 2021).

Moreover, the advent of financial technology (fintech) has emerged as a game-changer in the Islamic financial landscape. Technologies such as blockchain, AI, fintech and mobile banking hold promise to increase efficiency, accessibility and transparency in financial transactions (Litimi et al., 2023). While the rise of fintech in Islamic finance does present many ethical and legal complexities, a careful and practical approach must be adopted to maintain the principles of Shari'ah and the rights and interests of the consumers.

The fact that fintech is playing a major role in democratizing financial services and, thereby, promoting the inclusion of a larger population into the financial sector makes the implementation of additional safeguards and put in place the necessary measures that would ensure the Shari'ah compliance and positive benefit for everybody much more important (Yasini & Yasini, 2019). In this context, we have no other option but to equip the Islamic economics and finance professionals who work in the sector with the skills required by the high-tech industry and to prepare them for the challenges of the day to help sustain the Islamic financial industry. This will make it possible for them to equally test in practice the developmental significance of these institutions in near future.

After the Fourth Industrial Revolution is over, the concept of Industry 5.0 takes over, marking the beginning of a new era where human-centric technologies integrated with AI and decentralized decision-making process based on the big data are chosen as the dominant forces. Thus, Islamic finance is given more weight in this area, by specially using the state-of-the-art technology to materialize Islamic finance's own moral and legal requirements. AI in particular holds great promise to transform various facets of Islamic finance, especially in terms of risk management, regulatory compliance, customer service and product innovation. By leveraging AI-powered analytics and automation, Islamic financial institutions can augment operational efficiency, formulate risk hedging techniques and offer personalized financial solutions tailored to the diverse needs of stakeholders.

This era could even see AI-generated *fatwas* and automated Islamic finance product structuring tailored to provide optimal solutions that will be in line with Shari'ah principles, minimizing the so-called "costs of Shari'ah-compliance" (Ahmed, 2014). Generative AI models can be trained on all existing religious texts, *hadiths*, opinions, *fatwas* and Islamic financial contracts throughout the years, alongside with existing financial theories, models and product structures, to create innovative Shari'ah-compliant structuring models and perhaps even *fatwas*. With the advent of new technologies involving augmented reality such as metaverse, the very definitions of assets, property and even currency are being redefined due to their virtual nature, and the Islamic finance experts need to be academically equipped to explore these premises in conversations of the future.

Similarly, the concept of Islamic social finance, encompassing *zakat*, *waqf* and *sadaqah* can be used as a powerful tool to address social challenges and promote inclusive development. Through the mobilization of resources for community-based initiatives and philanthropic efforts, Islamic financial institutions can be a catalyst in improving the social and economic well-being of marginalized and disadvantaged communities (Ali, 2017; Mohseni-Cheraghlou, 2017).

Alternative positive screening methods that target the poor and the disabled should be coupled with the present method of negative screening to have a multipronged approach. This would lead to impactful goods which simultaneously take care of the society and environment without compromising on Shari'ah-compliance and profit. The role of Islamic financial institutions in this regard is to address poverty and underutilization of physical, human, and financial capital. Through these methods can foster entrepreneurial spirit and economic development boosting the overall well-being of the self, society and economy.

Finally, it can be said that the future of Islamic finance is at the crossroads of innovation with tradition, ethics, and profitability. In view of the turbulent financial environment that is gripping the world, it is crucial to stand firm on Islam's fundamental finance concepts while at the same time utilizing cutting-edge technologies and meeting the needs of sustainable development. Through the adoption of Industry 5.0, AI application, innovative concept of money and virtual realities exploration, the Islamic finance will have the chance not only to adjust to the digital era, but even to lead its transformation toward a more decentralized, fair and stable financial system. By aligning ideals and actions with the broader goals of economic prosperity, social equity and environmental stewardship, Islamic finance has the scope to truly realize its potential as a transformative force for positive change in the world.

References

Aboul-Enein, Y. H., & Zuhur, S. (2004). *Islamic rulings on warfare.* Strategic Studies Institute, U.S. Army War College.

Ahmed, H. (2014). Islamic banking and Shari'ah compliance: A product development perspective. *Journal of Islamic Finance*, *3*(2), 15–29. https://doi.org/10.31436/jif.v3i2.45

Ali, S. N. (2017). Moving towards community driven Islamic finance. *Journal of Islamic Business and Management (JIBM)*, *7*(1), 11–27. https://doi.org/10.26501/jibm/2017.0701-002

Anwar, S., & Suryani, M. (2022). The preliminary investigation of how barakah works. In *International Conference on Sustainable Innovation Track Accounting and Management Sciences (ICOSIAMS 2021)*, Bantul, Indonesia. https://doi.org/10.2991/aebmr.k.211225.013

COMCEC. (2022). *Standardization efforts in Islamic finance.* COMCEC Coordination Office. http://ebook.comcec.org/Kutuphane/Icerik/a5231a21-a35d-42fb-afbf-f29b4ec4e1e2.pdf

El Maghrebi, N., Mirakhor, A., Akın, T., & Iqbal, Z. (2023). Islamization of economics? An impossibility theorem. In N. El Maghrebi, A. Mirakhor, T. Akın, & Z. Iqbal (Eds.), *Revisiting Islamic economics* (pp. 209–240). Springer International Publishing. https://doi.org/10.1007/978-3-031-41134-2_6

Haneef, M. A., & Furqani, H. (2009). Contemporary Islamic economics: The missing dimension of genuine Islamization. *Thoughts on Economics*, *19*(04), 29–48.

Hassan, M. K., Muneeza, A., & Saraç, M. (2021). Need to redefine Islamic finance in the light of maqasid al-Shariah. In M. K. Hassan, M. Saraç, & A. Khan (Eds.), *Islamic finance and sustainable development* (pp. 11–34). Springer International Publishing. https://doi.org/10.1007/978-3-030-76016-8_2

Ibrahim, M. F., & Chek, N. M. B. T. (2020). The concept of Al-Falah maximization: Zakat and industry revolution 4.0. *Labuan e-Journal of Muamalat and Society*, *14*, 11–22.

Jan, S., & Asutay, M. (2019). *A model for Islamic development: An approach in Islamic moral economy.* Edward Elgar Publishing.

Kuran, T. (1995). Islamic economics and the Islamic subeconomy. *The Journal of Economic Perspectives*, *9*(4), 155–173. https://doi.org/10.1257/jep.9.4.155

Lamido, A. A. (2016). Maqasid al-Shari'ah as a framework for economic development theorization. *International Journal of Islamic Economics and Finance Studies*, *2*(1), 27–49.

Litimi, H., BenSaïda, A., & Raheem, M. M. (2023). Impact of FinTech growth on bank performance in GCC region. *Journal of Emerging Market Finance*, 09726527231218423. https://doi.org/10.1177/09726527231218423

Meera, A. K. M., Raheem, M. M., & Zambry, M. (2022). Making housing affordable through solar energy: A proposal for Malaysia. *Al Qasimia University Journal of Islamic Economics*, *2*(1), 223–248. https://doi.org/10.52747/aqujie.2.1.81

Mohseni-Cheraghlou, A. (2017). Financial inclusion and poverty alleviation in Muslim-majority countries: The role of Islamic finance and Qard Hassan. In M. Zulkhibri & A. G. Ismail (Eds.), *Financial inclusion and poverty alleviation* (pp. 141–197). Springer International Publishing. https://doi.org/10.1007/978-3-319-69799-4_4

Murtuza, A. (2002). Islamic antecedents for financial accountability. *International Journal of Islamic Financial Services*, *4*(1), 1–19.

Nasr, S. V. R. (1991). Islamization of knowledge: A critical overview. *Islamic Studies*, *30*(3), Article 3.

Raheem, M. M. (2021). A concept for funding universal basic income through a "National Waqf" scheme. *PalArch's Journal of Archaeology of Egypt/Egyptology*, *18*(13), 1251–1264.

Raheem, M. M., Meera, A. K. M., & Adewale, A. A. (2021). A model of a Shariah compliant credit clearing system to facilitate working capital management for micro, small and medium enterprises. *PalArch's Journal of Archaeology of Egypt/Egyptology*, *18*(13), 1383–1393.

Smolo, E. (2009a, October–December). Sustaining the growth of Islamic financial industry: What needs to be done? *Islamic Finance Bulletin*, *26*, Article 26.

Smolo, E. (2009b, December 10). Sustainable growth of Islamic financial industry (IFI): Some unresolved issues. In *Curtin International Business Conference, School of Business, Curtin University of Technology*, Sarawak, Malaysia, December 10–12.

Smolo, E. (2011, February). *Standard procedure: The future of Islamic finance industry lies in its consistency* (pp. 47–49). Business Islamica.

Smolo, E., & Habibovic, E. (2012). Barriers to growth of Islamic finance: Issue of standardization. In A. Trakic & H. H. A. Tajuddin (Eds.), *Islamic banking and finance: Principles, instruments and operations* (pp. 715–737). The Malaysian Current Law Journal.

Smolo, E., & Smajic, M. (2011, January 12). A road ahead for Islamic finance industry: A need for standardization. *Islamic Finance News*, *8*(1), 18–19.

Wang, K.-H., Zhao, Y.-X., Jiang, C.-F., & Li, Z.-Z. (2022). Does green finance inspire sustainable development? Evidence from a global perspective. *Economic Analysis and Policy*, *75*, 412–426. https://doi.org/10.1016/j.eap.2022.06.002

Yasini, S., & Yasini, M. (2019). Current trends and future impacts of fintech in Islamic finance. In U. A. Oseni & S. N. Ali (Eds.), *Fintech in Islamic finance: Theory and practice* (pp. 327–336). Routledge.

Index

Printed and bound by CPI Group (UK) Ltd, Croydon, CR0 4YY

15/09/2026

14962484-0002